# without frontiers
## the life and music of
# PETER GABRIEL

without frontiers
the life and music of

# PETER GABRIEL

daryl easlea

OMNIBUS PRESS
London / New York / Paris / Sydney / Copenhagen / Berlin / Madrid / Tokyo

Cover designed by Fresh Lemon
Picture research by Jacqui Black

ISBN: 978.1.78038.315.6
Order No: OP54516



Exclusive Distributors
Music Sales Limited,
14/15 Berners Street,
London, W1T 3LJ.

Music Sales Corporation
180 Madison Avenue, 24th Floor
New York,
NY 10016,
USA.

Macmillan Distribution Services
56 Parkwest Drive
Derrimut, Vic 3030,
Australia.



Printed in the EU

A catalogue record for this book is available from the British Library

Visit Omnibus Press on the web at www.omnibuspress.com

*To my darlings,*
*Jules and Flora Easlea.*
*Thank you for making my soul ignite*

# Contents

# Prologue

## A MAN WHO WOULD NEVER COMPROMISE HIS ART FOR ANYTHING

*"One of the things that turns me on is the sense you're on virgin snow"*
Peter Gabriel, 2007

*"Sometimes I'm proud of my mistakes, if they are done with conviction"*
Peter Gabriel, Star Test, 1989.

OCTOBER 1982. It is raining. Heavily. In the middle of England, six men are performing songs they had written over a decade previously, in order to salvage the dream of their former lead singer, who has rejoined the band for one night only. Contractually, they could not call themselves by their trading name, Genesis, and opted for the one-off soubriquet, 'Six Of The Best', an allusion to the fact that the group was founded at one of the UK's leading public schools, Charterhouse, renowned at the time for its use of corporal punishment. Only the Greek-style triangulated font used for their name on the programme, a font that first appeared as their logo on their 1974 album, *The Lamb Lies Down On Broadway,* gives a clue to these men's past.

The group's singer, Peter Gabriel, had left them seven years earlier moderately amicably and, to the wider world, surprisingly. As he had been their focal point, main spokesman and one of the principal writers between 1967 and 1975, few would have thought that the group could carry on without him. But, opting not to replace him, they had done so, and as a result were commercially far more successful after his departure than anyone would have ever imagined.

Gabriel's career since leaving the group had been anything but linear. He had pursued his art over commercialism, and had gained a new realm of admirers in the process. By this point he had recorded a mainstream rock album with the cream of US session players, an album partially recorded in New York that reflected the city in the era of new wave and disco, and most importantly, an album that would set the template sonically for his future work. This record also contained 'Biko', the track that would prove more meaningful for his career than anything he had recorded before, or since. Written about Steve Bantu Biko, the South African student leader who died in police custody in Pretoria in September 1977, it was overtly political and arranged with African drumming and the low-drone of bagpipes, an anthemic record that had the remarkable ability to stir the political conscience of its audience, and later, be instrumental in challenging apartheid. Gabriel was to call the track "a calling card announcing I was interested and prepared to get involved".

But now, Gabriel was suddenly in dire fiscal trouble. Never having been the most buoyant financially, Gabriel, in the words of Genesis' drummer and later vocalist, Phil Collins, was a great "um-mer and ah-her", content to follow his dreams first and worry about logistics later. He had pioneered a music festival that would bring together all of the musics from around the world in which he had a burgeoning interest. Accordingly, he put together an umbrella organisation, WOMAD (World Of Music, Arts and Dance), a vision borne out of his altruism and sincerity. At the same time, he was recording his fourth album, in his home studio in Ashcombe House, Bath, the first of his works that fully incorporated found sounds.

With his pioneering spirit, and a desire to work outside convention, Gabriel, with incredible zeal and vigour, had aligned himself with like-minded souls instead of tried music industry operators in order to stage a festival celebrating this music. As a consequence, the project lost money hand over fist. With debts estimated in the region of £250,000 (around £600,000 in 2013) it appeared that he and the fledgling organisation would be declared bankrupt. Indeed, the inaugural festival, held at Shepton Mallet in July 1982, was the epitome of a dream over financial reality, with audience numbers low and international travel bills sky high.

Aghast at the news that their old friend was in a parlous predicament and facing death threats from irate creditors, Genesis, and their manager Tony Smith, stepped in and offered something they knew would make big money – a benefit concert that saw the group back together onstage with their former lead singer.

Gabriel was overwhelmed with their generosity, yet was also acutely aware that for someone who only wished to look forward, it would be a hugely regressive step. However, there was little option but to take the lifeline offered to him by his old group. Six Of The Best offered the jolt in the arm that Gabriel needed. In the sodden atmosphere of the largely soulless Milton Keynes Bowl, 65,000 people joined the group for a great big roaring school reunion, with all the old boys playing to their strengths. They were introduced by their original mentor and ex-Carthusian Jonathan King, and for the encores, their guitarist, Steve Hackett, who had left the band himself in 1977, joined them onstage. To emphasise the irony of the night, Gabriel was brought onstage in a coffin.

Six Of The Best cleared the WOMAD debt, and ultimately set the organisation on the road to becoming one of the world's foremost boutique festivals. Within four years, Gabriel released an album entitled *So* that was a worldwide success, which meant that he would no longer need to rely on lifelines. By the end of the decade, based on the revenues of *So*, he had set up his own studio and label, Real World. With backing from Virgin Records, Real World would properly showcase his global appetite for new musics.

But the effects of the early Eighties would have a far greater impact on Peter Gabriel's future. His championing of world music and his receptiveness to new ideas meant that he no longer saw himself as a mere artist. His work would take on increasing political significance, leading ultimately to his establishing the Elders, an organisation of the world's most respected political figureheads, as a sort of think-tank to solve the world's big issues. He was awarded the Man Of Peace Award by the World Summit of Nobel Peace Laureates in Rome, recognising personalities from the world of culture and entertainment who have stood up for human rights and for the spread of the principles of peace and solidarity in the world, and made an outstanding contribution to international social justice. Few pop singers have achieved this with such stealthy, unassuming gravity as Peter Gabriel.

Gabriel, in his life and music, has frequently taken things to the very brink of the unknown, whether it be in a song, with art, or with bigger, broader concepts. The long defunct *Sounds* magazine said in 1987 that "he seems like a man who would never compromise his art for anything, the sort who would exile himself to a desert island rather than be forced in a direction not of his choosing". In 1982, by returning to Genesis, he *had* compromised his art for something, a means of survival. From that point on, he would ensure he'd never have to do it again. This is the story of one of the most sweetly uncompromising figures to have emerged out of popular music.

As readers will know, Peter Gabriel's first four solo albums in the UK were simply titled *Peter Gabriel*. His fourth was released as *Security* in the US, and at some point, colloquially, the preceding three albums became known by the shorthand descriptions of their covers, *Car*, *Scratch* and *Melt*. I soon abandoned my wish to keep the 'purity' of the UK titles for the first four after about a month of writing, toyed with the problematic 'PG1' 'PG2' labelling, so indeed, I refer to the albums as *Car*, *Scratch*, *Melt* and *Security*.

# Introduction

## A REALLY INTERESTING LIFE

*"Time leaves an indelible stamp on everything. When you revisit your past you can no longer live inside it, but you can walk around it, open up old memories and occasionally catch the scent of some place in which you lived."*

Peter Gabriel, 2012

*"Someone might look at your career and say, 'this man has committed career suicide. He had this gigantic breakthrough album in 1986, and then he waited six years to follow it up. Then he waited 10 years to follow that up, and here we are 10 years after that and the next one isn't even close.' . . . I'm sure that's correct, commercially. But I have had a really interesting life. And that seems to be a much more sensible goal at age 61. If I can still pay my bills, which does become an issue sometimes, then I'm a happy guy."*

Peter Gabriel
*Rolling Stone* 2011

PETER Gabriel said in 2012, "In our culture, masks are seen as something you hide behind, but in other cultures it's the vehicle in which you come out, that was how I came out." Masks have been used in ritual for over 9,000 years. They have been used for ornament, performance, protection and disguise. In African cultures, they have been extensively used in religious ceremonies evoking the spirits of ancestors; animal masks are worn to communicate with spirits.

US music magazine *Circus* ran a 'State Of Future Rock '75' issue in December 1974. In response to the question, "Do you find when you wear a mask the mask takes you over, that you become the mask?" Gabriel replied, "Yeah, I find that quite so. When I wear the mask I find it easier to be the part the mask is. I'm usually very inhibited, but behind the masks I'm not quite so." Peter Gabriel has spent a great deal of his career behind masks.

From the earliest theatricality of his Genesis outfits to the outlandish elegance of his painted face in the Eighties, Gabriel has worn the mask of a pop star for some considerable time. His 1983 video for 'I Don't Remember' begins with him putting on a mask that he finds lying discarded on the floor. The well-worn phrase 'will the real person stand-up, please?' remains problematic with Gabriel. In essence, it is impossible to find the real him. As a tremendously engaging and loving individual, there is no doubting his sincerity, honesty and steadfastness. As an innovator, businessman and campaigner against social injustice, there is no questioning his motives. Gabriel is a peculiar mixture, an emotional man who feels things deeply, married with strong work ethic and a painstaking attention to detail coupled with a classic upper middle-class desire to avoid confrontation. His work offers the closest clues to his personality, and in some instances, his soul-baring is incredibly overt. Yet, he is often hidden in plain sight. His desire to disguise himself on his album sleeves again makes one wonder where he is. Gabriel is, like his name suggests, a spectral, angelic presence. Masked, hidden, someone existing beneath a public exterior; this is the fundamental key to all of Gabriel's material.

* * *

To call him simply a pop star would be to call Salvador Dali a mere painter. Gabriel is one of the most talented, enigmatic artists that Great Britain has ever produced. Quintessentially English, he has had several careers, often running in tandem, and in all he retains a strict, painstaking quality control. He has enjoyed a long and varied solo career, and had a US number one single, 'Sledgehammer', in the Eighties. His voice – described by the *NME* as, ". . . a potent instrument. From a raven-throated croak to a searching treble it skids and arches through the music like alien speech lifted from myth" – is one of the most distinctive in pop. He diversified into writing and contributed to many best-selling soundtracks in the Nineties and new millennium. His audio-visual work has frequently been pioneering. He was one of the first artists to give pop a social conscience and has subsequently campaigned tirelessly on behalf of charities such as Amnesty International in his most understated, English manner.

He founded the WOMAD festival and can be attributed with helping popularise throughout Western Europe what became known as 'world music' through this festival and his label Real World, establishing a recording studio of the same name in Wiltshire. If this were not enough already, Gabriel has pioneered computer systems and was an early adopter in understanding how the music industry could harness the potential – and potential threat – of digital downloading.

For many, however, he will forever remain where his career began, as the front man with Genesis, that strangest of progressive rock groups that grew out of Charterhouse public school in Godalming, Surrey in the late Sixties. As DJ and writer Mark Radcliffe noted, Genesis "were the only prog band who were prepared to admit to a sense of humour and didn't shy away from the simple tune." As their initial, pastoral soul developed into something more ornate, Gabriel added – often to cover his acute shyness – theatricality into their shows with a variety of props and outlandish costumes which put him at the leading edge of innovation and stage performance.

After being courted by *The Exorcist* director William Friedkin to write a film script, he wrote almost every word on the group's 1974 double concept album, *The Lamb Lies Down On Broadway*, which told the tale of a Puerto Rican punk living underneath New York City, and that strayed away from the group's previous, more ethereal, themes. However, the stress levels within Genesis were getting too high and Gabriel, a young married man with a new baby, who had recently relocated from London to Bath, had had enough.

There was considerable shock when Gabriel quit Genesis in 1975 just as major recognition (and finally, financial solvency) for the group beckoned. Tired of the monolith he helped create, he retreated to the west country where he embarked upon what was to become an enormously successful and lucrative solo career, releasing albums without names, growing ever stranger with singles such as 'Games Without Frontiers' while embracing the latest technology. When he *did* give an album a title in 1986, *So* propelled him into the major league of fame and spawned two songs that would risk overshadowing his career – 'Sledgehammer' and 'Don't Give Up'. When this new success beckoned, many had no idea he had ever previously sung in a group.

His love and enthusiasm for global culture and politics led to a sincere and lifelong passion for sharing musics and cultures with the widest audience. As well as his work with Amnesty International, he founded WITNESS, a not-for-profit group that equips, trains and supports locally based organisations worldwide to use video and the internet in human rights documentation and advocacy. He has advised Nelson Mandela, and has met and discussed human rights with other world leaders, and, in 2006, was recognised by the Nobel Peace Prize Laureates as a Man Of Peace. In 2007, he was instrumental in setting up the Elders ("a global village needs village elders"), an organisation with Mandela, Desmond Tutu, Jimmy Carter and Kofi Annan.

Gabriel's ability to synthesise talents and work with the best possible people in all fields of his work has led to some remarkable collaborations in music, art, politics, charity and technology. His meticulous eye for detail means that he ensures the highest standards are brought to any work that bears his name. His influence can be heard today in groups such as Vampire Weekend (who name-checked him in their single 'Cape Cod Kwassa Kwassa'), Elbow and Hot Chip.

In 1992 *Rolling Stone* wrote a most compelling description of him: "Without question, Peter Gabriel's metamorphosis from pointy-headed, theatrical cult artist to canny, minimalist pop star is one of the most impressive transformations pop music has ever seen." This book is the story of that journey – his fascinating reinvention as an avatar of post-punk in late Seventies Britain meant that when *Trouser Press*, the rock magazine of the underground in America, was compiling its record guide of records away from the 'Commercial Mainstream', Gabriel – and indeed *So* – was in there, yet there was not a single entry from the Genesis catalogue.

Peter Gabriel operates with stuttering dignity. He thrives on collaboration. He has always been quick to acknowledge this; from his first partnership with Tony Banks at Charterhouse through to the support of Tony Stratton-Smith at Charisma Records, to hook-ups with Robert Fripp, David Lord, Daniel Lanois and later, the team at Real World, Gabriel has worked with some of the most mercurial talents, spurring on his own painstaking creativity.

The Charisma record label, "an organic, volcanic vat fizzing with fury from earthy lust to ethereal highs" and Stratton-Smith were the real beginning of Gabriel's flowering in 1970. In an atmosphere of encouragement and participation, Gabriel developed into one of the first great front men of progressive rock, borrowing from film, theatre, slapstick and art to create an otherworldly persona. There are those who can never get this image out from their mind, and this training, in the dormitory towns of

England's home counties to the ballrooms of Italy to the clubs of America, has led Gabriel to produce a series of ever-more spectacular live shows, whether it be with a conventional band, or as in 2010/2011, a 48-piece orchestra.

It's hard to put your finger on why Gabriel's music is quite so emotional, as often it is built methodically concentrating on sounds and feel rather than gung-ho emotion. Yet, he has wholly or partly written some of the most affecting songs in popular music: 'Supper's Ready', 'The Carpet Crawlers', 'Solsbury Hill', 'Don't Give Up,' 'Washing Of The Water,' and 'Father, Son' to highlight a mere few.

*Without Frontiers* is about the music, life and art of Peter Brian Gabriel. How many front men of progressive rock groups end up forming an association that deals with world issues? He inspires fierce loyalty from his friends, fellow musicians and associates, and he is seen as one of the kindest and most constant of human beings. Nile Rodgers, who has worked with Gabriel several times, speaks for many when he says, "We [Gabriel and I] live in a more ethereal world together, which is interesting for me as an artist, to have a friend who feels like your true friend. You may hardly see them, but when you do see them it's magical and special, and you keep going – it's like planets in the universe, they are out there doing their thing and every now and again they come into close proximity with each other. In my very humble opinion, Peter is the finest gentleman I know in rock'n'roll. He is that guy."

PART ONE

# From Genesis . . .: 1950–1975

# 1: Lead A Normal Life

*"My family arrived in this country from Spain at the time of the Armada, and the story goes we were adopted by Cornish peasants . . ."*

Peter Gabriel, 1974

*"My dad is an electrical engineer, inventor type, reserved, shy, analytical, and my mum's more instinctive, she responds by the moment – music is her big thing. And I've got both."*

Peter Gabriel, 2000

WHEN Peter Gabriel spoke of rather trusting a 'country man than a town man' in Genesis' 1974 song 'The Chamber Of 32 Doors', he could well have been talking about his own roots. For in his 63 years (at the time of writing), Gabriel has spent less than a decade living in a city. Although he keeps a residence in West London, Gabriel lives in rustic splendour at his home by his Real World studios in Box near Bath in Wiltshire, which echoes the rural idyll of his childhood in the Surrey countryside. The physical roots of his life could be a metaphor for his semi-detached relationship with showbusiness; near enough, yet far away. Surrey is less than an hour from London and his residence now is less than 15 minutes from the bustling city centre of Bath. He can get into the middle of things easily when he needs to, yet he remains far enough removed. It is not dissimilar to his relationship with the mainstream of popular music.

Whenever Gabriel has neared the big time (or indeed, 'Big Time', his 1986 hit single) he has been there just enough to receive acclaim and at times, stellar sales, before retreating back to the anonymous comfort of the margins. In this semi-detached atmosphere he thrives, creating works of great, lasting import. Getting a life, as he sang on his 1992 hit, 'Steam', with "this dreamer's dream"; for his family, like many of the post-war burgeoning middle class in the UK, encouraged dreams, just as long as they were grounded in a degree of reality and accompanied with a huge amount of hard graft.

Peter Brian Gabriel was born on February 13, 1950 at Woking Hospital. He grew up at his family home, Deep Pool Farm, Coxhill, just outside Chobham in Surrey, in the long, empty days of rebuilding and drabness less than five years after the Allied victory that signalled the end of the Second World War. However, although his father had worked with the RAF, it was almost as if the war had gone on somewhere else. The Surrey that Gabriel was born into was peaceful, leafy and well-to-do. Chobham is the epitome of the well-heeled satellite towns to the south-west of London. Originally listed in the Domesday Book as Cebeham, it was governed by nearby Chertsey Abbey. By the 20th century, it was still relatively rural and undeveloped, unlike its nearby neighbour, Woking, which burgeoned when a railway station on the London and South Western railway opened in 1834. With its green common, range of pubs and inns and the River Bourne providing the occasional flood risk, it looked every inch how an idealised British village should look.

At the time of his birth, Gabriel's mother, Edith Irene Allen, had been married for three years to Ralph Parton Gabriel. The family would be completed with the birth of his sister Anne in October 1951. Ralph came from a line of locally-based timber importers and merchants that traded under the name of Gabriel, Wade & English from 1925 onwards. Gabriel's great-great-great grandfather, Christopher Gabriel had founded the family business in 1770. He trained as a carpenter, initially making furniture before concentrating on the importation of timber in 1812. The business expanded greatly in the late 18th century.

The Gabriel family name in the UK is thought to go back to 1588, the year of the Spanish Armada, when ship-wrecked crewmembers found themselves on English soil. Elsewhere it goes back even further, deriving from the Hebrew name 'Gavriel', meaning 'God give me strength'. The name was used in the New Testament of the Bible, as the Archangel Gabriel was the harbinger of the news to Mary that she was to become the mother of Jesus. The family name became popular in the 12th century, and remained so throughout northern Europe.

Gabriel's ancestors had been fairly well-known in the 19th century as politicians and businessmen in Streatham, south London, from where the family timber business was run. According to census reports published in the *Daily Telegraph*, Gabriel's forefathers were, thanks to the success of their timber business, reasonably well off, keeping servants and attending the best schools. Gabriel's great-great-grandfather, Christopher Trowell Gabriel was born in 1797, and, in 1833, married Ruth, the daughter of billiard-table maker, John Thurston. Christopher's brother, Sir Thomas Gabriel, was London's Lord Mayor in 1866. When Christopher died in 1873, he left an estate in the region of £200,000. He and Ruth's son, Thomas, received the estate in Ely, while Ruth was bequeathed the possessions in the family residence, Norfolk House.

By the time of Peter's birth, Gabriel's family also ran a dairy farm. Although well-off, Ralph did not fit the image of the gentleman farmer, employing a bailiff and a tractor driver to look after it day-to-day. As Gabriel was to note, "my father was much more of a thinker than the rest of the family". Ralph was, in fact, something of a visionary. He became an electrical engineer after gaining a degree at the University Of London in the Thirties. Deep Pool Cottage, where he settled after his marriage, was part of the family farm and was the second and last dwelling of his 100-year life; it had been given to him as a wedding present by his father, and was across the way from Coxhill, the house where he was born. During the Second World War, Ralph worked on projects for the RAF. "The Germans developed this very clever system for guiding their bombers because of the blackout," Gabriel's friend and one-time Genesis tour manager Richard Macphail said. "They made a radio beam that would point at, say, Birmingham. All they would have to do would be to fly along the beam at a certain speed, and then at a given moment open the bomb doors. It was very clever. But Ralph was part of the team that figured out a way of bending the beam without the Germans knowing, so they would fly off course. He must have saved hundreds, thousands of lives, these bombs would drop harmlessly out in the countryside."

"My father was a quiet, thoughtful inventor and electrical engineer," Gabriel said in 2007. "He invented a thing called Dial-A-Programme in 1971, accessed through the dial of a telephone. I saw his passion, and I love to get involved with all sorts of techy things. All of this was entertainment on demand. My father was campaigning for the future."

Ralph would work for countless hours on new inventions in the workshop behind the house. He was often a little too ahead of his time: "He invented cable television for Rediffusion," Macphail adds. "He figured out how to get a television signal down the phone line but Rediffusion couldn't see why people would pay for television when the BBC were supplying it for free."

To counterbalance the methodical, eccentric, scientific approach of Ralph, Gabriel's mother inspired him musically. "My mother was the one who was interested in music and performing, running on adrenalin. My dad was more meditative. He would come back from a day working in London and stand on his head in the garden doing yoga."

It is clear that Gabriel senior is at the root of his son's lifelong restless inquisitiveness. For a man with the scantest of human vices, Gabriel's vice has become technology; early adopting. A man who, according to biographer Spencer Bright, bought a bio-feedback machine in the early days of Genesis and a floatation tank in the early Eighties. He learned sophisticated yoga techniques, and experimented wearing gravity boots and this before his pioneering, ground-breaking use of technology in music began. All of this can be traced back to his father's experimentation in the workshop at the family home.

Irene Gabriel, known to all as 'Ireney' was one of five sisters; two of them studied at the Royal Academy Of Music. The Allen family were musical, and Irene's mother had sung at the Proms, the world famous concerts established by Sir Henry Wood and Robert Newman in London in 1895. She could play the piano confidently, and her family had enjoyed certain luxuries as benefitted the daughter of the Chairman and Managing Director of the Civil Service Department Store in London's Strand. Her father, Colonel Edward Allen, was a sporty, self-made man who started off as a carpenter's mate, with a passion for gambling. He would take Irene and her sisters to places such as Monte Carlo so he could play the tables.

"Music was my mother's passion, she played piano, Christmases were always full of members of the family singing and playing different instruments, it was quite an occasion," Gabriel said in 2012. It was this clear combination of his respective parents' personalities and love of music that has coursed throughout his work. "His mum was a very strong character and she would dominate the proceedings with her easy charm," Charterhouse friend and future Genesis founder Anthony Phillips would say. "Peter and Ralph would be quite quiet in her presence. His parents were very generous; they'd often have us over for supper and they would trust Peter because he was always extremely sensible."

"Ralph was a fairly distant figure," Gabriel's future best friend, Tony Banks, adds. "He used to wander around in the shadows. He would come out with these little phrases. It's interesting how Peter has picked up his original thinking and inventiveness, and fortunately he has his mother's gregariousness and charm – he's got the right combination of the two."

Gabriel had a fairly idyllic middle-class childhood. As well as the love and support, there was also the withdrawn, stiff-upper-lipped demeanour that characterised many post-war families of similar stature. He had the run of the farm, he could watch and immerse himself in nature, playing with dragonflies, making fires with sticks, and damming the River Bourne. He would play with his sister and the children of the farmhands. However, with his sister sharing her mother's love for horses and ponies, Gabriel would often be alone from choice. Coxhill, the house on the farm where his father was born, was a big Victorian manor with, as he recalled to Armando Gallo in 1979, "wood panelling, a billiard room and a croquet lawn". The homely, yet slightly eerie detachment of the place would later inform his work. As a child Gabriel was quite convinced he could fly, running round four pear trees in his lawn flapping his arms to achieve lift off. "I was reading a lot of Superman comics at the time, so reality got a little confused." It is impossible not to hear his later songs, 'Willow Farm' or 'The Nest That Sailed The Sky', without this mental picture being evoked.

Although not a regular attendee of church, religion was a constant presence in Gabriel's upbringing, and the quest for spirituality, gleaned from perusing his father's books on eastern religions, would interest Gabriel throughout his career. Gabriel reflected on the place in which he grew up in 1978: "It's become Esherised. Reproduction print shops and reproduction antique shops taking over the local groceries." But then, although sleepy, rarefied and select, it was a strong working and farming community, not just a commuter suburb.

Gabriel attended Cable House primary school in Woking and then, from the age of nine, the year he holidayed for the first time in Spain, St Andrew's Preparatory School for Boys situated in a marvellous old building; Church Hill House in Wilson Way, Horsell. It was in his final year at St Andrew's that he became a weekday boarder. Although not a gifted academic, Gabriel would work hard and diligently to get results. Inherently shy, he found it relatively easy to get on with the other boys, but from that age, no doubt because of the influence of his mother, sister and the daughters of the farm-workers, preferred the company of women. "I wasn't a macho, sporty male," he was to say later. "I would prefer doctors and nurses with the girls behind the flower beds to cowboys and Indians." When he and his friends cycled to school, the working-class children of the village would regularly make fun of the 'posh boys'. As a result, Gabriel built up a thick skin.

"I had this dream when I was 11," Gabriel told Bright in 1988. "I saw a fork in the path where I could either be an entertainer or a singer, or a farmer . . . but I never thought that I would be a singer, because I didn't think I could sing. When I was young they thought I had a nice choirboy voice, but when I tried to sing rock songs, it sounded terrible."

It was while he was attending St Andrew's that teachers noticed Gabriel had some promise as a singer, and although he was ultimately to forego them, he spent some time following in his mother's footsteps by taking piano lessons. Gabriel had expressed an interest in drumming, and at the age of 10 had purchased from his friend's brother his first drum, a floor tom-tom for around £10. It was to be his first association with the rhythms that would so drive his work. Although on more than one occasion he has referred to himself as a 'failed drummer', throughout his career Gabriel has often returned to his first love: percussion. Even when he abandoned percussion altogether for his *Scratch My Back* concept in 2010, he made the strings sound like percussive instruments. Bill Bruford, drummer in so many key bands of the Seventies, opines that a gig with Gabriel was one of only three gigs that drummers would kill for in the late 20th century – the other two being King Crimson and Frank Zappa.

Gabriel wrote his first song, entitled 'Sammy The Slug', at the age of 12, and later joked that "everyone else was writing about girls and I was writing about slugs, which shows what I was interested in." This was the first example of his off-kilter approach to the art form that would one day make him his living.

Aware of her nephew's interest, one of his opera-singing aunties thought she would assist him on his path. Gabriel was later to recall, "She gave me £5 once to go and find out how professional singers sing." Gabriel bought the first Beatles album instead. He had first heard the Liverpool group's debut single, 'Love Me Do', on the radio in the back of his parents' car, and as he remembered "it was way more radical sounding than punk when I first heard it".

Gabriel was exactly the right age at the right time to absorb this new phenomenon. He was too young to have appreciated the first impact of rock'n'roll in the Fifties, after which the music scene quickly became somewhat staid. Soon after Gabriel turned 13, in March 1963, The Beatles released their debut album, *Please Please Me*. The impact it had on teenagers hearing it for the first time was simply enormous. That summer, as Gabriel came to terms with leaving the relative comfort and security of St Andrew's for the next stage of his young life, The Beatles seemed to be everywhere.

Although Beatlemania, as it became known, was yet to break, their first three singles, including their first number one, 'From Me To You', provided an intoxicating soundtrack to innocent days. And their debut album's somewhat eccentric mixture of self-written material and black American R&B covers (including songs by The Shirelles, Isley Brothers and Arthur Alexander) showed that it was acceptable to write your own songs, while also opening a gateway to mysterious, soulful artists who would provide a seed for Gabriel's intelligent, enquiring mind. To complement his floor tom, he was bought a snare drum by his parents. Gabriel was on the way to assembling his first drum kit.

The Beatles were number one in the UK charts with 'She Loves You' when, aged 13, Peter Gabriel began his first term at Charterhouse, a public school in Godalming, in September 1963. And it was to be their influence, together with other fellow travellers, that was to have far greater impact on Gabriel than anything merely academic.

# 2: Crying Or Masturbating, Or Both: Charterhouse

*"It's a complete misconception to think that Genesis existed as a group at Charterhouse. It didn't. It existed only as four songwriters."*

Ant Phillips, 2006

*"We were always straightforward in Genesis about our public school education. A lot of musicians, before us and since, have come from middle-class families and kept it concealed."*

Peter Gabriel, 2007

CHARTERHOUSE School was founded by Thomas Sutton in Charterhouse Square in Smithfield, London in 1611. It relocated and expanded to its current location in Godalming, Surrey in 1872. With its motto, 'Deo Dante Dedi' – 'Because God gave, I gave', the then all-boys school was the textbook embodiment of what one thinks of as an English public school. With its vast, stately main building designed by Philip Charles Hardwick, who had designed the Great Hall at Euston station, its position on a hill enforced its stature as a dominating and oppressive presence, the very epitome of imposing Victorian grandeur.

Attendance at the school was enshrined in Gabriel's family; his grandfather, Christopher Burton Gabriel, had been a boarder at Charterhouse in 1891. He was among illustrious company – poet Richard Lovelace, founder of Methodism John Wesley, composer Ralph Vaughn Williams, scout movement creator Robert Baden-Powell, playwright Ben Travers and poet and writer Robert Graves were all among its alumni. As his grandfather and father, Ralph, went to Charterhouse, accordingly the young Gabriel was 'put down' for the same public school at birth. The school encapsulated all that was held dear by the establishment – patriarchal values, rote learning, a system steeped in rarefied rituals that aimed to prepare its pupils for Oxbridge and, at the very least, senior positions in the city of London. Like many of these establishments, there was little patience for – and much exasperation with – boys who didn't wholeheartedly subscribe to its ethos, yet as the Sixties progressed more and more pupils looked to other ways to make a living beyond the conventional routes for which the school prepared them.

On leaving the relative comfort and close proximity to his home of St Andrew's, Gabriel was sent away to Charterhouse under some duress in September 1963. As he was already showing signs of becoming a strong-willed free spirit, he never fully fitted in at Charterhouse, and was always uncomfortable with its entrenched attitudes. However, to suggest he was a rebel would be to overstate the case; his respectful nature and strong sense of politeness meant that he caused little trouble. The revolution was to be inside his head, and that would be stirred by the music he absorbed and would soon start to make.

The impact on Gabriel and the fellow members of his future group of their time at Charterhouse has been well chronicled elsewhere, but Gabriel's vivid description of his first night at the school in *Genesis Chapter And Verse* graphically illustrates his feelings. Having become accustomed to the peace of the farm, the lights of passing cars through the curtain-less windows gave the impression of anti-aircraft lights, and "the air was full of boys either crying or masturbating, or both. It was 'welcome to grown-up school.'" And part of being in this type of 'grown-up school' meant occupying something of a parallel universe to the rest of the world, a universe with strong and established links to its foundation in 1611. Charterhouse had its own language; its pupils were known as Carthusians. Teachers were 'Beaks'; a lesson was known as a 'hash', evening meal was 'homebill' and the three terms, known as quarters, were the 'Oration', 'Long' and 'Cricket'. Gabriel never really fitted into the Charterhouse elite. He learned, he said, to survive without "being good at anything". "I was a bit of a loner. It was like *Tom Brown's School Days* – an atmosphere of fear and bullying – I didn't really fit in there."

And, as is so often the case in these establishments, outsiders meet outsiders. On the first day he was at Charterhouse Gabriel met Tony Banks, a fellow member of Girdlestoneites House, one of the four houses into which the school was divided. Named after its inaugural housemaster, Frederick Girdlestone, it had long been informally known as 'Duckites' as Girdlestone had walked with a duck-like gait. Without any doubt, the relationship between Gabriel and Banks was the foundation of Genesis, and also the reason why Gabriel left the group a decade after its inception. Born on March 27, 1950 in East Hoathly, Sussex, by the age of 13 Banks was already an accomplished pianist. "I said, 'Hello I'm Banks' and he said 'I'm Gabriel', because we just used our surnames in those days," Tony Banks laughs. "I remember thinking he was quite quiet, slightly fat sort of guy, serious looking. He didn't look threatening. Mostly harmless, as they say."

Gabriel and Banks were united in their distaste for the school. Richard Macphail, who was later to become Genesis' tour manger and remains a close friend of both, met them at the school. Macphail's view wasn't as bleak as some: "I'm just somebody who arrived on this planet with a very positive and optimistic outlook," he explains. "I know Tony had a ghastly time and really hated it, and it's putting it a bit strongly, but it probably scarred him. It was a fairly brutal regime. The senior boys were allowed to beat younger boys, not masters, but the boys. That was the way it was. Pretty wild, if you think about it."

"My first couple of years I found quite difficult, as it was quite oppressive," Banks admits. "I'd come from my previous school where I'd been quite successful. I went downhill in terms of my academic work. I didn't really get on with the teachers, and generally I was not particularly happy."

After getting to know each other, Banks and Gabriel would sit and make up songs, with Gabriel, a far less able piano player, trying to wrest keyboards from Banks at any given moment. "Peter won both ways really, because if I got there first, he would sing," Banks says. "We used to play these things with John Grumbar on clarinet. We used to play standards such as 'Quando Quando Quando' which taught me a lot about how music was constructed. Sometimes we'd have the sheet music and I'd bang away on the chords, other times I'd play it by ear. It was fun to do all that."

In this oppressive atmosphere Gabriel and Banks, inspired by the work of Lennon and McCartney, thought that they could one day become songwriters, performing material that they would eventually write. "I think Tony figured out that he didn't have a particularly strong voice and thought I had a better voice, so I suspect that was his main motivation for trying to work with me," Gabriel said in 2006. "And I certainly knew he had skills on the piano that I definitely didn't have."

The duo had no firm idea of wanting to form a band, as they were more interested in songwriting and looking at opportunities to create original lyrics and chord sequences. "Peter and Tony were both keyboard guys and they would both squabble over who was going to play the piano, and that is how their musical relationship got started," Macphail recalls. "Tony was a properly trained classical pianist and Peter was experimenting with blues chords. They had very different influences which is one of the good things that they brought to it – Banks was hymns and Bach, and Peter was Nina Simone and the blues, which is what really floated his boat."

"Peter and I were always looking for something a little bit different," Banks says. "He played me 'I Put A Spell On You' by Nina Simone, which we both loved; her voice was fantastic and the string arrangement and the chords were so evocative, and remains one of my favourites. We were both into the soul music thing. I loved Tamla Motown, and Otis Redding. We shared a lot of that: our musical taste was pretty close – I had a pretty catholic taste in those days. During the decade my tastes closed right up and by the end of the decade I didn't like *anything*."

The boys' time at the school coincided with the burst into colour that Britain experienced in the early Sixties: "It was obviously a period of huge change," Macphail recalls. "It was The Beatles and the Stones. We all arrived in 1962/3 and it coincided with everything going 'bang'. Everything went 'bang' at Charterhouse, too. People began growing their hair and wearing tight trousers and getting into the music." Ultimately, as Macphail recalls, "the thing that saved us all was the music. That's where I got my O and A levels."

As a lifesaver for the boys, there was a room in the basement of Duckites' House where, for an hour every evening, their housemaster would allow the Dansette record player to be turned up to full volume. It was here that Gabriel listened to the blues, R&B, soul, the Stones, The Yardbirds, The Beatles, whatever the boys purchased on their frequent trips into Godalming. Music became everything.

* * *

Anthony 'Ant' Phillips, who was in the year below Banks and Gabriel, was very much into bands. Born in Chiswick, west London on December 23, 1951, Phillips was a gifted guitarist. "People forget what a giant character Ant was," Macphail notes. "He was musically way ahead of everybody else even though he was younger than us." Phillips was friendly with Mike Rutherford (born on October 2, 1950), whom he had met early in his time at the school and had something of a reputation as a rebel. "I'd met Peter in our first year," Mike Rutherford recalls. "If you weren't in the same house you weren't that close. There weren't that many guys involved in music, so if you had an interest in music, you soon found like-minded people. Peter struck me as a very quiet person."

Rutherford's housemaster forbade him playing guitar, going as far as calling it "a symbol of the revolution". As guitar players were few and far between at Charterhouse, Rutherford and Phillips formed a fast friendship and they soon formed a group called The Anon, with bass player and Phillips' prep school friend, Rivers Job, on bass, as well as their good friend Macphail on vocals. "I never could imagine that I could write a song," Macphail says. "But I was a good mimic." Macphail had something of a Mick Jagger obsession. Whereas The Beatles were seen as good boys, Jagger's band, The Rolling Stones, were the bad boys of pop, channelling the delta blues and belying their rather posh Kent origins. Macphail loved the group so much that Phillips suggested that he should be known as 'Mick Phail' in the band. "I struggled all the way with my parents," Macphail laughs. "They seriously thought that Mick Jagger was the devil incarnate."

By mid-1965, the school had several groups, all of them inspired by The Beatles and The Rolling Stones' breakthrough into the world's charts and hearts. The League Of Gentlemen were arguably the best but Gabriel, who had been acquiring additional kit to accompany his tom-tom, began drumming in The Milords (sometimes referred to as The M'Lords) and subsequently a holiday band, The Spoken Word with friend David Thomas. "Peter was in The Milords with Richard Apsley," Banks recalls. "They mainly played trad jazz. They played a concert with Pete playing the drums and, on their version of 'House Of The Rising Sun', he played *and* sang. Now Peter has a great feel for rhythm, but he has no ability to keep it. His drumming was always pretty lethal. It was very exciting, he was playing every beat on all drums at the same time and shouting. It *sort of* worked."

Gabriel and Tony Banks were dragged further into performing together, away from their proposed writing factory, when, with friend Chris Stewart on drums, they formed a group for a prospective performance in the school hall in July 1966. Stewart also played in The Climax, formed by guitarist Rutherford with Mick Colman after Rutherford found The Anon's rehearsal regime a little too rigorous.

But The Anon were kingpins on the scene and Rutherford would soon rejoin them. There was rivalry between the bands. "If Rivers Job and I had not left Charterhouse in the summer of 1966, it's questionable whether Genesis would have ever got going," Macphail says. Although Job was set to leave, Macphail did not know at that point that he would not be attending Charterhouse the next term. He had the idea to bring together The Anon and the as-yet-untitled soul outfit led by Gabriel, who fundamentally only came into existence for this concert ("a funny little outing for what became Genesis" says Phillips, who briefly became their guitarist) on the same bill. "The concert could be seen as a symbol of social change and it felt like we were spearheading it," Rutherford laughs. "We did two sets, in two halves – they went on and we went on. It was fantastically amateurish." Job and Phillips would play bass and guitar for Gabriel's outfit, which had been hastily christened The Garden Wall. "I never knew we were called The Garden Wall at the time, someone later told me," Banks laughs. "The piano was too heavy to put onstage, so I played in front. No one knew I was there until I did the introduction to 'When A Man Loves A Woman', and they were all looking for me. We did very soulful versions of that and 'I Am A Rock', a few others and some improvised 12-bars. Quite humorously, I couldn't see the drummer Chris Stewart to stop the piece, and we'd run out of ideas, and we went round about five times before I managed to catch his attention. It was fun to do, and I have no idea what it was like."

Although Macphail was preoccupied with his own performance, he recalls, "Peter wore the funny tall hat he designed and had made. I don't remember him as being particularly wild, but he was definitely quirky."

The music master who sanctioned the event was Geoffrey Ford, by then into his tenth year as Director Of Music at Charterhouse. Although he was forward thinking enough to allow the event to take place, he had stipulated that he didn't want any announcements, which came as a great disappointment to Gabriel, Banks, Rutherford, Phillips and Macphail. The latter, by now 16, had started sloping off to see bands at London's fabled Marquee Club where announcing the upcoming song was all part of the magic ritual of performance. As the concert was in front of 600 people, the whole school, Ford was concerned that the groups would incite a riot. Gabriel was on his best behaviour and The Garden Wall got to finish their set, which was not to be the case for The Anon.

"I was sticking to the rules until we had a bit of an equipment breakdown," Macphail says. "I announced our song 'Pennsylvania Flickhouse' as I was so proud that Ant was writing our own material. At the end of it, Geoffrey Ford came and pulled the plug so we never got to play our last number. That 1966 concert was my pinnacle. I was over-brimming with overconfidence."

Rivers Job, a mercurial spirit, left Charterhouse and by the end of the Sixties, he would be playing bass in Savoy Brown. By the end of the Seventies he had committed suicide. Macphail was not to return to Charterhouse, and went to study at Millfield School in Street, Somerset. The Anon continued without him. Inspired by Cream, they became a power trio with Rob Tyrell on drums, Rutherford on bass and Phillips on guitar. Macphail was to remain in touch with his closest friend Phillips and kept an ear out for the latest developments.

Macphail's departure paved the way for the merger of the two outfits that would form Genesis, but, it is probably Ant Phillips' statement from 2006 that is the most telling: "It's a complete misconception to think that Genesis existed as a group at Charterhouse. It didn't. It existed only as four songwriters."

* * *

On September 18, 1966, Gabriel went to London and saw Otis Redding at the Ram Jam Club in Brixton. Although only 36 miles north east of Charterhouse, Gabriel could have been travelling to another planet. It was probably the single most important event in his life. The resonance of the occasion has echoed through interviews across his career. He told *NPR* on October 17, 2012, that "Otis Redding was the king for me and some of the Stax and that classic R&B soul . . . I managed to see Otis Redding in this basement and there were probably only three white faces in the whole place. And it is still, to this day, my favourite ever gig." His copy of the 1965 album *Otis Blue* had been played so much its grooves were almost smooth, but nothing quite prepared Gabriel for seeing the legendary performer in concert. Although only 26 years old, Redding – a minister's son from Georgia – knew everything about stagecraft, soul and timing. The wider world would get a glimpse of him when he played the Monterey Pop festival the following year.

Redding's performance had a deep and profound effect on Gabriel. He continued to *NPR*, "You felt your heart being opened when you were in his presence – I still feel all that emotion when I hear it. Say someone like Springsteen who has all that incredible energy as a performer, if you can imagine that times something you start to get near Otis. He'd stop it and be very still sometimes, but when he was on, it was like a factory of energy, love and passion." Redding's performance skills began to be incorporated in Gabriel's act around the school, and as a result, he and Banks began writing more material together.

* * *

Ant Phillips can be credited with bringing what would become Genesis together. He and Rutherford were working on some demos for The Anon at the studio of a mutual friend, Brian Roberts, and needed some keyboards. Phillips asked Banks to add the keyboards to his recordings, and, in turn, Banks suggested that Gabriel should come along to sing. During this period The Anon recorded 'Pennsylvania Flickhouse', the demo of which surfaced in 2011. Marking Phillips and Rutherford's debut recording, it showed a promising, if derivative beat-driven sound.

Banks thought that these sessions would provide a perfect opportunity to record the latest song that he and Gabriel had been working on, 'She Is Beautiful'. "I had the chord sequence and the bass riff, for 'She Is Beautiful'," Banks says, "and then Peter started singing on top and got the melody line and lyrics, so that was a reasonably common way of working. Later, I would write lyrics and melody lines, and Peter would write chords as well. We wrote a lot together over that period."

As Phillips was to comment: "Mike and I had the R&B, the raw side, Tony had the classical influence and the thing that Peter brought in, which the rest of us didn't have naturally, was the soul – that slightly soulful voice."

Gabriel told Paul Morley at *NME* in July 1980: "I felt I could repress the middle class English person with soul music . . . I wanted to sit at the piano for hours and hours and scream or whatever it was. Just to release emotions. This was one of the main attractions of rock music for me; perhaps another just being the raw excitement of it."

The exposure to performing, music and fashion opened up the young

Gabriel's mind. "That's something very common to musicians from England, people who are in that whole BBC thing; they all have that well-rounded knowledge of music, much more so than America," fan and future collaborator Nile Rodgers says. "In America it's more targeted, over there they still are concerned with educating as well as entertaining. But there is always an educational component that you are always turning people on – it's got to make you think as well as to make you react. Almost all the artists I've worked with from across the pond have that taste – and it's not just because a person may be better educated, I think it's something to do with the culture. People are socialised there and what they are exposed to. I see that pattern with musicians from there – I could be hanging with a guy like Johnny from Manchester, or Duran from Birmingham, Sting from Newcastle; a lot of these guys are from working-class backgrounds but they are sophisticated individuals, but they all do it young – they don't wait until they are 30 or 40, they are doing it between 15 and 17 years old."

Although Gabriel was certainly not working class, he *was* doing it between 15 and 17. Aside from his study and the band work, Gabriel, who would be known for his 'Motown' turn, frequently getting up and singing R&B on tables much to the joy of fellow students, also briefly dabbled in the world of fashion design. He would tie-dye shirts and sell them to fellow pupils and supply hats to sell at Emmerton and Lambert in the Chelsea Antiques Market that he had made up by Dunn & Co. in Piccadilly. The story resurfaced in 2011 in Britain's *Daily Mirror*: "I found these hats in my grandfather's dressing up box," he told them in September of that year. "I persuaded a gentlemen's outfitters in Piccadilly to get them made up in pinks and greens, hippy colours, and they were sold . . . where the Stones used to hang out. When I came back from school one day, I saw Marianne Faithfull wearing one of my hats on *Juke Box Jury* and I got very excited. Then the place called back and said Keith Richards had bought one too! That was worth many points at school." "I never did continue my career as a milliner," Gabriel said in 2007. "Although I have had a few silly things on my head since then. But I did possess an entrepreneurial streak, a determination which I really think helped Genesis at times."

Asked by TV programme *Star Test* in 1989 what his strongest memories of school were, he replied: "I was at school during the flower power days, so I was trying to be a hippy within the confines of an English public school, I was walking round with bells on my feet and throwing flowers in strange places. I think then it felt a quite oppressive, repressive atmosphere and music for me was a fantastic release. So that's when I really locked into channeling my emotions into music." One thing was for sure, as Richard Macphail notes, "Back then rock was not the typical pursuit of public school boys."

* * *

Their time in the albeit very small music scene at Charterhouse was a period of phenomenal growth and development for Gabriel and his bandmates. Gabriel was by now having the time of his life: his shyness abating, and his youthful puppy fat giving way to the lean, sinewy frame he was to sport for the next two decades, he was, like many Charterhouse pupils before him, finding that his real future lay in London. "I was 17 in 1967, and that was an amazing year to be entering adulthood," he said. "I'd sneak out from school and go down to the Electric Garden in Covent Garden, a basement club and you'd see all these oil projections on the wall, and it was Third Ear Band and all this psychedelia, really, the Indica Gallery, there was so much going on – *IT* and *OZ* magazines, there was this cultural explosion happening and there was this sense that youth, for the first time was taking over the world. Hypnotising, intoxicating, every barrier was being smashed down. And in our small, isolated little cell, we felt connected to that, me probably more than everybody else, but this sense of trying to do something in a new way." Gabriel was very much the fledgling man about town.

The Genesis story as we know it began when Jonathan King returned to Charterhouse for an Old Carthusians Day in January 1967. Since leaving the school, King had become well-known in the music industry. Six years older than Gabriel, he had taken the conventional route from the school and gone to Trinity College, Cambridge and, during a period of illness, written off to record labels seeking work in London. Impressed by his forthrightness, Tony Hall at Decca put him in touch with publisher Joe Roncoroni and Zombies manager Ken Jones. One of pop's curious and singular eccentrics, he was a talented writer, performer and producer, whose self-belief was unparalleled, a man who wasted no time at all reminding his audience of his greatness. By 1967, he was already known as a pop star for his 1965 Top 4 UK hit, 'Everyone's Gone To The Moon'.

With a mixture of youthful exuberance and arrogance, Gabriel and Banks looked at their options to get their Chiswick-made demo tape heard by the London music scene. The tape was recorded by a barely existent band that had never actually played live together, but the five players – Banks, Gabriel, Rutherford, Phillips and Stewart – knew they had something. They were aware that DJ David Jacobs' son was at the school, but felt that using the old boy network would possibly be more appropriate, and King was closer in age and outlook to the band than Jacobs, who was already well into his forties at this juncture. Gabriel enlisted their friend, John Alexander, to give King the tape as he emerged from his car at the school that day. With Alexander explaining that the group didn't even have a name at this stage, King rolled his eyes but played the cassette as he returned to London after his day at his alma mater. It was a perfect example of schoolboy chutzpah meeting the old music industry. And that was a powerful alliance.

Speaking in 2006, King said that, on listening, "I was absolutely staggered by the quality of Peter's voice. It had a smokiness to it, which is something I've always gone for . . . And Peter's voice was even better in 1967 because it was full of youth and enthusiasm." Gabriel said, "We were using the old boy network. And I think at that time King seemed quite happy to use the young boy network."

Initially little seemed to come of the tape they passed to King. However, that smokiness in Gabriel's voice remained in King's head and, after a period of months, King got in touch with Gabriel, via the phone number that had been scribbled on the cassette. He invited the band to London. King especially liked the song, 'She Is Beautiful', which pleased Banks no end, as that was the one that he and Gabriel had brought to the recording session in Chiswick. It was a song to which the group would frequently return in these early days, and it was finally released as 'The Serpent' on what was to become their debut album in 1969.

Gabriel would become the *de facto* go-between between group and mogul, going down to the nearest phone box to glean instructions from King. He gave them money to demo. "All the original demos King heard were with acoustic instruments which he thought gave us quite a novel sound," Gabriel was to say. "He was an interesting person and came up with a lot of outrageous ideas for us."

King signed the group – Banks, Gabriel, Phillips (who was 15 years old at the time), Rutherford and Stewart – to Jonjo Music and, through his connections at the Decca label, got the group signed to the label. The initial suggestion was for a five-year contract, which was changed to a year-long contract with option for renewal. Although money-wise, it was clearly paltry to the group, it was very much in keeping with the deals of the day. Most importantly, it got the group on the ladder and they enjoyed being in the reflected glow of King's stardom. "To make a record," Gabriel later said, "seemed like such a spectacular, exciting thing to do."

★ ★ ★

Decca Records was the heart of the establishment and had an illustrious history. Founded in 1929 by British stockbroker Sir Edward Lewis, the label was quick to diversify into the US market, and, as London Records in the States, it exported artists of the UK establishment such as Vera Lynn and Mantovani. By the Sixties the label was diversifying into popular music, and, after famously rejecting The Beatles in 1962, had clamoured to fill their roster with as many happening acts as possible, starting with The Rolling Stones, who were signed to the label on the recommendation of George Harrison. Jonathan King had signed himself to Decca in 1964.

It was King who gave this musicians collective their name. His first choice for the group was Gabriel's Angels, which Gabriel himself rather enjoyed, but it was quickly vetoed by the rest of the band. As Gabriel said, "When Genesis was suggested, I think we thought, 'Well, if this guy's going to pay for us to go into a studio, we'd better just go along with it.' " As Rutherford added, "We couldn't agree on anything, and we didn't have any great alternative to offer him, so that became the name. Genesis was never a name that I thought was very good, but after a while it is what it is and you get used to it, I mean, The Beatles is a crap name really, if you think about it."

One matter that all parties agreed on, given their name and the angelic moniker of the singer, was that there would be a religious undertow to their work. And Jesus was on the verge of becoming tremendously hip. Although establishment rocker Cliff Richard had publically declared his faith in the mid-Sixties, by 1967 religion was something more mystical and far-out, with The Beatles especially leading the way in embracing the Transcendental Meditation of the Maharishi Mahesh Yogi. Soon

Christianity would be wholly in on the act, with musicals such as *Jesus Christ Superstar* and *Godspell.* Gabriel, though ambiguous at best when it came to matters of faith, understood the redemptive power of religious music. "Hymns used to be the only musical moment at Charterhouse," he said. "The orchestra were really drippy people, and the choir was marginally less so, but the organ in chapel was magnificent and the playing was great . . . everyone would stand up and scream their heads off. It would be as moving as a Negro spiritual. It was really emotional, and people would come out of chapel feeling like they were on top of the world."

Jonathan King was very patient with the group – initially they wanted to be a songwriters collective and have their material covered by others, but King encouraged them to persevere. Throughout the remainder of 1967, the group recorded further demos, which resulted in their publisher Joe Roncoroni writing to the group stating that Jonjo were not impressed. Spurred on by this initial setback, Banks and Gabriel came up with 'The Silent Sun', a song that closely emulated The Bee Gees, to the point that Gabriel effectively delivered a Robin Gibb impersonation for the lead vocal. It was enough. King was greatly impressed. Genesis went into Regent Sound Studios and recorded the two sides in December 1967. It was to become the group's debut single.

# 3: Listen And Cast Your Mind Into The Sound Spectrum

*"We hope you won't find it pretentious or humourless because it was intended to be neither."*

Peter Gabriel, 1969

IN February 1968, the same month as The Beatles recorded 'Lady Madonna', Genesis released their debut single, 'The Silent Sun' backed with 'That's Me'. The group's name was nowhere to be found on the cover of the single. Released as Decca F12735, it was a sweet first record, with overdubbed strings by industry veteran Arthur Greenslade that heavily echoed The Bee Gees' 'Massachusetts'. 'That's Me' was a more pulsing, aggressive cut and featured fabulous guitar work by Phillips. The record was reviewed by *NME* on March 3, 1968: "I'm still not sure what the enigmatic lyric is about, but I gather it refers to a girl! Anyway it's certainly a thought-provoking song that holds the attention throughout. Competently handled by Genesis, with a beautiful flowing arrangement of violins and cellos. A disc of many facets and great depth, but it might be a bit too complex for the average fan."

The record received its first radio play from Kenny Everett on BBC Radio One and the single went into heavy rotation on Radio Caroline. The band duly rushed to buy outfits for *Top Of The Pops*. However, as *NME* recognised, it was indeed too complex for the average fan, and early success was not to be. Radio Caroline was forced off the air in March 1968, which effectively ended the only repeated airplay the single was receiving. It certainly didn't catch flame at the BBC. Jonathan King had a primetime Saturday night ITV show at that period entitled *Good Evening – I'm Jonathan King*, and there was an assumption that the group would appear on it but this again was not to happen.

Although the 45 failed to sell, King urged Decca to release a second single, and duly 'A Winter's Tale' and 'One-Eyed Hound' (Decca F 12775) appeared on May 10, 1968. While 'A Winter's Tale' was loaded with piano driven whimsy with Greenslade's brass band overdubs, 'One Eyed Hound' was a fascinating track, sounding not unlike early David Bowie (with whom the group were soon to appear on several bills). It had some actual aggression to it, with Stewart providing Keith Moon-like drum fills. Again, for all the hopes of the group and King, the single failed to connect with the public or the critics.

In the summer of 1968, King took the band into Regent Sound Studio B in London's Denmark Street (the fabled music industry Tin Pan Alley) for 10 days during their school holidays, to work on an album. They stayed for the duration at their old Charterhouse friend (and one time Spoken Word member) David Thomas' flat in Bramham Gardens, Earls Court. Thomas would join the group on backing vocals on recordings. Gabriel had been staying at Thomas' alone during that summer while he attended Davies Laing and Dick (DLD) College in Campden Hill, London, a 'crammer' to assist with Oxbridge exams, since he was not exactly shining in his formal academic work. "Peter was very quiet until he went to Davies Lang and Dick," Rutherford recalls. "It was a cool college, and that's when he changed and became the coolest of us by a long way."

"Pete did everything very slowly," Anthony Phillips remembers. "He's got the world record of O-Levels, because every time he did his A-Levels, he couldn't get his ideas down fast enough and would get O-Level passes. When Peter was doing his re-sits at DLD, he lived in London with David; Tony lived there for some of the time – it became the fulcrum place where we would all pitch up, not necessarily rehearse, but do stuff around the piano."

"Peter suggested I move in, if David and I got on," Banks says. "I was somewhat abrasive in those days, so it was quite an effort on my part. Fortunately David was equally abrasive, so we hit it off quite well, and he has remained one of my closest friends ever since. It worked out well, and the flat in Earls Court became quite a centre of Genesis activity for a while. When we were doing *From Genesis To Revelation* David had about 25 people in his two-bedroomed flat, with people in the bath. We had two days to do it and wanted to make maximum use of the time. It was an interesting house."

Chris Stewart, who later went on to be a successful author, left the band at this point and was replaced on drums by John Silver. Stewart, who was friendly with Gabriel and Phillips, signed away his rights for £300 in 1969. He wrote in 2007 that " 'Schoolboy drummer leaves band' is hardly earth shaking stuff, but for the schoolboy drummer in question it would have been pretty earth-shaking." The big issue for drummers at this point was that as a predominantly acoustic band, there was little for them to actually do in the studio, and they were not yet playing live. Silver knew Gabriel through his time at DLD, and the band were impressed as much with his energy as his record collection. Silver shared a love of The Beach Boys in common with Banks and Gabriel. They rehearsed their material at Silver's parents' house in Oxford.

Genesis worked quickly and industriously and the actual recording took a matter of days. Jonathan King produced the album, though he was only in the studio for some of the time; the album was engineered by Brian Roberts and Tom Allom. "[King] was a real enthusiast," Gabriel recalled. "When he's hot and getting into something, it suddenly seems everything's possible." However, when recording was finished, the album languished in Decca's vaults. The label, like the people that made it, were unsure exactly where it fitted. The period between recording and release was a time of great tumult for the band.

Banks and Gabriel saw The Nice together at London's Marquee club, another key moment for them. "It had a profound effect on us," says Banks. "I'm not sure we'd really thought about playing live particularly, I'd only ever listened to music on record, I didn't realise how exciting it could be. They were amazingly good. Keith Emerson was fantastic. It was so loud; I'd never heard anything like it in my life, we came out of it really buzzing. I know these days a lot of people in the business come from public school, but in those days it was a pretty rare thing to do. It really wasn't what we were supposed to be doing. I'd got a pretty clear path mapped out, going to university. Mike and Ant were the ones who wanted to go professional. We were just writing songs and seeing what we could do with them, hoping other people would cover them, and, as the story goes, no-one else would do them, so we started to do them ourselves, which was pretty much the truth. We didn't set out to be a live band, but things like seeing The Nice changed my attitude to how it could be."

Banks left for Sussex University, where he studied chemistry and then logic with physics. He also spent time at Gabriel's family home at weekends, writing, with Gabriel, sections of music that were later to be put to good use in Genesis. "I had my place at Sussex," Banks says. "The idea of making a career out of it was perhaps a little bit of a dream; but I'd never even thought of it even as a dream before."

Gabriel blossomed during his final days at Charterhouse. According to Phillips, "Once we'd broken down that thing of me being two years younger than him, we used to go out on double dates, when I was about 15 and he was about 17. He went through this strange transformation from being a bit of a plodder. He certainly wasn't one of the lads in terms of music or sport; he wasn't one of the dashing, pre-eminent ones. I often wondered if it was the same bloke, if he drank something or something, because he emerged slim and became very eccentric. Women adored him – there was that touch of mystery about him. He wasn't the rugged macho one, but he had this kind of mystique and detachment that women adored: he always got the cream. He was already with Jill then."

Phillips is referring to Jill Moore, with whom Gabriel began a relationship around this time. The union between Moore and Gabriel would last for 20 years and would inform some of his greatest material.

* * *

Decca discovered there was an American band with the same name as Genesis, and the label urged the group to change their name. Jonathan King refused. Instead he decided not to market the group's album under the name of Genesis, but to market it solely under its title, *From Genesis To Revelation*. Released in March 1969, as Decca SKL 4990, it was housed in a plain black sleeve – a possible answer to the plain white sleeve of The Beatles' self-titled release of the previous November, known universally as the White Album. Adorned with subtle gold writing in an old English font, it appeared to be a concept album, complete with a portentous note written by Gabriel on the back sleeve, explaining the situation with the American group of the same name that caused King's concerns over legal challenges.

Gabriel wrote, "The group started as Genesis, biblical centuries ago," before adding, damning themselves somewhat with faint praise, "it was intended to be just very pleasant" then stating where the band found themselves, at 17 and 18: "Those years between fifteen and twenty. No longer boy or girl, not yet man or woman. Confused by the bright light of age, remembering the hazy mellowness of youth. Years when one tries to go back, forwards, upwards, downwards – never to remain static, at peace in growing up." The conclusion had plenty of Sixties chutzpah, mixed with Gabriel's beautifully understated underplaying – "Listen and cast your mind into the sound spectrum. Hear what you hear – smile and enjoy, from the beginning to the end, from Genesis to Revelation." Perhaps the most telling line was: "We hope you won't find it pretentious or humourless because it was intended to be neither."

The album remains the curate's egg in the Genesis catalogue. It is not humourless, but possibly a little pretentious, sitting outside their canon, and often regarded as a work of juvenilia. It certainly lacks the bite and soulfulness of their early demos, and the grandeur that became their later trademark. "We wanted to try and write a whole thing," Gabriel told Armando Gallo in 1980. "King suggested that we should link it up to the beginning of the world, and that got us thinking a bit. It was terribly pretentious to think back on it – the history of Man's evolution in ten simple pop songs. Absurd, but we always liked biblical images."

Inspired by the orchestrations of Decca labelmates The Moody Blues, King took the group's fragile, skeletal songs and re-employed respected orchestrator Greenslade to liberally ladle strings across the tracks. The go-to arranger on the London musical scene in the Sixties, Greenslade had orchestrated works by artists as diverse as Billy Fury, Them, Dusty Springfield and Shirley Bassey. Nevertheless, the group was aghast when they heard their delicate songs bathed in sweetened strings. Banks was sanguine, seeing it simply as part of the process of record companies and seasoned producers; Rutherford was nonplussed; but Phillips was irate, at one point storming out of the studio. "I stormed out and went and lay down. My girlfriend had just left me just before and I remember thinking life couldn't get any worse, and quite soon after that, I got glandular fever!"

Of the original 12 tracks, there are few standouts, yet all have their merits. 'Where The Sour Turns To Sweet' emerges out of a bluesy piano figure and finger-clicks before turning into something more conventional, with The Bee Gees as a template. 'In The Beginning' and 'Fireside Song' are simple, naïve songs with catchy refrains. After another bluesy interlude, 'The Serpent' is based around 'She Is Beautiful', the song written by

Gabriel and Banks that had so impressed King in the first instance. 'Am I Very Wrong' is possibly the worst of the bunch, a whimsical confection complete with a chorus vocal from Banks and Phillips. However the introduction, all picked acoustic guitars and flute, sounds not unlike the future Genesis anthem 'Supper's Ready', so again, nothing ever really went to waste.

Heard through the prism of Greenslade's strings, 'In The Wilderness' is classic, fey, Sixties pop. With its joyous refrain, it is surprising this wasn't picked up by another artist – it could have so easily been recorded by the variety of established singers looking to the underground to prolong their career. It would not be beyond the realms of imagination to picture Matt Monro or Des O'Connor, or even King himself singing this poignant little throwaway. Banks' favourite track from the recordings, many takes were required before Gabriel achieved the desired vocal. Already marking out the path to his fastidious eccentricity, he would take showers between takes to get the best vocal performance.

For 'The Conqueror', the nearest thing on the album to straightforward rock, King asked Silver to play like Charlie Watts on 'Get Off Of My Cloud', a similarity that can be heard to this day in a song that owes a great deal to Bob Dylan and Lou Reed. Although much of the album is sweetly derivative, 'In Hiding' feels ahead of its time in the style of Crosby, Stills & Nash while 'One Day' is arguably the most Beatles-influenced of the songs.

'Window' was written by Rutherford and Phillips while staying at David Thomas' parents' manor house in Hampshire where they were inspired by the beauty of the countryside. 'In Limbo' has a startling coda, with Gabriel intoning 'Peace is floating in limbo' against the chorus vocals and Phillips' fuzz-drenched solo, the sum tentatively pointing towards the triumphs that lay ahead for the group. 'The Silent Sun' was re-recorded for the album, and remained as mellifluous as it sounded on first release. 'A Place To Call My Own' has a sweet and gentle coda to close the album.

*From Genesis To Revelation* sank without trace, reportedly selling less than a thousand units in the UK. As Banks was to say, "The album, after a year or so, had sold 649 copies and we knew all of those people personally. It wasn't a very auspicious start." But it *was* a start, and the group remained forever in Jonathan King's debt. As Mike Rutherford said in 1985, "He gave us a chance to do a whole record. You've got a bunch of musicians who were really amateur, could barely play well, were barely a group, and were able to go in one summer holiday and make a record." When interviewed in 1972, Gabriel said, "I haven't listened to it for a long time but it seemed to sell in very strange places. We've found people in Italy and LA that have either written to us or spoken to us who have got the record but the last figure we had was that it had only sold 600 copies so I don't know."

The album is actually brimming with ideas, and is sweet enough in itself, fizzing with potential. It was reviewed moderately favourably in *International Times* by Mark Williams (which delighted the band no end), saying "The album sets out to recall the memories of adolescence in all their fleeting naivety and it succeeds quite excellently. At times, however, the words border on the pretentious, but then one's teens are often pretentious anyway." Chris Welch was not especially kind to it in *Melody Maker.* Aside from its poor marketing, the record was simply out-of-step with the times. It was not grand enough to fit in with The Moody Blues' vision of acid-drenched symphonic pop, nor did it chime with the back-to-basics feel of records of the era by groups like The Beatles, The Band, The Rolling Stones or Creedence Clearwater Revival.

*From Genesis To Revelation* was not the sound of sweaty clubs and endless gigging, rather the genteel sound of well-to-do youth fortunate enough to get a significant break. Certainly the musical interludes between numbers that make it sound like a continual piece of music point the way to the future, offering a hint of something deeper within the band. Despite Banks accosting Tony Blackburn in the street and urging the Radio One breakfast DJ to play the final single taken from the project, 'When The Sour Turns To Sweet'/'In Hiding', (released in June 1969) it too failed to become a hit.*

Given the relative disappointment of the album, and, after a brief period of seriously considering whether or not they should call it a day, the band decided to turn professional in the summer of 1969. In one sense, they had

* *From Genesis To Revelation* would be reissued a number of times as Genesis' career took off. In 1974 it was issued again on Decca under the title *In The Beginning* and then in 1976 as *Rock Roots: Genesis*. In 2005, Edsel were to release the most comprehensive version of the album as a double CD with a second disc of singles, rough mixes and demos. For an album that sold less than a thousand copies on its first release, it has enjoyed a long afterlife.

little to lose and indeed, many thought that if they *had* had a hit with music that was not entirely representative of them, they would have been trapped on a never-ending cycle of attempting to follow up their smash.

"Thank God it didn't work," says Macphail. "Decca was the company who'd turned down The Beatles, they had dropped the ball. It would have been disastrous had Genesis had a hit back then, because they were just too young. Even though it was a slow build, it was a much better way to grow up, get your chops together and develop the way we did it."

Gabriel had applied for the London Film School and Rutherford was persevering at Farnham Technical College, yet the band decided to make a go of it. Banks left Sussex University. Gabriel was supported by his parents, despite their nagging doubts that he may not be making the right career choice. He told *Musician* magazine in 1986 that "They were disappointed that I didn't go to university, and then that I didn't go to film school . . . The film school seemed marginally preferable to them because their prime concern was not really that my lifestyle was rebellious – although we had traditional arguments about length of hair and so forth – but that I wouldn't be able to get a job later on and make a living." Naturally, his dogged determination to make the group succeed upset his parents' blueprint for their son's future. They put him in for an aptitude test in his early teens – he told *Entertainment UK* in the mid-Eighties that "the report came back saying the only thing I was good for was photography or landscape gardening".

It had been a fairly fruitless period for Genesis, trying to press their album into the flesh of disinterested radio producers. But they were, however, building a small and dedicated fan base. But it was small; very, very small.

# 4: Christmas Wishes

*"It was all cheek by jowl, but we were public school boys, so we were used to that."*
Richard Macphail, 2013

THE turning point for Genesis came in 1969 with the introduction of the 12-string guitar which not only moved Genesis forward but changed the direction of the band forever. Although there had been acoustic guitar on *From Genesis To Revelation*, it was only in early 1969 that Anthony Phillips and Mike Rutherford began playing their guitars in tandem. As Phillips was to say, "By complete accident, we found that for the first time in our lives we weren't really copying anybody." This sound, hit upon so spontaneously, would become the early trademark of the group and differentiate them from their peers. They incorporated it immediately into their writing, specifically a lengthy piece called 'The Movement' that was an immediate reaction to the three-minute pop songs they had been writing up to this juncture.

But before Peter Gabriel and his friends could achieve their dreams, there was yet more menial business to attend to. Genesis underwent another personnel shift after the release of *From Genesis To Revelation*. Under a great deal of parental pressure, John Silver left the band to attend Cornell University in America and study Leisure Management. He would go on to be a successful producer for Granada TV. With Gabriel taking the keenest interest – and still feeling that few drummers could rise to his personal standard of percussion – Genesis auditioned more drummers.

John Mayhew, who Rutherford tracked down after seeing him in his band, Milton's Fingers, had been playing drums professionally for a number of years in the East of England at air force bases, pubs and clubs. He had posted his number all over London as he was at a temporary loose end after leaving Milton's Fingers. During his audition, Gabriel and co. were impressed that he had his own kit and how his solo culminated in a cymbal crash, something perfected by Rob Townsend of Family, whom the group all admired.

★ ★ ★

The group already had a history of meeting and playing at a variety of houses, gathering new material, with stints at Rutherford's parents' and grandparents', at John Silver's and David Thomas' flat and at his parents'. Unashamed of their upper middle-class roots, theirs was an outfit not short of real estate in which to practice. However, it was at Christmas Cottage, owned by Richard Macphail's parents, that Genesis As We Know Them truly began. "Here they are deciding to take, what they call now a gap year," Macphail says. "Pete was going to go to film school, Tony was already at University, they all had plans. They decided to put it to one side and give it a shot." It was a gamble that was ultimately to pay off, although success seemed a long way away.

Former Charterhouse friend and one-time lead singer of The Anon, Macphail had reappeared on the scene in September 1969 and quickly evolved into the *de facto* road manager for Genesis, although at that point, they scarcely had a road on which to travel. Macphail had been in Israel on a kibbutz, and moved around elsewhere, but he'd kept a watching brief on his old friends. "I was one of the very few people who bought 'The Silent Sun' on the day it was released," he recalls. "I heard 'The Winter's Tale' when I was in Israel from the Forces' Radio from Cyprus. There was obviously no Internet or mobile phones, so it was all a long way away." Since returning to the UK, he had unsuccessfully auditioned for the Central School Of Speech and Drama in London. "It was a real *Sliding Doors* moment," he laughs. "The whole cottage and all of that wouldn't have happened if I'd got that place at Central."

Everyone, especially Gabriel, enjoyed being in Macphail's company, and he had excellent operational skills. "I was a mate from school who just helped out, and I was a good organiser. I was totally in awe of the fact that they could write their own songs," he said. "And they were just getting better and better. It just seemed to come to them."

With this growing songwriting skill, the group retreated to Christmas Cottage between late October 1969 and April 1970. Situated between Dorking and Abinger Hammer in Surrey, the house was a weekend retreat for Macphail's parents who bought it from *Born Free* actor Bill Travers' sister, Linden, in 1962. Macphail's family had moved in during the festive season, hence the dwelling's name, and it was where he had spent most of his teens, but its idyllic spell was broken for the family when the cottage was burgled in the summer of 1969, and as a result they wanted to sell. Macphail's parents were therefore more than happy to let the group have it as a place of rehearsal for it served the dual purpose of letting their son and his friends have some freedom, while also ensuring the further security of the property. Living with each other meant that the band formed a close bond. "I didn't get to know them until we all lived together at Christmas Cottage. I knew Ant and Mike but I hardly knew Peter and Tony at that point," Macphail says. "I knew Tony better because he came and stayed at our place in London when he got a holiday job at Harrods."

The group set up their equipment and began to rehearse daily. "We had had these two compositional blocks – the keyboard wing, Peter and Tony, which had started off as the dominant one; Mike and I were more derivative and more transitional in the early days," Anthony Phillips says. "For what was to become *Trespass*, Tony wrote on the organ, and Mike and I were more in the ascendancy." With Tony now composing on organ, there was less for Gabriel to do, as previously they had both sat together at the piano. "Peter didn't really have a power base; he would add a little flute line or add a vocal line at the end of it. It was difficult for him as he was exploring ideas and often we didn't listen."

"Sometimes Peter could be frustrating because he would go off at a tangent and it would break the mood completely," Banks says. "He will persevere with something – sometimes he has a lot of ideas that will come to nothing, but the one that comes to something is really worth having. He was an extremely slow worker and I was an extremely fast worker, so the combination of the two was one of the frustrations. I like to do things fast. He could be very dogged."

"The two compositional blocks came to blur and Peter must have felt very frustrated at times," Phillips continues. "Because he was slightly out of his comfort zone as he wasn't able to come up with songs at the piano; and come in later on the compositional ideas and not instigate as many. The basic part of 'Looking For Someone' was his and 'The Knife' was his and Tony's, but things were developed more by the instrumentalists and not the vocalist. That must have been difficult and quite frustrating for him."

"Peter was a perfectly reasonable keyboard player, but the trouble was, I was *only* a keyboard player," Banks says. "If these other guys started playing the keyboards all the time, then what was I doing? So I had to, in a fairly childish way, defend my patch. I didn't really like it if other people played because that's all I was really. Even if someone had written a piece on the instrument, I would still later play it on the record. It was difficult."

"Tony and Peter were competitive, much more than Anthony and myself. Tony was very possessive of the keyboards; so Peter didn't know what to do, I suppose," Rutherford says. "A lot happened in a short space of time. We were determined to prove ourselves musically. We were driven, and in life that's how you achieve things."

The band lived communally, with Macphail taking on the role of cook, while Gabriel would often sit in the cottage's converted porch writing lyrics and compiling lists of agents and promoters that he would go down to the nearby telephone box and contact, urging them to come down and visit. "Peter was very practical," Anthony Phillips recalls. "On the one hand you've got this very eccentric, fantastical man, and on the other you have this incredibly practical man, the one who sat down and made all the calls with his feet on the ground. He had this extraordinary amount of common sense – quite a dichotomy, really. There were two sides of him that would appear to be in opposition, but they were part of the same man."

Every other weekend the group would go home to their parents' houses. "Mike and Ant's mothers would send back these huge Red Cross parcels of food, of all this stuff that none of us knew how to cook," Macphail says. "I remember Ant's mother sent sweetbreads; I'm not even sure to this day quite what they are, and I had to cook them. I'd make yogurt and keep it in the airing cupboard, and everybody loved it." Gabriel and Banks shared what had been Macphail's room in the extension and the cottage had an open-plan kitchen diner where the band rehearsed. The dining room table was in the living room. "It was all cheek by jowl, but we were public school boys so we were used to that."

The new material that the group began rehearsing was getting heavier, longer and less song-based than the *From Genesis To Revelation* material, so at that point it became clear that Genesis and Jonathan King would have to part ways. "We started to get a little more adventurous," Gabriel said. "It got too out of mainstream, leftfield for Jonathan and for the publisher we were working with, Joe Roncoroni, so we parted ways."

The band practised for five months solid, rarely taking time out and only going home for any length of time to their parents at Christmas. There were no trips to the pubs, no physical activity, no countryside walks, just eating, sleeping and playing music. Phillips likened it to the band having taking monastic vows. "We loved the idea," he says. "We were going from this strange songwriting combo that made *From Genesis To Revelation,* we turned into this kind of crack fighting live unit through that incarceration period. Now the jury is out on whether it needed to be as abstemious and as hermetic as all that. If you don't get away from people you are going to get irritated; it's just a law of life unless you are all saints. We never got away from each other; we never had any breaks, we were all taking it *very* seriously. There was pressure from Peter and Mike from their women, so it did get pretty tense at times. I think if we had gone down the pub and had a few pints or a few laughs it may have been different. We didn't even go for walks or play football or really do anything to get away – there was no foil to the music."

Although the group hardly listened to music while at the cottage, there were clearly certain favourites that informed them. "You'd have influences on different sides of the group," Phillips says. "Mike and I liked guitar-based stuff; 'The Weaver's Answer' and *Music From A Dolls' House* by Family and Fairport Convention; the dual guitar playing of Richard Thompson and Simon Nicol. Tony was influenced by Keith Emerson. It's more difficult to pin down who influenced Peter; he really liked Tamla. He was probably the most original of us in many respects. Richard Macphail bought all of this stuff and we listened to his records. We listened to Simon & Garfunkel and *Astral Weeks*, which none of us got at all."

But from this time came a steady stream of material that challenged form and ideas – lengthy songs would be crafted by the band as a five-piece. It was here that material that would appear on record had its birth. 'The Knife', 'Stagnation' and 'Dusk' all come from the Christmas Cottage stage and the daily rehearsing meant that the group began to have the cohesion of a live band rather than the tentative nature of the *From Genesis To Revelation* recordings. "Peter wrote the words to 'The Knife' at the cottage," Macphail says. "I was in the kitchen, cooking, and I was surprised, as he was writing these words about violent revolution and it became a standard. Every now and again some of the deep stuff underneath would surface, but most of the time he was just terribly friendly and helpful and making tea – to this day it's the same. People want to dismiss him as an English middle-class public school boy, but he's so much more."

It was during this time that not one but two revelations occurred to Gabriel. One was hearing the album *In The Court Of The Crimson King*, by King Crimson. Released in early October 1969, coinciding with their arrival at the cottage, the album was, as they say in the early 21st century, a game-changer. As Crimson lyricist Pete Sinfield said, "In Crimson . . . we just refused to play anything that sounded anything like a Tin Pan Alley record. If it sounded at all popular, it was out. So it had to be complicated, it had to be more expansive chords, it had to have strange influences. If it sounded, like, too simple, we'd make it more complicated, we'd play it in 7/8 or 5/8, just to show off." It was this album, more than any other, that would define progressive rock.

*In The Court Of The Crimson King* played with form, comprising of five lengthy tracks based around structured improvisation to create something truly otherworldly. From its Barry Godber-designed cover inwards, it was something very, very different. It was about as far away from the mannered pastoralism of *From Genesis To Revelation* as possible. "King Crimson threw the gauntlet down for aspects of live playing," Anthony Phillips says. "That incredible tightness; the jazzy stuff in 'Schizoid Man'; the drama of the bigger tracks and the suggestion of theatricality as well. It was a blueprint album for being really exciting and really dramatic onstage and we were doing a lot of gentle, pastoral acoustic songs. And suddenly it gave us a kick up the arse in terms of making things really exciting, powerful, strong and dynamic."

"In the early days we used to feel that we were rushing things, though we struggled on playing how we wanted to play, and then King Crimson appeared on the scene, and we thought they were just magnificent; doing the same kind of things that we wanted to, but so much bigger and better," Gabriel said in 1971. The great art of Crimson's debut and the leisurely yet productive pace at the Cottage also hardened Gabriel's lifelong desire to never be rushed with writing or recording. "And we used to think, 'They'd never allow themselves to be rushed . . . why do we?', and we built Crimson up into giant mythical proportions inside our heads, because they were putting our ideals into practice – musically, and in the way they were being handled." Although all their influences were strong, from Banks' classical to Gabriel's R&B, and a shared love of groups such as

Traffic and Family, the group became obsessed with the Crimson album, arguably the last album they listened to as a collective as they became further absorbed in their own music and, subsequently, live performance.

Five days before the Crimson album was released, *Monty Python's Flying Circus* aired on British TV for the first time and, in its own way, it would have a similarly profound effect on Genesis, as it did on most British youths of the era. Nurtured through various strands of their Oxbridge upbringing, Python brought upper-middle class – just like the band themselves – mores to popular attention. Python chronicled small-town, small-minded Britain in an almost obsessive and entirely surreal way.

"Python influenced us in terms of day-to-day phrases and our ability to laugh at things," Phillips says. "I remember catching the third or fourth one and where Graham Chapman was strutting around staying 'stop this, it is getting silly' and there were blancmanges playing tennis. I thought he *was* Monty Python." Echoes of Python would find their way into Gabriel's increasing use of characterisations on the uniquely English trilogy of albums Genesis recorded and released between 1971 and 1973. Future characters such as 'Harold The Barrel', The Winkler from 'Get 'Em Out By Friday' and most of the cast of 'The Battle Of Epping Forest' could all be argued to have their roots in the surreal caricatures of *Monty Python's Flying Circus*.

"Python was fantastic for us," Banks says. "It was the unmissable programme, and we had the same sense of humour. Apart from John Mayhew, we had a shared language, and we developed these phrases that everyone used. Ant was a natural comedian, we had a lot of laughs, and a lot of fighting too, I can't deny that. We always like to have the light touch, right from the word go."

⋆ ⋆ ⋆

Peter Gabriel would phone and encourage promoters to come and see them rehearse. Those who did make the journey were fairly unimpressed. David Bowie's manager, Ken Pitt, came and went. "All these people were supposed to come down from London, and it's extraordinary the amount of punctures and accidents people had to stop them getting down there," Gabriel was to say. "There were more gangsters in those days, and less corporate, but there was also a lot of passion and enthusiasm and wonderful, colourful, mischievous characters." One such character was Marcus

Bicknall, who was starting out in the entertainment industry, and got the band some early shows.

Richard Macphail's father worked for Rank Hovis McDougall, and was able to get them an old Hovis bread van, which became their improvised tour bus. "My dad got us the old van, and John Mayhew made this wonderful bench seat for it, so we could put the gear in it and all sit in the back of it. He was a much better carpenter than he was drummer. And off we'd go but we had nowhere to go off to as we didn't have any gigs." To add to their bizarre fleet of vehicles, Gabriel bought a decommissioned London taxi for him and his girlfriend Jill to drive around in.

Gabriel's persistence eventually paid off. After a disastrous performance at a party for the Balme family, friends of Gabriel's parents – where they had to resort to playing the few Rolling Stones numbers they knew – Genesis played their debut concert at Brunel University on November 1, 1969.

The set contained 'In The Wilderness' and 'In Limbo' from the debut album, but the remainder was all new material. Despite not knowing how to actually arrange themselves onstage, the instruments falling wildly out of tune and repeated issues with the volume, the band impressed enough to get repeat bookings. They would start off playing acoustically before building into a crescendo with 'The Knife', now rapidly becoming their signature song. It was from these earliest shows that a Genesis trademark was born: "Peter's famous announcements happened because of breakdowns," Macphail said. "Not unrelated to the fact I'd never really learned how to do a solder properly. I was kind of self-taught. Our equipment was rubbish, a bit of a nightmare, so Peter would fill with nutty flights-of-fancy stories." This, and the fact Gabriel stood while the others remained seated, kicking a bass drum and wearing a long black cloak, already marked out their difference.

* * *

With their bread van, and Gabriel's decommissioned taxi, professional drummer and a brace of new material, Genesis truly were ready for the next decade and were desperate to find a label to fund their activities. Living on the piecemeal earnings from live shows was one thing, but a proper label bankrolling them was another. Also, they needed to get out of the Cottage soon before it did them irreparable damage: "As it went on, arguments started getting more tetchy and Pete unfortunately was the brunt of it," Anthony Phillips said. "He would come up with these ideas which were probably too good for the rest of us and because he was slow and not particularly articulate in explanation, he was suggesting ideas but not able to demonstrate them. We were quite dismissive, which I feel bad about in retrospect. He was probably way ahead of us."

After supporting Mott The Hoople (who, perhaps due to their Herefordshire origins, shared an outsider status from the London scene, and got on with Genesis famously) at the Farx club in Potter's Bar in early 1970, Ian Hunter recommended Genesis to Guy Stevens, the mercurial in-house producer at Island Records.

"We'd also played with Mott up in Sunderland," Richard Macphail recalls. "Ian Hunter listened to the set – he stood next to me at the mixing desk, and these people kept coming up to him asking what he was doing, he said 'I'm listening to Genesis'. He mentioned us to Guy Stevens and [promoter of Friars Club, Aylesbury] David Stopps. I phoned David to ask if we could play and he agreed, saying that Ian Hunter had tipped him off."

After some initial conversations between Genesis and Stevens, the deal went cold. "We went to Island at Basing Street Studios," Macphail says. "Island were just getting going, as we were in a room with no furniture in it, and we just sat on the floor and talked. Nothing came of it. He was fairly energetic, with his big curls. It would have been very different had we gone with them."

A tape of the material written at Christmas Cottage was heard by former Yardbird Paul Samwell-Smith, who in turn oversaw the group's BBC session in January 1970 for a projected programme with British painter Michael Jackson. The four tracks recorded, 'Provocation', 'Frustration', 'Manipulation' and 'Resignation', offered a glimpse of their new direction. And three of these tracks would later resurface in some of their best-known work. Industry maverick Chris Wright at Chrysalis was interested in them. But he had a policy that no women should join the band on the road, which went against the family-centric vibe that Genesis already believed in when they were on tour.

On March 11, 1970, Genesis played the Atomic Sunrise Festival in the Roundhouse, the huge, draughty former railway engine turning shed in London's Chalk Farm. They played on the bill with recent hit maker

David Bowie, whose 1969 single 'Space Oddity' already looked to have been a one-off novelty hit. Banks and Gabriel had followed his work since The Manish Boys.

By now, Bowie was fronting The Hype, a four-piece band featuring guitarist Mick Ronson and bassist Tony Visconti, playing one of their first ever performances. "We had no interaction with Bowie, it was another gig to us," Phillips remembers. "The stage was very small, and there wasn't a lot of atmosphere. I remember David and Tony Visconti wearing space-suits, but there was always a rush, there was never much time, we were always like ships in the night." Gabriel and Bowie would vie on the UK circuit for gigs for the next two years; both pushing boundaries in stage presence and presentation.

Mike Pinder of The Moody Blues had also declared an interest after seeing them in early 1970 for his group's newly-formed Threshold Records. According to Banks, he went so far as to record them. Banks played a wrong note at the end of 'Looking For Someone'. Pinder was fine to keep it in. Banks was not. Pinder was out. "We had a whole evening with Mike Pinder and he paid for a recording," Macphail recalls. "Tony didn't really take to Mike. It's funny because the Mellotron would never have happened had it not been for Mike Pinder, and Tony did great things with the Mellotron subsequently."

It was after supporting Rare Bird that things *really* began to change for Genesis. Of all the groups they had played with on the circuit, both Rutherford and Banks felt depressed after seeing Rare Bird because they were so very good. The London-based band, formed around Steve Gould and David Kaffinetti, performed pioneering organ-led pastoral blues-heavy progressive rock. It was through their keyboard player, Graham Field and their producer, John Anthony, that Genesis came to be introduced to the owner of Charisma Records, Tony Stratton-Smith, who would see them in London.

Genesis, working with promoter Bicknell, had found a residency upstairs at Ronnie Scott's fabled London jazz club in Soho's Frith Street, which ran on Tuesday nights for six weeks from March 3, 1970. It sounded more impressive than it was, as often there would be a mere handful of people in the audience, but it was to prove to be a turning point for Genesis.

Anthony told Armando Gallo in 1977 that: "It was like seeing five very young men who were somehow really timeless. And they all seemed to have every hang-up in the world, if you looked at them individually; they all seemed to be really struggling with whatever it was they were really struggling with, but the whole was so much bigger than the sum of the parts . . . I was pretty stunned." Anthony went back to Stratton-Smith and urged him to come and see them – and, in March 1970, the group met the man who was to change the course of their life. Stratton-Smith absolutely loved them.

"They were so incredibly good," Stratton-Smith said in 1977. "They were different. They had a language and feel of their own. You could see they had the possibility of being three-dimensional." Charisma Office Manager Gail Colson remembers it well: "Graham, the keyboard player in Rare Bird gave us a cassette of Genesis who had supported them at a gig somewhere and said that we should check them out. There were five of them onstage and about that in the audience; myself, my brother Glen, T.S.S., John Anthony and possibly my then husband Fred Munt. They were completely original, with Peter at the front, not only singing, but kicking a bass drum and playing flute. Incredible lyrics and beautiful intricate melodies, we were all really impressed."

Within two weeks, Genesis were signed to Tony Stratton-Smith's fledgling label, Charisma Records. The proximity of their performances at Ronnie Scott's to Stratton-Smith's Soho office was another one of those 'what-if' moments that coursed through the early career of Gabriel and Genesis, to add to what if Richard Macphail hadn't left Charterhouse in 1966, what if Jonathan King had not visited, what if Christmas Cottage had not become available. "If Ronnie's hadn't been round the corner from the office in Dean Street, it probably would never have happened," Macphail laughs. "John Anthony saw the band, and then dragged Strat along to Ronnie's. John said you have to see this band. Strat did and that was it."

"Strat liked us and thought we would work well on his label," Banks says. "We were out on the retainer of £10 a week – against future earnings, of course, and we were left to get on with it. That was fantastic."

# 5: The Famous Charisma Label

*"He is a remarkable singer, with a variety of tonal effects at his command from an unexpected soul shriek to clipped, precise phrasing; agonising howls to grotesque rolling accents delivered with theatrical venom."*

Genesis tour programme, 1972

1970 was to prove a pivotal year for Genesis. It would see the group sign to a supportive label, begin to play decent sized shows in front of appreciative audiences and Peter Gabriel would further hone his larger-than-life persona. It would find them settle on what, for many, will forever be their definitive line up and, most importantly, release an album that would encapsulate their new-found direction. However, it would prove too taxing for guitarist Anthony Phillips, ultimately leading to his departure from the group.

In Tony Stratton-Smith, Genesis found a staunch, loyal supporter who was prepared to allow the band time to grow at a pace best suited to their needs. As the head of their label, he was both encouraging and sympathetic and he also became, for all intents and purposes, the group's manager as well. One of pop's most idiosyncratic characters, stories about 'Strat', as he was affectionately known, are legion and legend. Born in Birmingham in 1933, he began his career as a sports journalist and, while working for *The Daily Sketch*, became the youngest sports editor in Fleet Street. While covering the 1962 Football World Cup in Chile, a chance meeting with Brazilian composer Antonio Carlos Jobim led Strat towards an interest in music publishing, which by the late Sixties had evolved into his becoming a band manager.

Stratton-Smith was a polymath. He had written a book, *The Rebel Nun* about Mother Maria Skobtzova, who had been killed at Ravensbruck for her role in the French Resistance during the Second World War. A fervent and passionate supporter of horse-racing, Stratton-Smith preferred to operate out of The Ship pub and La Chasse club just down from the Marquee on Wardour Street in London's Soho. He built a stable of acts who straddled the underground and mainstream – The Nice, The Creation, The Koobas and The Bonzo-Dog Doo-Dah Band were all on his roster. His second-in-command was Gail Colson, whom he had met while managing The Creation. Colson had been producer Shel Talmy's PA and had been instrumental in getting Talmy to offer an office to Stratton-Smith where he could establish his fledgling label. She became Stratton-Smith's PA and was later label manager at Charisma, the record label he formed.

Colson was to become one of the key players in Genesis and Gabriel's story. Former *Melody Maker* journalist Chris Charlesworth elaborates: "Gail was exactly what Strat needed, someone efficient to harness his recklessness. She was supremely efficient, an absolute sweetheart, absolutely down to earth and businesslike. When she hooked up with Strat she became his *consigliore*. She was the money person and made sure that what needed to be done was done. Strat would waft in and out. If it wasn't for Gail, god knows what would have happened to the bloody company! She was fiercely determined and put her foot down. She was incredibly charming as well."

"Charisma came into being through frustration at the way The Nice and The Bonzo Dog Doo Dah Band were being treated by Immediate and United Artists in the States," says Colson. "TSS and I thought that we could do a better job than either of them. We used to sit in either La Chasse or The Ship drinking and getting indignant about the whole situation with both bands. Tony and I were a good partnership, he would have all these wonderful mad ideas and my job was to try and rein him in and make them work."

Charisma Records was formed in October 1969 as a direct result of The Nice's label, Immediate, going bankrupt. Founded on an advance by B&C Records, who were initially to distribute Charisma's releases, he set up a community based on Berry Gordy's model for Motown Records, where he could sign like-minded artists who would work for the common good. In his initial press statement about the label he concluded, "The only central truth of the record business is that there is no substitute for talent. We intend never to forget that." Run as a family affair (Colson's brother Glen became the press officer, while her then-husband, Fred Munt, was later to run the management company), apart from Strat the team were all under 25, and through Stratton-Smith's many industry connections, gigs for the label were booked by the Terry King Agency. All of the groups on Charisma's roster had to be liked personally by Stratton-Smith.

As a result, Charisma was to develop into a wildly eclectic, occasionally highly commercial label. More often than not, Strat signed distinctive artists with a complete vision of their work, most notably his personal favourite, Van Der Graaf Generator, led by the mercurial Peter Hammill, who would prove to be one of Charisma's longest-standing artists. He also signed poets, sports commentators and Monty Python's Flying Circus.

"Charisma was really a one-man show," Glen Colson told *Mojo* Magazine in 2011. "Strat signed all the bands and we just sort of ran around listening to him. He was a drinker, you see. He was out every night until five in the morning. He was hanging out with MPs, he had racehorses. He was gay as well, so he used to really get around. I was into Jimi Hendrix at the time so I didn't think much of Genesis. But he just said, 'I like the look of these guys, I'm going to sign them.' Strat wanted one of everything. He wanted a classical band, a jazz band, a rock band, which used to confuse the shit out of everybody that worked with him . . . But he just wanted to sign acts that were the best of their kind. That was always his dictum."

Peter Hammill simply adds, "He was an extraordinary man." He also states that the label was "indeed, vibrant, strange and unpredictable, as was Soho at the time. Very interesting times. It was still the Wild West End then. I'm not sure that I saw that much of Peter and Genesis on Dean and Wardour Streets, though."

Genesis were part of the scene yet somehow distant. Theirs was not an on-the-tiles, 24-hour lifestyle. For ones so young, they were strangely detached and reservedly mature. They all agreed however, that Charisma was exactly what they needed. "Tony Stratton-Smith, our manager, is first class," Gabriel told *Melody Maker* in April 1971. "The situation before he came along was totally impossible. When we found him and vice versa, everything moved into a new scene."

This new scene was as strange and bizarre as some of the figments of Gabriel's imagination. "I knew Strat and the Charisma crew very well," says former *Melody Maker* writer Chris Charlesworth. "Charisma was a wonderful company. The word avuncular could have been invented for

Strat. He was quite fat, like some eccentric but kind uncle, but his flair and imagination, his bonhomie and lust for life, and willingness to take risks on music that was not necessarily in line with commercial trends, coupled with Gail's prudent business methods was a perfect combination. They never ever forgot that, in the words of [legendary music business PR] Derek Taylor, they were all working in the industry of human happiness and that if it wasn't fun it wasn't any good. Strat was in the office from noon onwards running things – and it was no exaggeration at all to say the whole staff would then move on to the Marquee or La Chasse, still doing business and then onto the Speakeasy, where they would all stagger out of there and go to bed at about three in the morning, often accompanied by the bands such as Van Der Graaf, Lindisfarne, and to a lesser extent, Genesis."

Paul Conroy, of the Terry King Agency, would soon join Charisma as their in-house booker. "Stratton-Smith was completely different to everyone else around at that time," he says. "He was extremely cultured and passionate about his music. I didn't agree with all his musical tastes, but he was someone who could take me out to lunch with Sir John Betjeman on one hand, or the Barrow Poets, and, through all his book contacts, that's how he became involved with Monty Python and people like that. I don't think he knew about rock'n'roll, but he knew an awful lot about emotion. Intelligence was a key thing with Strat. He'd been a journalist and author, he'd been best friends with Matt Busby. Jimmy Greaves asked Strat to represent him when he wanted to leave Milan, he was very pally with all of those characters, a good man and a good listener. I can't think of any other people who had such an interesting collection of artists."

Drinking in Soho was the bedrock of Charisma's business: "The Marquee was dry, you could only get Coca-Cola and tea and coffee there," Charlesworth notes. "So La Chasse became the private members club for those who wanted something stronger. It was about halfway between the Marquee and The Ship, over a bookies. There was one room with a bar in it, an old couch and a jukebox. People from the music industry used to hang out there. It was run initially by Jack Barrie who went on to manage the Marquee – there was definitely an affiliation between the two – and it was a good place to pick up groupies. Yes were the big news around there. Jon Anderson once worked behind the bar. Keith Moon was always in there, as Track Records' office was just around the corner in Old

Compton Street. Moon would famously enter through the roof, he'd get out of the skylight of Track and make his way across the roof tops. Strat was always in there - he used to drink neat vodka, and drink like a fucking fish – he could consume huge amounts of booze without being affected."

In the booklet accompanying the Charisma box set released in the Nineties, *Melody Maker*'s Roy Hollingworth recalled that as a writer in the early Seventies he was "bombarded with hype and shite, wading knee-deep in a bog of snakes and lizards and horrible little things called press officers and publicity geeks and promo gooks who peck and and nip and salivate and smarm all over me. Driven with despair I seek sanctuary at Charisma where bullshit is a banished word and shouts of abuse greet my arrival and can settle for an hour or two to talk footy, art, women, whatever and sit back and listen to stuff and make my own mind up about it."

It was clear that Genesis, and Gabriel in particular, would thrive in this environment. Indeed, Charisma could not have been more different than their previous label: "The comparison between Decca and Charisma is amazing," Gabriel enthused in 1971. "Charisma is like a family, but we used to go to Decca, give our name at the door, and the man at the desk would phone up and say, 'the Janitors are here to see you'. Our sales figures seemed to fluctuate rapidly too – we'd be told a record had sold 1,000 one week, then 2,000 the next week and so on; then later they'd say it had sold a total of 649. They eventually caught on to the way that other labels like Island were scooping all the sales and we got a letter from them saying 'we now have an artists relations manager – come along and chat to him whenever you want', which seemed a bit like waving the flag when the ship's sinking." It was far more ad hoc at Charisma. "How Charisma existed in the first place was a mystery to me," Chris Charlesworth says. "It was Strat's vision. Money didn't really matter, whether he had any or whether he hadn't. He just seemed to surf the rock business without a care in the world and he never stopped – I don't think he had any life outside of Charisma."

Tony Stratton-Smith respected the band, and, most importantly, could understand their potential. They were good, but they were not there just yet. He wrote in 1982: "From the start, the Genesis subversion was subtle, its tone literary and the effect of its warm music haunted rather than provoked. Using fantasy as metaphor, wryness rather than bluntness, never escaping a certain gentility in approach – their themes were nonetheless easily revealed as modern and impressive: individuality, the need to believe in something, justice, compassion, fraternity."

* * *

Paul Conroy became Genesis' first proper booking agent. The same age as them, he was particularly in tune with their needs and would spend the next three years working closely with them on tour. He'd been social secretary at Ewell Teacher Training College where he'd booked bands for student shows, and his contacts led to the job at Terry King's booking agency. "I was there with my NUS book, booking out the bands on the roster such as The Fortunes, The Foundations and Caravan. They had the Charisma roster then, which was mainly Rare Bird, because they had had a hit with 'Sympathy'. Genesis' booking sheets were remarkable empty, with the exception of a few Sundays down at the Angel in Godalming." This was all soon to change thanks in no small measure to a club in the Home Counties.

On April 13, 1970, the group played their first gig at Friars in Aylesbury, Buckinghamshire, the venue with which they would become most closely associated. Opened in late 1969, Friars was the brainchild of Robin Pike and David Stopps who'd leased the New Friarage Hall in Walton Street. By early 1970, the 400-capacity club had gained something of a 'go-to' reputation in rock circles.

By booking them, David Stopps was to play a pivotal role in Genesis' career. "The first time I met Peter was in April 1970," he says. "I still have the contract for it; I booked them through Terry King. We were always scanning *Melody Maker* and *NME* for what other venues were putting on." Stopps, like Stratton-Smith, saw something in Genesis and especially in their singular, shy and in turn, spectacular, front man: "They were clearly different. The first thing you noticed was Peter's bass drum. There was the drummer and there was Peter giving a bit extra. Nobody had done that before, so that set them apart immediately, and they had all these stories that he would tell between the songs; nobody else was doing that."

Stopps became an ardent supporter of Genesis and, later, Gabriel would appear at Friars on his solo tours.

Ian Hunter's blessing endeared them to 15-year-old club regular and future music writer, Kris Needs. "In 1970, both Mott and Genesis could have been considered outsiders, if that means standing out with your own personal vision flying above the standard fare on offer, which was very much rooted in 30-minute guitar solo ego indulgences. Mott and Genesis might have seemed polar opposites but they had that extra ingredient which made them firm favourites at our club which, it has to be mentioned, gave David Bowie enough of a reception in 1971 to catalyse the birth of Ziggy Stardust as first unveiled there the following year."

Needs recalls feeling the early power of the group: "Genesis blew your socks off. You weren't expecting much but they had had one dodgy album out and I don't think *Trespass* had been released yet. Peter Gabriel comes on telling these five-minute stories and [has] the crowd hanging onto every word. By the end of the set with 'The Knife' it was all mayhem again!"

Needs, who designed the membership card for Friars, can recall being at the club on April 13, 1970, when he was 15. "The poster says Nick Drake supported but I don't remember anything about him. They were startling and captivating with something special about them. The songs Genesis were doing at that time were most of the debut album: 'Visions Of Angels', 'Twilight Alehouse', 'Looking For Someone', 'The Knife', each one like a mini-movie. At Friars, I was a stalwart of what became known as Leaper's Corner, where the ancient art of idiot dancing was practiced. This entailed jumping in the air while flinging every limb in different directions, in a kind of fitful frenzy. The madder the band, the better their score on the 'Leapometer'. Genesis were considerate enough to intersperse their mad bits with stretches of sepulchral calm, so it was possible to get your breath back and dry off."

Paul Conroy could spot the group's intelligence right from the off: "Genesis already had a very religious sort of following, as we were moving to a time of the concert rather than the gig. People got into all that. The band didn't like having to do shows with other people, because of their equipment." These early shows, although tentative, had a passion and intensity that was breathtaking.

With Charisma's money behind them, the group purchased the must-have instrument of the late Sixties/early Seventies, the Mellotron. Initially popularised by The Beatles on 'Strawberry Fields Forever', and in the work of Mike Pinder in The Moody Blues, it had reached its apogee on King Crimson's debut album, *In The Court Of the Crimson King*. In fact, Genesis were to purchase one directly from King Crimson leader Robert

Fripp himself. "We bought our first Mellotron from Crimson," Richard Macphail recalls. "The case had been damaged in a fire and someone had slapped some matt black paint on it. Fripp came over when Charisma was in Old Compton Street and it was the first time I'd met him. The deal was done and we picked up this beast of a thing. It was so heavy – it had this whole left hand where you push the thing down and it plays for eight seconds."

Tony Banks set to work incorporating it in the ever-developing sound of the group. The time it took to tune onstage gave Gabriel ever more time to expand his stories.

★ ★ ★

Buoyed up by their increasing live reputation and their new deal with Charisma, Genesis moved into Trident Studios in June 1970 to record their first album for the label. Trident, in St Anne's Court at the heart of London's Soho, had been built by Norman and Barry Sheffield, and in less than two years had already established a fine reputation. One of the first studios in London to boast eight-track recording capabilities, The Beatles had briefly abandoned Abbey Road to record parts of what was to become the double album, *The Beatles* there, most notably the single released during that period, 'Hey Jude', which they recorded at Trident on July 31, 1968. David Bowie had recorded 'Space Oddity' there while Marc Bolan cut early Tyrannosaurus Rex records at the studios.

Stratton-Smith favoured Trident for their relaxed attitude to recording, coupled with state-of-the-art equipment, the 'can-do' approach of the mixing team, not to mention its proximity to his favourite Soho drinking dens. Working with John Anthony and supported by Robin Cable, the group ran through the material they had been writing at the cottage, taking the best from the now one-and-a-half hours of songs that they had honed on the road. It wasn't as if, as Phillips was to say, the group had been 'emancipated from some odious yoke' by leaving Jonathan King, as they still had to work with a producer. They had considered going back to some of the material they had jettisoned, but they needed to work relatively quickly.

"*Trespass* was our first album as a band. *From Genesis To Revelation* was really a bunch of kids in their holiday time," Mike Rutherford was to say. It was the only album ever – aside from the occasional song – that Genesis would play live before they recorded it. Already, Gabriel would take as much time as possible to get his performance right. "When he was in the studio, he wasn't slow because he was lazy," Phillips would say. "He'd spend a lot of time getting the right sound, and the rest of us were more impatient. Tony and I were impatient – Peter really did need his own space to be able to devote a lot of time to these ideas and follow these hunches, which is why he came up with some very original arrangements."

With the album completed, further personnel issues dogged the group, and this time the schism was deeply serious. "After the recording sessions, I felt like a bit of a zombie," Phillips said in 2007. "And then we started again on the road and I was nowhere, absolutely nowhere. By now I wasn't paralytically nervous, but my heart had gone out of it. I just couldn't get back into it." He had suffered from a spell of glandular fever and then bronchial pneumonia, undoubtedly brought on by the intensity of his work with the group and how deeply and passionately he took everything. He was not a natural performer and suffered from bouts of stage fright. Phillips opted to leave. He'd simply had enough.

The reaction of the rest of the band was one of shock, and surprise, as they were finally moving into a period where their hard work seemed to be paying off. Drummers were one thing but Phillips had been the very core of the group. He'd been there, playing with The Anon at Charterhouse when Banks, Rutherford and Gabriel were just finding their feet. "We did a gig at Hackney Technical College and Ant freaked out," Macphail sighs. "There was no-one there and he freaked out and fell apart. He got glandular fever, and he quit. He has never played in public at all since then. He's totally immersed in music but he has never played since."

Anthony Phillips' final show with Genesis was in front of around 25 people at the King's Arms, Hayward's Heath, Sussex, on July 18, 1970. He had played over 60 gigs with them. It felt like the end of an era. "That was the biggest blow we've yet suffered," Gabriel told *ZigZag* magazine in May 1971. "He didn't like the road, felt too nervous playing in front of people, and he thought that playing the same numbers over and over again, night after night, was causing it to stagnate. But you just don't get the opportunity to keep changing your repertoire when you're in our position." The band was shell-shocked, and, as they did a year previously in the wake of the indifferent response to *From Genesis To Revelation*, briefly considered splitting up. "When Anthony Phillips left the band I actually left [too]," Banks told *Sounds* five years later. "But you quickly realise that you must be realistic, you must go on. What's the point of breaking up?"

Phillips' departure had a huge impact. "It was potentially a death wound as he was so important," Macphail recalls. "One of the last gigs was at the Marquee, and we had to go through this little courtyard in Richmond Buildings, and we were loading in, I was in the van with Peter, Mike and Tony and they were discussing whether to go on or not. In my mind, there was no question, they *had* to go on and find a replacement for Ant. It was too good now to let go. I said that to them. They later reported that that was the moment they decided to go on. They'd done OK, but they needed that confidence that I unwittingly provided. It was at that point that Tony said, if we are going to go on, we will need to get another drummer."

Anthony Phillips remained on excellent terms with the rest of the group and, after studying classical composition for years, returned to music with his enigmatic solo album, *The Geese And The Ghost* in 1977, which contained a selection of material that he and Mike Rutherford had written at Christmas Cottage in 1969. Phil Collins sang on two tracks, and Steve Hackett's brother, John, played flute. Phillips also played on Peter Gabriel's first demos after leaving Genesis in 1975. "It's amazing, because nobody's ever heard of him, he's made a very good career for himself as a writer, he's got a studio at home," Richard Macphail says. "He's ploughed his own furrow, but being in a band on the road was really not for him."

⋆ ⋆ ⋆

Genesis used the opportunity to have a spring clean, and sensing the need for definitive change, Gabriel supported Banks' decision to jettison John Mayhew, who had never really fitted in with the group. His departure was not entirely unexpected and, frankly, they had got through enough drummers already in their brief existence not to get *that* attached to him.

Gabriel and Rutherford fired him in a coffee shop in the West End of London. Gabriel did most of the talking at the dismissal. As Mayhew was to note, the news was "delivered . . . in his usual stuttering way, but he did it with a lot of dignity. [He said] 'John, I think it's time you left the band.'" Gabriel isolated one of the main reasons for his departure while talking to Al-Jazeera in 2011 – his speed. Mayhew was a slow learner and, by his own admission, not a natural drummer. Mayhew continued playing professionally until the mid-Eighties, when he retrained as a scenic artist and furniture craftsman, emigrating to New Zealand and then Australia. He died in 2010.

With *Trespass* on Charisma's autumn release schedule, it was again time to audition for new members. Gabriel and the group realised that for the aggression they were achieving onstage in the rapturous closing section of 'The Knife', they needed a natural, fearless drummer.

* * *

Former child actor and Flaming Youth drummer Phil Collins joined Genesis in August 1970, after responding to an advert in the classified pages of *Melody Maker*, which said Tony Stratton-Smith required "a drummer sensitive to acoustic music and 12-string guitarist".

While in Flaming Youth, Collins had commented to his manager that Genesis were always in the gig listings, while his band was not. Restless, he began auditioning for groups such as Manfred Mann's Chapter Three and Dada. Collins knew Stratton-Smith through the Marquee, where he would help set out chairs in return for free admission, and the Russell Hotel, a regular hang-out for musicians. He asked Stratton-Smith about this band who needed a drummer and was told they were 'quite picky'. Strat said he couldn't elbow him in, but he could get Collins an audition.

Accompanied by Ronnie Caryl, the guitarist from Flaming Youth, Collins went out to audition at Deep Pool Farm. "We drove there in Ronnie's Morris Minor, drums in the back, heading down to Chobham through all these tree-lined drives," he said in *Genesis: Chapter And Verse*. "Of course, coming from Hounslow, it was like suddenly cruising along Fifth Avenue if you'd been living up in Harlem." Gabriel, forever the frustrated drummer, had devised a series of tests for potential drummers to play. There were 15 drummers to see in total, so Gabriel told Collins and Caryl to have a swim in the family pool while waiting.

As the auditions were being held in the drawing room, with doors opening onto the patio, Collins was able to absorb what the drummers were playing, and by the time he came to audition he knew what was expected of him. Collins recalls hearing the music, and that with their harmonies, he sensed a strong Crosby, Stills & Nash influence. Though at first he thought that Genesis were "a bunch of Noel Cowards", he got the job. Rutherford was initially reluctant, but Banks and Gabriel were in favour: "I was convinced from the first moment," Gabriel said in 2005. "I knew when Phil sat down at the kit. Before he'd played a note [I knew] that this was a guy who really was in command of what he was doing, because he was so confident. It's like watching a jockey sit on a horse." He added, "I used to have a lot of fun telling drummers some of the drum parts. When Phil came along, that finished."

Collins was cut from an entirely different cloth to the other members of the group. Born in West London on January 30, 1951, he was a world away in class terms than his new band mates. His father worked in the city and his mother ran a toyshop, and he'd been drumming since the age of five. He had appeared in *Oliver Twist* in London's West End, and had bit parts in *A Hard Day's Night* and *Chitty Chitty Bang Bang*. His easy, amiable and extroverted persona was a contrast to the introspection of the public school boys in the band, a fundamental difference in temperament that acted as a positive influence on everyone. "When Phil came on board, there was a sense of lightness restored, a new lease of life. It was fun to play, exciting to jam," Gabriel was to say. "He was a real drummer – something I was never convinced of with Chris Stewart or John Mayhew. Up until then, we were a group of fairly ramshackle musicians, trying hard to communicate through our music. Phil . . . changed our attitudes and brought us closer together as a band."

Genesis took a two-week break and then reassembled on August 24 to rehearse at the Maltings, an old oast house in Farnham, working initially as a four piece as they were unable to find a suitable guitarist. Although he would sit in on one of their forthcoming shows, Ronnie Caryl was deemed too bluesy for the outfit. The band began to rehearse and write, with Banks playing electric lead guitar parts on his keyboard when needed and Rutherford standing in on guitar. "The Maltings was semi-derelict," Richard Macphail recalls. "I was sleeping on the floor in there. We set everything up and Mike taught the songs to Phil. It is unimaginable the difference that he made – it was just astonishing. As a four piece, we had Ant's amp, with Tony on an electric piano, playing his solos. It was because Phil was just a giant that made it possible." Rutherford enjoyed the fact that it immediately put the group on their mettle.

Collins would soon become aware of rivalries and tensions that lay within the group, and learned just how much of a mediating role Phillips had played. "After Ant left," Banks says, "Peter and I used to argue quite a bit, as we both had very strong opinions. Most of the time we agreed, but we'd then argue about a C#m or a 17th chord, but a lot of it *was* that, we were still quite immature." It accelerated Collins taking the role of peace-maker in the band.

"They were always very driven, and when Phil came in from Flaming Youth, who'd had some success, he was *very* driven" Paul Conroy laughs. Collins was also a workaholic. "If there was a chance of a session at two in the morning at Olympic, Phil would be there. He was a great catalyst to them all – but he knew his place – he knew when to back out and he was always a little sensitive that he wasn't an 'original member' as such, that the public school Charterhouse set was the main thing."

It was during this period that two songs that would shape the next phase of Genesis' career took shape: 'The Musical Box' and 'The Return Of The Giant Hogweed'. The group worked for a while with guitarist Mick Barnard, who had been recommended by Friars promoter David Stopps. Barnard had played with a group called The Farm, and although technically proficient, ultimately, Genesis found him too reserved. However, they needed an ensemble performer, someone who would be able to contribute and develop the writing process.

The group had to cancel a series of concerts as Collins had to honour commitments with Flaming Youth. He made his live debut with Genesis on October 2, 1970 at Medway Technical College in Chatham, Kent. Although these early shows were tentative in the extreme, a new bite and drive was discernible for the group. For one thing, Gabriel could stop worrying about the drums and concentrate further on his performance, and he was soon introducing a new level of audacity to his performance.

"He announced at the beginning of the set [at Friars] that the audience could judge the music by how much they boo'ed," David Stopps says. "Somebody came in late and asked what the hell was going on as the songs seemed to be being received really well, but they just couldn't make head or tale of it. It was very funny. They did a gig somewhere else and a lot of Aylesbury people started booing as well, which shocked the locals there."

By now Gabriel was almost always doing something unusual. At the Princes Risborough gig at the British Legion Hall on October 6, their equipment broke down. "It was one of the first gigs that Collins had played with them," says Stopps. "Pete started this chant, just him and his tambourine at the microphone. It sort of morphed into 'Biko' later on. He did it for what seemed to be 10 minutes."

For Gabriel, nothing would go to waste.

# 6: If Keith Emerson Likes Them, They *Must* Be Good

*"Spotty, poorly defined, at times innately boring, and should be avoided by all but the most rabid Genesis fans"*

Review of *Trespass*, *Rolling Stone*, 1974

WITH their line-up still in a state of flux, Genesis' debut Charisma album, *Trespass* was released on October 23, 1970. Recorded only four months previously, it felt like it had been made a lifetime earlier. With just six tracks, the shortest of which clocked in at just over four minutes, the album epitomised the group's new vision of pastoral progressive rock. When Peter Gabriel sang 'Looking For Someone', it was the start of his career, as we know it today.

Indeed, 'Looking for someone' were the first words heard on their first proper album, on which Gabriel's soulful voice, the slight quaver of the vocal, set him on the course for the next 40 years and more. Initially written by Gabriel, with later assistance from all members of the group, and with Anthony Phillips singing the chorus vocal, it has all the trademarks of what was to become the Genesis sound, most notably its extended instrumental passage, echoes of which could still be heard throughout the best of their Seventies work.

The introduction to 'White Mountain' sounds not unlike something that would, just a matter of years later, be brought home by package tourists from a Balearic island, with a nod to 'Those Were The Days' by Mary Hopkin. The album's title track of sorts, it swung over a two-note Hammond refrain by Banks before breaking down to the soon-to-be-trademark intermeshing double 12-string work. Gabriel's whistling at five and a half minutes was unusual and unexpected, giving it the feel of incidental music from a TV detective show.

'Visions Of Angels', written largely by Phillips, was a leftover from *From*

*Genesis To Revelation*. A delicate pop song with a plaintive piano riff and a heavily treated Gabriel vocal, it features some of Banks' best Hammond work before culminating in an early use of the Mellotron for the group. The coda of 'Stagnation' again pointed to a great deal of future Genesis work – the shift to major chords at six minutes gives a triumphant air to the record, halted by a brief flute breakdown by Gabriel before a full-on coda that the band would emulate onstage, ultimately incorporating it into the closing sections of their 1973 single, 'I Know What I Like (In Your Wardrobe)'. Gabriel described 'Stagnation' as a 'journey song', away from the standard verse-chorus format. 'Dusk' provides a sweet interlude, the closest in spirit to Crosby, Stills & Nash, and had begun life as 'Family', which had been played incessantly at Christmas Cottage and during their early gigs.

Although added to the running order only at the last minute, 'The Knife' set Genesis on their course. Written by Gabriel and Banks, it was inspired musically by The Nice (its working title actually *was* 'The Nice'). Keith Emerson's habit of throwing daggers into his Hammond organ onstage had a deep impact on Gabriel and Banks. With its barnstorming, springy beat, 'The Knife' became a live favourite for the group, and would be played regularly throughout the coming five years. Aggressive compared to the rest of the album, its lyrics were inspired by Gabriel's deep admiration for Mahatma Gandhi: "The lyrics for 'The Knife' were partly me being a public schoolboy rebelling against my background," Gabriel said in the 1970s. "I'd been heavily influenced by a book on Gandhi at school, and I think that was a part of the reason I became a vegetarian as well as coming to believe in non-violence as a form of protest. And I wanted to try and show how all violent revolutions inevitably end up with a dictator in power." The song had a strange, if slightly skewed commercial potential, and Stratton-Smith demanded it be released as a single (CB 101), which was issued in May 1971. Although it sold next to nothing, it became one of the most sought-after of all Genesis/Gabriel collectibles.

The six tracks of *Trespass* marked out the territory that Genesis were to inhabit for the first decade of their career. Although frequently overlooked in Gabriel and Genesis' work, *Trespass* is an exceptionally strong album, borne out of months of intense rehearsing, and according to Rutherford, the only album where all members contributed equally to the recording process as opposed to writing in pairs as they had done before and subsequently. Given that the band were barely in their twenties, it sounded mature and accomplished. Reviews were few and far between, but tentatively appreciative in the UK. When the album was reissued in America in 1974, *Rolling Stone* encapsulated the gulf between the US and the UK approach to the group: "Recorded well before the band was in full command of its craft . . . It's spotty, poorly defined, at times innately boring, and should be avoided by all but the most rabid Genesis fans." It is clear that this was not easily-definable music, with its classical references and strange time structures.

Peter Gabriel was, as he is today, obsessed with detail and exactly how a release should look. Tony Stratton-Smith had introduced the band to Paul Whitehead, an artist and graphic designer he had met through John Anthony. Whitehead, one of the founders and art director for London listings magazine *Time Out*, began designing artwork for Van Der Graaf Generator and subsequently for Genesis. His three album covers with Genesis have now become legendary. "With Genesis, I became a sort of 'art director' for them," he told Jim Christopulos in 1997. "I got to know them and as time went on I would introduce them to different artists and styles and books. Whenever I went to meet them I'd have an armful of books with me and say, "Look at this, isn't this neat?"

Engaged by the group for the sleeve of *Trespass*, Whitehead came up with the ornate, almost Middle English sleeve design of a couple standing between colonnaded windows looking out across a mountainous landscape. But adding 'The Knife' had significantly altered the mood of the album, and it was felt by Gabriel that the artwork would need to be amended. Whitehead came up with a quick, effective and memorable solution. He slashed his canvas with a dagger, leaving the knife in the artwork for all to see on the reverse of the gatefold. The impact of the art is striking, and perfectly encapsulated the menace beneath Genesis' pastoral stylings. Banks has said that the album sleeves worked very well: "You see them as one thing, but there's another thing going on." Although it barely sold in the UK at the time, Gabriel reassessed *Trespass* on the album's reissue in 2007: "I think it was a good start . . . it was the first thing that set us apart."

* * *

In the same month in late 1970 that he got engaged to Jill Moore, Peter Gabriel spotted an advert in the small ads section at the back of *Melody Maker*: "Imaginative guitarist/writer seeks involvement with receptive musicians, determined to strive beyond existing stagnant music forms." The advert had been placed by Pimlico-based guitarist, Steve Hackett.

Hackett's working class, council estate background placed him in a different realm to the Charterhouse core of the band. Quiet and studious, from the age of 16 he had wanted to be in a band; a self-taught player, he was equally influenced by blues and beat as he was by Bach and baroque, and was looking for an opportunity to combine all together. He had briefly played with bands Sarabande, Steel Pier and Canterbury Glass. He'd been placing similar adverts in *Melody Maker* for the best part of a year. His last band was called Quiet World, a 'quasi-religious' outfit signed to Pye and centred around three South African brothers, John, Lea and Neil Heather, but when that came to nothing, a reworded version of the advert was again placed.

Gabriel phoned Hackett and, on learning that the guitarist had not seen Genesis, recommended that he listen to *Trespass*, singling out the track 'Stagnation' in particular, as it gave the clearest indication of the direction in which he wished the band to head. Hackett felt there could be something synchronous in the fact that both he and Gabriel used the word 'stagnant'. Hackett and his younger brother John, both ardent admirers of King Crimson as well, listened to *Trespass*. Hackett found it 'interesting'. Banks and Gabriel instigated an informal audition at Hackett's family flat in London's Victoria, a dwelling far removed from the leafy climes of Surrey. Hackett and his brother played a guitar and flute duet, and Hackett was in the band. Gabriel told Hackett: "If you join us you'll be joining a songwriters collective."

"I remember Pete doing most of the talking." Steve Hackett recollects in 2013 of the meeting. "Tony seemed thoughtful. I played them three styles of music along with brother John on flute and on guitar when I switched briefly to harmonica. Styles were from pastoral to atonal to blues. Pete liked the more melodic, pastoral music. We both shared a love of twelve string guitars."

To demonstrate how willing the group were to get a gig, they played a special performance at Aylesbury Grammar School on December 16 that year: "Every Christmas, there was a Christmas dance for the sixth formers at the school, organised by one of the teachers, Robin Pike with help from David Stopps," Kris Needs recalls. "1969 had seen Mott demolish the hall and bemuse the toffs. 1970 saw Genesis in that first flush of Friars appreciation, possibly the furthest you could get from a school dance band but enthralling the crowd to the extent most sat down for the first half of the set. Being in a school hall seemed to bring the story-teller out even further in Peter, who rose to the occasion. Some of the Friars hardcore had sneaked in too, which added an interesting ambience. I think David got them for 30 quid. It was a roaring success; packed out, with the group absolutely on form."

On a festive roll, Genesis played the Lyceum on December 28, 1970, one of their final shows with Mick Barnard guesting on guitar. Hackett was in attendance, and soon after, joined the band full time. Gabriel said in *ZigZag* in May 1971: "We've had two new lead guitarists in the last two months and we've had to rehearse a lot, but this latest one is permanent we hope . . . he came to us through a *Melody Maker* ad and seems to fit in very well." Hackett may never have been fully accepted in the way Phillips was, but he did a great deal to shape the Genesis sound.

Although he was to find an affinity with all the group's members as time progressed, Hackett found the first rehearsals both bewildering and amusing: "They definitely spoke their own language," he told biographer Alan Hewitt. "Somewhere between Venusian and Vulcan and Charterhouseisms. I didn't know what they were talking about. All I knew was that I felt the music was very interesting, texturally." His initial acute stage fright and lack of stagecraft meant that he would sit down to play, and at their first serious gig at the Lyceum together in January 1971, he had to be helped off the stage by Richard Macphail, as he was still sitting there after the show had finished. "Steve was so focussed on the two mistakes he'd made," Macphail stated. "The show finished and he didn't know what to do, so I had to help him off. It was the beginning of the golden era."

With Hackett slowly integrating and Collins' much needed personability offering light relief, the band were soon back out on the road. "There was also Phil's earthiness to counterbalance the Charterhouse aspect," Hackett says. "Once they'd accepted me, I was invited to spend a night with Pete at his parents' place, where we played each other our favourite records. In doing that, Pete helped me to feel comfortable. He seemed to be very open to new ideas. Although his background was public school he didn't seem typical and there was a feeling of empathy. He was warm." Hackett was exactly one day older than Gabriel, which gave the pair an affinity: "We shared a love of blues and Nina Simone. We had a similar sense of humour. Both of us wanted to experiment and break the mould."

As Richard Macphail says, 1970 had been a climactic year with Ant Phillips departing the fold. "John Mayhew was dispatched, and we got Phil. And then came Steve, and there you have the classic Genesis. It's completely true that Tony and Peter were the grit in the oyster. But that's not to sideline the richness of talent of the others. Most bands had one or two writers, but they were *all* writers."

* * *

Paul Conroy began taking a much more active role in Genesis' bookings: "You could see they had that following, they'd played public schools, but it was really only in the Home Counties that there had been any interest, so I became their agent. Charisma management didn't think Terry was doing a good enough job, and they liked me, and they wanted to start an agency, so we went off and started Charisma Artists."

Conroy surveyed the Charisma roster that he now presided over: "Van Der Graaf Generator were, by now, ahead of the pack. Strat was very keen on his Midnight Courts at the Lyceum on a Thursday night." The Midnight Courts were a series of late-night shows in London that brought an anarchic spirit and a mixed bill to after-hours bohemians. Keeping in line with this ethos, a plan was hatched which culminated in one of Stratton-Smith's greatest enterprises of all time: the 'Six Bob' tour. Three of Charisma's leading acts, Van Der Graaf Generator, Lindisfarne and Genesis were to play the country, all for 30 newly decimalised pence (six bob in old money) admission fee, captalising on the national furore of moving away from pounds, shillings and pence in the UK on February 15, 1971. "We came up with the idea of the package tour," Conroy says. "With the exception of the Home Counties, there was no question that Genesis were going to be third on the bill. I think they quite liked it because they could get their sound check and set their stuff up so it couldn't be moved, because it was always a little more sensitive. I did the compering-cum-DJing with Andy Dunkley. It became their first real shot."

A pecking order between the bands was established. Rod Clements from Lindisfarne, speaking in a documentary on the subject, said: "The layout at the beginning of the tour was Van Der Graaf Generator at the back of the bus getting up to all sorts of strange exotic practices that we knew nothing about at all. Genesis were occupying the front seats of the coach with bottles of sherry and mineral water and cameras to take pictures of the countryside and pointing out cathedrals." This left Lindisfarne, who were at that juncture the genuine pop stars of the label, to occupy the middle of the tour bus. Camaraderie developed between the acts. "The tour was a great tribute to Strat's inventiveness," Mike Rutherford says. "We were very lucky to have him. It was great fun, although we were definitely the junior team."

Hackett saw the tour as a baptism of fire. His view of the time was, "If you wanted to talk about the meaning of the universe, life and death, you went . . . and spoke to Dave Jackson, Peter Hammill, Guy Evans and Hugh Banton. If you wanted a drink at lunchtime, you . . . sat down with Lindisfarne and discussed the merits of Guinness versus Newcastle Brown Ale." Genesis learned their craft on that tour – with Gabriel claiming the middle ground between the good time fun of Lindisfarne and the challenging, uncompromising music of Van Der Graaf Generator. Observing Van Der Graaf Generator, Rutherford suggested that Genesis learned to structure a set by doing the opposite of VDGG, who put their quiet and loud songs together in blocks.

Richard Macphail felt the band needed more guidance at this stage: "Most bands have a manager and a record company and it was like this triangular relationship. But Strat was both. I asked him how he felt about that. It occurred to me that people thought I wanted to be the manager, but I never had aspirations. Whatever was lacking in that dynamic, Strat made up for in so many other ways, like the six-shilling tour, because we got to play at all the venues, and it was cheap, and the venues were full. It was chalk and cheese. Lindisfarne would drink bucketloads of Newcastle Brown. As we had lots of technical playing, there was no way we could play drunk or stoned."

Genesis were the relative unknowns on the tour so had the least to lose. Friendships were formed, Gabriel especially hitting it off with Rod Clements from Lindisfarne and Peter Hammill from Van Der Graaf Generator. The two would frequently cross paths for the remainder of their career. Hammill says that Genesis, "were, of course, from the word go, a very tight band. A lot of their work was very impressive. But obviously, we were also in competition with each other in a way so would always look to our own work rather than that of others."

Paul Conroy adds: "I loved all the bands in different ways. Anywhere north of Sheffield was Lindisfarne country. South of Sheffield and the Midlands was Van Der Graaf's territory, and home counties would be Genesis. Usually Lindisfarne went on last as they were more crowd-pleasing, and then we would switch VDGG/Genesis. But it was usually Genesis on first." "The Six Bob tour was like a strange ongoing works outing really," adds Hammill.

"I have to say I put my money on Lindisfarne," says Chris Charlesworth, who saw the tour on a Charisma-sponsored charabanc trip to Brighton Dome in February 1971. "Lindisfarne were instantly successful, far more so than Genesis. They were the stars of the label, thanks to Alan Hull's songwriting, and Genesis looked as if they were always going to be a niche band. I thought they were a bit po-faced. My colleague Chris Welch was really the man who supported them. He was a lone voice initially. He liked their long rather ponderous songs that appeared on their early Charisma albums, which were always proceeded onstage by a long shaggy dog story told by Gabriel. They didn't have enough power or punch as my favourites The Who but weren't as funny or sing-along as Lindisfarne."

Much was made, often derisorily, about Genesis being the 'toff lads' who would turn up on the tour with a hamper. Far from it being prepared by mummy or daddy, it was a necessity to cover their abject £10-a-week stipend. "We used to go on the road with a hamper because we were so poor," Macphail laughs. "There was no way we could go to a café and afford bacon, egg and beans. I used to bake some potatoes and throw a lump of cheese in them. Cold sausages: That's what we lived on, and everyone used to think it was so funny, and they wrongly made the connection with the public school thing, that we had our hamper to go off to see the rowing at Henley."

"I think our stage act is very different from our records, and mainly we favour song writing," Gabriel said in 1971. "We're really into composition and arrangement, and our ultimate ambitions lie in that area. Live, we have various songs we couldn't get across without showmanship. I think showmanship is justifiable if it adds drama and doesn't swamp the music."

"I was never a natural performer," Banks says. "I was always hiding behind the keyboards; I never felt really comfortable out there and I was always very grateful for having someone as good as Peter up there who the audience could focus on. When Peter first went onstage, he didn't really know what to do and he developed his persona. Some of it was by chance, but otherwise he had to tell his stories as we kept having equipment breakdowns and 12-string tunings. He started acting out songs, and then he thought about the characters, which took the emphasis off him doing other things. He could carry it off, he really became very good."

⋆ ⋆ ⋆

Amidst all this tumult, Gabriel and Jill Moore married on March 17, 1971, at St James' Chapel, London, with the reception at St James' Palace. Moore was the daughter of the Queen's assistant private secretary and former Deputy High Commissioner in Singapore, Philip Moore. Strikingly attractive and pleasingly outgoing, she was a tremendously popular figure amid the hubbub of the group. Her parents lived in Grace and Favour accommodation at Kensington Palace, and family visited Balmoral every year. On one occasion Peter and Jill went along and found themselves dancing with Princess Anne and Prince Charles respectively, a further indication of how removed Gabriel was from the rest of the music industry. It was on his wedding day that the band learned that *Trespass* had climbed to number one in Belgium.

On June 11, 1971, during an enthusiastic version of 'The Knife' at Aylesbury Friars, Gabriel jumped offstage and broke his ankle. "By now, the club had moved from its original venue to the Borough Assembly Hall in the Market Square [the same one David Bowie was pushing through in 'Five Years']." Kris Needs recalls. "A year had elapsed since Genesis had last played Aylesbury and they were greeted like returning heroes, with a set now straddling the first couple of albums. We witnessed this band which had started off so shy and unassuming the previous year, now on the obvious cusp of major success. They were on fire that night and around encore time Peter suddenly came sailing right past me and landed on some pissed-up bloke who was doing some form of idiot lurching before hitting the deck."

"I was nearby when he went down," David Stopps laughs. "It was quite a high stage at the Borough Assembly Hall. For some reason during 'The Knife', Peter ran to the back of the stage and ran as fast as he could to the front and he leapt into the audience at a great height. I think he thought people would catch him. But people saw this heavy weight coming towards them at high speed and with gravity playing its part, the crowd parted to get out of the way in self-preservation. Peter fell on the floor quite awkwardly from about six or seven feet in the air. We picked him up and got him back onstage and he somehow completed the song. I don't know how he did it – he was sitting on the floor with the microphone, and he was just left there. The band went back to the dressing room and nobody came out to help him off. To this day, he's still pissed off about it! Talking to him later he said, 'The bastards stayed in the dressing room and nobody came out to help.' "

"We bundled him back on but he'd obviously hurt his foot," Needs recalls. "It was a classic case of adrenalin from the gig taking over to the extent of blocking pain. He finished the set on his knees." Gabriel had to have a pin fitted in his ankle. "As far as I know, Peter has still got that pin in his leg, so a piece of Friars Aylesbury goes with him at every show he ever does. He wrote a bit for the Friars magazine in 1972 saying, 'I had the best screw I ever had at Friars, it's five inches long, it's in my leg and it will be with me until the day I die.' "

Stopps was amazed at the variance in character between the respectful, quiet man offstage and the extrovert onstage. "Peter was very polite, charming, very friendly. When he got onstage it was a very different matter. You had to have a release somewhere and that was onstage for him; offstage he was thoroughly charming."

"At that time it was possible to get bombarded by anything from Van Der Graaf Generator's epic psychodramas to Mott The Hoople reviving the teenage rampage of Jerry Lee Lewis, but those first incarnations of Genesis presented something else altogether," Kris Needs recalls. "[They were] based on a sense of innocence, largely due to Peter's lengthy story-telling introductions and increasingly alien image and, quite simply, some beautifully crafted pieces of music to go with them. 'The Knife' was always the no-holds-barred closer. For a teenager in love, there were also some very melodic, even romantic elements." Gabriel was gathering together the elements to become one of the most important, charismatic and idiosyncratic front men in rock.

★ ★ ★

In one of his first full interviews, with long-term supporter Chris Welch in *Melody Maker*, Gabriel said in 1971: "We'll be a better band in the summer." Welch was by now an avid champion of the group, and he, like fellow *Melody Maker* writers, Roy Hollingworth and Chris Charlesworth, enjoyed a good relationship with Charisma Records and would actively seek interviews with acts signed to the label. This bonhomie was largely down to their affable press officer Glen Colson: "Charisma made themselves very popular with the music press," says Charlesworth. "Chris Briggs and Glen endeared themselves to the press because they were always buying us drinks and they were friendly, and they were funny. Glen didn't like Genesis much; he liked the lesser bands, he would call them rubbish. It endeared him to us, because we knew he was sincere, and this made a lot of difference to us journalists who were sick and tired of PRs ear-bashing us about dodgy acts, which happened all the time. The acts were friendly too, so they got a lot of positive press."

With support growing in the UK, Genesis repaired to record their follow-up to *Trespass*. They spent much of the summer of 1971 at Luxford House in Crowborough, Surrey, Tony Stratton-Smith's country home. Although the writing process was a little strained to begin with, with the old timers missing the input of Phillips, ideas began to flow. Richard Cromelin, in a *Rolling Stone* review, picked up on the overall strangeness of the whole thing: "The countryside cottage in which (it says here) Genesis regrouped their creative energies must have had a lot of strange stuff coming out of the walls to have been worthy of hosting this new contender for the coveted British weirdo-rock championship."

He wasn't wrong. Luxford, once in the ownership of the Beaverbrook newspaper publishing dynasty, was another of the great country houses that littered Genesis' career. Chris Charlesworth was one of many writers to take up Strat's invitation to visit. "It was a beautiful, rambling country house with lots of small rooms," he recalls. "It looked 17th century; beams, low ceilings. He'd invite the bands down there, and it was all very lovely. A lot of dope was smoked."

Steve Hackett concurs: "It was, for a cottage, large indeed! It had a great atmosphere and fabulous garden where we also wrote and played sometimes."

"We took the summer off really much to our agent's disgust," Gabriel told *Sounds* in 1972, "but I think it was very necessary then because it was the first album we'd worked on with Steve and Phil and they were playing a very important part."

It is a trifle disingenuous to suggest that the group took the entire summer off as there was a smattering of gigs, including a return to Friars, as well as their first Reading Festival. Genesis were becoming a better band, especially by the time the group returned to Trident to cut their next album, again with John Anthony producing. *Nursery Cryme* – with its wonderful Paul Whitehead gatefold sleeve – was released on November 12, 1971, and although today it is viewed with mixed reactions within the Genesis camp, it was a significant step forward from *Trespass*. It is the sound of a band on the cusp of greatness, full of assured faith.

The album opened with 'The Musical Box', arguably one of the group's most important tracks. Written as a four-piece before Hackett had joined them, it quickly ranked alongside 'The Knife' as one of their early anthems. It weaved in the pastoral, progressive storytelling of *Trespass* with a harder, more aggressive edge with The Who's influence clearly apparent. It also introduced the searing lead guitar of Steve Hackett, and the insistent, complex drum fills of Phil Collins as well as his assured vocals: double-tracking and responding to Gabriel, adding sweet to Gabriel's salt. The middle section positively springs out of the speakers, using the most exaggerated sections of 'The Knife' as its very starting point.

The song, which was to inspire Paul Whitehead's legendary album painting, came with an explanation on the inner sleeve, which began "When Henry Hamilton-Smyth minor (8) was playing croquet with Cynthia Jane De Blaise-William (9), sweet smiling Cynthia raised her mallet high and gracefully removed Henry's head." Cynthia later discovers Henry's beloved musical box in his possessions; as it played 'Old King Cole', a small 'spirit figure' appeared: Henry as an old man, expressing his life's desires, and trying to instigate sexual congress with Cynthia. The story culminates with his nurse arriving in the nursery, throwing the musical box at the old man and destroying them both. Many generations removed from chart pop, the song gave Gabriel his first genuinely striking stage characterisation: as he played the ageing Henry, he put on an old man's mask and in it became someone else entirely. "The old man routine on 'The Musical Box' is genuinely disturbing," writer David Buckley says, "particularly the end, as it has that horrible sexual charge where he's licking his lips and rolling around in the mask".

'The Musical Box' visited the realm of fantasy, the furthest so far in Gabriel's writing. By regressing to childhood, he conjured what he called, "a dream world, I suppose. It was about mood and atmosphere. I pictured my grandparents' house, and some of the underlying feelings I had about that place." Speaking to *Uncut* magazine in 2007, he added: "They didn't have a croquet lawn but it was a Victorian house, with dark wooden panels, and it had a mood that fed the lyric of that song. I think it was sex trying to break through it all. The feeling of constraint . . . the feeling that somehow fertility, vitality and sexuality were all connected, and the old world of control and order was on the other side of the spectrum. And was something that had to be broken through."

The sex trying to break through it all was like a metaphor for Gabriel's quiet rebellion at Charterhouse, the feeling of the new shattering the old. It certainly struck a chord. Writer Buckley said, "Because I'm a working-class Liverpool lad, to be introduced to these upper-class croquet matches where people's heads fall on the floor, it was like *Narnia*, and it was a bit like class as fantasy which I found beguiling." And it was. It paraded the group's upper-classness perfectly, exaggerated and like songs from a particular drawing room. Black Sabbath this was not.

After such a definitive opening, the rest of *Nursery Cryme* basks somewhere in its shadow. 'For Absent Friends' was brief and interesting as it featured lead vocals by Phil Collins and was one of the first songs written with significant contributions from Hackett and Collins. Stage favourite 'The Return Of The Giant Hogweed' again showed how the new band was shaping up – a remarkable introduction with Banks' organ tracked with Hackett's guitar and intricate, compelling cymbal work by Collins, before Gabriel's voice positively rips through the speakers. Again, a killer weed that threatens mankind was not a go-to subject in popular music but Gabriel sings with honesty and sincerity. Gabriel liked to bring a soulful number to each album, and 'Seven Stones' is no exception, sweet and tender but with added bite, and its breakdown was one of the first opportunities for Banks to introduce his trademark Mellotron sound.

'Harold The Barrel' was an early indication of the pop brio that Genesis incorporated into their work, and demonstrated the development of the story song that the group had begun during *From Genesis To Revelation*. Now it was developed into broad comedy, with vocal characterisation and a great deal of mirth. "We had lyrics that were tongue-in-cheek," Banks says. "Peter was the best exponent of that. 'Harold The Barrel' is so quirky and off-the-wall, it tells you that this isn't ELP. It was very important for us. We didn't ever want to be seen to be taking ourselves too seriously." 'Harlequin' was a beautiful, touching 12-string interlude, a nod to Crosby, Stills & Nash and also the finger-picking style of The Beatles' 'White Album', though Genesis had been doing this themselves for a considerable time already.

'The Fountain Of Salmacis' closed the album in almost the same remarkable, grandiose fashion that 'The Musical Box' started it; a breathless mesh of sound, with Banks' Mellotron, Hackett's guitar tapping and, amazingly, a brief bass solo from Mike Rutherford. Taking its story by Ovid from Greek mythology about the attempted rape of Hermaphroditus by Samacis, and the subsequent intertwining of their bodies, the song broke new ground, combining the classical pretensions so admired by Banks and Hackett with passages of full throttle aggressive rock.

Charisma advertised *Nursery Cryme* in *Melody Maker* using a paragraph of commendation by Keith Emerson, now a superstar in ELP, complete with his picture and signature – culminating in his phrase "no bullshit: their new album really is incredible". The band were delighted with such patronage, especially given Gabriel's admiration of Emerson's old band, The Nice. "People are a lot more swayed than one thinks. They think 'if Keith Emerson likes them, they *must* be good'," Gabriel told *Disc & Music Echo*. "I know it influences people because I am as bad."

That said, the album received a cautious response. In America, where it was released on Buddah almost a year after its UK release, Richard Cromelin wrote: "It's definitely a type of music that skulks down back alleys far from the beaten path, but if Genesis . . . learn how to gear things up to explosion level and manage to develop their ideas a bit more thoroughly, they could be the ones to successfully repopulate those forgotten passageways."

He did take issue with the album, however: "*Nursery Cryme*'s main problem lies not in Genesis' concepts, which are, if nothing else, outrageously imaginative and lovably eccentric, nor with their musical structures – long, involved, multi-movemented frameworks on which they hang their narratives – nor even with their playing, which does get pretty lethargic at points. It's the god-awful production, a murky, distant stew that at best bubbles quietly when what is desperately needed are the explosions of drums and guitars, the screaming of the organ, the abrasive rasp of vocal cords." *Rolling Stone* suggested that it offered "Mother Goose tales in the ten-minute 'The Musical Box'." Robert Cristgau wrote: "God's wounds! It's a 'rock' version of the myth of Hermaphroditus! In quotes 'cos the organist and the (mime-influenced) vocalist have the drummer a little confused! Or maybe it's just the invocation to Old King Cole!" Gabriel as the 'mime-influenced' vocalist had a job of work on to convince the Americans to accept his group.

Chris Jones, a lifelong fan, who wrote for the BBC opined: "We end up with a series of mini suites about murder by croquet mallet followed by psychosexual haunting ('The Musical Box'), Armageddon by enraged plant life ('The Return Of The Giant Hogweed') or hermaphroditic tales of caution ('The Fountain Of Salmacis'). All of it delivered with a panache that wouldn't quite put them in the big league but was a large step towards making their mark."

Dave Gregory, who within eight years would be the guitarist in XTC and contribute to Gabriel's third solo album, was typical of many new fans in this period. Initially unsure, their inquisitiveness was to pay off. "At the time I was into guitar-based rock. And then I heard 'Harold The Barrel'. I was aware of Genesis as they always seemed to be playing Friars in Aylesbury, but I thought they were an arty-farty folk band. I remember then seeing an article in *Melody Maker* which had a picture of Peter Gabriel holding his tambourine with the headline 'Don't Miss Genesis This Time Around' and I was strangely drawn to his charisma."

Gabriel was clear how the band should sound – he told *Disc & Music Echo*: "As listeners we have all been bored to tears by bands improvising and doing endless guitar solos. With us, everyone plays a pre-rehearsed part like an orchestra, so basically if anyone starts jamming around with their own part, it's going to sound very messy. Anyway, it's very difficult to improvise unless you're playing something very simple and we don't play anything very simple." *Nursery Cryme* sold about the same as *Trespass* in the UK. It was an underground hit and a common room favourite, but in Belgium it truly struck a chord. For Genesis to be a bigger success, they would have to cultivate their overseas audience.

One thing was certain, the band were not making any money whatsoever. "Richard Macphail would come in once a week and get the salary off Fred," Paul Conroy remembers, "and they were seen as the posh boys, and one of Strat's favourites, but they were not seen as having the obvious success that they wanted."

"It's a big question how long any other record company would have stuck with the band," Richard Macphail says. "Because success did not come quickly. Lindisfarne was the cash cow and all that cash went into Genesis. We are talking hundreds of thousands of pounds, and Strat was prepared to let that happen."

It was clear that Genesis and Gabriel had all the potential needed to break through. With their strange and skewiff tales referencing art, history and mythology, their strange otherworldly art and their bizarre-looking singer and impeccable playing, well, it would just take some time.

# 7: Always Worried About Something Or Another

*"I don't mind how they react as long as they react – it's if they didn't react at all that I'd be upset."*

Peter Gabriel, 1972

HE was hardly running with a wild bunch of hard-rocking reprobates, yet Peter Gabriel was already setting himself apart from the rest of his group. A barely-drinking, non-drug taking married vegetarian inspired by Ghandi and *The Whole Earth Catalog*, he was developing into a charming, intense and otherworldly man who was already being seen as the public face of this most introspective of all progressive rock groups. "On one tour I remember getting up early in the morning with him and rowing around the canals in Sheffield," Paul Conroy remembers. "In Italy he'd go off and find time to go to art galleries. Completely unlike other bands who'd be in bed until 4pm nursing a hangover each day."

A great deal seemed to happen very quickly for Genesis in the wake of the release of *Nursery Cryme*. The album had been a huge hit in Italy, reaching number four there. To support this, the group embarked on their first overseas tour in April, playing throughout Italy before stopping off for shows in Germany and Belgium on the way home.

In many respects, Italy was the making of them. Here, the band arrived fully formed and played to an audience with little knowledge of the personnel schisms that had bedevilled them. No longer playing to indifferent crowds at the bottom of a bill, here the group were simply Top Five recording artists. They didn't have to worry about billing and it was simply 'Genesis In Concert'. Some nights there was an acoustic act to open the show, but there was no rush to set up their equipment and the crowd was attentive and familiar with their material.

Paul Conroy went with them and, for this tour, took on an unofficial role of road manager. "Going to Italy really opened it up," Conroy recalls. "It was such a massive opportunity for them. There was a gaggle of three or four Italian promoters who used to get into the Marquee and snaffle up acts to take to Italy. One of whom was Maurizio Salvatore, who brought Genesis over. It was a bit like the Wild West over there. Uriah Heep went to Italy and wouldn't play on small stages. The promoter blew the wheels out on the van telling them that they weren't going anywhere. The first time I went with Van Der Graaf, outside they were rioting on the streets."

Genesis and Conroy bonded during the tour: "They were pleased to see me in Italy. I travelled with them and listened to everything going on. It was the art school dance goes on forever, really – all hands to the pumps helping out." It was all a little cut and thrust and somewhat removed from the rarefied air of concerts in the home counties. "We used to do two shows: one would be about three o'clock in the afternoon, so girls could come, and then we'd have a later show as well, and we'd have dinner in between," says Conroy. It was a great learning experience for the group: "To play every night over a two/three week period was fantastic for them, because they never got that opportunity in England. You might get the occasional Friday and Saturday night gig, but there weren't the shows for them, really. They were a difficult sell because they didn't want to play in a lot of clubs in England, like the Penthouse, Scarborough or the Penzance Winter Gardens because of the equipment situation. They played some of the bigger places like the Van Dyke club in Plymouth, but it was the David Stopps of this world that had kept them going."

For Gabriel, the tour was the beginning of a love affair with all things Italian that three decades later would culminate in him buying a hotel in Sardinia. "The strong melodies and church influences in our music seemed to appeal to the Mediterranean areas," he was to say. "We generally found the further south we got the warmer the welcome." And the warm welcome proved most conducive to them: it was during the sound check at their show at Palasport in Reggio on April 12 that the group devised the song 'Watcher Of The Skies', a cornerstone of the next phase of Genesis.

With its strange arrangements, early afternoon performances, and between-show dinners that culminated in a show in front of 20,000 people in Rome, Italy was a great step to Genesis the live act as we know them. Painstakingly perfectionist, the group would pull apart the previous night's performance as they moved on to the next city. "Every time I travelled with them, we had to listen to last night's performance in the van," Conroy laughs. "There would be quiet moments when they would reckon Tony Banks had gone out of tune, they were perfectionists. And in down time they'd play The Shadows in the van after we'd got through four hours of last night's gig."

"There was always an intention to improve," Steve Hackett adds, "which probably appeared like a post mortem!"

"We were getting nowhere. And then, this little ray of light appeared in Italy," says Mike Rutherford. "It was hard work, very uphill. To suddenly find a country that likes you – it doesn't take much goodwill to make you feel that it is all worth doing."

* * *

Back in the UK, the group's touring schedule was relentless, but Conroy ensured there was accord between Genesis and the agency: "I remember Peter rang me up from a coin box in Whitley Bay. I'd sent them out for a gig on a Friday night but it had been cancelled, and I'd forgotten to tell them, at least the next night they were in Sunderland, and the agency had to cough up for a hotel for them, but I think that was the only one time we fell out." There was little time *to* fall out: On May 29, the group played the Great Western Festival at Bardney, just outside Lincoln. The festival was a quagmire thanks to incessant rain, and Genesis played on the main stage between the Sutherland Brothers and boogie labourers Status Quo.

The festival was notable for Gabriel launching a new look, a sort of heavily mascara'd Egyptian prince with a section of his head shaved (either a subconscious desire to join the Hare Krishna movement or a nasty shaving accident, he was to quip). In an era when Marc Bolan and David Bowie wore make-up, it was not *that* out of the ordinary but Gabriel somehow managed to look striking, weirdly off the radar for a rock singer and very strange. The set was notable for the live debut of 'Watcher Of The Skies', and a now well-honed selection of material they had taken around the continent. The damp weather played havoc with the Mellotron, and the band struggled manfully with the afternoon slot, but it showed how polished they were becoming. Though Gabriel's look was quite remarkable, Tony Banks claimed in 2004 that the crowd failed to appreciate their efforts. "They didn't like us. We were on in the afternoon and there was no atmosphere, nothing. It was raining, it was crap. I never felt we were a good festival band, the music was just too complex, really."

The Genesis tour van continued to traverse the motorways of the UK, yet there was little room for excess. Gabriel and Jill would often travel separately from the rest of the band, as would Banks and his soon-to-be wife Margaret, leaving Macphail, Collins and Rutherford to get up to more traditional hi-jinks. "Peter, Jill, Margaret and I were very much a social unit," Tony Banks says. "We did a lot of stuff together. Margaret and Jill still get on well. So much has changed across the years, it's difficult to go back to all that. We were young. We were also extremely naïve and very green. A person of 19 these days can be pretty streetwise, and together. We *still* haven't reached real maturity. At 17 we were like 13-year-olds are today, if that. We'd come out of the public school system so we were incredibly ill at ease, and shy."

"Mike, Phil and I would be the ones to spliff up," Macphail says. "Only on the way home from a gig, mind. There was a certain sign on the M1 that was our skinning up signal. Phil often used to come with us in the van. We had a Hillman Imp, Gerard Selby and me. Phil would come as he'd want to get there earlier and I had a cassette machine and he would make these amazing mix tapes full of John McLaughlin and Yes."

"Richard was immensely central to it all," Hackett says. "He was all things to the band at that time. He undertook all jobs great and small with a smile."

On June 16, 1972, at one of the Friars' gigs, the group arrived at a landmark in their career. "I was the first person on the planet to pay them £100," says Stopps. "It was at Bedford Corn Exchange." He had gradually been increasing their fee from the £10 they received for their first show in Aylesbury. "Peter came and shook my hand onstage – I was the first person to have paid them a three-figure sum." The £100 would be worth just over £1,000 today. It was good money if you were working every night of the week, but not enough to subsidise the group's mounting debts. The money worries, coupled with a lack of equipment and their work being respected but not necessarily catching fire, led to a degree of uncertainty. Perhaps Gabriel should have gone to the London Film School, after all.

Just over a week later, on June 28, Stopps gave them another significant boost by promoting a special show at the Watford Town Hall. Realising that they would soon be too popular to play his venues, the show was in appreciation of the business they had brought his way, and a nod to how he had nurtured Gabriel's nascent showmanship. But it also was a confidence booster for them. "They went through a very weird patch; their gear was always breaking down and they just needed a bit of investment: some proper gear or an extra road person who understood *not* to get gear that kept breaking down all the time. I was worried that they were going to split up as they were such an important part of what we did. We thought we'd do this special gig and call it the Genesis Convention and that was the Watford Town Hall show."

Stopps invited *Melody Maker* journalist Chris Welch, along with various other notables, to the Convention and Gabriel made rosettes to scatter among the audience, exactly like those that could be found at gymkhanas, emblazoned with 'GENESIS 72' on them. Adverts were placed in *Melody Maker* with headlines such as 'Home Counties Genesis Freaks Unite!' On the night, their equipment broke down, again. "But somehow Chris Welch wrote this amazing review even so," Stopps says, "and it did get them wider recognition via the *Melody Maker*."

Stopps was aware that with Stratton-Smith occupied with his label, Genesis lacked strong management to propel them to the next level of success. "I suppose you could say I was doing a manager's job really with the Watford convention," he says. "I was a promoter but what I was doing was management. It didn't occur to me, I didn't see the opportunity and the conversation never took place."

Paul Conroy helped set up the first Genesis fan club, The Hogweed Appreciation Society, which was operated by Amanda Gardner out of the market town of Winslow in Buckinghamshire, just outside Aylesbury. "I remember going up to Charisma's Soho offices to visit Paul Conroy with two local girls," Friars veteran Kris Needs recalls, "who wanted to start their fan club but seemed more concerned with getting nearer Peter. At the time, I'd been helping with Bowie's before taking over Mott's so couldn't do it myself."

Genesis would return again to Italy and play to larger crowds that August. "Italy was very important," Hackett says in 2013. "It gave us the confidence that we could be accepted on a mass scale." They took along *NME* journalist Tony Tyler. "We'd graduated to a three-ton truck," Conroy recalls. "It was very serious. But the acoustics in the sports arena venues were hideous. The Italians loved it. It was amazing the way the

Italians emotionally connected to the music. They would suddenly burst into spontaneous applause in the middle of the song, something would just take them. On the second tour at the last show in the Palais de Sport in Rome, there were at least 10,000 people there. The following Sunday we played a basement club in Peterborough to about 20 people. If that had gone on without Italy, we may not have continued. The band were stars from the word go there."

Genesis played their final gig at Friars Aylesbury on Saturday September 2, 1972. "They would be different every time they played but the opening song was always very dramatic," Kris Needs recalls. "Particularly when it was 'Watcher Of The Skies'. The whole place was in uproar right from the start." Offstage, however, Genesis were the epitome of gentlemen. "They were always very pleasant and polite." Needs recalls. "They were only a few years older than us but, when you're that age even a year makes all the difference, so I must have seemed like a burbling kid. I just remember Peter seeming very shy but always really nice and accommodating to the fans. He started recognising the Aylesbury regulars and always took time out to talk. Looking back, we would have been their first enthusiastic pocket of fans."

⋆ ⋆ ⋆

To underline their increasing success, the band was invited in to record a John Peel session for his *Sounds Of The 70s* show on September 25. Although somewhat subdued, it showed how capable the group was becoming – 'Twilight Alehouse', 'Watcher Of The Skies' and 'Get 'Em Out By Friday' were all previewed.

Gabriel himself had candidly announced in an interview that Genesis was about £14,000 in the red. Conroy recalls, "As *Foxtrot* was coming out, one of the questions that seemed to be asked was 'should we continue?' That was their third album and it was really a case of 'blimey, can we afford this luxury?' The big issue was that although they were getting a fair old following, they *still* weren't getting press attention. To get Genesis out on tour properly by this point, their demands were increasing, needing more equipment and bigger PAs." Something had to be done to draw attention to them.

Things changed for the group – and for Gabriel personally – on September 28, 1972. It was the night when Gabriel wore his wife Jill's red

Ossie Clark dress and a fox's head onstage at Dublin Stadium. Within a week, they had appeared on the cover of *Melody Maker* and had doubled their fee. "I had a conversation with Paul Conroy, who was booking gigs for us," Gabriel said in 2005. "He was suggesting that we employ a person to walk round wearing a costume of the character Paul Whitehead had drawn for the album cover, the fox in the red dress, as an extension of the illustration. But then I thought, 'Right, I'll try putting that on, I'll see if I can get a fox's head made.' " It was to provide an amazing spectacle during the closing section of 'The Musical Box'.

"Glen Colson had said something like, 'Well, you are just too boring' for the [*Melody Maker* journalist] Roy Hollingsworths of this world," Conroy recalls. "Genesis weren't gritty rock'n'roll, they didn't fit in with the Uriah Heeps of this world. Peter was all for the dress. We were a little worried as Lou Reed had done something along those lines, and then the fox's head came up; Peter had already shaved the front of his head, and it was like, 'hello?' " Gabriel did not tell the rest of the band of his intentions beforehand. It was just easier not to. "We'd have put up some 'hang-on-a-minutes'," Mike Rutherford laughs. "I'm sure we wouldn't have said yes, or at the least we'd have made it complicated for him to do."

"He knew if he'd told Tony he would have vetoed it," Macphail says. "So he just went off in the middle of 'The Musical Box' and came back on wearing the fox's head and the red dress. What could Tony do? Walk off, stop playing? He probably would have thought of it. The place was just a riot. Fait d'accompli. That's Peter, just a fantastic visionary. They all wanted to play behind a black curtain, they wanted the music to do it and gradually, Peter realised it wasn't going to go anywhere unless somebody, him, started to put on a bit of a show."

Gabriel recalled the reaction: "You could feel the horror. I thought, 'Oh, this is exciting!' " Gail Colson, talking about her brother Glen's role as Charisma's press officer recalled that, "One day Genesis were moaning at Glen about why he couldn't get them any press and he was saying, 'Because you're boring fuckers, and there's nothing going on.' And the next minute Peter put on a fox's head, wore one of Jill's . . . dresses, there they were on the front cover of *Melody Maker*."

Chris Charlesworth wrote in *Melody Maker* on October 7: "Gabriel dons a fox mask – remarkably lifelike too – and a long red dress. The effect is frightening but wandering minds are jolted back into life as bright flashes of burning magnesium explode on either side of the stage. 'Musical Box' and 'Giant Hogweed' are greeted by the crowd like old friends and Genesis leave the stage to a standing ovation." In 2013, Charlesworth added: "I could never work out whether they did it for artistic reasons or to draw attention to themselves. Whatever, it worked."

Of course, Gabriel wasn't the only performer who was experimenting with performance and make-up in 1972. Glam rock was in full swing thanks to the appropriation of Eddie Cochran guitar riffs by feather-boa and make-up wearing Marc Bolan, recycling it to hordes of excited girls. David Bowie, who had played with Genesis on the Atomic Sunrise bill at the Roundhouse in 1970, was also heavily associated with Friars in Aylesbury, and it was there in June 1972 that he premiered his new creation and alter-ego, Ziggy Stardust. Some commentators noted a similarity between the Bromley-born maverick and Gabriel himself. "It never occurred to me," says Kris Needs. "Bowie didn't come along with Ziggy until 1972 and Peter was well away by then. Peter did seem to be wearing more eye-liner when they played in September 1972, but that would've been the extent of it. If anything, Bowie might've borrowed a couple of ideas from him." The similarities between Peter Gabriel and David Bowie were marked; in fact David Buckley states in his Bowie biography *Strange Fascination*: "If Bryan Ferry was Bowie's equal as art-rock *agent provocateur*, then Gabriel was, to many, Bowie's equal as a showman."

The group, Banks especially, had been aware of Bowie since Charterhouse. "I liked 'I Can't Help Thinking About Me' because of its use of adventurous chords and it had a good melody," Banks says. "I even followed him through his Decca period, when he was like Anthony Newley. I loved everything up to *Hunky Dory*. I like everything since but not to the same degree. He moved away and went into minimalism."

"I was a big Bowie fan," Gabriel told Buckley. "Strangely enough, Tony was the first person to pick up on Bowie when he released one of his early singles . . . and I picked up on him in his second incarnation. Bowie's capacity for reaching into atmosphere and character and the arrangements and what he did with the vocals, I really enjoyed that a lot. I think we were riding somewhat similar paths . . . And then we had a sort of spurt ahead of Bowie, and then came Aylesbury and mock blow jobs and all the rest, he shot ahead. We were still strong and warmly loved but he was definitely the phenomena."

"Peter's decision to shave his parting and wearing the masks and take off in more theatrical, Bowie-like direction made a hell of a difference," Ant Phillips says. "And it was a vital part of his act."

"Peter was always experimenting with that sort of thing," says David Stopps. "I think Bowie influenced him to some extent; we were very involved with Bowie, with us debuting Ziggy Stardust. I think Peter was influenced by the personas that Bowie experimented with in Ziggy and Aladdin Sane. He certainly didn't copy it, but was inspired. He thought it an interesting area to get into – his different masks and looks were all part of that sort of identification development. I used to smile and think we're in the entertainment business and this is all part of it. Whereas Bowie actually became the person, Peter used a mask."

Bowie didn't appear on *Top Of The Pops* with 'Starman' until July 1972, after Gabriel had already appeared in his make-up at the Great Western Festival. The early 1973 Genesis tour brochure suggested that "Peter Gabriel's stage act has been described as more fearsome than Alice Cooper, more delightfully camp than David Bowie, but once again it is a natural rather than a contrived grace of movement that personifies the characters about whom he sings, and captures the hearts of audiences." With the characters that Gabriel was to take on, they seemed part of the song, multiple personalities rather than Bowie becoming one central figure. Gabriel deeply admired Bowie, but public love was never reciprocated from Bowie, and Gabriel always trod carefully in interviews when discussing him, such as when the subject came up in US magazine *Circus* in 1974.

> "Circus: Are you influenced by Bowie's costumes?
> Gabriel: I think we were headed in that direction before he was, though I'm not sure.
> Circus: Do you think he was influenced by you?
> Gabriel: No, I wouldn't say that either.
> Circus: What would you say the basic differences between Bowie's costumes and yours are?
> Gabriel: As far as what I understood about his costumes, they were done for a desired effect rather than for a relevance for the material, whereas what we did was we tried to materialise some of the characters in the lyrics"

* * *

Gabriel quickly took to his new persona. Asked about it by *Melody Maker*, he said of his audience, "I don't mind how they react as long as they react – it's if they didn't react at all that I'd be upset. Hopefully it should appear as either strange or humorous." Strange and humorous it was. Gabriel suddenly became a series of multiple personalities onstage. He added to a journalist in LA that, "It's easier to write about the masks than it is the chord progressions and people generally don't want to read about that, because they don't understand or it's just not very readable."

"The trouble you had is that you can't really write much about music," Mike Rutherford laughs. " 'Pounding bass', 'thumping drums' – where do you go after that? Anything visual was so much easier to describe. Peter's costumes and presentations and, later, screens, slides and light show meant it always gets more coverage. It never worried me that much."

Gail Colson looked on: "Nothing really shocked me and Peter has a very vivid, fertile imagination." Hackett waited avidly to see what Gabriel's next thrilling instalment might be: "I found it all more fun than surprising! I was right behind him. I approved the showmanship."

Gabriel was ready and available to promote the band. He and Jill lived in Campden Hill Road, Notting Hill. "Peter was a good-looking boy and very bright," Conroy recalled. "He used to do a lot of the PR; he was very much the front man, and Peter was always a lot more around London, rather than the others who lived out in the sticks."

It was certainly the masks and visuals that took Genesis to another level. "It was very photogenic, with the result that Genesis probably got a disproportionate amount of media coverage than their popularity deserved," says Chris Charlesworth, now *MM*'s News Editor and partly responsible for whatever appeared on its cover. "It was great having a picture of him dressed as an old man or a fox in a dress or as a sunflower, that looked great on the front page, very striking, very dramatic. I have no doubt that Genesis benefitted an enormous amount from *Melody Maker*'s sympathetic coverage of them."

Chris Welch, one of the band's earliest admirers, wrote about when they first met in his book *The Secret Life Of Peter Gabriel*: "I found him not only charming, but helplessly vulnerable, strangely mysterious and at times, possessed by an oddly eerie presence. I felt he was quite capable of using the power of his mind over people, as he fixed them with a penetrating look and a smile that seemed to hint at an intuitive knowledge of dark forces. Then he'd release the spell with a creaky laugh and the mood he could conjure at ease would dissipate into the ether."

Gabriel's presence and persona was certainly beguiling; as Phil Collins said, "Pete was always very vague. To the onlooker, it would seem as if he was stoned out of his head, although in fact he was as straight as a die."

Paul Conroy adds, "I remember when he had the house in Campden Hill Road and he never partook in any of that, although he did mix with some fairly interesting characters." Charlesworth sums up the informal feelings of many about Gabriel in this era: "Peter was a very serious bloke, the most serious of the lot. Always had a permanent look of worry on his face, he always seemed worried about something or another."

Gabriel brought an earnestness and consideration to what he did. Never the most fluent of communicators with friends and family, let alone journalists, Gabriel would worry about his relative penury and the pressures of being a young married man in a touring rock band; as well as the constant pressure of deadlines and, most notably for him, to deliver his lyrics. And there was a song he had been trying to finish, based on a real-life event that was proving particularly taxing.

# 8: Part-James Brown, Part-Chamber Of Horrors, Part-Camp Seaside Revue

*"I've a feeling that when the rock analysts of the next decade go circumspectly about their business, they will find great difficulty in omitting Genesis from their chronicles"*

Jerry Gilbert, Lindisfarne/Genesis tour programme, 1972

CHARISMA remained totally supportive of Genesis. At this point, the label was enjoying a remarkable period of success, with chart hits from Lindisfarne, credibility for Van Der Graaf and much kudos for signing Monty Python, the uber-hip wags whose TV shows were essential viewing for just about everyone who was switched on. But while Charisma's reputation as a boutique label *par excellence* continued to grow, Genesis remained a huge financial drain on the label. They desperately needed an album that sold well, to repay the faith that Stratton-Smith had shown in them.

The group were striving to capture their crisp live sound in the studio, and fast coming to the realisation that John Anthony was not achieving this. After some aborted sessions with Lindisfarne's producer, Bob Potter, they worked with David Hitchcock, who had recently worked with Caravan. They moved out from Trident and recorded at Island's Basing Street Studios in Notting Hill. The sessions were fruitful, enlivened by a lengthy suite of songs that included 'Supper's Ready', the song that would define Gabriel-era Genesis and the one that, for many years, all his future work would be judged against. A 23-minute-long patchwork in seven movements, it was an incredible piece of work, complex, strange, moving and disquieting.

Released on October 6, 1972, *Foxtrot*, of which 'Supper's Ready' occupied an entire side, was the album that in many respects provided Genesis with their platform for longevity. "To this day *Foxtrot* is a magical album," future Gabriel guitarist Dave Gregory, who bought the album in the same week he bought his first Gibson guitar, said. "'Supper's Ready' became like an addiction. It had such a great sound, and enough mystery to make you want to hear it over and over again. I had to listen to it at least once a day. And when you look back at it now, they were barely out of short trousers. To this day, I will never tire of it. How did they piece it all together? It's up there in my Top 10, without a doubt. It certainly helped me as I was then playing in a country and western band around Swindon."

But it sat among an album of many highlights. *Foxtrot* can be viewed as the first *real* album of the classic Genesis era, with the band fully working as a collective. 'Watcher Of The Skies' was an enormous, signature song; conceived by Banks in Italy, it looked at the thoughts of an imaginary alien arriving on planet Earth, only to find it deserted by humanity. With Banks' innovative use of the Mellotron the group had bought from King Crimson, it immediately added a touch of drama and attack to the group's live set, another pinnacle up there with the closing sections of 'The Knife' and 'The Musical Box'. The sweet and touching 'Time Table' is arguably the most overlooked of all Gabriel-era Genesis songs. Unmistakably written primarily by Banks, it sounds like something that would grace Genesis albums in the later Seventies.

'Get 'Em Out By Friday' continued the thread established by 'Harold The Barrel' from *Nursery Cryme*; a play in a song, devised by Gabriel, allowing him to experiment with characters and provide a social commentary. Allegedly inspired by issues that the Gabriels were having with their landlord in their Campden Hill Road flat, the song's setting is distinctly prosaic Harlow, a new town in north-west Essex, one of the original ten towns devised in the 1946 New Towns Act, a social experiment to provide living for the overspill of war-ravaged cities. Geographically opposite the leafy area of Surrey where Gabriel was raised, Harlow, like many of its contemporaries, was a sea of concrete modernity, and by the early Seventies these dream towns were beginning to decay. The setting provided the backdrop to the tale of private landlords clearing dwellings, evicting tenants on low-rents with a mixture of inducements and fear to live in high-rise blocks.

This was a familiar topic in the early Seventies, and raised the spectre of London property developer Peter Rachmann who evicted existing tenants in West London on low rents to house immigrant families at exorbitant, self-fixed prices. Gabriel plays three characters, John Pebble of Styx Enterprises, Mark Hall, known as the 'Winkler', his 'heavy', and Mrs Barrow, a tenant. Hall's wages depend on his successful eviction of the residents. Barrow is offered a new home at a high-rise block, and reluctantly goes, only to find her rent increased. The song ends in 2012, when a message from the mysterious Genetic Control informs that a height restriction of four feet has been placed on 'humanoid height', so more people can be fitted into dwellings. Pebble, now Sir John De Pebble of United Blacksprings International, sends the Winkler out to do his work again. The song's coda is delivered by 'Satin Peter', very much a glam saint, suggesting that humankind seems happy indulging in such nefarious practices, yet guilt can be assuaged by investing in the church. With its theatrical builds and attacking, multi-character vocal, the song again demonstrated how far Gabriel was prepared to travel outside of the conventional subject matter.

The sweet 'Can-Utility And The Coastliners' had been around in various forms since the Christmas Cottage days: originally known as 'I've Been Travelling All Night Long' and later 'Rock My Baby' and 'Bye-Bye Johnny', it was reworked by the group for the album. After a brief, sweet guitar introduction by Steve Hackett, 'Horizons', *Foxtrot* was all about 'Supper's Ready', the song that rightly became their anthem. For a brief period in the Seventies, it formed part of a holy trinity with Led Zeppelin's 'Stairway To Heaven' and Pink Floyd's *Dark Side Of The Moon*, as the go-to common room records.

The piece was ambitious – spanning 23 minutes, it was split into seven movements. Fortunately, everything within these movements is in good measure – it is akin to seven short(ish) songs threaded together with incredible élan. Inspired by a sober, chilling, out-of-body experience that Gabriel, Jill and producer John Anthony had had at Jill's parents' flat in London the previous year, and a similar occasion when Gabriel thought that he had witnessed shrouded men walking across the lawn, the song explored the basic tenets of good and evil. Richard Macphail recalls the wonder of first hearing it: "No matter what we were doing, we'd have to listen to 'Supper's Ready' all the way through; it became a daily ritual."

The patchwork of the songs was established before the group reached the studio. "As I was part of the process of joining my bits to other people's, it was a growing experience," said Steve Hackett. "Both Pete and I insisted there needed to be plenty of interesting aural and visual detail." The detail is stunning, creating an exciting, sometimes baffling but ultimately rewarding experience. The 23 minutes simply fly by. Gabriel was quoted in Tony Palmer's story of popular music, *All You Need Is Love,* as saying that 'Supper's Ready' represented "the ultimate cosmic battle for Armageddon between good and evil in which man is destroyed, but the deaths of countless thousands atone for mankind, reborn no longer as Homo Sapiens." It begins with 'Lover's Leap', directly inspired by the out-of-body experience – of lovers lost in each other's gaze and transformed into another male and female entirely – before they go off on a journey of the mind. They come to a town dominated by two contrasting individuals – a benevolent farmer and 'The Guaranteed Eternal Sanctuary Man', in Gabriel's words, "the head of a highly disciplined scientific religion". We encounter Gabriel's own emotional pull between nature and science that would be a recurring theme. Would he wish to be out in the trees damming the stream or in the workshop inventing?

The Guaranteed Eternal Sanctuary Man is indeed a false prophet, and it is suggested he contains "a secret new ingredient capable of fighting fire". Ikhnaton and Its-a-con and Their Band Of Merry Men appear to the lovers, "clad in greys and purples, awaiting to be summoned out of the ground". They rise from the earth and attempt to attack those without an 'up-to-date "Eternal Life Licence" ', which was available at the religion's headquarters. It could be seen as an astute, if oblique, commentary on the racial tension conjured up in the wake of Enoch Powell's 'Rivers Of Blood' speech in April 1968 which had already indirectly inspired Paul McCartney to write 'Get Back' for The Beatles. In 'How Dare I Be So Beautiful', after the battle, the lovers find a lone figure, fixated on his own image, akin to the Greek myth of Narcissus. They watch his transformation into a flower as they are pulled into their own reflections, to find Willow Farm, a place where 'life flows freely' and all is 'mindlessly busy'.

The song builds perfectly to its sixth section, 'Apocalypse In 9/8 ('Co-starring The Delicious Talents Of Gabble Ratchet')'. Originally intended by Banks as an instrumental, Gabriel added his climactic vocals when the others were out of the studio. Banks' initial displeasure was quickly dissipated by the absolutely stunning majesty of the vocal. Gabriel wrote in the supporting notes for the song that "the lovers become seeds in the soil, where they recognise other seeds to be people from the world in which they had originated. While they wait for spring, they are returned to their old world to see Apocalypse of St John in full progress." As the chaos builds, the song reverts back to the theme of 'The Guaranteed Eternal Sanctuary Man' for 'As Sure As Eggs Is Eggs (Aching Men's Feet)' and the suite ends with the triumph of good over evil, as the couple are led towards the New Jerusalem, as referred to in the Book Of Revelations.

In its review of the album *Sounds* said, "Sufficient to say that it is difficult to follow Peter Gabriel's thought patterns at the most logical times and the whys and wherefores of his words are best left unchallenged . . . 'Willow Farm' . . . taxes the imagination more than Maggie's farm ever did, 'The Guaranteed Eternal Sanctuary Man' . . . heads rather obliquely in the direction of Bowie and seems to be about a supersonic space age farmer. Finally 'Apocalypse In 9/8 (Co-starring The Delicious Talents of Gabble Ratchet)' . . . sort that one out if you can."

Gabriel had been reading Zen teaching, and there was certainly a Zen introspection to 'Supper's Ready' – as he explained to Jerry Gilbert in *Sounds*: "Well, you see I just met up with Zen completely by chance and it seemed to me that I was reading this approach to life which seemed to fall in with all the things I liked before – Spike Milligan, Monty Python, Don Quixote, *Alice In Wonderland* and stories. There's a book called *Zen In The English Literature* which is tremendously entertaining – very exciting . . . but spontaneity isn't the sort of thing you can strive for. One of the great troubles with the mind is that it's always lost between two extremes. That's partly what 'Willow Farm' is all about – cement between two bricks, and wherever you are and whatever you do there's always a left and right, an up and down, a good and bad and if everyone's good there must automatically be some bad."

'Supper's Ready' became a centrepiece of Genesis' live shows and finally unleashed the power of the group on record, something that had only previously been hinted at. Its mixture of fantasy, sprawling yet economical musicianship, flashes of social and spiritual realism also had a remarkable grasp of its audience. To underline the song's significance, a sheet would be handed out at shows with the lyrics on it, plus an explanation of the song by Gabriel.

"It did feel like we captured some emotion there. Particularly at the climax," Gabriel told Chris Roberts of *Classic Prog* magazine in 2012: "For my part it was influenced by John Bunyan's *The Pilgrim's Progress* – as was

*The Lamb Lies Down On Broadway*. It was the idea of a journey. And we were then trying, consciously, to break out of tradition: throwing together different ideas and influences to see if there was a fresh way of putting them together."

Its sleeve, again designed by Paul Whitehead, illustrated both 'Supper's Ready' and incorporated Gabriel's fox stage look. "The whole fox thing became irresistible," Gabriel said. "Whitehead had picked up on it from hearing the American term for woman, and then added it into the painting he was working on for the album's cover. With the hunters on the seashore, as foxes were always being hunted, Whitehead thought, 'Why not have the fox disguise himself as a woman, to get away." It worked. It added mystery and depth to the group – and to Gabriel in particular.

The band was firing on all cylinders. *Sounds* said: "Lyrically and musically *Foxtrot* comes across as a total mind trip, with imagination and musical ideas being allowed to run wild and in turn stretch the imagination of the listener. Genesis have taken a lot of chances, but these days they have the full courage of their convictions to back them up. They're in a territory all of their own and picking up supporters all the way – I hope that this outstanding album receives the patient, repeated listening that it deserves."

'Supper's Ready' was premiered in the group's live show in November 1972. Gabriel appeared in triangular box headgear with lights for eyes in 'Apocalypse In 9/8', before the show climaxed with him in luminous makeup holding only a fluorescent light tube as the rest of the stage fell into darkness for 'As Sure As Eggs is Eggs'. All agreed it was one of their most mesmerising, transfixing performances yet, building the show into complete theatre. The tour came with its own programme, explaining that "A Genesis gig is like watching a pantomime against the background of an orchestra".

"I was conscious by the time we got to *Foxtrot* that Peter was getting all the attention," Tony Banks says. "It didn't really bother me, except it pissed me off that everyone thought Peter wrote everything. I was very happy to have someone who was as charismatic as that with me in the group, but beyond that, why it had to mean everything else, I don't know."

★ ★ ★

There was now the opportunity to play America, and the band were ready. Or so they thought. "We weren't straight ahead rock'n'roll," Gabriel told Philip Dodd in 2007. "We were a bunch of limey poofters and our music was full of classical references. So we attracted this quirky, eccentric, following."

Tony Stratton-Smith was later to state: "Like most groups, the ambition was to 'make it' in a Nixon-led America which continued to have its nose bloodied in Vietnam and where the State was regularly going over the top in containing its young radicals. Incipient Genesis saw their 'time' as a general assault on the human spirit and maybe they were . . . right."

The band's first show in the US was at Brandeis University in Boston on December 16, 1972, followed by a performance at the Carnegie Hall in New York the following evening. Although they were dogged with technical issues, they had a friendly supporter in Ed Goodgold, formerly manager of Fifties rock'n'roll revivalists Sha-Na-Na, who was Charisma's US representative and worked for Buddah Records.

Goodgold listened diligently to the band's existing catalogue that Stratton-Smith had spoken so warmly about, but was not enamoured by the 'mountain of noise' he heard. Wondering how to tell Stratton-Smith that he didn't want to manage them, he gave 'Supper's Ready' another listen. "I heard the musical light," he wrote in 1998. With typical American flourish, he went on to say, "The aural colours their music created were particularly dazzling. The group reminded me of Berlioz." His willingness to look after the band in America was cemented when he saw them, at Stratton-Smith's request, play London. "I realised the band were conducting a religious service, a high mass for the rock faithful. That night, they didn't have an audience, they had a congregation. Their followers wanted a hint, a taste, a sense of awe and the band did not disappoint them."

In the era of Jesus freakery and the huge American success of *Jesus Christ Superstar*, Genesis' quasi-religious overtones led many in the States to believe they were part of the same piece. "We got home just before Christmas, and there was this rave review in *Cashbox*. Things started to change from then," remembers Macphail.

★ ★ ★

It was the show at the Rainbow in London's Finsbury Park on February 9, 1973 that was to prove one of the most significant in Genesis and Gabriel's career, a landmark performance that showed just how the band was moving forward. "It was really *Foxtrot* that gave it that lift, and with Peter's characters," Conroy recalls. "Adrian Selby had designed all these sets for the Rainbow show and would come in and have a flaming row with Fred Munt about the cost of them. They all had theatrical friends, and certainly Peter had a load of people. Peter would find people to make things for him, and then come up with a massive bill, which Peter was always very good at and he was great at getting stuff sorted."

It was this melting pot, cross-fertilisation of ideas that spurred the band – and especially Gabriel – on. The magical performance at the Rainbow, the rapture of Italy, the indifference of Lincoln, the shock of Dublin all fed into a band comfortable with their material, pushing forward. The full house agreed, as did virtually all of the music press who were there. Selby's sets, complete with a white gauze curtain and ultra violet light, marked the group out as a must-see live spectacle. The amps went behind the curtain and when the light shone on it, all the equipment, the trappings of a conventional rock concert, disappeared, placing the emphasis on the theatrical aspect of the work.

The show marked the debut of Gabriel's batwing head-dress which he wore for the opening 'Watcher Of The Skies'. "The Rainbow was one of our best ever shows," Banks says. "Other people did stuff just with costumes, but we tended to use the whole stage. When you went to a Genesis concert, you saw the gauze curtains, and then the dry ice, which I know is a cliché now, but it wasn't then. You saw the bat wings and the eye make-up. You heard the Mellotron sound, which was really early stereo. It couldn't have been any other concert in the world at that point. The power was so strong in those first 10 minutes. I think we were one of the first groups to truly appreciate that, using simple visuals and music. Some of it was luck and chance, and some of it was Peter's ability to carry it off.

"It was all Peter's thing," Macphail recalls. "He found Guy Chapman, who made him all the masks that came with 'Supper's Ready' and *Foxtrot*, and the black cloak." Part-James Brown, part-Chamber of Horrors, part-camp seaside revue, Gabriel came into his own. "'Watcher Of The Skies' is pure *The Cabinet of Dr Caligari*," says writer David Buckley.

"Genesis tapped into that very English Lewis Carroll-esque 'chop-off-your-head' nursery rhyme brutality, which no other group at the time came anywhere close to nailing."

Now in a field of their own, what was truly astonishing was the stage dramatisation, for want of a better word, of 'Supper's Ready'. Gabriel lived every section of the song, most notably (and the image that stuck with his audience) the Chapman-designed flower head for 'Willow Farm'. Partially inspired by the character of 'Little Weed' from BBC TV's ever popular children's programme *The Flower Pot Men*, it highlighted Gabriel's sense of playfulness and longing to return to childhood. "When he put on the flower mask, he took on this music hall persona," Banks said. "And he became even more the centre of attention."

"The flower head should be hamming it up. It's consciously supposed to be unreal," Gabriel told *Circus* Magazine in 1974. "I don't specifically want to frighten. Let's say I would prefer to be Fellini. In fact, the flower walk was probably more influenced by Shirley Temple, which is better than ripping off Eric Clapton."

Gabriel realised the importance of creating a spectacle, telling director and writer Tony Palmer: "At the moment, we are still at the first stage of the audio-visual, in much the same state as those first stereo engineers who experimented with trains passing from one speaker to another. We do not intend to create a Hollywood song and dance spectacular, however, but a concept whose visual and musical aspects can be expressed at the same time." The Genesis live show over the next two years would further explore audio-visual elements to the fullest extent.

* * *

By the time Genesis returned for their second tour of America in 1973, they had grown tighter and more accustomed to the stage. In April that year, they played the New York Philharmonic Hall. Ron Ross from *Phonograph Record* was one of the first American journalists to note their prowess, his lengthy review concluding with: "If they never have a hit single, and it's unlikely that they even listen to hit singles, Genesis could be a tremendous commercial success for many of the same reasons as Bowie, Alice Cooper, the Moody Blues, Yes or Jethro Tull. They make the most of that transcendent Britishness that has kept us with the Move and the Kinks for so many years, and now that pop is having its brightest day since

1965, it's good to see a band that appreciates 1967 and the kind of intelligence which once made the Airplane great, without having to create an asshole like *Aqualung* to prove it. And then there's the one they do about the hermaphrodite fountain . . ." He also opined that Gabriel "looks roughly ten times better in a jumpsuit than Mick Jagger and doesn't have to foam at the mouth to impress his audiences."

Larry Fast, who would later play with Gabriel for the best part of a decade, was part of a team that interviewed Gabriel for college radio in Pennsylvania where Fast was studying law, although as a keyboard player and synthesiser pioneer, he was more interested in speaking to Tony Banks. He recalled talking to Gabriel at this time: "I was struck by the difference between the Peter that I saw onstage and the quiet, polite and more introspective Peter after the show. I suppose that is something that I came to understand better in the years working with Peter. In my previous experience with more conventional musical personalities I found more consistencies between the onstage and offstage personas. Yet Peter didn't strike me as though he was simply being theatrical and playing an onstage role as an actor. It was something rather more special with him inhabiting the music he created. Though I didn't recognise it as such at that time it was a type of performance art. In a sense, both the onstage and offstage Peter are the real person; just different aspects of him."

One of the more bizarre interludes was Genesis' brief tour supporting Lou Reed, then enjoying something of a fleeting commercial moment off the back of his David Bowie-produced album, *Transformer*, and now billed as 'The Phantom Of Rock'. They shared a bill at the Massey Hall in Toronto, a show Steve Hackett recalled to *The Guardian* in 2011: "There were people who wanted to watch Genesis, and people who wanted to watch Lou Reed. And that deteriorated into a punch-up between the Lou Reed fans who were on downers, and the Genesis fans who were more into Earl Grey tea. Tony Banks started up his Mellotron introduction to 'Watcher Of The Skies' and someone shouted out, 'Sounds like fuckin' Beethoven!' They just wanted a boogie."

Among those at the show was Bob Ezrin, a young Canadian producer who would later play a significant role in Gabriel's career. Ezrin had made his name producing theatrical American rock icon Alice Cooper, and had shifted his sound from the dense, Mothers Of Invention art-rock to songs like his iconic 1972 hit, 'School's Out', which fused art and glam together.

"I had been asked to produce Lou Reed. I went to Massey Hall with the A&R man from RCA," Ezrin recalls. "I said, 'Look, I love Lou and I'm really pleased to be doing his album, but can you introduce me to the guy with the flower on his head. He's amazing, I need to meet him! I'd became a fan of the British avant garde through Alice, who loved Syd Barrett and Marc Bolan, and was very much a fan of what became known as progressive rock. I was aware of Genesis, but I'd never seen them. And to see Peter emerge with this flower on his head, it was absolutely brilliant – I fell in love with them very early on. We went back stage to see Lou, and I was allowed to go into Genesis' dressing room and I told Peter how much I thought they were amazing. It was about a 30-second encounter." Within four years, Ezrin and Gabriel would get to know each other very well.

To capitalise on their growing success in the US, the group was recorded by the *King Biscuit Flower Hour*, which syndicated live performances of groups to 300 radio stations in the States. Two concerts were recorded, at the DeMontfort Hall in Leicester and Manchester's Free Trade Hall. As the band were working on their new album, and *Foxtrot* was over six months old, he persuaded the band to release an edited version of the concert on a new budget imprint on Charisma, the CLASS series. Released at the end of July 1973, the five-track album, minus the 23-minute 'Supper's Ready' recorded at the shows, was attractively priced at just over a pound, and not only took Genesis into the UK Top 10 for the first time but acted as a calling card in America.

With its eerie, otherworldly sleeve featuring a blue-tinted live shot of Gabriel performing 'Apocalypse 9/8', taken by Bob Gruen at Princeton University, *Genesis Live* became a student staple. "You looked at that cover," Banks laughs, "and you thought what the hell was that?" Inexpensive, it ensnared fans world-wide. Erik Neuteboom, a fan writing on progarchives.com in 2005, captured the simple essence of this bizarre album: "When I saw the cover of *Genesis Live* with the blue light and the mysterious figure with the cloak and the mask, I realised that this had to be something special."

It also demonstrated how accomplished Genesis had become as a live band. Its five tracks – 'Watcher Of The Skies', 'Get 'Em Out By Friday', 'The Return Of The Giant Hogweed', 'The Musical Box' and 'The Knife' – focused on the snappier aggression of the group's live set, and as a result, many felt a power was lacking on the group's studio albums. *Rolling Stone* said: "This album goes a long way toward capturing the gripping power and mysticism that has many fans acclaiming Genesis as 'the greatest live band ever'". It was high praise indeed. The group was getting noticed. When the CD was being worked on for its 21st century release, Gabriel dropped in on mastering at the Farm (Genesis' studio) and was taken aback by the energy he heard from the band.

The rear sleeve also contained a short surreal essay by Gabriel, based on one of his onstage between-song riffs. For many, this added to the album's budget allure. The title-less tale concerned a woman in a green trouser suit standing up on a crowded tube train that gets stuck in an underground tunnel. Calmly she walks to the middle of the carriage, unbuttons her green trouser suit and continues to remove all of her clothes until she is stark naked. She then searches for a zip between her legs and peeling apart her body, she reveals a golden rod, a flagpole without a flag. The vividness of the writing, the comedy, the smuttiness and the metaphor seemed to strike a chord, and again confirmed Gabriel's place as the band's Renaissance man. It attracted many fans, including the film director William Friedkin, and added to the strange mystique of this strange band.

On the back cover of *Genesis Live* there was a small picture of Gabriel's dear friend Richard Macphail, taken by Margaret Banks, saying the album was dedicated to him, as he had departed his role as tour manager, sound engineer and all-round band fixer in April 1973. The ambiguity of the band's statement led to some confusion. "People thought I was dead," Macphail laughs. "It was rather unfortunately worded. There are many thousands of people out there who don't know who I am but they think I'm dead. It's very odd." Although Macphail was very much alive and well, and would go on to play a key role in Gabriel's future, another tangible link with Genesis' Charterhouse roots was cut.

# 9: Love, Peace And Truth Incorporated: *Selling England By The Pound*

*"We're closer to cartoons than the conventional rock band. As far as other bands go, I think we're in a little puddle all by ourselves"*

Peter Gabriel, 1974

IN November 1972, Peter Gabriel was interviewed, alone, by Jerry Gilbert for *Sounds* Magazine. In the interview, Gabriel outlined a passion that was to continue with him for the next two decades, to create some form of futuristic theme park: "One of my ambitions which I'd like to get off the ground is . . . to create a sort of Willow Farm in reality. It's what I'd like to do if I accrued large sums of money, buy a hundred acre farm in North Wales and turn it into a cross between Disneyland and an art gallery where the visitor goes through a tremendous amount of first hand experiences which would completely upturn his points of relativity and put him through a series of changes." This concept was seldom to leave Gabriel over the next 20 or so years; at any opportunity he had to dream he returned to this fun-filled, artistic scheme. It was another example of how far he wanted to travel from the conventional route of being a singer in a rock band; another frontier to cross.

Genesis were now at last moving to where they wanted to be, with critical and finally some commercial success. There was interest in their material in the US, and their UK tours were now guaranteed sell-outs. Charisma too was expanded, although the commercial success of their first number one band, Lindisfarne, was abating, and the label was diversifying further into records and films. The label was still a financial house of cards, with Stratton-Smith's love for his artists often blurring fiscal sense. But Genesis' fortunes were on the turn, and it looked likely that through a series of fortuitous opportunities, Gabriel's vision would soon be shared by more people.

In America, Genesis came to the attention of Ahmet Ertegun at the fabled Atlantic Records, who was developing the label's core business of soul and R&B into something more progressive. Atlantic had an incredible soul, R&B, blues, jazz and more recently, rock tradition, and many of Gabriel's favourite R&B artists had made their name at the label, including Ray Charles, Aretha Franklin, and through their distribution of Stax-Volt, Otis Redding. Lately, though, their biggest successes had come from Led Zeppelin and Yes from the UK, and Crosby, Stills, Nash & Young from the US. Buddah had looked after Genesis' US releases to that date, and although in Ed Goodgold they had a vociferous supporter, Atlantic would offer more nationwide promotion and support.

"When we signed them, Genesis was a band that had a very small but very fervent following in America," Ertegun said in 2001. "With every release we expected them to break bigger and bigger, and finally they did." Achieving widespread US success was still some distance away, but with every release, every tour, their fan base was increasing. The band was still starving though, and were now somewhere in the region of £200,000 in debt. The release of their next album, *Selling England By The Pound*, changed all that.

What was to become *Selling England By The Pound* was rehearsed during the early summer of 1973 in the living room of a group friend's house near Chessington Zoo in Surrey, punctuated by complaining neighbours, and recorded in three weeks in August at Basing Street Studios in West London. The band and Gabriel wanted to look at aspects of how traditional England was being subsumed in the modern world. They asked John Burns, who had worked as engineer on *Foxtrot*, and also helped assemble *Genesis Live*, to produce. Burns was of a similar age to them, and had already had considerable experience, working with Blind Faith, Jethro Tull, Spooky Tooth and Free. "I never thought the power of the band had been fully captured on record," said Richard Macphail. "It wasn't until John Burns came along that he really captured the essence of them as a live band in the studio." Another key factor was that they "started to get some better equipment".

In 1973, Britain was at a crossroads. Edward Heath's Conservative government seemed to be losing control of various industrial disputes that raged in a union-dominated workplace, and inflation was spiralling due to the increasing global economic crisis. Value Added Tax (VAT) was introduced at the start of April 1973, and the cost of living was a contentious topic of conversation. With credit cards becoming ever more popular and national debt on the rise, writing about beheadings during games of croquet seemed now perhaps too frivolous, too escapist.

Pink Floyd's *Dark Side Of the Moon*, released in March 1973, contained 'Money', a song that parodied the financial system yet made the band wealthier at last. *Selling England By The Pound* was an attempt by Gabriel to reassert the band's roots and "look at Englishness in a different way." It is infused with a whimsy, a Britain-at-sunset, looking to see how it can move forward in shifting times. And the use of the word 'pound' in its title was key: aside from the obvious pun between currency and weight, the pound sterling was one of the hottest political topics in recent history. In the preceding decade it had been devalued, decimalised and floated. Harold Wilson's 1967 phrase, "the pound in your pocket", when the pound was devalued by 14 per cent to foreign markets (but remained worth the same in the UK) had stuck in popular consciousness. A collective focus on thrift and economy, set against the financial crisis, gave the album's title a resonance with the English public and nodded to the state of the nation. "*Selling England By The Pound* is our best album title ever," Mike Rutherford says. "The feel and the look of it and the social approach was interesting."

Although ostensibly an eight-track album, it offers five significant pieces and three shorter fillers. Originally entitled 'Disney', 'Dancing With The Moonlit Knight' was a bold introduction, marking a clear line in the sand between *Selling England By The Pound* and their previous work. Looking to marry traditional folk with contemporary band arrangements, Hackett described the song as "a still, tranquil lake, with every player disturbing the surface". Gabriel wrote the melody for the opening section, while the rest of the band contributed to later sections of the song. But the subject matter was the most overt in reflecting the commercialisation of a troubled Britain, with Gabriel singing a folk madrigal as Britannia, posing the simple but effective question at the album's very outset, "Can you tell me where my country lies?" Father Thames has drowned, but the population are too preoccupied to notice, as they digest their Wimpy burgers*, spending pounds to gain pounds.

* Since the Thirties Wimpy had been the premier fast food outlet in the UK before McDonalds arrived in October 1974.

The Arthurian legend is invoked, and the final cry of calling the 'Knights of the Green Shield' to 'stamp and shout' is a pun on the long defunct Green Shield spend-and-stamp reward system. This call for an uprising to reassert Britain's place in the world delivered forlornly by Britannia is one of Gabriel's most poignant (and pun-filled) lyrics. Where other writing at that time was heading off into space, this seemed grounded in reality, albeit shrouded in a mist of fantasy. Musically, it begins gently before heading off into battle, showcasing the road-tested confidence of the players. "We were an English group of a certain kind," Banks says. "And the way it starts with the folky introduction, I think the album is the best example of the early Genesis. I think using that phrase [*Selling England By The Pound*] was a really good idea."

Where *Selling England By The Pound* differed from previous Genesis albums on Charisma was that it had actually had a short, snappy commercial number that could act as an accessible calling card to the album's knottier core. 'I Know What I Like (In Your Wardrobe)' came from a guitar figure that Hackett had been toying with for a while, and in this one single, glam rock and progressive music came together, giving Genesis a point of accessibility with the wider market.

For all their 22-minute, multi-parted symphonies, Genesis always knew a good pop tune when they heard it, and that was the very thing that attracted them to Jonathan King and Decca in the first place. And 'I Know What I Like (In Your Wardrobe)' is a *fantastic* pop song. Hackett kept playing a Beatles-influenced guitar riff through Banks' Leslie cabinet at rehearsals for *Foxtrot*. Collins and he would jam on it, but the band were not particularly interested. By the time of *Selling England By The Pound*, there was a paucity of material and when Hackett and Collins played it again, Banks began improvising around it. Soon the others jumped on it, welcoming a touch of light relief from the more opaque material that was their bread and butter.

In rehearsal, it frequently reached 20 minutes. Gabriel came up with a melody line and a lyric inspired by what was to become the album's cover painting, *The Dream*, by Betty Swanwick. 'I Know What I Like (In Your Wardrobe)' is the tale of external pressure on Jacob, a young man (allegedly Genesis' roadie Jacob Finster) to conform. The line "there's a future for you in the fire escape trade" echoes the line from Mr McGuire (Walter Brooke) to Benjamin Braddock (Dustin Hoffman) in Mike Nicholl's 1967 film, *The Graduate*, "There's a great future in plastics". Like Braddock, Jacob eschews the advice; he is simply content to mow lawns for a living and doze in the sun at lunchtime.

With Banks' irresistible chorus, Rutherford playing an electric sitar and Gabriel's to-die-for synthesiser riff to close, it all scuttles along with tremendous panache and humour. The unusual percussion sound at the start came from Gabriel's talking drum that producer Burns had brought back from Nigeria. A stage favourite for the band in both Gabriel and Phil Collins eras, with the former dressed as a yokel meticulously miming mowing and the latter furiously banging away on tambourine, 'I Know What I Like (In Your Wardrobe)' makes a case for the tiny sub-genre, glam-prog. The lyrics even wittily referenced the Garden Wall, the first band that Gabriel, Banks and Chris Stewart had been in back at Charterhouse. As a single, 'I Know What I Like (In Your Wardrobe)' had a great influence and impact on its listeners. As *Sounds* said, "'I Know What I Like (In Your Wardrobe)' conjures up amazing visual possibilities with its childlike quality of far-away images." The record reached number 21 in the UK in April 1974, their first showing in the singles charts.

After the levity comes the gravity. One of Banks' greatest and loftiest creations, 'Firth Of Fifth' was stitched together from three separate pieces of music left over from *Foxtrot* and became one of the group's most loved songs. After Banks' grand piano introduction, the power of their arrival still surprises. Featuring Hackett's single best guitar solo with the group and Gabriel's full-throated singing and delicate flute work, it returns to the world of fantasy with suggestions that the sands of time are being eroded by the river of constant change, an echo of the uncertainty of 'Moonlit Knight'. 'More Fool Me', with Phil Collins on lead vocal, was a curio that pointed towards the future; a two-minute love song that closed the first side and owed its inclusion to producer Burns who thought this simple piece offered a pleasant contrast to the high drama found elsewhere on the record.

But there were also signs that Gabriel was outgrowing the band. 'The Battle Of Epping Forest' proved controversial, as it was simply one long showcase for his voice and characterisation, a sort of modern Gilbert & Sullivan operetta, with all parts played noisily by him. And as for subject matter, gangland warfare on the fringes of North East London was a resolute departure from the usual leafy meanderings from the fringes of London's South West. Gabriel had talked about it in an interview with

*Melody Maker* in July 1973: "About two or three years ago I read a newspaper item about a gang battle that took place in Epping Forest. I like to collect cuttings from newspapers about any odd happenings. In this case I kept the cutting for ages, but could not find out any more about the battle. I even put an ad in *The Times* and checked in newspaper libraries. But the story had disappeared off the face of the earth. Even my original cutting seems to have disappeared." This rich and vivid story of gangland life seemed meat and drink to Gabriel, who constructed another mini-operetta in the style of 'Get 'Em Out By Friday'.

The track, deceptively long at 11 minutes, is akin to a Monty Python sketch set to music, complete with myriad voices, generous double-entendres, camp academic stereotypes ('Harold Demure, from Art Literature', indeed) and little room for the instrumentation to breathe. Banks, for one, was never a fan. "'The Battle Of Epping Forest' was a fight between the vocals and the music," Banks says. "The music is great, and the vocals are great, but both together are a bit too much." "On 'The Battle Of Epping Forest', there were too many good ideas going around," Mike Rutherford adds. "That's why it got easier each time, as we became a four piece and then a three piece."

'The Battle Of Epping Forest' obliquely echoes the album's theme of searching for a lost England: corrupt reverends, antique shops, judgements based on what a person owns as opposed to who they are, and increasing commercialisation. There is a dig at the death of the hippie dream, with a new 'pin-up guru' every week, turning alternative lifestyles into simply another commodity, 'Love, Peace & Truth Incorporated'. It became a staple of their live set from the end of 1973 and into 1974, giving Gabriel the opportunity to don stocking masks and act out some violence. The song, unbelievably, was adopted as a chant at West Country football derbies.

Artist and photographer, Julian Woollatt, a fan from childhood, would sing 'The Battle Of Epping Forest' on the way to games: "Very often it would all be about adopting voices; you'd have this old English thing, like 'The Battle of Epping Forest' or they'd talk like they were from *A Clockwork Orange* or Monty Python, a creative language in a way." A language of the underground developed and Gabriel seemed to be tapping into it: "It was weirdly patriotic," Woollatt continues. "I'm not sure it comes just from the music of the Sixties, but from that phenomenal imagination that was in Sixties television, too. You've grown up with *The Prisoner* and *The Avengers*; the aftermath of Sixties drug culture and it all fuses together as this kind of theatrical mass, without the peace. It was that sort of aggressive culture with elements of hippiedom and dark English humour." Gabriel was certainly flirting with something that was in the air – whether it be David Bowie's sailors, fighting in the dance hall, or Elton John suggesting that Saturday night was indeed alright for fighting.

'After The Ordeal', an inconsequential instrumental composed largely by Hackett, acts as a bridge between "The Battle Of Epping Forest' and the other major piece on side two, another 11-minute long opus, 'The Cinema Show.' The only song here that echoes the Genesis of *Trespass*, the lyrics – largely written by Banks and Rutherford – tell of a modern day Romeo & Juliet romance which references Tiresias from Greek mythology, who lived as both a man and a woman, a blurring of gender that harks back to 'The Fountain Of Samacis' and the union of the lovers in 'Supper's Ready'. With his often camp stage persona, Gabriel was tapping into the sexual politics that were permeating the Seventies, just a handful of years after homosexuality had been decriminalised in the UK. Bi- and homosexuality had become a popular topic of discussion in music after David Bowie's 'coming out' to Michael Watts in *Melody Maker* in early 1972. Shortly before six minutes, the track abruptly shifts gear from its dreamy CSN-style acoustic mid-tempo as the band move into a slow-building and soon to be free-wheeling jazz-rock instrumental that builds into a climactic closing section.

The theme of the state of the UK comes into focus again with the closing 'Aisle Of Plenty', a short song which reprises the original melody of 'Dancing With The Moonlit Knight', introduced by Hackett's tender acoustic work. The short verse offers a series of puns about UK supermarkets and concludes with Gabriel watching 'the deadly nightshade grow'. Was England going to be left under a carpet of the alluring yet poisonous plant while everyone is too busy buying things? He and Collins call out a series of prices of consumer goods with price reductions and special offers. This minute-and-a-half drifts by and links the album back to where it began, the cash-strapped British economy of 1973.

*Selling England By The Pound* was released in October 1973. Strikingly complex, yet often deceptively simple, it heralded a different Genesis. It even looked different, moving away from the band's now trademark gatefold sleeves and Paul Whitehead illustrations and offering instead something far more direct. Gabriel had persuaded Betty Swanwick to add a lawnmower to her painting, *The Dream*, which had inspired 'I Know What I Like (In Your Wardrobe)', and for it to be used as the cover. It retained the English whimsy of the previous releases, yet looked more in keeping with a modern jazz album.

*Selling England By The Pound* was well-received. Long-term fan Barbara Charone wrote in *NME*: "Genesis stand head and shoulders, above all those so-called progressive groups." Genesis were progressive as they were reflecting on the state of the nation, be it the bully-boy gang warfare on the fringes of London, or the threat to national identity. As a result of the global energy crisis, spurred on by Arab nations embargoing the sales of oil to America for their support of Israel and the work-to-rule of the British coal industry, Britain went into the Three Day Week, limiting commercial consumption of power. The ethereal nature of much of the album's material seemed to chime perfectly with the times and its lyrical message seemed to reflect clearly contemporary issues. By the end of 1973, *Selling England By The Pound* was top three in an album chart populated by Slade, David Cassidy, Status Quo and Peters & Lee.

As Genesis had seemingly come from nowhere, it was inevitable that some thought they had merely aped a variety of styles that were currently on offer. Gabriel told *NME* in October 1973: "I think some people have a rip-off concept of us, which goes something like this: they see us as a band who were sitting around doing nothing, and who looked at who was pulling in the money in the music market, so they think we ripped off Yes's music, Alice Cooper's visuals, and we came up with Genesis . . . And just because I was dressing up, people assumed I was imitating Bowie. But the thing is, the characters I play are things talked about in the lyrics, and they do occur. Bowie's a great writer, but I don't always think his costumes are relevant to his music."

Every costume Gabriel wore or prop he used was there to propel the dramatic narrative of the songs. It was in the air, this spirit of adventure, the liberation provided by The Beatles and the Stones, the impact of drugs on popular culture, the permissive society was all coming together. And now, Gabriel's escapist vision, married to the increasingly impressive musicianship of the group, was providing a suitable antidote to the increasingly grim economic landscape in the UK.

The concerts that supported *Selling England By The Pound* saw Gabriel's costumes and props becoming all the more otherworldly and elaborate, to the point that fans came to the shows believing Genesis was fundamentally him and a backing group, an assumption that irked the other four members, Banks especially. There was now even a lawnmower brought onstage to assist in the narrative of 'I Know What I Like (In Your Wardrobe)'. "I did a lot of helping Peter with all of the early toys they got," Paul Conroy remembers. "I got the first lawnmower for him from the back of someone's garage, and we used to bang them in the three-ton truck."

The venues were getting bigger and their support act was now almost always a solo performer so the stage was ready for their set. To underline their growth, one venue no longer on the itinerary was the Friars in Aylesbury: "They left us behind by the time *of Selling England By The Pound*, because we just weren't big enough," David Stopps sighs. "I should have pushed it a bit harder, actually. We were the venue that really helped them, so come back and give us some support, but it never really occurred to me."

The *Selling England By The Pound* tour opened in Manchester on October 6, 1973 and saw the band playing 2,000-seater venues and filling them comfortably. On the road Genesis maintained their dignified, grown-up conduct, and there was little gossip or backstage shenanigans. "Tony was married as well [as Peter], so he didn't hang with the muso types," Conroy says. "Mike would hang more with Steve and Phil, but Tony would go back to the hotel. Peter would always be involved with some ne'er-do-well fan who would want him to speak to the local fanzine and he was always around for that, but they weren't backstage swilling ale like some groups we could mention." Gabriel was to send up the band onstage years later at the *Six Of The Best* concert at Milton Keynes: "We would creep into a Holiday Inn bathroom, all of us, in the dead of night, unwrap a bar of soap, and leave it unused the following morning. There was one incident when the birthday boy [Mike Rutherford] travelled up and down on a German hotel lift."

Their concert appearances were now eagerly anticipated and warmly received. "I saw Genesis at the Bristol Hippodrome in 1973, and they were everything I thought they would be," Dave Gregory, later of XTC, was to say.

The group filmed their live show at Shepperton Studios at the end of October, highlighting the new Gabriel characters and opening the show as Britannia for 'Dancing With The Moonlit Knight'. The film emphasises quite how un/surreal the band looked, with three seated performers looking like they are conducting an intense scientific experiment, with Collins on drums undermining them by wearing his overalls. And then Gabriel, looking every inch the malevolent eccentric, strutting out using every inch of the stage as his playground, either with his lawnmower, his old man mask or his batwings. It was like a circus with Gabriel as the ringmaster.

* * *

During 1973, Tony Stratton-Smith, busy with his interests in racehorses, the wider Charisma label and a much-anticipated diversification into films, relinquished his day-to-day control overseeing Genesis' career. The band, still teetering on the verge of financial chaos, asked Tony Smith, their tour promoter, to be their exclusive manager. Smith was a powerful industry presence, who had assisted his father John with arranging one of The Beatles' first tours of the UK. "I was becoming ensconced in pub rock, but I helped with Tony Smith coming over to manage them," Paul Conroy recalls. "He'd been the promoter that we had used on the Charisma tours. He had seen them and knew that they were good, but we persuaded him and gave him every opportunity to come in. Tony took a real chance. He didn't have a lot of money to pump into them. He had quite a steady income from promoting gigs."

After consideration, Smith accepted, working on a profit share with the group. His direct, no-nonsense approach and financial savvy meant that he would leave the band to make the music, while he took care of business. Smith's management and the personal, professional relationships he built with them, would take the group to the next level. Smith had long been impressed by them. Speaking in 2000, he said he was initially drawn by "Peter's persona onstage . . . was really quite unique and lyrically they were also pretty unique, the only other band at that time I picked up on from a lyrical point of view in the same manner was the Syd Barrett days of Floyd, where the lyrics were pretty bizarre." Gail Colson said that "Tony Smith is totally different [to Stratton-Smith]. Quite reserved, solid, organised, a safe pair of hands."

A safe pair of hands was exactly what the group wanted if they were to develop further beyond the theatre circuit to which they had now graduated, especially as their foothold in America was getting stronger. After their short tour in December 1972, Genesis had returned in March 1973 before beginning a major North American tour in November of that year. Maintaining the Charisma links, Peter Hammill, now a solo artist as Van Der Graaf Generator were on hiatus, supported them there. "[It was] mainly on their Canadian tour, where they were gracious enough to ask me," he recalls. "To be frank I had quite a lot of chutzpah to go on before them in the ice stadiums with just an acoustic guitar. Peter helped me out by personally introducing me. Very decent."

Genesis was treated with bemusement by sections of the rock audience, but the press began to sense something of great note was happening before their eyes. Al Hudis in the *Chicago Sun Times* proclaimed: "They are masters of the magic that Alice Cooper and David Bowie are crudely (by comparison) grasping toward – theatre." In America they seemed to be offering a vision of exactly what British people should be; deeply eccentric, quirky. This was reinforced by Gabriel's self-deprecating persona and British wit. When being interviewed in America about the group's Charterhouse roots, he said, "We all took courses in pretentiousness." It was that sort of approach that endeared them as classic limeys abroad.

Larry Fast, then at University in Pennsylvania, could understand their appeal. He was "impressed with Peter's lyrical and performance contributions. Who wouldn't be . . . my focus as an electronic composer was with the entire sonic package presented by Genesis. I felt that Peter had found the right support and setting for the imagery he was projecting with the combination of instruments and musical approach that the rest of the band provided. What might have seemed to be disparate musical genres and elements were combined with the unconventional songwriting to create something truly unique."

From December 17, 1973, the 'truly unique' Genesis performed another landmark series of concerts, six shows across three nights at the fabled Roxy Club on Los Angeles' Sunset Boulevard. Playing the plush club, owned by industry mogul David Geffen, was, according to Gabriel, "Really amazing. We got there for the first show, thinking we were going in really cold and it was one of the best welcomes we have ever had. And they still liked us when we went away. And as I said, some stayed for all six performances – poor suckers! It was our first time on the West Coast and we found we had a sort of underground mystique."

The shows were well reviewed, with a feeling that Genesis could indeed be the last of their generation of underground bands to break through. And although it didn't translate into a significant chart breakthrough, it did mean that the records were selling well, and that they had seemed to have, like the Aylesbury crowd years before, a cult following coalescing around them.

* * *

With this recent experience under their belts, the definitive series of shows of the first era of Genesis, and indeed, for many, the end of their imperial phase, was when they played the Theatre Royal in London's Drury Lane for five nights from January 15 to 20, 1974. It was a watershed moment – the group would not play the UK again until May 1975, by which time virtually all of their material would be different. Drury Lane will always be remembered because, during the final section of 'Supper's Ready', Gabriel was hoisted by harness high above the stage like a pantomime fairy. Chris Welch, reviewing the concert for *Melody Maker*, wrote: "[It] proved that rock and theatre can mix and have a validity outside of mere exhibitionism. The band are currently playing at a peak of their ability, and while Peter Gabriel is a show in himself, the sheer musicianship of the individual players has never been more stunning."

Steve Hackett: "I think Pete had star quality, which is indefinable. He also worked at it and was always working on possible opportunities. He was a grafter." The strange aura that people spoke of when they met him, and which was seen onstage was, according to Hackett, simply "a stage persona. He was friendly, approachable and unassuming offstage."

Unlikely as it might seem, Genesis were becoming hugely influential on the next generation of musicians and sometimes surprisingly so. Saxophonist Lee Thompson from Madness was so inspired by Gabriel's flight onstage at Drury Lane that he was to emulate it six years later in the group's groundbreaking video for their 1980 UK top five single 'Baggy Trousers'. Mick Geggus from Oi! Band, The Cockney Rejects, recalls seeing Gabriel on TV and being profoundly moved; not that it showed in the respective groups' music, but his stagecraft was at once shocking, eccentric yet also profoundly moving. Writer David Buckley adds, "I know from talking to Martyn Ware and Ian Craig Marsh . . . both cite seeing Genesis in Sheffield in 1973 as a real influence on The Human League – and this is something that is not in the Jon Savage or Simon Reynolds history of popular music."

With 'I Know What I Like (In Your Wardrobe)' reaching number 21 in the UK in April 1974, the group seemed on the verge of a major breakthrough. Kris Needs was still in thrall: "I looked forward to seeing what Peter would be wearing next. The first few gigs, he was just in black, then his increasingly-sculpted hairdos crept in, along with head-gear, then costumes, which were in full swing by the time I went to see them at Oxford Apollo around 'Supper's Ready' time. That box thing on his head and the greenhouse monster outfit."

Historian Dominic Sandbrook, writing in his illuminating history of the Seventies, *State Of Emergency, The Way We Were: Britain 1970–1974* suggested that "Gabriel wore costumes so ludicrous – fluorescent bat wings, a flower-petal mask, a diamond helmet – that he would have made a first class monster on *Doctor Who*." He absolutely would, and the connection many fans made with Gabriel's performances and the realms of the popular TV fantasy show endeared them to him further. There was no-one else really doing this at quite such a level of intelligent, knowing ludicrousness. "Genesis permeated working class culture," Buckley adds, "especially in the north of England for the community of *Dr Who*-watching people who loved David Bowie, loved Genesis, and would later love the Human League for almost the same reasons."

'I Know What I Like (In Your Wardrobe)' would have gone even further had they appeared on *Top Of The Pops*; however the band were in America, which ruled out a personal appearance, so the footage of them at Shepperton was readied for use. Genesis vetoed it. After seven weeks in the charts, the single quietly slipped out. However, the single and album had made them more popular then ever before – *Selling England By The Pound* was on the UK charts for 21 weeks, 11 weeks longer than their previous best, *Genesis Live*, which had the benefit of its lower price, and amazingly, the attention they had received meant that *Nursery Cryme* finally charted in the UK. It may have just been for one week, and it may have been just at No. 39, but the appetite was clearly there. They were voted 'Top Stage Band' by readers of *NME*'s annual poll, placing them ahead of all the other bands they struggled for billing with several years previously, ahead of scene leaders such as The Who and Yes.

After a short European tour, Genesis then headed back to the US. Their legend was growing, and on certain playbills, typified by the one for their April 27 performance at the Century Theatre, Buffalo, it appeared as if audiences were actually going to see a Victorian travelling show: "A special 2½ hour concert starring Genesis – A Group That Combines Serious Theatre With Rock, Real Explosives And The Most Intricate And Complex Of Light Shows. And For A Finale – The Lead Singer Blows Himself Up!" In some respects, it was easy to understand why there was a growing unease among the serious-minded members of the band that their beloved music was being reduced to that of a mere freak show.

After returning from the US Tour in May, the band were scheduled to begin writing their sixth album. The tour had been enlivened by the news that John Lennon 'loved' *Selling England By The Pound*; Hackett recalled his singer dancing around the dressing room in response to the ex-Beatle's comments on New York radio station WNEW. That said, Gabriel was already struggling with the pace of events. The forthcoming album was to be Peter Gabriel's last with the group. He told US underground magazine, *Crawdaddy* in March 1974 that "It's good to be able to travel around and take in different places, but the pace we have to keep is frustrating. You begin to forget where you are and what day it is. I can't really see myself doing this for more than another year or two."

# 10: A Yellow Plastic Shoobedoobe – *The Lamb Lies Down On Broadway*

*"There were too many people in the group for all sorts of reasons by the time we got to* The Lamb Lies Down On Broadway. *Arguments were a bit too frequent."*
Tony Banks, 2013

*"I don't know what it's about. I'm just the drummer.* Ask Peter . . ."
Phil Collins, 1975

WHEN Steve Winwood-led rock group Traffic moved out to a cottage in Aston Tirrold in the Berkshire Downs in 1967, they set in motion the trend for bands to get out of town and live communally in order to hone their craft. For the first time since their sojourn at Christmas Cottage in 1969, Genesis revisited the idea, relocating to Headley Grange in Hampshire in 1974 to start work on their next album. But they were no longer 19-year-olds with everything to prove; they had grown older and, as men in their mid-20s, they had a variety of responsibilities and commitments that were simply not present five years previously.

As a result, the recording process for what was to become their sixth studio album, *The Lamb Lies Down On Broadway*, was difficult and convoluted. The group decided to release a double album, realising that the extra length would give them time to stretch out and join together their songs with linking pieces and that their fans would relish this abundance of material. The double album of original material had travelled a long way since Bob Dylan had released *Blonde On Blonde* in June 1966; they had become common currency in rock music for those with weighty, extended statements to make. In 1973, The Who had released their second double set of their career, *Quadrophenia*, and Yes, arguably closest rivals of Genesis in UK progressive rock, had released *Tales From Topographic Oceans*.

Genesis convened at Headley Grange to begin the writing and rehearsal process. Headley Grange had an illustrious history. Originally entitled the Headley 'House of Industry,' it was built in 1795 at an estimated cost of some £1,500 for the parishes of Headley, Bramshott and Kingsley, to shelter their infirm, aged paupers, and orphan or illegitimate children. There had been a notable 'poor house riot' there in 1830, when farm workers revolted against the clergy as a result of falling wages. Over a century later, the house was rented out as a studio, chiming in with the mantra of the times for 'getting it together in the country.' It had been owned by Aleister Crowley, which had drawn devotee Jimmy Page of Led Zeppelin to record there. By 1974, it was in a state of some dilapidation with rats scurrying from room to room. The album was to be sketched out with the band playing and delivering material to Gabriel who would write his lyrics in a separate room.

It was not a happy time for Gabriel or the band. Gabriel was swayed by two key things, which demonstrated to the others that the band, for the first time in his life, was not his key motivating force. Personally, his wife, Jill, was having severe difficulties with her pregnancy, and after the birth of their first child, Anna-Marie on July 26, 1974. "Around the time of *The Lamb Lies Down On Broadway*, Anna was born. At that point, in band decisions, which was the way they had always worked, increasingly there was 'the band' and there was 'Peter.' They were up for touring the album in America for as long as it took. Naturally, Peter wasn't, because he and Jill had Anna and it had been a difficult birth," Richard Macphail says. This conflict between Gabriel's professional and personal life wasn't a new issue but had been managed well in the past. "There had been times he was frustrated being stuck down in the cottage [in 1969] and worrying that he was losing Jill," Macphail adds. "There was always those conflicts, but Peter was right in balancing the issue of growing his relationship with Jill and the band becoming a cohesive unit." But now it seemed different; there were life-changing events happening around him.

"Jill and Peter were the first ones to have a baby," Mike Rutherford says. "When Angie and I had a baby and Tony and Margaret had theirs later, we realised it was life changing. Pete's came very early on and we were not good at change. We were very unsympathetic towards him. That was a big part of the problem really. It all came to a head with *The Lamb Lies Down On Broadway*; as you talk it through now you can see it pretty

As Harold Demure et al from crowd (and band)-splitting 'The Battle Of Epping Forest', 1973. MICK ROCK

Revelatory: Decca Records promotional picture, 1968 – Anthony Phillips, Mike Rutherford, Tony Banks, Gabriel, John Silver.

The old man from 'The Musical Box' develops – on stage, 1973.
MICHAEL PUTLAND/GETTY IMAGES

Dublin, 1972. Richard Macphail: "The place was just a riot. Fait d'accompli. That's Peter, just a fantastic visionary."
BARRIE WENTZELL

Two sides of 'Supper's Ready' – Gabriel starring in 'Willow Farm' and 'Apocalypse 9/8'. MICHAEL PUTLAND/GETTY IMAGES, MICHAEL OCHS ARCHIVES/GETTY IMAGES

Happy smiles belying the tensions underneath. Genesis during recording of *The Lamb Lies Down On Broadway*, Headley Grange, July 1974. MICHAEL OCHS ARCHIVES/GETTY IMAGES

"A subconscious desire to join the Hare Krishna movement or a nasty shaving accident." Gabriel maintaining his look, 1973.
REX/GEORGE HARRIS/ASSOCIATED NEWSPAPER

Genesis at Headley Grange at the beginning of the sessions for *The Lamb Lies Down On Broadway.* DAVID WARNER ELLIS/REDFERNS

"He was... like some eccentric but kind uncle... his flair and imagination, his bonhomie and lust for life, and willingness to take risks on music that was not necessarily in line with commercial trends." Tony Stratton-Smith in his office, Soho, with Brecht looking on, 1972. BARRIE WENTZELL

'Dancing With The Moonlit Knight' was a wistful look at Britain at sunset and offered Gabriel yet another costume opportunity. BARRIE WENTZELL

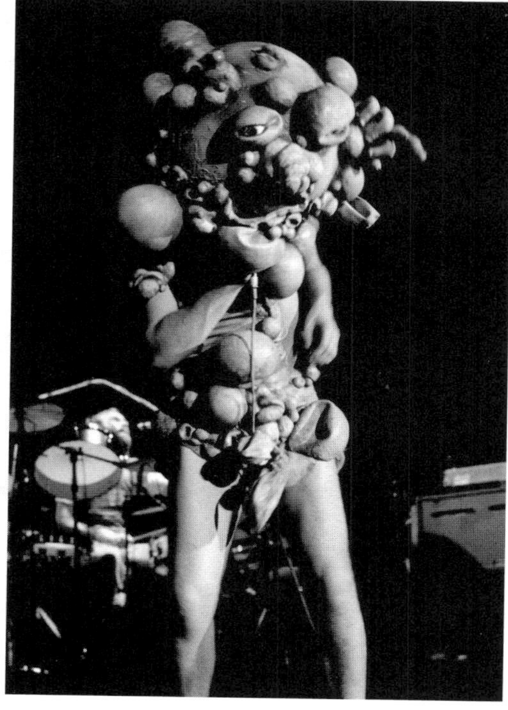

The Slipperman outfit was Gabriel's most controversial outfit of all. JORGEN ANGEL/REDFERNS

Genesis in 1974. DAVID GAHR/GETTY IMAGES

Tony Banks: "You saw the bat wings and the eye make-up. You heard the Mellotron sound, which was really early stereo. It couldn't have been any other concert in the world at that point."
BARRIE WENTZELL

One Gabriel's most unsettling performances: 'The Musical Box
LAURENS VAN HOUTEN/FRANK WHITE PHOTO AGENCY

The Egyptian Prince on his flute, 1972. MICHAEL PUTLAND/GETTY IMAGES

'I Know What I Like (In Your Wardrobe)', Shepperton Studios, October 1973. FIN COSTELLO/REDFERNS

NOT another boring old Knebworth. Gabriel takes to the stage, September 9, 1978. DENIS O REGAN/GETTY IMAGES

The Broadway Melody of 1973: Ahead of their Felt Forum concert that night, the group partake in a little Thanksgiving celebration.
WARING ABBOTT/GETTY IMAGES

clearly really. We'd done a double album that was always rated by the fans but was not much fun to make for lots of reasons. A double album is a lovely idea, but it's hard to make on a good day, without having all the problems and the worries of what all went down."

Professionally, too, there were distractions for Gabriel. He was seriously influenced by an offer from film director William Friedkin who had read Gabriel's essay on the rear sleeve of *Genesis Live* and wanted Gabriel to join him as an ideas person, and come up with different thoughts and concepts for a new film. Friedkin was then at the absolute peak of his game. One of the new wave of film directors that had attained popularity in Hollywood in the late Sixties, he had cemented his reputation with his 1971 Oscar winner, *The French Connection*. He had just delivered the world's then-most controversial film, *The Exorcist* and was white-hot. "He was trying to put together a sci-fi film and he wanted to get a writer who'd never been involved with Hollywood before," Gabriel said in 1984. "We were working at Headley Grange which I felt was partly haunted by Jimmy Page's black magic experiments, and was full of rock'n'roll legend. I would go bicycle to the phone box down the hill and dial Friedkin in California with pockets stuffed full of 10p pieces."

While these calls were taking place, two ideas had been suggested for the theme of the next Genesis album. Influenced by Alejandro Jodorowsky's 1970 Mexican cult movie, *El Topo* ("a rough, visceral, cowboy, spiritual film" – Gabriel, 2007), Gabriel came up with the character of Rael, a Puerto-Rican street punk who embarks upon a form of *Pilgrim's Progress* in New York. Alongside Gabriel's concept of Rael, there was another idea – principally supported by Mike Rutherford, to write a concept album based around *The Little Prince*, the 1943 novella by Antoine Saint-Exupéry. Gabriel was vocal in sidelining Rutherford's plan, as he sensed something was in the air: "I thought that was too twee," he told Hugh Fielder in 1984. "This was 1974; it was pre-punk but I still thought we needed to base the story around a contemporary figure rather than a fantasy creation. We were beginning to get into the era of the big, fat supergroups of the Seventies and I thought, 'I don't want to go down with this Titanic.'"

With the idea for *The Lamb Lies Down On Broadway* established, and the initial writing sessions at Headley Grange completed, the band decamped to Glaspant Farm, near Beulah, Newcastle Emlyn, Wales to work further on the music. Meanwhile Gabriel to-ed and fro-ed with both Friedkin's storyline and the weighty, portentous plot for *The Lamb*, between the hospital in London, his family and the far-flung location in which the group had chosen to record. "When they did *The Lamb Lies Down On Broadway*, the band were all out there on the farm recording the music and Peter would be separately writing the lyrics," Macphail recalls. "They had no idea what he was going to come up with. This crazy business, it was a voyage into his unconscious."

Without Gabriel's full-time presence, Banks, Rutherford, Collins and Hackett worked on a great deal of the musical ideas with John Burns who did such a great production job on *Selling England By The Pound*. Using half-finished instrumentals and jams that began to weave into the patchwork of the album, the group waited for Gabriel to arrive. Gabriel's insistence that he held onto all the lyrics and the artistic flow-through of the story created further divisions between them. "We had written a lot of stuff," Banks said. "90 per cent of the record was there, so we just carried on the idea of the album. Peter left for a day. He was getting difficult, and suddenly he had a different attitude. The group was central and suddenly it wasn't to Peter anymore, and there were all sorts of reasons for that, but nevertheless, it was very difficult to live with. And from that moment it wasn't as much fun – there were good moments obviously but it was a difficult period."

It was one thing for Gabriel to moonlight, but the band had other reasons for their disgruntlement. "Another thing that rubbed the band up the wrong way was that Tangerine Dream were going to do the film score for Friedkin," Gabriel said to Fielder. "The others thought I was using the group as a springboard to jump off for my own personal success and wasn't even bringing them along with me. But Friedkin didn't want Genesis. He only wanted me for weird ideas, not for music. I just wanted a month to do this script outline. So I walked out. There was a big eruption with Charisma and I think Strat had to come out of his watering hole to help resolve it."

With the pressure mounting, his desire to be with his wife and child and the Friedkin idea looking as if it was about to fizzle out, Gabriel asked if he could take a break from the album: the group were unforgiving and refused to let him. "Suddenly Peter came up and said, 'Do you mind if we stop for a bit'," Phil Collins told Hugh Fielder in 1984. "And we all said,

'No. Of course we don't want to stop.' It was a matter of principle more than anything else. So he said, 'OK, I want to do the film, so I'm leaving.' I remember we were sitting in the garden by the porch saying 'what are we going to do? We'll carry on. We'll have an instrumental group', which for about five seconds was a serious idea because we had a lot of music written." With both Stratton-Smith and Smith working out a middle ground for the group, Gabriel was urged to postpone writing his script and ultimately did not work on the project, which in the end became *Sorcerer*, with Tangerine Dream providing the music. It was a film that would see Friedkin's Hollywood crown slip.

Gabriel obsessed about the storyline for *The Lamb Lies Down On Broadway* and was adamant that it should be all his own work: "My argument was that there aren't many novels which are written by a committee," he said. "I said, 'I think this is something that only I'm going to be able to get into, in terms of understanding the characters and the situations'. I wrote indirectly about lots of my emotional experiences in *The Lamb* and so I didn't want other people colouring it. In fact, there are parts of it which are almost indecipherable and very difficult, which I don't think are very successful. In some ways it was quite a traditional concept album – it was a type of *Pilgrim's Progress* but with this street character in leather jacket and jeans. Rael would have been called a punk at that time without all the post-'76 connotations. The Ramones hadn't started then, although the New York Dolls had, but they were more glam-punk. *The Lamb* was looking towards *West Side Story* as a starting point."

After recording the basic tracks in Wales and Headley Grange, Gabriel's vocals and final overdubs for *The Lamb Lies Down On Broadway* were completed at Island Records' Basing Street Studios in Notting Hill, West London. The sessions have a reputation for being fraught. "Yes sometimes they were," Hackett says. "It wasn't easy for Pete. His ideas were really important to him for that project." And Gabriel's main idea was Rael.

Rael. One of Gabriel's most loved, debated and discussed characters. "Yes, of course there was a bit of me in Rael . . ." Gabriel said in 2012. "The thing is: he was freer than me to live out things that I was never going to be able to." One of the most obvious, political statements was Rael's look, an absolutely integral part of the concept. Gabriel wore an open leather jacket and white t-shirt, with his hair cut short. It was something that progressive rockers were not doing in 1974. Although his character was rooted in the supernatural and at times, the mythical, this was about as far away as he could get from the romanticised England of the previous release. It was a clear underlining that he wanted things to be different. Setting his tale in New York at once gave the music a link to the classic songwriters that had so inspired him; to Frank Sinatra, as well as the burgeoning underground and art scene. This was also the New York that incubated punk and disco that Martin Scorsese was to capture in his era defining film *Taxi Driver*; a grimy, dangerous place that was synonymous with murder, drugs, prostitution and violence.

Gabriel said in 1975: "The New York setting is a device for making the character more real, more extroverted and violent, as the kid goes through these fantastic changes. Adolescence is the time you adjust yourself to the world, you either find a slot or reject a slot; you're questioning most things around you. But this guy is slotless; his name is supposed to be raceless. He feels as if he's a waste of material, part of the machinery. He doesn't even think about his position in society. All he can do is escape or give up. He's very aggressive. The point of Rael being accessible, earthy and aggressive is that he provides an earthy response to these fantasy situations." When you look at all the information now available about his circumstances at the time, it was clearly Gabriel speaking about himself, a slotless part of the Genesis machinery.

Rael is also a fantastically unreliable narrator – books have been written about the inconsistency in the tale, but that in many respects makes it all the more memorable. *The Lamb Lies Down On Broadway*'s linear/non linear story line, introduction of spurious characters and sometimes clunking plot devices make it endearing. It must have made for interesting group meetings when Gabriel was introducing the group to the concept.

As a result, the music on the album is somewhat schizophrenic. Gabriel's contributions seem to echo what he had said earlier in 1974 after the band's experiences in America: "Spending time in America might well change our music for the better by making us seem less isolated in our opinions. Soul music excites me more than rock'n'roll. There's more emotion and I like the rhythm better. A lot of rock'n'roll seems to be working at a high speed, but not a high intensity." Hence the melody and aggression of 'Back In NYC', the title track and 'The Chamber Of 32 Doors' echo his sentiment, while music for 'In The Cage' and a variety of others bear the progressive trademark chords of Banks and Rutherford.

The album was dense, and, the title track, 'Counting Out Time' and 'Carpet Crawlers' aside, it was hard initially to find obvious tunes within the dense mass of music contained on the double album. Given its problematic inception, the first two sides of *The Lamb Lies Down On Broadway* rank among the very best music the group had ever recorded. The epic, catchy, title track was the final song that Tony Banks and Gabriel wrote together, closing an eight-year writing partnership. "I had the fast piano and introduction, and Peter had the chord sequence," Banks says. "It worked rather well using the same sort of idea. We developed it from there. It would have been nice to do a bit more, but by that time, he was drifting into other regions, and we never wrote together again." It leaps from the title track's succinct pop to the show-stopping, dark 'Fly On A Windshield', which has, in Banks' opinion, Genesis' single greatest moment where the full weight of the band slams in. 'Broadway Melody Of 1974,' a track on which all five members contributed, took its title from the old Busby Berkeley movies. It catalogues American cultural icons at a time when their magic was fading, as the old vanguard of Groucho Marx and Howard Hughes was being challenged by the thinking of the late Lenny Bruce and the intellectual assessments of Canadian media commentator Marshall McLuhan. The sensitive, bridging 'Cuckoo Cocoon' leads into the dramatic, climactic eight minutes of 'In The Cage', which demonstrates how far the group were prepared to upholster Gabriel's concept.

Gabriel's desire to move out of his past was signalled by engaging sound avatar Brian Eno to assist with *The Lamb Lies Down On Broadway*. Of late, the former Roxy Music synthesiser player had embarked on an intriguing art-rock career, with his debut album *Here Come The Warm Jets*. Eno was also working at Island Studios (on his forthcoming work, *Taking Tiger Mountain [By Strategy]*), when Genesis were recording *The Lamb Lies Down On Broadway*. Gabriel and he hit it off immediately, and he asked Eno to add some sonic effects to a couple of tracks on the album – most notably on 'The Grand Parade Of Lifeless Packaging,' the final track on the first side, on which he put Gabriel's vocals through his ARP synthesiser. It was hardly John Lennon bringing Yoko Ono into the studios, but the centre of the band felt somewhat affronted by this mercurial incomer. Gabriel credited Eno for 'Enossification' and Tony Banks felt that it was rather too much. "His contribution to the album is minimal actually," he said in 1992. "I often wonder why we even credited him, because what he did was very little."

If the first side of *The Lamb Lies Down On Broadway* was remarkable, the second side is possibly Genesis' greatest and most sustained side of music in their entire career. 'Back In NYC', aside from its ornate middle eight, is one of the hardest things the group ever recorded, and clearly pointed the way for Gabriel's later solo career. The song was a tough, violent venture that updated the 'Apocalypse in 9/8' section of 'Supper's Ready' with Gabriel performing his roughest, earthiest vocal to date, moving frequently from a scream to a whisper (as writer David Buckley notes, "like a honking horn"). 'Back In NYC' is one of the few songs that stands alone within *The Lamb Lies Down On Broadway* and has been covered by both Jeff Buckley and, in 2012 by Tin Spirit, a modern progressive rock band formed by ex-XTC guitarist Dave Gregory. "It was clearly written on 12-string, probably by Mike Rutherford," said Gregory, who would later contribute to Gabriel's third solo album, *Melt*. "The key changes fall to the fingers very easily. It's tremendously fun and challenging to play." After the tender Hackett and Banks interplay on the instrumental 'Hairless Heart,' the record takes an unabashed commercial turn with 'Counting Out Time,' one of the few songs almost entirely written by Gabriel on the project; a close relative to 'I Know What I Like (In Your Wardrobe)', it is a jolly paean to puberty and early sexual exploits, based on Gabriel's real life experience, referring to using a sex manual in his teens. The book that Rael follows, *Erogenous Zones and Difficulties in Overcoming Finding Them*, was loosely based on this.

If 'Counting Out Time' is poppy, tricksy and unusual then 'Carpet Crawlers' is arguably Gabriel's greatest, most succinct Genesis-era song. One of his best-ever melodies, 'Carpet Crawlers' is the indisputable highlight of Genesis' most impenetrable album. Unlike other material on the 90-minute-long suite, 'Carpet Crawlers' was written very quickly, developed by Banks and Rutherford.

Gabriel added the lyrics and the melody, written on an old out-of-tune piano at his wife's family home in London. The song comes at a point in his "punk *Pilgrim's Progress*" when Rael finds a red-carpeted corridor, full of people on their knees heading up to a hidden chamber. Beyond the narrative aspects of the song, it has been said that its haunting, repeated refrain, "you've got to get in to get out" represents the need for sperm to fertilise an egg in order to produce a baby, 'a carpet crawler' if you will. However, if you don't wish to interpret a blind word of what Gabriel is on about, just listen to the beauty of this song – the whole band play with passion and, importantly, restraint. Gabriel is at his most soulful and Collins' chorus vocal is memorable.

'Carpet Crawlers' is Genesis for people who despise progressive rock, weaving as it does an idiosyncratic yet inclusive soul-folk path. Although unsuccessful as a single release, 'Carpet Crawlers' serves as a five-minute distillation of Genesis' glory. It was to become one of the group's best-loved numbers and was played as the final encore on their 2007 reunion tour.

The following 'The Chamber Of 32 Doors' contains one of Gabriel's most soulful performances – lyrically, it reflects the dream that Gabriel had when he was 11, of whether he wanted to be an entertainer or a farmer. When Rael states that 'he'd rather trust a country man than a town man' and you 'don't need any shield, when you're out in the field,' it seems to hark back to Gabriel's simpler dreams but also to precipitate and indeed celebrate his move from London to Wiltshire.

The remainder of the album suffers from the strength of the opening disc. It is confused, shining, difficult and brilliant, as the tale meanders through Rael and Gabriel's psyche. Based on 1969's 'The Light', 'Lilywhite Lilith' charges in, again betraying the influence of The Who on the group, with the chorus vocals reminiscent of The Beatles on *Abbey Road* before the song reintroduces the motif from 'Broadway Melody of 1974'. Gabriel drew inspiration from the 1895 pre-JRR Tolkien fantasy *Lilith* by George MacDonald, that had been reprinted by Ballantine Books in the early Seventies.

Originally recorded in the dark with all manner of sound effects and improvisation, including Gabriel blowing into his oboe reeds, 'The Waiting Room' provided an opportunity for the band to stretch out musically, and it developed into the 'Evil Jam', which would extend for up to ten minutes onstage. 'Anyway', one of the most musical numbers in the second half of the album, reaches back to the *Genesis Plays Jackson* sessions of early 1970, with the song 'Frustration' rewritten. The playfulness of Hackett's 'Here Comes The Supernatural Anaesthetist' sets up for the major work of the third side, Banks' 'The Lamia', taking its name from Greek mythology's beautiful queen who became a child-eating demon. The closing 'Silent Sorrow In Empty Boats' is another mournful instrumental.

The complex and knotty 'The Colony of Slippermen' is split into three sections – 'The Arrival'/'A Visit To The Doktor'/'The Raven'; dealing with Rael's final steps into, as Spencer Bright noted, 'sensual gratification.' We then meet Doktor Dyper, who castrates Rael (using almost nursery rhyming, Dyper whips off Rael's 'windscreen wiper'), and with incredible portent and a rich seam of humour, the disembodied private part is stolen by the bird of ill omen. 'Mr Raven' is also a central character in MacDonald's book, *Lilith*.

'Riding The Scree' contains 14 seconds of the funkiest Genesis ever got on record. Gabriel appears two minutes in, telling of Rael trying to escape the rapids; the album again screams its modernity with references to the daredevil, audacious motorcycle stunt man Evel Knievel, who in 1974 was in his full pomp. "Evel Knievel, I think, is a great folk hero, he's the stuff that myths are made of," Gabriel told *Circus* magazine in December 1974. "I like that. There have been many plays and books theorizing on the possibilities of attracting world wide attention through suicide or possible suicide. And he really realised that, for the first time ever as far as I know. The fact that he got all the media coverage that he did is obviously because of the fact that he might die, so I find it fascinating from that point of view." 'In The Rapids' is a linking piece, which brings Rael the realisation that the body of his dead, drowned brother is actually his own, summed up by the line "That's not your face, it's mine . . ." It dawns upon Rael that it is himself, not his brother that he has been searching for.

*The Lamb Lies Down On Broadway* concludes with '*it*', captured at Island Studios in the final days of recording, with the band working in day shifts and night shifts. It is all acoustic guitars and showboating, with Gabriel's pun on the then-current Rolling Stones single and album, *It's Only Rock'n'Roll*. Gabriel's coded line that 'if you think that *it*'s pretentious, you've been taken for a ride," which at once provides the enormous wink that even he doesn't want the whole 90 minutes to be taken *too* seriously.

* * *

*The Lamb Lies Down On Broadway* was finally released on 18th November 1974, just over a year after *Selling England By The Pound*. Go-to 70s album designers, Hipgnosis, designed its arty, angular photographic sleeve, featuring male model Omar as Rael. The sleeve had a modern, futuristic feel – shot in black and white, it was a huge step away from the other-worldly paintings of Betty Swanwick or Paul Whitehead. With George Hardie's graphics – including a new, line drawn logo that the band would use on at least two further sleeves – and his graphically stunning inner bags, the sleeve, shot in Wales and in the vaults and tunnels under the Roundhouse in London's Chalk Farm (where the band had played in 1970 as part of the Atomic Sunrise Festival), offered purchasers a cornucopia of stoned interpretation.

What added further to the density of the concept was Gabriel's impenetrable, imponderable text laid out across the album's gatefold sleeve. Whereas on *Genesis Live* he had told his story in a couple of paragraphs, here were five columns of tiny, tiny words, telling the story of Rael, and his struggles in subterranean New York to locate his brother John. The reader is introduced to characters such as the Slippermen, Lillywhite Lillith, the Lamia and Doktor Dyper. "I think some of the lyrics are great," Banks says. "But I don't enjoy the story as a whole. It owes quite a bit to Kurt Vonnegut's *The Breakfast Of Champions*. It encourages the idea that the album was dark and dense, and it isn't really, it's got some quite light pieces. The whole thing is tainted in my mind." "It's like a poem everyone can read differently," Mike Rutherford adds. "It lacked cohesion. It was a wonderful journey, but I feel that a conversation should be able to be explained in one long sentence or in a paragraph and you can't really with *The Lamb Lies Down On Broadway*. It was a wonderful imagination run riot. Lyrically, it's fabulous, as is some of the music; I'm just not sure it holds together that well personally."

It was some body of work, and an album that would challenge its audience: Tony Banks said on its release, "People think we're more airy-fairy than Yes or ELP, you know, more *fey* because we don't sweat as much. I think this album will end all those comparisons entirely." Of all the things the album was, fey was not one of them; sure, there were some pretty linking passages, and the middle eight of 'Back In NYC' was delicate, but that was about it. It was not 'Visions Of Angels'. Of course, people compared it to Yes's double concept album of the recent past, *Tales From Topographic Oceans,* released in December 1973. The only things they had in common were that they were both by five-piece English bands *and* were both stretched over four sides of vinyl. John Burns had delivered a muscular, close-mic'ed production, that clearly benefited from the live sound of the studio barn the group recorded in down on the farm in Wales. If anything, with its black and white imagery and recurring musical themes, its closest relative was the Who's *Quadrophenia*, released in October 1973, which told the story of a dysfunctional central character, Jimmy the Mod. Artist Julian Woollatt says that "In the days before the punk divide, we didn't know what progressive rock was, and to us listening, we saw *The Lamb Lies Down On Broadway* as a sister album to *Quadrophenia*. It was hard, aggressive and melodic."

With its sheer wealth of material and its impenetrable plotline, *The Lamb Lies Down On Broadway* was not, however, accepted warmly at the time. *Melody Maker* journalist Chris Welch, one of the group's most ardent supporters in the UK, seemed to lead its detractors: "There is a vast amount of music to wade through, with some 24 titles and only a few themes worthy of such interminable development. The musicianship is all that one would expect from a group of such calibre, and yet it is instrumentally lacking in character, as they tend to plod through the arrangements, with little fire or purpose. I like the opening tune, while 'Broadway Melody' has affinities with John Lennon's 'Walrus', and 'Counting Out Time', has some neat, clever tricks. Genesis have given us so much, and deserve respect for their efforts. Perhaps we must be patient and wait for the *Lamb* to grow on us. But I have the feeling it is a white elephant." Patience was indeed what was required with the album.

Was it a white elephant? The concept of the album continues to vex, perplex and delight fans of Genesis and Gabriel in a manner that none of their other work does. Retrospectively, Paul Stump, writing in *The Music's All That Matters*, suggests that, by and large, "the album consisted of ramshackle and discrete songs constructed unpretentiously but originally around hastily arranged melodic fragments bound together over four sides of vinyl to tell, or (to put it more succinctly and accurately) *intimate* a story." It was one of Dave Gregory's, later of XTC, favourite albums. "When I did meet Peter . . . I had to say how I felt that *The Lamb Lies Down On Broadway* got such an unfair kicking in the press. He was very humble about it. I think even Mike Rutherford said that Hitler got a slightly better press."

Writing in 1998, British DJ and writer Mark Radcliffe wrote, "The exact intention of the piece remains unclear to this day. It revolves around some kind of journey being undertaken by the hero Rael through New

York. It may be some kind of transcendental awakening, it might be a nightmare vision of the future, it may be a foetus on a fast track to birth or it may be a load of old toss." Radcliffe was clearly taken by the album, and expanded upon the theme in *Reelin' In the Years: The Soundtrack Of A Northern Life*, his 2011 autobiography through his favourite records, one per year from his birth to the present day. In the book, he says "Even at the time of its release, certain members of the band professed to be mystified at aspects of the saga and this turns out to have been fair enough, as talking to Peter Gabriel recently, he cheerfully admitted that he wasn't entirely sure either. And it was his idea."

Scholarly tomes have been written on the subject: in 2008, Ashgate Press published a phenomenal text, *Genesis And The Lamb Lies Down On Broadway*, written by Kevin Holm-Hudson, the Associate Professor of Music Theory at the University of Kentucky. He says: "*The Lamb Lies Down On Broadway* is – along with the 26-minute epic, 'Supper's Ready' – regarded as the apex of Genesis' progressive ambitions." When interviewed by *Rolling Stone* in 1975, the band themselves remained cagey on the subject: Banks said that it was "not really a *concept* album. It's probably closer to the lyrical content of *Tommy*, rather than *Tales From Topographic Oceans*." "Well, it certainly isn't Peter Gabriel's life work," Gabriel said, "It's more a *plot* album than a *concept* album." "I don't know what it's about," Phil Collins shakes his head, "I'm just the drummer. Ask Peter . . ."

*Ask Peter.* That is what everyone was doing. Even his mother, Irene. Richard Macphail recalls being at Woolley Mill, the Gabriels' new residence outside Bath, one night just after the album's release and Gabriel receiving a phone call. "It was Irene – and it was this 45-minute conversation where he was trying to explain the lyrics to her. It's all about his sexual psyche and his unconscious, you know, 'The Lamia' and the two personalities; it was deep stuff." It made for an interesting phone discussion. Many theories have been posited, but the most likely is that Gabriel is trying to reach out to himself – there is no brother John, it's the other half of Rael's personality.

The album was conceived for live performance. Gabriel had said early in the Seventies to Tony Palmer that "Our role as musicians is somewhere between the orchestra in the pit and the old-fashioned, but out-front rock'n'roll group. Instead of the band being the focus of attention, therefore it will be the mime or dance or whatever we are orchestrating. I appreciate that this may well be providing bourgeois escapism." *The Lamb Lies Down On Broadway* was Gabriel's ultimate realisation of this but the spikiness of the music at times and the overall density of the plot made it difficult for the live show to be escapist.

The complexities and issues thrown up by the 102-date tour that supported the album are well documented. Firstly, as with Neil Young on his *Tonight's The Night* tour before them, there will always be issues, no matter how devoted your fan base, with playing a new album in its entirety with hardly any concessions toward older material. In Genesis' case, it was a double album of material that cut the cord from a lot of their earlier work. As Steve Hackett said, "we simply weren't doing the old tunes, we had become a new band." Historian Dominic Sandbrook, writing in his illuminating history of the 1970s, *Seasons In The Sun: The Battle For Britain 1974–1979* marvels that the tour required "seven slide carousels holding 1500 pictures, allowing them to project the images of, say, 'a greatly magnified and grotesque insect against a stolid Fifties Ford', or 'a snowy white feathered heart nestled in crimson satin drapery'." He adds that Gabriel wore "a string of outfits that might easily have got him locked up, including a clinging body suit designed to glow under the stage lights." But for many, Sandbrook concluded, the piece de resistance, or the step too far was Gabriel in his Slipperman costume – "a kind of lump-encrusted sub-*Doctor Who* monster suit, complete with inflatable genitals."

The live show was to prove problematic from the very start. Gabriel had devised a multi-media show for the album at least a decade before there was equipment sophisticated enough for it to be performed without a hitch. The show demanded the album be played start to finish to follow the evolution of Rael as a character. "There are people who believe that the costumes, props, and slides we use are crutches to hold up crippled music," Gabriel said in 1974. "But if the visual images are conceived at the time of writing, and you don't use those visuals, then you're not allowing the audience to listen to the song in the full strength of which it was created. And that's what we're after, to give the listener as much in a song as we get from it. Visuals are rubbish unless they are integrated with the continuity of the music." The group was to endure similar problems to The Who during their staging of *Quadrophenia* the previous year – getting all of the material to run in sync with the visuals.

The slides, which were projected on three screens across the back of the stage, were designed by Australian-born new media pioneer Jeffrey Shaw with assistance from Theo Botschuijver. Gabriel engaged Shaw and was thrilled with his work, which Shaw had to sell to the rest of the band. The slides were extremely impressive, but needed to truly run in sync. Collins was later to comment that this would happen on average once in a hundred shows. Problems enough, perhaps, but running with a simultaneous slide show and several costume changes – most notably Gabriel's notoriously cumbersome Slipperman mask – was an operational nightmare. For a band that enjoyed stretching out musically onstage, the technical constraints led to ill feeling between Gabriel and the rest of the group.

The tour programme announced: "To convey the complex story line of the new album, visual aids will be used on three backdrop screens, hinting at three dimensional illusions, slowed down slides will also add to an animated feel. As always, these new technical improvements will serve as painted landscapes adding to the fantasy and clarifying the story line. While the emphasis remains on the music and players the show will be theatrical and exciting, the music and imagery will not be separate, but whole, working together to pull the listener into the Genesis fantasy and out of everyday street realities. What Genesis are working towards is the future and their present flirtation with multi-media concepts is only the beginning of a whole new world. Welcome." It was clear that this would be a different kind of show – and its discussion of multi-media put the band many years ahead of its peers. Gabriel would appear out of a blow-up phallus as the Slipperman, and often he wouldn't be miked properly, as he crawled around the stage; and in the descending, swirling cloak that accompanied 'The Lamia', the cloak would get caught around his microphone stand.

To compound matters, when the tour started, the album hadn't even been released, and audiences, especially US ones, who had just acclimatised themselves to the group's material, were confronted with unfamiliar, complex songs. Collectively, they had heard about the man with the flower and the old man's head and the bat wings and they wanted to see some more. Instead they were confronted with a bewildering array of images, music quite unlike anything recorded by the group to date, and the lead singer, initially, looking like a short-haired street punk. "*The Lamb Lies Down On Broadway* was terribly late," Macphail recalls. "It was all a ghastly disaster – they played this huge long show and even the most dedicated fans hadn't heard the music."

*"The Lamb Lies Down On Broadway* was an extreme tour all the way round," Mike Rutherford says. "It was weird to play music just from one album; apart from everything else going on, when you did shows you did things from different albums. The trouble with that album was that there were good and bad songs. Some of the songs from *The Lamb Lies Down On Broadway* are rubbish to play live, but you are stuck with it. It wasn't much fun to play. It was a funny tour to do. We felt slightly separated; we still hung out, but there was this shadow over the tour."

"I saw them perform *The Lamb Lies Down On Broadway* in New York in December 1974," *Melody Maker* writer, then their American correspondent, Chris Charlesworth, said. "I found it rather dull and rambling. Mainly because I was unfamiliar with the music and it went on far too long. It was at the Academy of Music on 14th Street, they weren't up to stadium strength at that point." If journalists were having problems with the density of the music, fans who hadn't yet heard the music would be feeling similar.

There is no denying that when the band were on form, and the material worked, they put in some of the best performances in their career. When it didn't there was a feeling that, although playing so much music, they were somehow short-changing both themselves and their audience. Steve Hackett said in 2002, "At the beginning of the tour, we were playing two hours of music nobody knew, including me. I felt the story line was hard to swallow, it wasn't always fun to play. The slide show was a good idea, it was like a film. The rest of us were still sitting down playing, like a pit orchestra, while Pete was the focus." With Banks' view that some of the songs were never meant to be played live, and Rutherford's disgruntlement that the show left room for only one or two encores of their classic material, and certainly no room for 'Supper's Ready', you glean a picture of not the happiest group moving around on the road. To add to this, Gabriel was simmering at the band's lack of understanding of his need for time off to be with his family and how his filmic dreams had been thwarted by them.

* * *

Three dates into the eventual start of the tour, at the Swingos Hotel, on the 25th of November, 1974, Gabriel told the band of his decision to leave them. A famed rock'n'roll pit stop in Cleveland, Ohio, Swingos was the sort of hotel that was used as a pleasure den for bands such as Led Zeppelin and The Who. In an orange-walled hotel room, Gabriel announced his intention at a meeting hastily convened by Tony Smith. Gabriel said in 2007: "The hotel was part of rock'n'roll culture and I realised, 'I'm part of this machinery and I don't feel this is where I should be or who I am.' I could feel the pressure mounting and I had to punch my way through it."

Hackett recalls the meeting well: "I was very disappointed as Pete was such an integral part of the band and I tried to dissuade him." The band initially thought it would pass, and went into a form of denial, as he agreed to honour all of the touring commitments that lay in front of them into May of the following year. He also agreed to leave the band most of his equipment and also his tape archive. He was definitely out, happy to sever all ties.

"I wasn't surprised by that stage," Tony Banks says. "After the tour, I had a long conversation with him, and tried to persuade him to stay, because I thought we could get over it – if he wanted to write more lyrics, we could have accommodated that, but by then, he had psychologically moved on. He'd probably had enough of the fights and he just wanted to be on his own. He was the only person in the group at that point who could have gone and had a solo career and the question was could the group survive without him. The way it was perceived was very much 'Peter' and 'the band'. It was a strange time." Banks had lost his old friend and sparring partner. "In some ways I felt a sense of personal loss, but it was a relief as well, I can't deny that. We then had something to prove, which gave us a new goal. Fortunately the audience wanted to stay with us."

Tony Smith was sanguine about the shock news: "I always said you could virtually replace anyone in the band other than Tony," he said in *The Genesis Songbook* DVD. "Tony is the sound of Genesis – those big chord changes and sequences, there's only he that does that."

Genesis then entered a strange six-month limbo period where all parties knew that Gabriel was leaving, yet nothing was to be said to the press or public, fearful that Gabriel's impending departure could lead to a slump in ticket sales. Fortunately, the shows got better and better as fans became more aware of the material and some of the glitches were ironed out.

Of all of Genesis' work, *The Lamb Lies Down On Broadway* is the one that people keep returning to, an ultimate vindication of Gabriel's toil.

Tony Stratton-Smith, writing at the time of the 'Six Of The Best' reunion, wrote glowingly and perceptively about *The Lamb Lies Down On Broadway*. "*The Lamb* is a hymn to the integral innocence of the human spirit meeting the bacon slicer of a corruptive society; a forerunner to the 'street music' of the late Seventies and far better crafted. That's why the legend of the piece grows stronger through the years while much rival material has gone swiftly to the dumper." Someone who was impressed by what he saw was a young Jim Kerr, who caught the tour in Glasgow. "If it wasn't for Peter Gabriel I don't know if I'd be in a band," Jim Kerr told Q Magazine in 1991.

Gabriel looks back at *The Lamb* with great affection; he told *Classic Prog* Magazine in 2012: "I'm not sure if the story made much sense to most people, but it did mean something to me, in essence, it was about an awakening. He was on a journey to find himself, in a seductive, magical place. Strangely, it seems to resonate with people around their early 20s, the age we were when writing it." Mark Radcliffe said, "It's easy to laugh at the pomposity of some these records now, but *The Lamb Lies Down On Broadway* still holds thrills driven not only by nostalgia but by a genuine appreciation of the ambition and scale of the thing." The tour eventually ended in France in May 1975.

"We went too far on some of *The Lamb Lies Down On Broadway* stuff, but we were all involved in that," Tony Banks said. "The idea of doing a big show ended up coming from all of us, we all chipped in as to how we were going to show it. I didn't really like the gauze effect in 'The Lamia', that wasn't great for the song. I'd written this rather romantic song, which was already saddled with a difficult lyric, and all of this was happening onstage. The same with 'The Colony Of Slippermen', which obscured the musical content. *The Lamb Lies Down On Broadway* never really worked properly. We were doing this whole thing to an audience where half of them had never heard it. It was not the happiest year – and then suddenly in the middle, Peter said he was leaving. It was all a bit of a disaster. It was one of the least happy periods of my professional life."

Gabriel retreated to Bath, and, after a short break, the remainder of Genesis regrouped to commence work on their seventh studio album. It was time to go public about his departure.

* * *

In late July 1975, Gabriel issued a statement to the press outlining his future. It was a deeply personal, frequently amusing statement that he delivered by hand to the UK music press, entitled 'Out Angels Out', a pun on the 1970 Edgar Broughton Band single, 'Out Demons Out.' The letter was a witty exposé of a band that were just on the verge of actually achieving the success that they had craved, but in the process of doing so, to Gabriel's mind, had lost their spark. The statement opened, "I had a dream, eye's dream. Then I had another dream with the body and soul of a rock star. When it didn't feel good I packed it in. Looking back for the musical and non-musical reasons, this is what I came up with", before he got into the body of the text. He continued, "The vehicle we had built up as a co-op to serve our songwriting had become our master and cooped us up inside the success we had wanted. It affected the attitudes and spirits of the whole band. The music had not dried up and I still respect the other musicians, but our roles had set in hard." He talked about how, as an artist, he needed to "absorb a wide range of experiences."

After suggesting he had had his ego stroked enough and had attracted 'young ladies', he talked about growing cabbages and suggested he would at some point return to music and that there was absolutely no animosity between him and his old friends. The letter concluded with a characteristically amusing and theatrical finale: "The following guesswork has little in common with the truth. Gabriel left Genesis:

1. To Work in Theatre.
2. To make more money as a solo artist.
3. To do a 'Bowie'.
4. To do a 'Ferry'.
5. To do a 'furry boa around my neck and hang myself with it'.
6. To go see an institution.
7. To go senile in the sticks.

I do not express myself adequately in interviews and felt I owed the people who have put a lot of love and energy into supporting the band to give an accurate picture of my reasons. So I ask that you print all or none of this." Of course, the papers printed the witty press release in its entirety.

When the news went public, long time supporter Chris Welch translated the feelings of many into prose: "No more will that slim, strangely shy figure with the ability to rivet audiences with blazing eyes and bizarre costumes strut and posture in a variety of guises. No longer will Peter startle his fans with apparitions, kinetic structures, and theatrical trickery of every description."

In August 1975, Genesis issued a simple statement to counteract Gabriel's: "They are now looking for a new singer. They have a few ideas but nobody has been fixed. The group are all currently writing material and rehearsing for their new album, and they will go into the studios shortly to record. The album will be released at Christmas and Genesis will go on the road in the New Year." Steve Hackett realised ultimately that it was for the best: "I understand, though, in retrospect that he needed to leave the band so he could fully realise his own potential."

Original guitarist Anthony Phillips, who had started to reacquaint with Gabriel, was not surprised when he heard the news, and thought back to that dynamic that the group had had at Christmas Cottage. "The difficultly, as with a lot of these people and I don't know if one should use the word 'genius' with Peter, but not every idea is genius and that's the point; it was trying to work out which stuff was genius, and which stuff wasn't. Sometimes with the great men, it's not all brilliant stuff. We tended to be too impatient to work out which idea was genius and which one wasn't. And I think that's partly one of the reasons that Pete left. He was beginning to acquire a feeling for a modus operandi within music that there was no room for it within Genesis. His furrow was being ploughed elsewhere and he was right to leave them."

And that was it. In another of his many reinventions and departures, Gabriel had, in one long, protracted blow, cut the ties from his old group. The group he had played with in the school hall at Charterhouse; that had badgered Jonathan King to get them a recording contract; the outfit with which he had realised all of his early dreams. It was now time for him to go it alone and realise his potential, and importantly, in the short term to be with his young family. "When Anna and Mel were young he was quite pioneering taking time out with them," Richard Macphail says. And that is what he wanted to do. And he did.

PART TWO

# I Will Show Another Me: 1975–1986

# 11: Walked Right Out Of The Machinery

*"I don't particularly want a Peter Gabriel solo career as such. I'd like to develop the writing and the video thing"*

Peter Gabriel, 1975

IT was time for Peter Gabriel to go into the unknown, a five-year period when he would fully establish himself as a solo artist. Meanwhile, Genesis wasted little time in regrouping, and after working on the instrumentals for what would become their next album, *A Trick Of The Tail*, they began to audition vocalists for the position vacated by Gabriel. Numbers vary about how many vocalists tried for the role – figures have been quoted from as many as 400 to less than 10. Mick Rogers from Manfred Mann's Earth Band came close; Mick Strickland from Witches Brew auditioned; Nick Lowe, then looking for a job as his group Brinsley Schwarz had folded, sent an audition tape. Richard Macphail learned long after the event that he had seriously been considered for the role.

At his then-wife's suggestion Phil Collins, who had sung so many key backing parts during Gabriel's era, live and in the studio as well his two solo vocals, decided to have a go, singing on a new demo called 'Squonk'. When Tony Stratton-Smith heard the demo he said simply, "I realised Phil could do it – he sounded more like Peter Gabriel than Peter Gabriel did!" Collins was Genesis' new front man, and it was decided that the band augment their live work with an extra drummer, initially Bill Bruford from Yes and King Crimson, with whom Collins had been working in his offshoot project, Brand X.

Although Genesis and Gabriel had been aware of the split for nearly a year, when the news broke in the papers in the summer of 1975, it came as a huge shock to the wider world, and the remaining group had to finish recording with the media carrying all sorts of post-mortems for them. "What's a drag is people writing the band's obituary," Collins told *Sounds* in September 1975. "All that talk about they *were*, they *did*. We're not dead."

"Phil eventually becoming the singer was a bit like the goalkeeper becoming the striker," Paul Conroy says. "He always was the cheeky chappie, but to think he could suddenly don that role, was remarkable."

"Yes, it was a big surprise when Peter announced that he was leaving," Gail Colson adds. "I have to admit that it was really only Tony Stratton-Smith who believed in them 100 percent and predicted that they would be bigger without Peter. He always felt that as long as Tony Banks and his melodies were there that there would also be a Genesis."

In February 1976, eight months after the announcement of Gabriel's departure, Genesis released *A Trick Of The Tail*, a clean, airy, fairly straightforward album, which had more in keeping with *Selling England By The Pound* than *The Lamb Lies Down On Broadway*. Using songs that they had stored from as far back as 1972, it established their credentials as a sort of credible, commercial pop Mahavishnu Orchestra-lite. It also became their biggest seller to date, and their concerts, which began in Canada in March 1976, saw Collins stamp his everyman authority on the proceedings so successfully that all calls of 'where's Pete?' from the audience quickly stopped. For a band that just over a year ago were being billed in America as "*Genesis – Featuring The Total Theatrical Flair of Peter Gabriel*" much to the chagrin of Banks and Collins, they could now concentrate on the music.

Gone were the costumes, and in came the light show. And, aside from the material from *A Trick Of The Tail*, the group did not shy away from tackling the songs Gabriel held most dear; material from *The Lamb Lies Down On Broadway* and, nestling towards the end of the set as it had done from 1972 to 1974, the song that will forever be most closely associated with Gabriel, 'Supper's Ready'. "I had more confidence in Genesis continuing than they did themselves," Gabriel said in 2007. "And the reason was because we were a group of songwriters, and the songs would continue coming out. It's a funny thing, but when I was the singer, everybody thought I created everything and wrote all of it. Of course, when I left the band, they were way more successful without me. Everybody then assumed, ah, okay, he did nothing."

Eventually, Gabriel saw Genesis on tour at London's Hammersmith Odeon, and was impressed by what he saw. The group's success without

Gabriel assuaged any guilt he had at leaving the band. Although Collins may have missed Gabriel's subtleties when delivering some of his, at times, intensely personal lyrics, Collins' stage school training and overall demeanour offered a connection with the audience that hadn't necessarily been as obvious during Gabriel's era. "I think my reference points were more out of film and more noir and Phil's were from comedy, theatre and music hall," Gabriel mused in 2007.

"For a short while after leaving Genesis I was still attached to some things I had written," Gabriel said. "A real test for me was watching Phil singing 'Supper's Ready.' I had reminded myself that I had chosen to leave the band rather than the other way round and that if I cared about the number in the first place it was better that he did it his way with his convictions." Collins said in 1983, "When Peter saw us just after I started singing, he said, 'You sing 'Supper's Ready' and 'Carpet Crawlers' better than I do, but you'll never sing them like I do.'" Although Peter Gabriel and Genesis would only ever unite twice officially again over the following three decades, the two would be forever linked. As the reissue business took hold in the late Nineties, the group would be in each other's company on an intermittent basis.

* * *

Gabriel returned to Bath at the end of the *The Lamb Lies Down On Broadway* tour on May 22, 1975, and somehow dissolved into the community. As he was to say as late as 2012, he took "two years off growing cabbages and children". The impact of this disappearance was remarked on in the weekly UK rock press who as ever needed to fill column inches. It was hardly Brian Wilson's retreat into his sandbox, but for some reason, it absolutely fascinated the papers that a star, suddenly about to achieve what he had ostensibly craved for, would turn his back on it at the age of 25 to pursue family life.

It wasn't that Gabriel was a recluse: he would materialise sporadically. On June 7, 1975, he returned to his roots and appeared at a Stackridge concert at Friars Aylesbury where he leapt out of a birthday cake. There were no costumes, slide shows or synchronization to worry about, just a bit of old-fashioned spectacle. "We made a big cardboard cake and he jumped out," David Stopps laughs. "Peter knew Stackridge from the circuit; they were quirky in the way that Genesis had been quirky, there was clearly some resonance between the bands. He wished everybody a happy birthday and that was it. It was a great evening!"

By the end of the year, Jill was pregnant again, and Anna-Marie was now a healthy 18-month-old. Life was good, and the pressure of the music business seemed a long way away. Chris Welch interviewed Gabriel at the end of 1975 for *Melody Maker*, and found a deeply reflective man, getting away from the pressures of being in the spotlight. Gabriel had been exploring possibilities of alternative lifestyles. "I've also been trolling around seeing different people in various communities," he said. "It's very ironic but I was doing an audition for a group of people the other day, called 'Genesis'. One of the possibilities I've got on ice at the moment is joining a commune. It's not your drug-ridden sex orgies, but a group of people working together in a lot of areas, and one of the communes is called, by complete coincidence, Genesis . . . I can't get away from them. Let me out! There's another place in France I'm going to have a look at. I'm thinking of joining with my family." Although this wasn't to be, Gabriel was fully in tune with alternative lifestyles and finally took the opportunity during his sojourn to experiment with drugs. It was to prove a short-lived experience. "There had been no excess," Richard Macphail says. "Peter has never been a druggie at all. He once ate some hash cake at Ashcombe and typically, he got out a tape recorder and taped himself. He wanted to get back to Woolley Mill and he didn't want to walk down the road because he didn't want to meet anyone he knew because he didn't think he could string two words together. So he got down to the stream, walking over fences, through fields crashing into stuff, recording himself all the way. I have that tape – it's very funny – he could have written a load of lyrics from it." In a 1981 interview with Mick Gold, when the subject of drugs arises, Gabriel is candid, and through a joke, says a great deal. "I've had minimal drug experiences because of fear. I would be afraid of losing control. I can trust machines, yet I can't trust pills . . . a machine you can always switch off, or get out of . . . whereas when a pill gets hold of your metabolism, you have to ride through." A loss of control would simply never do.

* * *

Gabriel's first forays back to music came with thoughts of a collaboration with lyricist Martin Hall. Hall was a poet of renown; he and Gabriel had become friends back in the early Seventies, when they were introduced through producer John Anthony. Tony Stratton-Smith had published his book of poetry, *The Stan Cullis Blues* on the Charisma Books imprint in November 1974. Gabriel had actually first talked of getting together with Hall as far back as the 1973 tour to support *Selling England By The Pound*: "I do have things I'm interested in outside of the band. There is a song-writer called Martin Hall and there is a possibility of my doing an LP with him. As it is – the band comes first." In a break from *The Lamb Lies Down On Broadway* in 1974, Gabriel had sketched out some demos with Hall at Anthony Phillips' parents' house, Send Barns in Woking, with Hall on guitar, Phillips on piano and Phil Collins on drums: 'You Get What You Want (When You Rip It Off)', 'Firebirds' and 'You Never Know', a whimsical, comedic piece pondering the mysteries of life.

"I got to know Martin quite well," Phillips recalls. "Martin was not from our social scene – he was a big Wolves fan, and a good lyricist. Looking back you have to question why Peter was working with someone who was essentially a duplication, because Martin's strength was as a lyricist and Pete was already a brilliant lyricist; I think ultimately that combination was doomed. He probably made Peter look at lyrics in a slightly different way. A lot of these combinations in life are about foils; you need somebody – and sometimes people cancel each other out."

One of the more unusual things that Gabriel did do in 1975 was bring this new co-write with Hall to vinyl. But 'You Never Know' was not *his* first solo statement, or a release by one of his music industry associates, but a single by . . . Charlie Drake. A diminutive comedy star who had been popular in Britain for the best part of two decades, Drake relied on an everyman demeanour he had built in the Fifties and on the TV show *The Worker* between 1965 and 1970, and like other comedians of the day he'd enjoyed several hit singles. Produced by Beatles production maestro George Martin, 'Splish Splash' and 'My Boomerang Won't Come Back' had both been UK Top 20 hits and were the sort of novelty songs destined to be on compilations of children's music for years to come. Gabriel and Hall had toyed with the idea of making an animated TV series around Drake and this new track could have been its theme song.

How Drake found himself in a room at AIR Studios in Oxford Circus with Gabriel, ex-King Crimson guitarist Robert Fripp, jazz pianist Keith Tippett, Phil Collins, Collins' Brand X bandmate Percy Jones and supreme folk vocalist Sandy Denny is far more prosaic than the wonderful mêlée of talent in one place may suggest. Charisma was based in the heart of Old Compton Street and that is where Drake, who lived in nearby Leicester Square, came to record. All the musicians were nearby and easy to call on. Phil Collins seemed as puzzled as the wider world about it. He wrote on his website after Drake's death in 2006: "How he ended up with this line up I have no idea. It seems the most obscure set of people to make a comedy record. On the day Charlie, who was quite small, turned up with a brand new denim outfit for his rock debut . . . it was quite touching to see him at it." Fripp was later to comment, "This was arguably the strangest session of the entire era."

The tune picked up from where 'Willow Farm' left off, and was an easy and amusing record to make. To hear Sandy Denny playing the role of a groupie and Fripp, who was by then in the first phase of his self-imposed exile from the music business, playing simple chords, make this a charming footnote. It is ironic, and somewhat telling that when David Bowie got his first flush of success and was able to produce artists, he chose Lou Reed and Iggy Pop; Gabriel chose Charlie Drake. Gabriel was nothing if resolutely his own man, and in this instance, every inch the English eccentric. The single, credited to the production team of 'Gabriel Ear Wax' was backed with 'I'm Big Enough For Me', the theme to Drake's recent children's TV series *Professor Popper's Problems*, was released on November 21, 1975 and promptly did nothing.

And nothing came of the partnership with Hall either, aside from 'Excuse Me', another collaboration they were demoing at this time. It was finally used when Gabriel came to record his first album proper. "I collaborated with Martin . . . with the intention of composing songs for other people," Gabriel told Armando Gallo. "But this . . . proved frustrating as we had difficulty in getting the right people interested and I was unhappy not to be in control of the arrangements." If 'You Never Know' *had* struck a chord, and the partnership with Hall had been more successful, Gabriel may have delayed returning to his serious music.

As he toyed with returning to the business, Gabriel considered the idea of a multi-media rock opera: *Mozo*, a 'mercurial stranger', based obliquely on the character of Moses. Inspired by the *Aurora Consurgens*, a mediaeval work that Carl Jung, with whom Gabriel had recently become infatuated, had attributed to St Thomas Acquinas, Mozo was to be a fictional character that came from nowhere, made changes to people's lives and then abruptly disappeared. Gabriel would grapple with this over-arching idea right through into the *So* album in 1986. The character of Mozo is introduced in the opening track of his second album, 'On The Air', by name, yet there is evidence that 'Down The Dolce Vita' and 'Here Comes The Flood' from the first album were also at one point intended for use in this concept. But concepts were not where it was at as 1975 turned into 1976 – there was a change in the air for music, and before punk rock was to rip up the rulebook, the arrival on British shores of Bruce Springsteen would have a profound effect on Gabriel.

On November 18, 1975, Gabriel went to see Springsteen and his E-Street Band perform their UK debut concert in London's Hammersmith Odeon. "I remember Peter phoning me and saying he'd gone to see Springsteen and that he was very impressed with him," David Stopps recalls. "He was overwhelmed with how good he was live; it had a major effect on him. I later saw Peter at Hammersmith Odeon on his first tour and you could see the influence of Springsteen on his show." Gabriel's writing could now absorb all his influences, away from the constraints of his band and the demands placed upon him.

Additionally, his home in Bath was conducive to his work, and the town became something of a magnet for like-minded arts and crafts bohemians. "I think Peter moving here was a huge catalyst," local resident and studio owner David Lord, who would later produce him, said. "And then a lot of people he worked with followed in his wake either to work with him or use our studios. Bristol was always very jealous because although it was a much bigger city, it was always overshadowed by the Bath scene." Gabriel had a restful, peaceful arty place in which to spin his ideas.

"I began to contemplate returning to the hurly burly of the music business," Gabriel reflected in 1986, a full decade on from his sabbatical. Charisma, of course, wanted a solo album from one of their most mercurial stars, and Gail Colson and others from the label had kept in relatively close touch with him during his break. In the meantime, he had contributed a heartfelt version of 'Strawberry Fields Forever' to the soundtrack of the ill-fated film, *All This And World War II*, which married stock footage of the Second World War and old MGM film clips with a soundtrack of cover versions of Beatles songs. It was originally intended for The

Beatles themselves to supply their catalogue as a soundtrack, but Lou Reizner decided it would prove more lucrative to have well-known artists provide cover versions. It underlined Gabriel's significance when you look at the company he was in: Elton John, Rod Stewart, The Bee Gees, Bryan Ferry, Frankie Valli and Tina Turner were just some of the stellar names involved. Although the film was withdrawn from cinemas after just two weeks and it has never had an official DVD release, the soundtrack album was a modest success, reaching number 23 on the UK albums chart in November 1976. It thus became the first official Peter Gabriel solo release.

# 12: The Expected Unexpected

*"The rock business is a strange hybrid of hypocrisy. You get to the point where you're not really being yourself. You're selling something. You get the feeling that the rock star is some sort of teenage creation realised by people who are no longer teenagers."*

Peter Gabriel, February 1977

TWO events would shape Peter Gabriel's 1976; one was the arrival of his and Jill's second daughter, Melanie, on August 23; and the second was his serious return to recording, marking the formal commencement of his solo career. When Gabriel began writing in earnest, he strove to arrive at material that was as different from Genesis as possible. However for his first foray into the studio, he assembled a surprising line-up of players for his experiments – his closest friends in Genesis: Ant Phillips was on piano, Mike Rutherford on bass and Phil Collins on drums. It was interesting that he didn't choose Tony Banks, who was his oldest friend but most fractious (yet genteel) sparring partner and Steve Hackett, who was also busy with a solo career.

"I used to go and watch Genesis gigs, but contact with Peter had drifted off a little," says Anthony Phillips, who had subsequently studied music since leaving Genesis in 1970. "I was closest to Mike and I used to see Peter occasionally. Once he left the group, we got closer. We got together again in late '75. He knew that I had studied piano. In the days of the group, I was a three-finger merchant, but didn't have a great amount of technique. Pete saw me as somebody that (a) understood his music and (b) was a safe pair of hands and (c) wouldn't argue. And that was really what he wanted." They had worked well together on the demos at Phillips' parents' home the previous year, and the first meetings for the new demos took them even further back: to David Thomas' flat in Earls Court. "I was staying at a flat in London that didn't have a piano at that stage," Phillips continues. "So, we used to rehearse things like 'Here

Comes The Flood' there. It was great fun working with him, and then we worked with Mike and Phil as a rhythm unit. It was so good. John Goodsall, nice chap, slightly eccentric, was on guitar."

In the long, parched summer of 1976, Gabriel took some ideas into Trident Studios in London's St Anne's Court, a familiar and warm stamping ground. The piano demos he had recorded at home were interesting and diverse. 'Howling At The Moon', 'Funny Man', 'No More Mickey' and 'God Knows', all recorded at this time, have never turned up on any subsequent Gabriel recording.

"I remember doing 'Here Comes The Flood', Phillips continues. "We were back in Trident where we had done *Trespass*, playing at the piano that The Beatles had recorded 'Hey Jude' on. It went very well. I always got on well with Peter. He was full of talk about the future and what we were currently listening to. Although he used Mike and Phil, essentially it was a new broom for Peter. He was finding his feet. We didn't meet and socialise – the group was never a clubbable, pubbable sort of band where we'd go and have long chinwags – it might have been a lot more relaxed if it had been ironically."

"There was a natural musical admiration between everyone in the band," Mike Rutherford recalls. "John Goodsall was lovely. By the time 'Here Comes The Flood' came out, it had changed so much I could barely recognise it. He got us for free; we were unpaid."

It did seem strange that Gabriel would rush headlong back to his old Genesis compadres. "I thought it was pretty ironic, but then I was nervous enough about my piano playing to not dwell too much on it." Phillips says. "It did seem like the obvious choice, as he really hadn't come across a lot of other musicians at that point. He'd worked with Martin and done those songs, but outside that, Genesis had been a very closed shop, apart, of course from Phil playing with a lot of people; Pete simply wouldn't have had a milieu of people to choose from. As he was leaping into the unknown, he wouldn't have had the contacts to plough a new furrow. If I was a safe pair of hands, they were a mighty safe rhythm section." The ideas were fleshed out, but it was clear that what he was recording sounded, unsurprisingly, just like Genesis.

'Get The Guns', Gabriel's second Martin Hall collaboration, was covered by Alan Ross for a super obscure RCA single produced by Tony Visconti in 1977. Gabriel later took some of the melody of it for another new song he was working on, 'Down the Dolce Vita'. The other material, 'Here Comes The Flood' and 'Excuse Me' would form a key part of his forthcoming album. 'No More Mickey', a light and fairly commercial tune allegedly about his dear friend, Richard Macphail, had been offered to Charisma as a single in 1975, and was rejected. 'Funny Man' was an interesting take on a fading entertainer, made to perform his act repeatedly, with its refrain – "Funny Man, be the death of me, give that performance that we're all dying to see" – parallels could easily be made between Gabriel's former persona, as he was there trapped in his flower head, the element of surprise removed.

While demoing this new material, Gabriel went to see the band Strange Days at the 100 Club on London's Oxford Street, round the corner from Trident Studios. A now long-forgotten progressive rock outfit featuring Eddy Spence, Phil Walman and Graham Ward, they were supporting a group that had begun to make waves in the UK music press. Gabriel was enthralled by the pre-EMI Sex Pistols. With the band wearing the Vivienne Westwood-designed Cambridge Rapist T-shirts, Gabriel, already enamoured with the stripped-down bombast of Springsteen, saw that this was another part of the jigsaw of change. Something new, that he could identify with, was in the air. Although hardly ready to go to Pistols-like extremes, it was time for Gabriel to attempt something different.

Gabriel began casting his net for a producer for his new work. He liked the idea of someone outside the UK production system, with different ideas and a wider vision. His first choice was the mercurial Todd Rundgren: "Peter came up to Bearsville Studios," Rundgren told Paul Myers in his book, *A Wizard, A True Star: Todd Rundgren In the Studio.* "And we discussed me doing the record . . . He was a very quiet, shy guy, and it seemed like he was in this transitional space and not super confident about where he was going with everything. I think he was looking for me to give him something 'certain' to hang on to, but I didn't know exactly what it was he should do at that point." Gabriel and Rundgren would bump into each other at intermittent intervals for the next 30 years, with continued talk of collaboration.

On the other side of the Atlantic was producer Bob Ezrin, who had seen Gabriel at Massey Hall in 1973 supporting Lou Reed. "When Tony called and asked if I would be interested in working with Peter as a solo artist, I didn't hesitate for one second," Ezrin says. "I told Tony I thought Peter was a brilliant man and that I would love to work with him."

Gabriel's hook up with Ezrin as producer for his first solo outing was, and still is, a curious choice, but one that was to prove ultimately successful. Ezrin was an outgoing Canadian who had been in production since he was 19 working with his friend, Alice Cooper. More recently he'd been assisting cartoon-rockers Kiss in their world-conquering path, fashioning the shiny rock veneer of their keynote album, *Destroyer*. Ezrin had also worked with Reed on *Berlin*, his critically lauded, black-as-pitch 1973 masterpiece, a record that acted as a pointer to some of Gabriel's work.

It was imperative that they work fast and that Ezrin had a hand in selecting Gabriel's team. To that end, Ezrin chose virtually *all* of the album's players, trusted session hands used to working at speed with demanding artists. "I had developed this crew of regulars that I would work with," Ezrin says. "I put them together for when I worked with solo artists who didn't come with their own band. They were very versatile – some of them were New York session players I had encountered in different situations, but in whom I'd seen a spark. These were the outlaws of the studio musician set, the guys who often felt constrained by what they were trying to do, and liked to stretch out."

Drummer Allan Schwartzberg, for one, had a fine pedigree – a one-time member of fabled Mountain, he was a much in-demand session player. He had added the remarkable shuffle behind Gloria Gaynor's disco hit 'Never Can Say Goodbye' in 1974 and was one of the players credited with arriving at the distinctive disco drumbeat. Percussionist Jimmy Maelen was a true character. "As most percussionists are, he was a lunatic of the best sort," Ezrin says. "He was a creative genius, very highly strung and focused – many of the percussionists I've worked with are also martial artists, and Jimmy was one of those guys – he had the focus of a zen martial artist, but also the unfettered imagination of an *avant garde* painter. That was his thing, he like to paint aural pictures – he added a tremendous amount to Peter's record, almost more to the spirit in the room than even the things that he played."

It was through Ezrin that Gabriel met one of his longest serving and most trusted players, bassist Tony Levin. With his shaven head and seal-like moustache, Levin was already a player of some renown, and embarked on a career that would find him playing with King Crimson, David Bowie and John Lennon, as well as going on to play on almost all of Gabriel's albums.

Gabriel chose two other players on the album: one was Larry Fast, who Gabriel had first met when Fast interviewed him at the College Radio station at Lafeyette College in Pennsylvania in 1973. A talented keyboard and synthesiser player, Fast also met Rick Wakeman from Yes and as a result was invited to assist with programming on their *Tales From Topographic Oceans* album, which led to a recording contract with Passport Records. Playing in the band, Nektar, he had released his ambitious solo album, *Electronic Realisation For Rock Orchestra*, in 1975 under what was to become his brand name, Synergy.

Gabriel was impressed with Fast's innovation and asked him to contribute to the album. Fast was ready to go with Peter's experiments. He had followed Genesis, and reckoned that "the acoustic folk sounds combined with the massive Mellotron and pedal bass sounds were so creative. The guitar and synth soloing were drawn from other traditions in rock music, so the combination didn't sound like any other band out there. The wide dynamic changes in sonic structure supported Peter's contributions well. However by the time Peter left the band, I believe that his interest in exploring that particular route had been satisfied and he wanted to take the learning experience of his Genesis years and apply it to covering new territory."

Freed from his old group – or as Fast says, "the self-imposed restrictions of the Genesis 'style'" – it allowed for some more conventional high-energy rock, world music, minimalist experiments and so on. It wasn't that Gabriel had left everything behind, as Fast suggests, "Many of those lessons in evolving a musical style found a way into Peter's solo career, but often in much more subtle ways. Unusual time signatures didn't call attention to themselves. The dynamic changes in musical intensity were used less frequently for shock value and more for guiding the musical journey."

Gabriel's cultural radar was in tune with the time, as Fast recalls: "Peter and I went to see the Ramones playing in Toronto during the recording of his first album, as they were part of the same label group that I was signed to. I had been to CBGBs with Seymour Stein to see Talking Heads when they were still a three-piece band. Seymour later signed many of the important acts coming out of that New York scene and named it new wave. I connected with the art-rockers like the Heads and Blondie who would become more new wave than punk. The Ramones were a little more hardcore and raw than anything I wanted to do, but it was good to be exposed to all of it."

Gabriel relocated to Canada to Nimbus Studios in Toronto to start work on the album. With the new producer in place, and in a strange country with a new band, Gabriel looked to someone with whom he felt comfortable, specifically his old friend, Robert Fripp. Like Gabriel, Fripp had been laying low since leaving the outfit that had made his name. Fripp, a natural practical intellect, liked to, in his own words, 'travel light'. Like Gabriel too, Fripp's new ideas were coming from outside the standard rock and pop straightjacket.

"He thrived on the characters," Ezrin said. "He negotiated with me, asking if he could have one Brit: I felt we were doing a sports deal, like a football club, needing a striker. I agreed. He said 'Can it be Robert Fripp?' It was an exciting thing that he brought Robert into the fold, and Robert perfectly rounded out this group of misfits and musical outlaws. He was the proper Brit, in total contrast to the improper Americans that we had on the date – and we had Canadians too, it was a very ecumenical date."

Fripp was to say: "I actually said to Peter when he asked me to play on the album, 'I'll come along and make the record on the sole proviso that if it's not appropriate for me to do it I can leave after three days.' Peter agreed. But after three days, having discovered it wasn't appropriate, I didn't want to leave. I didn't want to leave my friends to be ravaged."

★ ★ ★

The sessions were conducted in a brisk, business-like fashion: "It was much more of a studio 'factory' operation than I had expected," Fast recalls. "I had done many of these kinds of sessions with formal structures, union players, and so on in New York. Very professional and hours of intense work often followed by good meals at fine restaurants. It was closer in nature to some of the dates I had done for big pop and R&B singers. So it wasn't an unfamiliar scenario to me, but compared to my work with Nektar in France and England, and being at the studio during some Yes sessions it was a bit of a surprise to find it so 'old school'. The other bands, and my own Synergy recordings used the studio process as an experimentation zone looking for new sonic avenues and perhaps a bit of rambling in structure. *PG1* was closer to the fine craft of making pop records."

Fast was given a great deal of latitude "to add what I came up with during the recording of basic tracks, and that was a departure from the real old school sessions. And after hours, when the rest of the session players were off the clock, I had the opportunity to do overdubs to add electronic parts. The signature horn line of 'Solsbury Hill' was done that way as was the electronic orchestration at the end of 'Humdrum' and several others."

The album is a peculiar and not at all unpleasant addition to Gabriel's catalogue and was enough of a statement to distance himself from his old band and commence the next chapter. It's the closest Gabriel ever came to becoming a straight down-the-line stadium rocker, full of interesting quirks smoothed out to create a holistic, upbeat rock sound.

'Moribund, The Burgermeister' guides the listener into Gabriel's world. It is the most Genesis-esque number on the album, and placed at the start of the record, it made it clear to the listener how much a part of the group he had been; in some ways it sounded more like his old group than their two albums since his departure. Initially similar in sound to 'The Grand Parade Of Lifeless Packaging', it explodes into a wall of majestic guitars and synthesised starkness.

'Solsbury Hill' was quickly lifted from the album as its debut single. With it, Gabriel wrote his first solo classic, a record that proved he had more than enough commercial *nous* to go it alone. As Gabriel said at the time, "It's about being prepared to lose what you have for what you might get, or what you are for what you might be. It's about letting go." A thinly veiled reference to his departure from Genesis, it was set over an infectious, acoustic guitar-driven folk groove. Its optimism is heart-warming, and its manifesto is clear. To succeed, you have to take risks. Fortune favours the brave. His choice of the line 'walked right out of the machinery' echoes his 1975 interview where he says that Rael "feels as if he's a waste of material, part of the machinery".

Ezrin used a little of his studio magic to make the single happen. "It became the hit once we got it to the floor," he recalls. "Steve Hunter came up with that guitar part, which in my mind is as important as the melody. We took away Steve's electric guitar and gave him a 12-string that he hadn't played in a long time. This is another situation where I wanted to change the environment because I felt that the song required a different approach than a conventional band approach. I took

Schwartzberg's cymbals away and I covered up his drums, gave him a shaker and a telephone book and one drumstick; Larry made this fake drum kit on his keyboard that we called a 'synthibam' and so we came up with this part that held the seventh; to make it feel natural not awkward. The minute that Peter started singing, it all started to fall into place; you knew that this was an important song."

But for Ezrin, it had one notable problem – the hook line that Gabriel had originally written for the chorus didn't work for him. "It went 'Son, make your life a taxi not a tomb'. At which point I said, 'STOP'. I loved the sentiment of it, but I thought the language was ugly. Symbolically, we could have done something a little more poetic – we almost have a hit song here but we don't have a hit chorus; and we're not going to put it out until we have a better chorus, but we cut it anyway." It was only during the final mixing that the vexed question of the lyrics of 'Solsbury Hill' were finally mastered: 'Son, make your life a taxi not a tomb' became 'Grab your things, I've come to take you home.'

'Solsbury Hill' was released as a single, ahead of the album in February 1977 and soon was sitting in the UK Top 40. It became the first release associated with Genesis to reach the Top 10 singles chart. With it, Gabriel gained his first solo anthem.

With its crashing guitar and rather flashy, splashy, synthesisers, 'Modern Love' was arguably the most conventional foray into rock that Gabriel has made in his career to date. It is hard to deny the influence that Bruce Springsteen's work had on Gabriel. In fact, he had tried to secure the services of the E-Street Band's keyboard player, 'Prof' Roy Bittan, but to no avail as Bittan was prevented by Springsteen's management from playing on the album. Josef Chirowski, from Toronto based band, Mandala, who had worked previously with Ezrin, stepped in instead. The track, which was understandably selected, as the follow-up single to 'Solsbury Hill' was superb, noisy rock – having most in common with the upbeat and jagged moments of *The Lamb Lies Down On Broadway*. Concerned that Gabriel could not nail the appropriate emotion for the vocal line, Ezrin resorted to novel and dramatic measures to tease the best out of Gabriel.

"We had discovered gaffer tape," he laughs. "Which was amazing for a number of things. We always were practical jokers and doing pranks on each other; and Peter was an easy mark, as he was this gentle, innocent, polite English person who would never think somebody would do such a thing to him. We were doing 'Modern Love' and Peter was just not nailing the chorus. He was being too polite for my taste and he wasn't getting the energy that I was looking for. I half jokingly said, you get three more tries and if we don't get it, you're going up the pillar." 'The pillar' was one of the concrete supports holding up the Nimbus studio roof.

"I'm sure Peter didn't believe it. After his three tries, I said, 'That's it boys, he's going up'! Brian Christian, my engineer, 220 pounds of solid Southside Chicago muscle, who looked more like a bodyguard than an engineer went out along with Jimmy Frank, the assistant engineer, took Peter up a ladder and we gaffer taped him under his armpits to the pillar. We took the ladder away and left him dangling. We miked him up, and that's the performance on the record. I was used to creating environments for Alice Cooper that were a little bit wacky and shook him out of studio brainlock, I'd just change the environment and get a really good performance. Sometimes it would backfire of course, but that time it didn't."

After his sojourn up the wall, Gabriel later shot a video for the song with director Peter Medak, whose 1972 film, *The Ruling Class*, he had greatly admired. The video was shot in the West 12 Shopping Centre in Shepherd's Bush, West London, where they had just installed new escalators. This allowed Gabriel's futuristic ninja-warrior/American footballer-style character to rampage on the moving walkway. Surprisingly perhaps for such an upbeat, shiny single that sounded at once contemporary, it failed to make the UK Top 50.

Aside from the Charlie Drake 45, the only other significant recorded evidence of Gabriel's work with Martin Hall was the witty, barbershop based, 'Excuse Me'. With Tony Levin on tuba, it could indeed have been sung by any British music hall vaudevillian. In the tradition of the UK novelty song, it is the album's 'When I'm Sixty-Four' or 'Honey Pie'. It could be seen as another veiled reference to his departure from Genesis, as Gabriel sings "I'm not the man I used to be, someone else crept in." It certainly provides a moment of levity after the intense rush of the album's opening trio of songs.

*Rolling Stone* said that the album's next song, 'Humdrum', opened "as a hypnotic ballad as hushed as a falling raindrop" before "then snapping into a Caribbean tempo". Fella's deft with the lyrics, too: "Out of woman comes a man/Spends the rest of his life getting back in again". It showed the pull of ideas with the tempo changes, the traditional Gabriel ballad being treated and arranged in manners that would hitherto not be considered, a departure from the big block chords of Genesis that Anthony Phillips had previously talked about. The magazine added that the following track, 'Slowburn', was "a heavy orchestral pastiche that shifts so fast and furiously it leaves me with heartburn". The Springsteen influence again lies heavy; his opening line suggesting that he is a 'character actor' from the 'Tower Of Babel' was a sly reference to one of the more well-remembered tales from the book of Genesis.

It did not all necessarily work: 'Waiting For The Big One' is a strange singular entry in Gabriel's solo canon. With its lazy bar-room piano, and aggressive rock guitar riffs, it is a big, daft bluesy number, which owed a debt to Randy Newman. Gabriel had been introduced to Newman's music by Ezrin during the recording in Toronto and had fallen in love with it. Recording 'Waiting For The Big One', they got Fripp, pop's arch theorist, to play against type. "You should have seen him the other night," Gabriel laughed to Barbara Charone in *Sounds* in 1977. "We got him drunk and he was playin' *blues* guitar! 'Fuckin' good' he kept saying!" But with all its false starts, ends and breakdowns, the cumulative effect is somewhat pointless. It is a triumph of form over content, and for once, the 'more is more' approach seems unnecessary.

However, it is only a minor detour. With its huge portentous London Symphony Orchestra orchestral overture, the slamming rock of 'Down the Dolce Vita', one of the *Mozo* songs, predicts the funky progressiveness of Jeff Wayne's *War Of The Worlds*, and it is a rather splendid, daft addition to Gabriel's canon. It was on this track that Ezrin brought all of his power to bear, constructing a marvellous soundbed for Gabriel's slight song.

'Solsbury Hill' aside, 'Here Comes The Flood' was the album's showpiece. "All I know is that Peter played me 'Here Comes The Flood' in the middle of my living room on our first meeting," said Bob Ezrin. "I was in the middle of producing albums for Kiss and Alice Cooper. In the midst of all *that* I went to bed singing 'Here Comes The Flood' instead of my own records!" Gabriel was currently fascinated with short wave radio, and was amazed by the manner in which signal strength would become stronger as daylight faded. All of this fed into the tale of barriers in individuals' thought processes being broken down so anyone can see into other people's minds and, as Gabriel said, "those inclined to concealment would drown in it." The flood, of course, was in the Book Of Genesis in the Old Testament. The God Of Israel cleansed the world of its evil past and recreated a new one with a chosen band of survivors.

Gabriel recounted in 1977 how it was written. Inspired by the writings of Carlos Castaneda and recent reading on the American Indians, he recalled: "It was a warm summer evening and I was on the hillside above my cottage. With my eyes closed I used to run for a hundred paces and see where I found myself and look for plants and animals of significance . . . I felt as if I had found an energy point on the hillside and after a burst of meditation stormed down the hill to write. In the case of 'Flood', it felt as if the song was writing me rather than me writing it." It is an amazing, intense experience that demonstrated how distinctive Gabriel's writing was, and exactly what he had brought to Genesis. "'Here Comes The Flood' is spectacular, an amazing song," Ezrin tells me in 2013. "There's so much brilliance in this record, coming from a man in his middle twenties, the depth of wisdom and sensitivity, not to mention how musically brilliant he was then (and is still)."

The initial recording had been intense and so very different to the way in which Gabriel had worked in his old group. There was, as demonstrated by the 'Modern Love' gaffer tape incident, a rich seam of humour running through the sessions, and Gabriel was delighted to take part: "The *other* Peter Gabriel gaffer tape incident was when he was sitting in one of the rolling chairs in the control room," Ezrin laughs. "I can't remember what precipitated the moment, but we gaffer taped him to his chair and then we wheeled him outside, down the ramp onto the street. Instead of attempting to come back in, he took off down the road in his chair. And then I started to get scared, thinking he's going to get killed and it's my fault. A car drove alongside him and rolled the window down and said do you need any help, and he said, yes – can you tell me the way to Bay Street please? And they gave him directions and he kept going. He has one of the best senses of humour of anyone I've ever worked with."

After the sessions finished in Toronto with a riotous meal and prize-giving ceremony at the Napoleon Restaurant, recording moved to London for further overdubs and sessions with the London Symphony Orchestra whose work on 'Down The Dolce Vita' and 'Here Comes The Flood' was stunning and suitably grandiose. They returned to Canada for final mixing.

It was important for Gabriel that the album looked, sounded and played differently to the material he had last recorded with Genesis. Ezrin was the right man for the job: "Bob's a very smart man with good instincts," Gabriel said in 1986. "At the time of the first album I was nervous recording without the structure of a band, and was quite happy to let Bob take a strong role. I think it worked well on most tracks. We wanted an acoustic, homemade quality to the music." Ezrin said of Gabriel: "Compositionally, I thought some of the material rambled but I wasn't listening that much 'cause I was so captivated. The pure presence of the guy was magic. I was so knocked out with his personality that I found him totally hypnotic."

Larry Fast adds: "Bob was a very forceful individual back then. He actually wore a whistle, like a coach, around his neck while he paced the studio during song rundowns. He knew what he wanted and you had better give him that unless you wanted the whistle in your face."

Robert Fripp was retrospectively unhappy with the album. "It was a very demoralising and a depressing experience," Fripp told Allan Jones of *Melody Maker* in 1979. "I found it difficult to work with the producer. I liked him as a man, but I couldn't express myself fully in the circumstances. Neither could Peter. It wasn't Robert Fripp on that album."

"I didn't encounter any issues while we were there, but I heard there were issues after the fact," Ezrin says. "I believe that while Peter and Robert were in England after having left Canada that Robert may have sowed a few seeds of doubt in Peter's mind about how things were done and the end result. I don't know because I wasn't there, but these are things I had heard – personally I had a great time with Robert. He was so creative and so different to the very American other members of the team. It was just a wonderful combination of personalities. I was very pleased with how the album turned out. I thought musically it was exciting, innovative and a great reflection of Peter as an artist and a great way to start."

* * *

The album, titled simply *Peter Gabriel*, was released in the UK on February 25, 1977 and encased in a Hipgnosis designed sleeve; a heavily colourised image of Gabriel sitting in Storm Thorgerson's rain-soaked car. It had an other worldliness about it, distant, strange and mysterious. It gave the album its simple, colloquial name of *Car*.

With a tag-line of 'Expect the unexpected on the new Peter Gabriel album', Charisma, then distributed through Phonodisc, put considerable weight behind it: Radio commercials were made for Capital, LBC, Piccadilly, BRMB and Clyde; 300 record shop window displays, 500 posters on the London underground and full-page ads in *Melody Maker*, *Sounds* and *New Musical Express*. It reached a respectable number seven in the UK (ironically the same position as Genesis reached with *Wind And Wuthering* there) and number 38 in the US. Gabriel was pleased with this performance: "Success no longer holds the key to happiness for me," Gabriel told Barbara Charone at *Circus* magazine. "I wanted it badly once but it's an experience I had. I've got complete control now. The rock business is a strange hybrid of hypocrisy. You get to the point where you're not really being yourself. You're selling something. You get the feeling that the rock star is some sort of teenage creation realised by people who are no longer teenagers."

Reviews were generally favourable. Stephen Demorest, writing in *Rolling Stone*, said: "The English have an expression for excess – 'over the top' – which I think applies here on occasion. Gabriel's more symphonic tracks, some with five or more movements, are so complex they can become staggering. Sometimes, when a particularly lovely bit vanishes too quickly, one wishes his compositions would stop fidgeting. It's probably just restlessness bursting from an unusually ambitious artist, though, for this is an impressively rich debut album. And I still don't know what to expect from him next."

Anthony Phillips wrote an interesting piece on the album in *Melody Maker* to coincide with its release: "It was important that Peter went to America to record because, in fact, Mike, Phil and I did some demos for Peter here and of course it sounded terribly, terribly like Genesis. And I thought at the time, hell, what's he gonna do? So America was absolutely necessary. I think Pete will produce a REAL masterpiece when he is reunited, hopefully, with his own country, 'cos he's very English."

*Car* was released two months after Genesis' *Wind And Wuthering*, but they were now seen as completely separate entities. Gabriel reinforced his modernity with his album, trapped in a sort of alien style behind the glass of his windscreen, while Genesis was still pursuing a heavily-illustrated windswept, autumnal feel. Both albums seem to have a sense of longing at their heart. Both produced catchy hits: learning from the lesson of 'I Know What I Like (In Your Wardrobe)', Genesis had 'Your Own Special

Way', while Gabriel's 'Solsbury Hill' was a heavy duty, *proper* pop hit.

Interviews were riddled with questions on his feelings about his old group's success: "The only thing that used to upset me a lot," he told *NME* in 1977, "was when with things that I'd written with the others or done [a lot of] work on, such as 'Supper's Ready', or 'The Lamb Lies Down', it was glossed over that I'd been involved with those songs at all. I used to get angry, but I knew they had a very good chance of doing well. I didn't know it'd be quite as easy as that. I'm probably biased about it, but I don't like their lyrics too much. But I think that in terms of production and playing they're really very good."

He continued: "It's a lot less competitive ego-wise, and it's now easier to try different styles. In Genesis we were all putting in material to a polished band arrangement, whereas now I'm trying, as a writer, to arrange things differently. It's nice just to be able to realise some of the ideas that I was going for. In the group it was a compromise. You'd hand over your idea to a band interpretation, but now if I hear some things in my head it's possible just to try them out and see how they work. It's a lot more enjoyable for that reason."

"The first album was hard to judge as he'd just left the group and there was a bit of competiveness there," Tony Banks added in 2013.

Gabriel's prolonged absence, for the whole of 1976, from the pop eye, seemed an eternity at the time. In the 21st century a year off is seen as fairly common, longer is positively expected to allow tour cycles to finish and marketing departments to work through any residual magic or life there may be left in a product. "Generally, there's only one golden egg in a band, as far as business goes," Gabriel reflected. "It's very rare when people split up or break off that you get two successful acts. The chances are remote. The longer I didn't do anything the bigger the question mark. I wouldn't describe myself as a golden egg yet. But I'm in a strong position; certainly much stronger than I was a year ago."

Gabriel also seemed to have escaped the enormous backlash that progressive rock was getting in the media; it was as if he jumped off the juggernaut exactly at the right time. With punk's 'year-zero' revisionist approach, many of the new characters on the scene, almost all of whom were of similar age or only slightly younger than the bands they referred to as 'old farts', pretended they had no time for and, indeed, had never owned much of the music they had spent the previous three years listening to. Gabriel was pleased that *Car* was displayed in Malcolm McLaren and Vivienne Westwood's SEX shop in the Kings Road and that Nick Kent, then the hottest, most revered rock critic was onside with his new work.

★ ★ ★

In March 1977, Gabriel went on the road, almost two years after his last *Lamb* show. Titling the American leg of the tour 'Expect The Unexpected', he assembled a band of top session players and old friends. When Barbara Charone caught up with him in Toronto during rehearsals for his first tour, he said: "I feel like a completely free man. I don't feel I have to cater to any preconceptions or any roles. Nothing is particularly expected of me, so anything has to be a bonus." On bass was the mercurial Tony Levin, who had played on the album and became the only player to remain with Gabriel through to 2012. Allan Schwartzberg, Larry Fast, Steve Hunter and Jimmy Maelen reprised their album roles, while Phil Aaberg joined on keyboards. Surprisingly, Robert Fripp played guitar, billed under the pseudonym, Dusty Rhodes. Fripp would often play from behind the speakers or sometimes offstage, such was his distaste for the touring rock machine.

The tour began at the Capitol Theater in Passaic, New Jersey on March 3, 1977 and continued through North America and Canada into April before heading to the UK. Audiences were treated to live versions of the album, plus, as a lovely nod to Gabriel's soul roots, versions of Marvin Gaye's 'Ain't That Peculiar', 'I Heard It Through the Grapevine' and the Temptations' 'Ain't Too Proud To Beg'. Dipping back further the beat boom's influence on him is writ large by his raucous, almost metallic cover of The Kinks' 'All Day (And All Of The Night)'.

It seemed a hoot. "It absolutely was," Larry Fast attests. "The band was professional and without the petty issues that often cloud a self-contained band. That made it lighter and even more enjoyable than I had expected. The R&B covers were a lot of fun. I had done many sessions for soul and R&B artists so it was rewarding to transplant that background to a respectful English aficionado like Peter. The tour infrastructure, crew, management, travel arrangements, were all handled professionally which took a huge load off of my mind as a performer."

Atlantic Records, who retained Gabriel as a solo artist in America, put a great deal of promotion behind it, as, in the main, the album had a super-lean US sound to it. "When Gabriel's first solo album came out, Atlantic threw a dinner for him in New York that I was present at," writer Chris Charlesworth recalls. "There was about 20 of us. Ahmet and the top brass was there." Nancy Lewis, who organised Charisma's US operation oversaw the launch.

His six shows over three nights at Los Angeles' legendary 500-capacity Roxy Theatre in April 1977, where Genesis had been received so warmly in December 1973, were eagerly awaited. The shows marked Gabriel's coming of age as a solo performer; pointedly, he wore a grey sweatsuit, about as far away as you could get from the theatre of his previous group. LA radio station K West broadcast the show. You could hear the excitement and vitality – stripping the bombastic album versions of their production and orchestras to show a tight, aggressive band.

He opened the set with 'Here Comes The Flood', pared down to just Gabriel's voice and piano and Fripp's guitar. It was as understated an opening as possible, considering that LA audiences had last seen him at the Shrine just over two years earlier dressed as the old man in 'The Musical Box' at the end of *The Lamb Lies Down On Broadway* concert show. The synthesiser drive of new song 'On The Air' referenced The Who, the long-term touchstone of Gabriel. Songs like 'Moribund, The Burgermeister' had located their swing, while Fripp was introduced as the 'immaculately obscure' Dusty Rhodes on guitar.

"I was following Peter on the tour in 1977," Anthony Phillips recalls. "The first gigs, he tried to be 'Peter Gabriel', the guy sitting at the piano being a normal kind of an artist. It didn't work properly because he wasn't that messianic presence. It took a while for him to realise you're going to have to switch into that persona and act that commands people's attention – people quite liked some of the songs, but he wasn't this spellbinding stage presence that he'd been before and was eventually to become again; it was a brief experiment in 'I'll just be good old me' and it really didn't cut the mustard. It was fascinating to see that and then see him begin to project more."

By the time of the second leg of the tour, which began in September that year, Gabriel had shifted personnel, and added Bayette on keyboards, Sid McGinnis on guitar and a performer who was to greatly influence Gabriel for the next decade, drummer Jerry Marotta. In December 1977 they were mistaken for members of the Baader-Meinhof gang while on tour in West Germany, the situation eventually alleviated by the band singing a close harmony version of 'Excuse Me'. Proof, if needed, that going solo would be full of unpredictability and excitement. Gabriel himself had to expect the unexpected.

# 13: Keeping It Small

*"One moment he looks rakishly sensual, the next like an untouchable buddah. He is reserved, but the slow-burn look in his eyes must light a few fires. He's the kind of man who will open a door while carrying a heavy box of groceries and insist you go before him. And you do so, since to refuse would be churlish."*

Caroline Coon, *Sounds*, 1978

GABRIEL said in 1977, after completing *Car*, "For me this album is a run-in for the second project. This album is more a bunch of songs while the next one will be more experimental, musically and conceptually. On this first album I just want to make a niche for myself as a songwriter. This way people will get a chance to make a musical assessment before they get any visual overload."

He discussed the album too with old friend Richard Macphail: "I remember being on the phone to Peter, talking about his career at that point," Macphail says. "He talked about Bob Ezrin, his all-American band, Fripp – I just recall saying that I'd love to come back and work with him and he jumped at it. I was there for all of *Scratch*." Macphail returned to be Gabriel's road manager, a safe pair of hands for the next album and the subsequent gruelling tour schedule. By now, Macphail was living in the 'squatter's republic' of Frestonia in north-west Notting Hill, West London. He'd been employed by Tony Smith and Gail Colson as a tour manager, and he had worked with Genesis on their 1976 tour, as well as tours by Bill Bruford, Brand X and Peter Hammill.

With Macphail coordinating the proceedings for Smith and Colson, the second Peter Gabriel album was recorded at the fastest pace of any album in his career. Robert Fripp was to produce, the complete opposite of Bob Ezrin. As Eric Tamm notes in Fripp's biography, "If *Peter Gabriel* 1977 sounds like it was recorded in a heavenly cathedral, *Peter Gabriel* 1978 sounds like it comes out of a dingy garage: Fripp persuaded Gabriel to cut back drastically on the electronically induced spaciousness and instead opt for the close, tight, dry, realistic 'live' type sound King Crimson's recorded music had nearly always had – the production strategy Fripp was later to call *audio verité*."

His second album, also titled *Peter Gabriel* became known as *Scratch* because of its distinctive, Hipgnosis-designed sleeve, and its sound put Gabriel amid the current milieu of post-punk and scintillating new wave. Although partially recorded at Relight Studios at Hilvarenbeek in the Netherlands, which seemed to be the go-to studio in this period, its sound primarily was that of New York, where the remainder of the album was recorded at the Hit Factory on West 54th Street in Manhattan. This album could sit nicely with Talking Heads, Television and Patti Smith. It's sparse, harder and emotional, with Gabriel's writing becoming more direct and his vocals less tricksy though for all intents and purposes, it is still a rock album. Fewer musicians were in the studio and the band gelled; Tony Levin, Fripp and Larry Fast were back. Jerry Marotta, then playing with Orleans, came in on drums and would become another long-serving foil of Gabriel's. Gabriel got his wish and Roy Bittan was released from the E-Street Band to add his unmistakable piano line; Sid McGinnis came in on guitar; Rhodes specialist Bayete (Todd Cochran) added keyboard textures and Timmy Capello provided saxophone to a couple of numbers.

As writer Paul Stump was to say, "Where Genesis mollified, Gabriel wanted to disturb. His recruitment of Robert Fripp and his audio-verité approach to the production console for his second solo album atoned for his Genesis aestheticism, as did his much publicised appearance at punk festivals in 1978." "Robert was very keen to get everything fresh," Gabriel said in 1978. "We kept a lot of early takes and kept the production very dry. The second album is more spontaneous. There are some with rough edges and some mistakes but leaving them in makes it more alive."

Larry Fast outlined the differences between the two Bobs: "Both have strong musical personalities, but those personalities and what they impart to the recordings are quite different," he said. "Bob Ezrin is more in the classic Phil Spector mould. Find the best session players, build up a large band, tweak the sound to be as big as a rock orchestra as needed and then record the tracks, mostly live. Overdubs were not the usual mode of working. The basic recording of a given song was probably more than three-quarters finished at that point. Even the live scratch vocals had a somewhat final sound at times. It was a big, live wall of sound. Bob took command of the sessions and there was little discussion about taking any other approach to the tracks. Later, there were huge orchestra overdub sessions for some of the songs that were so over the top that most of them were not used. The emphasis was on big."

Fripp, however, was very different. "Robert Fripp at that time was working in his *audio* verité mode. That was a very stripped down, spare and dry sound; quite minimalist. It was in many ways the polar opposite of the Ezrin sound and approach. Robert did not take on the role of a military commander taking his troops into musical battle as Bob did. But he was steely, in a quiet firm way, in defending his approach from any challenges from the musicians and even from the artist. I spent a lot more time doing overdubs on the second album, though not nearly as much as the third album a year later. The end results, though were a much dryer, pointillistic and intimate sounding recording which is what Robert wanted." Gabriel told Spencer Bright, "the playing on the album is . . . very hard edges . . . there's actually more synth on the second album but it's used in a different way. It's used less like a string section."

The album crashes in on a sea of synthetics for 'On The Air', another segment of Gabriel's suggested Mozo concept. Mozo lives in a rubbish skip and inhabits a fantasy world created by short wave radio; musically it is reminiscent of *The Lamb Lies Down On Broadway*, taut and clean. Gabriel told Spencer Bright that "through short-wave radio he [Mozo] becomes whoever he wants, but in real life, on the street, he's totally ignored." Fading in slowly, emerging with crackling, popping atmospheric synthesisers, it ends similarly, sounding not unlike Pete Townshend's post-*Tommy* work with The Who. Its five-and-a-half minutes are neatly answered by the two-and-a-half minutes on 'D.I.Y.' which, with its crisp snare snap and acoustic guitars, follows on where 'Solsbury Hill' left off. It is another plea for independence, while also chiming with the 'do it yourself' ethos of the new wave movement. Change can be affected at any level if people are mobilised to do something. It gleefully parades Gabriel's personal freedom with the message that if an individual wants control, 'you've got to keep it small'. It was almost as if with Fripp he had left another piece of the machinery in Ezrin. The track is one of Gabriel's very best, yet it failed to connect with audiences when released as the album's lead single, missing the charts on both sides of the Atlantic, even when a 12″ mix was prepared with extra horns and choruses.

Nick Kent likened Gabriel to Travis Bickle from the film *Taxi Driver* after hearing the lyric he'd co-written with Jill for 'Mother Of Violence'. In an extraordinarily beautifully arranged setting, Gabriel delivers one of his best vocals over Roy Bittan's piano and Robert Fripp's incessant yet low key guitar squall. The gentle reggae skank of 'A Wonderful Day In A One Way World' gives way to the incredible 'White Shadow'. Sounding like subversive AOR, it arrives with all of Fripp's floating ambience based on Larry Fast's swathes of synthesisers.

'Indigo' reads like a progress report of Gabriel's well-being and future intent; opening with a growing feeling of personal obsolescence, the track sounds like a long goodbye note, caught amid great personal change. There seems little hope, yet love is offered as a form of redemption. It was the closest the album got in sound to any Genesis material. 'Animal Magic' was a song of virility that took its inspiration from army recruitment slogans. An update of the Charles Atlas-type 'make you a man' adverts of the Fifties, the protagonist decides to prove his masculinity to his ex-lover and her new partner by joining the army. Mere romance cannot get to him now he is a trained killing machine. It explores the 'lover' or 'fighter' idea – which one was Gabriel?

'Exposure' was another segment from the Mozo piece and is one of the album's highlights. Introduced by Fripp's unmistakable guitar, it is a dense, brooding funk that appears from nowhere and seems to linger forever, featuring one of Tony Levin's greatest bass lines. A re-recorded version was to become the title track of Fripp's first solo album the following year. 'Flotsam And Jetsam' is a sweet moment in a dense album, yet points to another doomed relationship where little is as it seems; 'Perspective' was blazing rock, full of Timmy Capello's saxophone and charging beats. It sounded like a hybrid of new wave and Bruce Springsteen.

'Home Sweet Home' closed the album on another subdued note. Starting as a conventional piano ballad, Gabriel then sings in his higher register, sounding almost identical to early Seventies John Lennon. An emotionally turbulent tale of the doomed relationship of Bill and Josephine, who marry because of her pregnancy and invest their money in an apartment in a soulless block, the resulting isolation leads to Josephine taking their child, Sam, and throwing herself and the child out of their eleventh floor window. The resulting insurance money that Bill receives feels 'dirty', so he gambles it on roulette, and, confounding the bleak lack of expectation set up by the gloomy subject matter, wins money beyond his wildest dreams. He ends up alone in a country house with his memories. Even the good in the song turns sour. It conveys the same skull-beneath-the-skin reality of Roxy Music's 'In Every Dream Home A Heartache'. With Gabriel revelling in tales of doomed relationships, a pattern establishes that when Gabriel seems settled emotionally, his subject matter turns ever darker.

*Peter Gabriel* was released in June 1978. Lyrically downbeat, musically often bright and snappy, at best it demonstrated an artist moving forward and growing in stature. One thing it wasn't was commercial. The sleeve was again assembled by Storm Thorgerson and Peter Christopherson from Hipgnosis. Christopherson, by now moonlighting as a musician in avant-punks Throbbing Gristle, took the moody pictures of Gabriel in the snow-heavy streets of New York, while it was Storm's idea to have Gabriel tearing down the artwork of the sleeve with his clawing fingers, thus providing the album with its colloquial name of *Scratch*. The fact his albums gained two names underlines a key aspect of his work; Gabriel is a 'Gemini' character – seemingly always facing two directions. When you see one thing, you are really getting another: a settled man writing about emotional traumas; an intensely private showman, happy to divulge a great deal of personal information without revealing *anything*.

* * *

The reviews were generally favourable: *Sounds* concluded: "This new Peter Gabriel album is absolutely *it*. It hasn't left my turntable yet and doesn't look like it's going to. It couldn't happen to a finer artist. Just listen." Caroline Coon wrote: "Robert Fripp's production is feelwise less intense than Ezrin's and there are fewer moments of transcending brilliance, but the inspired, well structured and arranged songs, consistently infused with elegiac sensitivity and emotion, are ample compensation."

Retrospective reviews see the album as something of a curate's egg: *Allmusic* said "By the end, it all seems a little formless. It's not that the music is overly challenging – it's that the record is unfocused." Yet Richard Cook in *NME* in 1982 said that with *Scratch*, Gabriel "found himself in a raw area that kept exploding into colour as he touched it – that second LP, with its cropped and screwball run of songs, sounds brilliantly excitable still." Brilliantly excitable and often unpredictable is an accurate summation. Although superbly played, it sounds far less professional and had greater spontaneity than the first album.

Eric Tamm, in his biography of Robert Fripp concludes: "Peter Gabriel 1978 shows us a very Frippicised Gabriel, as though Fripp was doing his utmost to incorporate Gabriel into his own scheme of things. In the long view, I think we should be thankful he didn't succeed." "Robert was very keen to get everything fresh," Gabriel told Spencer Bright. "We kept a lot of early takes and kept the production very dry."

Although not perfect, *Scratch* was another step towards Gabriel shedding his masks. Its to-the-bone subject matter and experimental playing demonstrated Gabriel's growing confidence: he was over the band thing; had completed the slick, professional album, now it was a further leap to the next phase. It was often uncommercial, and certainly raised eyebrows at Atlantic in the States, who were looking for more singles of the calibre of 'Solsbury Hill'. Instead he was singing doom-laden songs of suicide, mysterious strangers and fear. There was a feeling of letting Gabriel have his head before he delivered his real commercial triumph.

Then a surprising thing happened. Gabriel unexpectedly joined Genesis onstage for the final encore of 'I Know What I Like (In Your Wardrobe)' at New York's Madison Square Garden on July 29, 1978. Gabriel was in town recording for the forthcoming Robert Fripp album, and Atlantic felt it would be good publicity for his solo album. Nancy Lewis, who'd worked with Genesis when they were at Buddah, and had now moved across to Atlantic, negotiated an upgrade to Concorde if Gabriel would do it. It showed there was no animosity between the band and Gabriel, and by now both had established sufficiently separate identities for it to be seen as nothing more than what it was, a bit of fun.

But in the public eye, Gabriel, a 28-year-old father of two small children was to take a much weirder turn. The showman in the mask was about to shave his head completely and take to wearing high-visibility jackets on tour while singing nursery rhymes and delivering punk versions of rock standards. It really was time to expect the unexpected.

In the period since Gabriel had first seen the Sex Pistols and the Ramones, and since the release of his first album, punk rock and its artier counterpart, new wave, had preoccupied the music press that previously hung on to Gabriel's every word. The phrase 'boring old fart' became common parlance for those who dared to wear their hair too long, or admit to owning albums that just a handful of years before were held dear. Although new wave had yet to make any enormous commercial in-roads, the shape of the charts was changing, and as discussed previously, it seemed as if all the old bands were falling by the wayside, or adapting. The smartest of the old guard moved forward: Yes, Genesis and ELP, now reviled by the papers that once loved them, all scored their biggest hits, shortened the length of their songs and cut their hair. Pink Floyd, who had always stood outside prog, found that Roger Waters' bitter, hand-biting catalogues of gloom chimed with the times. Others, such as Caravan, Gentle Giant and the like soldiered on, soon to implode. Gabriel, like his friend and less commercial ally Peter Hammill, seemed to have an added dimension that kept them on the right side of the press; never seeming too old fartish or embarrassing, they were able to move ahead, enjoying the liberation of the form.

Gabriel welcomed the punk movement. It had provided a shot in the arm for music and it took him back to the ethos of rehearsing in school. "He saw the Pistols at the 100 Club," Macphail recalls. "He wasn't into it musically, but he really appreciated the spirit of it and what they were up to. He'd seriously moved on by then." To show how far he was able to flirt with punk, in 1978 he shaved off his hair. Not the semi-circle at the front of the *Selling England By The Pound* days, but a head-wide grade one, and now Gabriel looked aggressive, which he had never looked in his life before. He was stripped clean, a symbolic shaving of the lamb. "People react to a shaved head differently to how they do to a soft hairy one," he said with some understatement. This was borne out by the surprised public reaction to him when he took various photo shoots in London tube stations. He joked with German rock television programme *Rockpalast* that he shaved his skull because he liked the sound of raindrops falling on his head.

Gabriel could see punk was just the next wave breaking, as he had seen first with The Beatles and then the next wave with Family and King Crimson. "I think it's important for every generation to have its own identity in music – I like the energy of it," he said. "In terms of pure energy it is a focal point for anything else to be compared to. I don't really feel it's had a tremendous influence other than providing me with the idea for a new version of 'A Whiter Shade Of Pale'."

The new version of Procol Harum's 1967 number one was to be showcased in the tour to support *Scratch*, which began in Oxford in August 1978, taking in the States and Europe before closing at Hammersmith Odeon in December of that year.

For Larry Fast, the band was quite distanced from punk. "For the most part, we were quite separate from it. We tried a kind-of sort-of punk arrangement of 'A Whiter Shade of Pale' during the 1978 tour. It was fun, but we didn't really identify deeply with the punk ethos. I don't think Peter or the band really connected with at the true visceral level what punkdom was all about. We were from a very different world so all we could do was mimic some of the superficial elements, though perhaps understanding the deeper underpinnings that others were doing. I always felt like I was more of an observer from a musical and sociological-anthropologist viewpoint. Peter's separation from the most self-indulgent aspects of the progressive movement right from the outset of his solo career allowed him to evolve on his own terms without having to answer to the musical fashion of any year be it punk, prog or any other style-of-the-moment."

Dave Gregory caught Gabriel on tour at Oxford Playhouse with Sid McGinnis and Tim Capello on saxophone in 1978 and was amazed at the power of the band, the toughness and the strength – complete with Capello's showmanship on saxophone and keyboards. The experience of the tour was a complete flushing away of his previous personas. It was just Gabriel, his shaven head and overalls; the most simplistic that he had ever appeared onstage. This was new territory and Gabriel was working from an open-minded palette, which would soon be reflected in his method of working and writing new material.

The apogee of this era was two concerts that Gabriel played in September 1978 at Knebworth House and Battersea Park; the former on a bill with Frank Zappa, the latter as principal support to The Stranglers. The Knebworth Park concerts had become a key event in the rock calendar by 1978. Held in the grounds of the stately home since 1974, the 'Bucolic Frolic' offered the likes of Van Morrison, Tim Buckley and The Doobie Brothers, before hosting Pink Floyd in 1975, The Rolling Stones in 1976, and earlier in 1978, Genesis, making their only UK concert appearance that year.

By the September 9 concert, the mood of the times had reached Freddie

Bannister, the concert promoter. Billed as 'not another boring old Knebworth', the show reached out to audiences who, if not wholeheartedly punk, certainly leant towards its immediate musical successor, new wave. The full bill featured Gabriel playing alongside The Tubes, Zappa, Boomtown Rats, Rockpile, and mercurial ex-Dr Feelgood guitarist, Wilko Johnson's new outfit, The Solid Senders. Showcasing a mixture of material from the first two albums, Gabriel's set also included a tryout for 'I Don't Remember' and his very-much-of-the-moment punk cover of one of progressive rock's most revered baubles, 'A Whiter Shade Of Pale'.

The concert captured the iconoclastic spirit of the age, and for Gabriel, it was a showstopping showcase that illustrated just how experimental he was prepared to be. On the negative side, some sections of the audience saw it as a too-near-the-knuckle parody of punk and Bob Geldof in particular. Gabriel was met with a barrage of abuse. However, he played a version of 'The Lamb Lies Down On Broadway' to provide his long-term fans with a brief glimmer of the artist formerly in Genesis.

Gabriel's position on the bill at The Stranglers concert at London's Battersea Park the following week was even more overt. The Stranglers were seen as the shady and dangerous elder brothers of the punk movement as they were older and more seasoned than a great deal of their contemporaries. Gabriel played on a bill that included The Skids, Spizz Oil, The Edge and compere Johnny Rubbish. His 11-song set was very much of the moment and showed exactly how far Gabriel had travelled in the three years since he played his last concert with Genesis. While his old band had finished their last tour playing the conventional arenas to which they had become accustomed, here he was out in the park on a late summer Saturday amid a new wave crowd, who understandably went wild for his version of 'A Whiter Shade Of Pale'.

"The tour for this record was one in which we were all dressed in sort of road workers' fluorescents," Gabriel later said. ". . . We used to do a sort of punk version of 'Whiter Shade of Pale', which is probably safely eroded in the mists of time, and a version of 'Me And My Teddy Bear' which I think was the first song that I performed as a kid and was one of the few songs that I could remember the words to." Gabriel looked astonishingly malevolent. With his dyed black skinhead crop and fluorescent jacket, here was a man rebelling against his upbringing, wearing the uniform of an authentic, classic road worker; a real job of the working class. Not so much the bucolic Chobham life, but more his years in the dormitory town of Genesis, all serried rows of trees and well-informed men, never truly displaying their emotions. It was as if Master Peter was metaphorically leaving the croquet lawn to go to work.

★ ★ ★

Gabriel and Jill's relationship during all this was fractious; his personal growth seemed to run parallel with the disintegration of their marriage. Richard Macphail encouraged them to attend EST. A controversial practice, Erhard Seminars Training (EST) encouraged participants to confront their deepest feelings, relationships and motives across two intensive 30-hour weekends – often by sharing their emotions baldly with others in a small group situation.

EST training had begun in 1971 in San Francisco, crossing over to London six years later. Macphail encouraged the Gabriels to go along with him and his then girlfriend. Although not wholly sold on all of its aspects, Gabriel took its central tenet of taking responsibility for one's own actions and that people are not victims. Macphail noted one other, deeply significant effect it had on Gabriel: his lyrics became a lot more straightforward, leaving behind the symbolism of Genesis and relying less on third party stories. "It was a deeply affecting thing, for Jill, Peter, me and my then girlfriend," Macphail says. "I don't think we'll ever get over the depth of bond we cemented. We both had this interest in the human potential movement. That was a very intense time. I think EST was absolutely pivotal to his art. To this day I'm a huge fan of it. People talked about brainwashing and that's bullshit – it was designed to go deep." In small groups, through discussion, participants would aim to shed themselves of their past, accept responsibility and fully embrace the present.

"It was very controversial. It's designed to get past your mind and get to the essence of you. It made a huge difference to Peter and I." Gabriel was receptive to all of this; he had looked at communal living and flirted with the Silva Mind Control technique. "He'd already been making a journey into his unconscious with *The Lamb Lies Down On Broadway* which was the most extraordinary journey."

It was at this point that Gail Colson, who had risen to become the MD of Charisma, came across to manage Gabriel. Colson, who had worked so dedicatedly for Tony Stratton-Smith and then for Tony Smith, relished the responsibility for managing Gabriel. "Charisma was breaking up and her golden handshake was managing Peter Gabriel," Chris Charlesworth recalls.

"I suppose things started to change for me around 1976 when punk arrived and I could see that things were going to change and that we could not just rely on one band, Genesis," Colson says. "Among some of the artists I wanted to sign were The Boomtown Rats, Elvis Costello and Devo – Tony didn't 'get' any of these. So, Genesis got bigger and bigger. Around March of 1978 I was in the States looking for a producer for one of our artists and was only away for about a week but when I returned Tony had signed two acts without any discussion with me and having listened to them I didn't 'get' either of them, they were Razar and The Blue Nile. We had a bit of a disagreement and I handed in my notice, I gave him three months and left at the end of June when Genesis headlined Knebworth. I always joke that that was my leaving party."

Colson took on the management of Peter after his first album had been released and when he was in the middle of touring, initially working out of Tony Smith's offices. "At that time, because Tony had been a promoter before taking over the management of Genesis, he did not use an agent and booked the tours direct himself. I remember that my main challenge was how the hell was I supposed to book a European tour. I found myself an agent, Steve Hedges, and hired him to take over the booking of the European tour."

Colson then had two artists in her small stable – Peter Gabriel and Peter Hammill. Gabriel was to quip to Mick Gold in 1981 that she "only manages artists called Peter". "They are very different people," she said in 2013, "but there is a definite mutual respect for each other." With Gail Colson taking special charge of Gabriel, her ruthlessly efficient, never-less-than charming manner ensured that his operations ran smoothly.

* * *

The next step on Gabriel's transition from "pointy headed, theatrical cult artist to canny minimalist pop star" came with his involvement on Robert Fripp's first solo album, *Exposure*, the sessions for which ran concurrently with the recording of Gabriel's second solo album. Fripp, who in 1975 had disbanded King Crimson ostensibly for good, had, after three years studying, re-merged with a plan for what he entitled 'the drive to 1981', which would involve a series of releases and productions. Although he had worked with Gabriel on his first two solo albums, Fripp was now a long way removed from the progressive rock scene that he had helped create. Describing himself as "a small mobile, intelligent unit", he had been living in a small flat in the Bowery, New York. He was involved with new wave and became a go-to art guitarist on a select series of releases, most notably adding the haunting guitar figure to the title track of David Bowie's *"Heroes"* album. Discussed as an 'autobiography of sorts', Fripp had intended *Exposure* (originally titled *The Last Of The Great New York Heart-throbs*) to be part of a trilogy of releases that included *Peter Gabriel* (*Scratch*) and *Sacred Songs* by Daryl Hall, both of which he had produced.

As Fripp told *Melody Maker* in 1979, "*Exposure* deals with tweaking the vocabulary of, for want of a better word, 'rock' music. It investigates the vocabulary and, hopefully, expands the possibilities of expression and introduces a more sophisticated emotional dynamic than one would normally find within 'rock'." Intended as part of another trilogy with an album of Frippertronics and one of Discotronics (the two albums would come out as one – *God Save The Queen/Under Heavy Manners* in 1980), *Exposure* showed how a selection of artists could work together under Fripp's strict guidance and create some of the most thrilling art-rock ever committed to tape.

And the line-up was rather special indeed: alongside Fripp and Gabriel, there was Peter Hammill, Daryl Hall, Phil Collins, Narada Michael Walden, Brian Eno, Terre Roche, Barry Andrews. Blondie were to have appeared providing a reworked version of Donna Summer's 'I Feel Love', had their record company Chrysalis not stepped in and aborted it. It was interesting that a lot of the key performers were not those naturally given to frequently appearing on the albums of others (aside, of course, from Collins and Eno). Fripp was questioned by Kris Needs of *ZigZag* in 1979, he said: "There's a style of English artist where they're un-producable. They determine their own situation, nothing can change it. Bowie, Eno, Fripp, Gabriel, Ferry, Hammill – these are the names that spring to mind." Fripp had seen similar in Daryl Hall. He originally intended Hall to be the lead voice on *Exposure*, continuing the remarkable working relationship they had developed during the making of *Sacred Songs*. However, RCA Records and Hall's manager, Tommy Motolla, were horrified with the results (of both *Sacred Songs* and Hall's contribution to *Exposure*). Hall with his partner, John Oates, epitomised a middle-of-the-road, blue-eyed soul but his work with Fripp was too left-field for his image, and it was largely removed from the album, replaced in part by Peter Hammill.

Peter Gabriel was involved directly and indirectly with *Exposure*. He can be heard on the album's 'Preface', after Daryl Hall's choir vocals and before the ringing of the telephone. The track, 'Exposure', that he had written with Fripp for *Scratch* was re-recorded with Terre Roche on vocals. Sid McGinnis laid down the disco-funk guitar over Tony Levin and Jerry Marotta's watertight rhythm section. Fripp added Frippertronics and he and Brian Eno spoke out the letters to the word, exposure. However, it was in the album's final moments that Gabriel delivered one of the greatest performances of his career. Convening in the Hit Factory in New York in March 1978, Fripp recorded Gabriel performing 'Here Comes The Flood', the closing track from *Car*. The song, which Gabriel had commented was "writing me rather than me writing it", had felt the full force of Bob Ezrin's orchestral production on the album. Here Fripp took it back to Gabriel's original intentions.

Small, intimate and personal, it was recorded just with Fripp and Eno present, adding the subtlest sound textures to Gabriel's emotional tale of feelings laid bare. It was beautiful and direct, and this, combined with the EST training that he and his wife Jill had recently been through, provided Gabriel with a clear idea that simplicity in his sound should be the way forward. Eric Tamm said it was a "simultaneously heartbreaking and terrifying reading of a song he had originally recorded for his first solo album in a heavier rock arrangement." Gabriel was to move ever further away from rock in the next decade of his career.

It was a fertile era for collaborations, and Gabriel was, by now, fully enjoying his freedom. He had met new wave artist Tom Robinson in 1977 and the two got along famously. Robinson wore his social conscience fully on his sleeve; an out-gay man who refused to play to a stereotype – an exceptionally rare commodity in the public eye in the late Seventies. Robinson and his band had become known for their rousing Top 5 single '2-4-6-8 Motorway' and the controversial anthem 'Glad To Be Gay'. Although Robinson was perceived as from the generation that replaced Gabriel and his ilk, he was in fact only a handful of months younger than Gabriel and they had much in common.

Gabriel and Robinson collaborated on two songs together, 'Merrily Up On High' and 'Bully For You', which was a centrepiece of the album Robinson was working on. Gabriel and Robinson put on a joint show in 1978 the week before Christmas at Hammersmith Odeon, 'Rob and Gab 78'. After their first show on December 20, they headed east and performed vocals, dressed in long overcoats to 'Hello It's Me' in Todd Rundgren's shows at The Venue, in Victoria. Rundgren, whom Gabriel had approached in 1976 to produce his debut album, had just finished producing Robinson's album. It again demonstrated Gabriel's desire to experiment and think outside the box. But what was to happen next would truly establish Gabriel as an innovator without masks or frontiers.

# 14: Happy In The Dark

"Peter Gabriel III *runs the gamut of all emotion. It begins with a burglary and ends with an anthem, with all human points in between."*

Dave Gregory, 2012

*"Young people listen to rock music and to have that attention and that possibility for giving out information and not to use it for anything other than saying who you laid last night is, I think, a waste of time."*

Peter Gabriel, 1987

BEFORE Peter Gabriel could properly start work on his next album, there was still some unfinished business that had haunted him for the past five years and would continue to hang over him for several years to come. Gabriel had copyrighted the story and the lyrics to *The Lamb Lies Down On Broadway* at some point in the late Seventies. In 1979, he found director Alejandro Jodorowsky in Paris and wanted him to direct a film of the story. Jodorowsky had directed *El Topo*, which had had a tremendous impact on Gabriel. He had worked up a 12-page draft based on *The Lamb*. Charisma Films, which had been established with some vigour by Tony Stratton-Smith, looked to raise the proposed budget of £5 million. Jodorowsky came to Ashcombe House and worked with Gabriel for about a month, persuading Gabriel not to appear himself in the film as Rael.

However, when Gabriel was dropped by Atlantic (for reasons we shall come to), the funding stalled, and by the mid Eighties, *The Lamb Lies Down On Broadway* film had faltered. Perhaps once and for all. "Unfortunately nothing came of it," Gabriel told Armando Gallo in 1986. "Charisma Films, with whom we were dealing, were unable to raise the necessary finance. I was very disappointed at the time but it could have been very complicated in that some of Genesis were reluctant to have it resurrected."

"It's Pete's baby," Mike Rutherford says. "A film presentation needs to be explained simply. It's not a body of work that stands up cohesively, and that's what you need for a film. Someone could write the book, as they call it, but that would mean giving stuff up. It needs a heavy hand to drive it somewhere."

* * *

The third Peter Gabriel album began in earnest when, after demoing tracks and ideas in Bath, Gabriel located to the Town House Studios on West London's Goldhawk Road, which was then owned by Virgin Records. "The Townhouse was a well-run facility with then-state of the art equipment," Larry Fast recalls. "I had worked at other London studios such as AIR and Morgan, but I found that I liked the atmosphere and professionalism at the Townhouse quite a lot."

Gabriel's choice of producer Steve Lillywhite and engineer Hugh Padgham was pivotal to the making of his new album. Bringing in a young team meant that ideas could easily flow. Gone was Ezrin's bombast or Fripp's studied-yet-speedy approach. Here was something new. The then 24-year-old Lillywhite had been working in UK recording studios since 1972. His stock rose after working on the first Ultravox! album with Brian Eno. Lillywhite had become a go-to producer in new wave and post-punk, working with Siousxie & The Banshees, and most notably at this point, Swindon avant-punkers XTC.

Gabriel loved XTC. They had created a unique, distinctive sound; initially described as Britain's answer to Talking Heads. They soon established themselves as credible performers, and possessing two great songwriters – Andy Partridge, and to a less frequent extent, Colin Moulding. On their groundbreaking 1979 album *Drums And Wires*, Lillywhite had demonstrated how he could sweeten their herky-jerky angular noise into a palatable proposition without losing any of its edge and had shown what an inventive, electric sound he could get. Padgham was the same age as Lillywhite and had begun as a tape-op with bands such as Yes and Emerson Lake & Palmer, before moving to the Town House in 1978, and supporting Lillywhite on his XTC work, among others.

XTC had been working on *Drums And Wires* at the back of the Town House, where their guitarist Dave Gregory recalls: "It was the home of the famous 'Stone Room', where Hugh got that drum sound that Peter was to use on 'Intruder' and Phil Collins was later to use on 'In The Air Tonight'.

Andy (Partridge) always used to ask for louder drums, you can hear it on 'Roads Girdle The Globe' from *Drums And Wires*. As we were doing the session, Steve Lillywhite got the call from Peter Gabriel's office, asking if he would be interested in producing him. Steve was unsure. He hadn't really heard of him. I told him that he *had* to say yes – I couldn't think of a better producer to work with him. I could see that Peter was anxious to be part of the new wave, he was forward thinking and that Steve would be the perfect man. As a jolly aside, I said, 'If you take the job and need a guitar player, you know whom to call.'"

XTC came back from an Australian tour to learn that their producer was indeed working with Gabriel. "We were about to remix our track 'Real By Reel' for a possible single and Steve came back in, bouncing off the walls," Gregory laughs. "He was so happy, saying things like, 'There are no cymbals, I've never worked with anyone like this'. It was so exciting. He said that although he had no idea how successful it was going to be, it was one of the most exciting things that he had ever worked on."

Dave Gregory would be one of a stellar cast that was to work on Gabriel's next album. Gabriel was working from an exciting, varied palette: guest artists (and this is still probably his most star-studded album) drop in and out, never once detracting from the overall sound and shape of the record.

The choice of producers and players made the album much more organic-sounding than its predecessors. "There was just the right amount, for the first time, of letting Peter-be-Peter to unleash his creativities while having top shelf engineering and production talent that held things together without getting in the way," says Larry Fast. "Steve and Hugh provided a very good balance in coordinating and capturing Peter's creativity without impressing their own obvious stamp on it." The album featured a considerable amount of innovation, and certainly for Gabriel's writing, the drum machine was key. "The creative work was advanced more by the programmable drum machine which was new and had been used by Peter as a core to his writing process for the first time," Fast adds.

Also on the album was someone who would become one of Gabriel's longest serving players, David Rhodes. Gabriel had met Rhodes through his band, Random Hold. Originally entitled Manscheinen, the group were formed around former Dulwich College alumni Rhodes and David Ferguson, who met in 1976 at a concert by 801, Roxy Music's Phil

Manzanera and Brian Eno's occasional side project. After an early interview by Allan Jones in *Melody Maker* that trumpeted their ability and innovation, the group were signed by Polydor in 1979.

Random Hold had been spotted by Tony Smith and Gail Colson. Smith signed them to Hit And Run for publishing, and Colson signed them to Gailforce Management, the name she had chosen for her new company. The group arrived to record at Gabriel's barn in early 1979, to find it flooded. Although the two had met at a Rock Garden show earlier that year, the first sight that Rhodes had of Gabriel was him digging a ditch with two roadies to drain the water off. The carpets were saturated, but the band – Rhodes, Ferguson, Bill MacCormick and drummer David Leach – rehearsed for several days. Impressed with what he saw, Gabriel asked Rhodes to assist him on the recording of what was to become *Melt*.

"Going into the same barn some months later was much more daunting," Rhodes recalled on his website. "At least the first time I had been with my friends. This time Peter had a mobile studio there, with the producer, engineer, and musicians Jerry Marotta and John Giblin. I felt most inept when we started up, as the standard of playing was so high, but Peter was kind and supportive, and really helped me to get through it."

One of the key aspects of the relationship boiled down to simply this: "Maybe it was just the fact that I didn't play like most other guitar players, because I couldn't; I was technically so inept that I was more interested in ideas and sounds." The partnership has continued through to 2013. The interest in ideas and sounds was to come to the fore on this recording, and remain the central tenet in Gabriel's career for all future recordings.

Whereas *Car* was the sound of an artist finding his feet, and *Scratch* was experimentation, still very much within the standard rock format, this third album was the first full cohesive solo work recorded by Gabriel. The album contains two of the most significant pieces in his work, 'Intruder' and 'Biko'. The tracks book-end the album, and offer the fullest picture of Gabriel's manifesto.

'Intruder' was Gabriel at his most sonically adventurous. He was determined not to have any cymbals on the album, finding them too splashy and detracting from the core of rhythm. In Gabriel's permanent role as an ex-drummer, it was the percussion that mattered more than anything.

"Peter had spoken to me about the no-cymbals idea even before the first album was recorded," Larry Fast says. "But I suspect that the first two producers saw that as too outside of their comfort zone to allow. Steve, with Hugh's engineering, embraced the concept. That was a welcome departure." Gabriel had asked his old friend Phil Collins to come and experiment with some drum sounds for the new album. Collins was initially sceptical about Gabriel's demands for cymbals to be dropped. "I told him that there are times when using cymbals is good," he said later. "Yet he remained steadfast in wanting no metal on the album whatsoever, so I said 'all right' and got along with it."

"The worst thing you can say to a creative person, I think, is 'You can do anything'," Gabriel said in 1977. "That is the kiss of death. You should say to them, 'You can't do this. You definitely can't do that. And under no circumstances can you do that.' Then they'll start thinking in a different, more creative way." Removing and withdrawing, forcing the situation. Gabriel's motto when recording the album was simple: no middle ground.

It was due to this lack of cymbals that Collins began thrashing around to a Gabriel song entitled 'Marguerita' and, so accustomed to using cymbals, was hitting the air when he would have been playing a cymbal. Gabriel suggested that he hit the drum when he would have traditionally and instinctively gone for the cymbal. Padgham, delighted that they would not have to worry about the resonance of the crashing metal, was, as a result, able to place microphones closer to the drum kit. Padgham was aware of the ambience of the room contributing to the unusual sound that he was receiving. Running the blare through the studio's pioneering Solid State Logic (SSL) console, Padgham fed the compressed sound through a noise gate, which led to the reverberation stopping abruptly and strikingly rather than continuing on, creating a strange, loud and unsettling sound.

Padgham was to say in 2006, "When he stopped playing it sucked the big sound of the room into nothing." The revelation that the studio itself could be part of the sound of the record was something that appealed greatly to Gabriel, and the technological advance of the desk added fully to it. "The B series installed there had the built-in dynamic section noise gates which allowed that 'drum sound' to happen." Fast recalls. "I loved the live sound of the UK studios, especially in contrast to the very dead sounding spaces that were being designed and built in the US at the time. It's not exciting to me recording in a carpet-walled anechoic chamber."

Gabriel took the rhythm track straight back to Ashcombe House where he had set up a home studio, recording with the Manor Mobile and began composing what was to become 'Intruder'. The loud, aggressive 'boom, boom, tsh, boom' sound is the first thing the listener hears. It seemed at once revolutionary. 'Solsbury Hill' it ain't. Although similar to some of the drum sounds being achieved by Tony Thompson in CHIC by Nile Rodgers, Bernard Edwards and Bob Clearmountain thanks to the ambience at New York's Power Station studio, Collins and Padgham's experimentation at Gabriel's insistence set a template for Eighties pop to follow. "I remember Phil coming in to the rehearsals for *Duke* (Genesis' 1980 album) with a tape of the drum loop they'd done," Tony Banks recalls. "With the gated reverb. Phil played it to us, and he told us Peter was writing a song on top of it. I thought it was fantastic."

The sound was of course popularised the following year when Collins and Padgham worked together on Collins' debut solo album, *Face Value*. 'In the Air Tonight' – a song that took the menacing mood of 'Intruder' – became a hit of huge global import, and the drum break at 3.41 in the song has arguably become Collins' best-known contribution to popular music. Later, Gabriel was, by unknowing souls, accused of plagiarising the sound that he had been instrumental in creating.

The sonic possibilities opened up by the removal of metals was acute. It gave the record a cavernous vacancy that could at once be filled with eerie otherworldly noises, most often Gabriel's vocal tics, or random percussion. With its tense, claustrophobic sound built around the drum pattern, Morris Pert's strange percussion and quirky xylophone solo, Fast's unsettling synths and Rhodes' scratching noises on the fret board of his acoustic guitar over Gabriel's block chords on piano, 'Intruder' drew the line between past and present. Gabriel's deranged, monotone whispered vocal demonstrated how his role-playing had developed from the amateur dramatics of, say, 'The Battle Of Epping Forest', seven years earlier. "There's a transvestite element, a clothes fetish," Gabriel told John Doran in 2011. "There's part of me in that but there's also a rape metaphor. It's definitely dark but real. I always used to enjoy performing it."

If the opening wasn't strange enough in itself, the record swooped into 'No Self Control', a blacker-than-pitch view of schizophrenia and paranoia. With the dense, looped guitar of Robert Fripp (making it his third consecutive appearance on a Gabriel album) providing the loud introduction and then the melody veritably floating on the sea of Morris

Pert's xylophone, 'No Self Control' was bizarre. Gabriel's maniacal *sprechgesang*, a spoken-sung whisper is supported by the track's remarkably insistent backing vocals, provided by Gabriel's new friend and collaborator, Kate Bush.

Bush was to add backing vocals to both 'No Self Control' and, importantly, 'Games Without Frontiers'. Gabriel first met Bush when he guested at the memorial concert for Bill Duffield, her 21-year-old lighting engineer who had previously worked for Gabriel. Duffield died from injuries sustained from a fall after the opening show on Bush's first and only UK tour, at Poole, in Dorset on April 1979. A memorial concert was planned at the end of Bush's tour on May 12 at Hammersmith Odeon. The evening was an emotional *tour de force*. Gabriel, with Cockney Rebel avatar Steve Harley, who too had worked with Duffield, duetted with Kate Bush on versions of her recent hits, 'Them Heavy People' (where both men dressed as Bush's dancers in raincoats and mackintoshes) and 'The Man With The Child In His Eyes'. Bush joined Gabriel on a version of his still-to-be released 'I Don't Remember' and they all sang a version of Beatles standard, 'Let It Be', to close.

Gabriel and Bush hit it off immediately. Bush had built a reputation for writing quirky songs with stunning and obscure narratives sung with a passionate exuberance that belied her teenage years. Like Gabriel, she seemed to operate outside the music industry, although, being signed to EMI and having enjoyed a number one hit with her debut single 'Wuthering Heights' in early 1978, she was definitely at the heart of it. The meeting with Peter Gabriel had a profound effect on her.

Gabriel would appear on Bush's TV Christmas special that December, recorded in October 1979 at Pebble Mill Studios in Birmingham. The pair duetted on Roy Harper's 'Another Day' and Gabriel sang a heartfelt, emotional version of 'Here Comes The Flood'. Their association would continue, with Bush clearly influenced by Gabriel's ability to follow his heart and merge art with rock. "I'm sure she was influenced a lot by Peter, and subsequently she went on and made art her career," Steve Lillywhite told Bush's biographer, Graeme Thomson.

The mollifying minute-and-a-half interlude 'Start', a showcase for regarded British jazz saxophonist Dick Morrissey, at once ameliorates the strangeness and discomfort provided by 'No Self Control'. As Morrissey extemporises over Gabriel and Fast's synthesisers, it is the closest the album came to easy listening; a brief moment of respite before the discord at the end of it tumbles into 'I Don't Remember', a song that had been around since early 1978, and was frequently included in Gabriel's live set. Dave Marsh later commented in *Rolling Stone* on the pairing of the two tracks: "The solace of Dick Morrissey's sax solo – the record's one moment of pure sweetness – is immediately devastated by the goose-stepping bass drum and interrogative terror of 'I Don't Remember', which smacks down hope with the rubber hose of the third degree." The traumatic loss-of-memory number kept in pace with the totalitarian threat that seemed to hang over popular culture at this juncture (see also Pink Floyd's *The Wall* and the paranoia of new synthesiser phenomenon Gary Numan), a reflection of the conservative backlash to the seemingly doomed liberalism espoused in the Sixties and Seventies.

Producer Steve Lillywhite did indeed come good on Dave Gregory's throw-away line and Gregory was to spend a day in the studio (October 16, 1979) adding detail to Gabriel's painstaking working process. "Sure enough, I got the call from Steve," Gregory says. "Peter had been asking for a wiry rhythm guitar sound on a track, not heavy or broken up." The day did not get off to a good start for him: "I turned up an hour and a half late, which is the worst thing in the world you can do, yet Peter was so accommodating and friendly. I played my 1963 Stratocaster through a Roland JC-120 with a chorus effect switch on it with a stereo pan, something that Peter had suggested. He told me that he couldn't get enough power on the downbeat, and we experimented with tuning so I was playing the chords that Peter had arrived at on his piano and hitting the open strings.

"I played to a track with Tony Levin's stick, Jerry's drums and some of Larry's electronics on it. That was it. The track before I added anything was remarkable. The power chords in the choruses were played on a 1963 Gibson ES-335 through my 1962 Fender Tremolux amp, in regular concert tuning. Many years later I discovered that my old 335 is the same guitar formerly owned by Eddie Phillips, late of The Creation. There is, I think, a symbiotic beauty in the knowledge that it links 'Genesis' with 'The Creation'! It was a little bit nerve wracking – having to get into this groove from scratch. I can hear my nervous twitches all over it." The combination of Gregory's lucid jangle with Rhodes' rhythm guitar and Fripp's powerful lead made the track one of the most propulsive of

Gabriel's career. It also demonstrated how the new toy, the Fairlight CMI synthesiser could be incorporated into conventional rock, with its sampling of bricks being banged together and milk bottles being smashed, adding to the otherworldliness of its sound.

Gabriel was one of the first musicians in the UK to use the Fairlight, which, within a matter of years would completely transform the way music was made. The synthesiser, which could sample natural sounds and play them back at a variety of pitches and tones, seemed truly revolutionary. It had been invented in Australia by electronics engineer Peter Vogel and synthesiser enthusiast Kim Ryrie. They took its name from the hydrofoils that crossed Sydney Harbour outside their office window. "The instrument only showed up for a day here and there, already well into the recording," Fast recalls. "It was very useful for its sampling capabilities, but these were laid into already existing songs."

As a single computer was in the region of £10,000, this wasn't a commitment that could be entered into lightly: Vogel and Ryrie spent a week at the recording sessions when they continued at Ashcombe House, and, as a result, the synthesiser was used on *Melt*, and Gabriel agreed to distribute it in the UK. Gabriel invested in the Fairlight and persuaded his cousin, Stephen Paine, to come in with him. The company Syco Systems was established by him, importing and distributing the instruments in the UK. "It was one of the early Fairlights, and in typical Gabriel style, you know, if I want a pint of milk I buy the cow," Gabriel told *Uncut* magazine in 2007.

'Family Snapshot' was a standout track: it stemmed from Gabriel reading *An Assassin's Diary* by Arthur Bremmer, who shot Alabama Governor George Wallace in May 1972. He did not shoot at the Governor for political reasons, although he was a controversial figure of the far right, but simply, as Gabriel put it, because Bremmer "was obsessed with the idea of fame. He was aware of news broadcasts all over the world and was trying to time the assassination to hit the early evening news in the States and late night in Europe to get maximum coverage". The book also inspired Paul Schrader to write the screenplay for Martin Scorsese's 1976 film, *Taxi Driver*.

'Family Snapshot' ends with the assassin-narrator going back to his childhood, and Gabriel for one of the first times on record introduces the listener to some explicit psychotherapy. "It is a film device, but I don't think I've seen it done in a rock song before," Gabriel told Phil Sutcliffe. "As to the psychology of it, all that I can say is that some clichés are true – patterns of behaviour begun in childhood do carry through, I see that in my own life." Seeing that in my own life: although Gabriel had been open and emotional in his writing before, the effects of the EST training that he had attended with Jill and Richard Macphail were beginning to permeate his work. Dave Gregory also played on 'Family Snapshot'. "It was more conventional. Peter wanted a bit of chunky rhythm guitar, so I played my Strat through a Mesa-Boogie amp." He was thrilled to contribute. "It was probably the best musical company that I've ever been in."

The recording process at the Townhouse and Ashcombe was punctuated by the occasional drop-ins of Gabriel's US A&R man, John Kalodner. Kalodner, whose website today bears the legend "He is his own one-man act when it comes to Artists & Repertoire", was a heavily bearded Californian, whose job as Atlantic's Head of A&R was one he took very seriously. Kalodner had an extremely impressive track record with bands such as Foreigner, and he had worked with both Genesis and Gabriel in the past. He loved Gabriel's first album, as to him it was, as Gabriel told writer Mick Gold in January 1981, 'on the money'. The second album was where the 'English weirdoes' were tolerated, but Kalodner was unsure about this new direction.

Kalodner's presence, although greeted with the customary extreme politeness, was a divisive one. He talked Gabriel and the band through a new track, the more conventionally rocky 'And Through The Wire', and instructed them how to make it sound more like the Doobie Brothers. Manager Gail Colson left the studio in disgust. Gabriel's reaction to this advice was simple: he called in Paul Weller, then still an angry young man fronting The Jam, that most English of new wave bands. Weller was in an adjoining studio at the Townhouse. He added, in *Sounds*' Phil Sutcliffe's words, "some distinctly non-Californian chords". Steve Lillywhite recalls the team playing pranks on Kalodner such as turning the heating down when he was coming, even though he expressly liked warm rooms.

'Games Without Frontiers' was chosen as the album's lead single. It was a remarkable track, taking the template of 'No Self Control' and rendering it commercial. Gabriel was inspired by the daftness of the long-running primetime BBC TV programme *It's A Knockout*, the British version of the pan-European show *Jeux Sans Frontiers*. Described as a 'school sports day for adults', the premise of the show was that teams from all over Europe would dress up in silly outfits and perform a series of equally silly challenges, invariably involving greasy poles, pools of icy water and the likelihood that participants would humiliate themselves. The idea for the programme allegedly came from French President Charles De Gaulle, who commented that a fun competition between everyday people of France and Germany would lead to a greater understanding of both nations' cultures. Gabriel thought the symbolism of the show was ripe for exploring, and that all of this jollity cloaked simmering resentment. The threat of old rivalries was never far from the surface. He wanted to show that war was still the silliest game of all.

One of the best assessments of the futility of aggrandising nationalism ever to reach the UK Top Five, the song offered a fine example of Gabriel's new sonic landscape. With its drum machine, unusual synthesiser sounds and whistling provided by Gabriel, Lillywhite and Padgham, it was a jarring listen, buoyed up by one of Gabriel's most commercial choruses. Arguably the most memorable part of the song is Kate Bush's repetition of the phrase 'Jeux Sans Frontiers' which many misheard as 'she's so obvious' – it contributed to the finely esoteric sound of the track. Gabriel could experiment and still deliver one of the biggest hits of his career.

With its full-on sonic assault, 'Not One Of Us' is, alongside 'I Don't Remember' and 'And Through The Wire', one of the last vestiges of conventional rock on the album. Over John Giblin and Jerry Marotta's taut rhythm section, lyrically the song explores the subject of fear of the 'other', whether it be racism, feminism or homophobia, talking about how unwelcome others are in the 'land of the blind.' 'Lead A Normal Life' suggested mental illness. The sister track to 'No Self Control', it pits a repeated nine-note piano riff from Gabriel against the repetitive march of Morris Pert's xylophone, with hints of Marotta's drums and Rhodes' best squalling Robert Fripp impression. After a minute and a half, Gabriel intones the song's six lines about a patient in a rehabilitative unit, who has clearly undergone some significant trauma. After less than 30 seconds of vocals, we return to this gentle, repetitive instrumental punctuated by a brief cacophony of guitar tempest, which resembles a desperate cry. Although the lyric and the vocal delivery is a trifle RD Laing meets Monty

Python, it is a completely chilling number that offers the listener little hope whatsoever.

But ultimately the album, for its entire sonic advance, is about one track; the closer, 'Biko', the song that would have the biggest significance for Gabriel and his future direction and which marked the beginning of the next phase of his career. He had been finding rock rhythms progressively limiting, and by setting this slow African-inspired rhythm, it created a hypnotic pattern. "The rhythm is the spine of the piece," he said on *The South Bank Show* in 1982. "If you change that the body that forms around is changed as well. The style of writing which I was attracted to put with it was very different to what I would have done with a normal rock rhythm, if that had come from a regular rock pattern on a rhythm box or a rock drummer. A lot of rock rhythms are built up around four in a bar, and a lot of non-European work more on a pulse basis – and they perhaps have different instruments which are like pieces of a jigsaw which form a pattern, a whole, of which an individual part cannot provide you with. The variation and the range are a lot more stimulating." He thrived on the different responses that different rhythms gave; one morning Gabriel was trying to listen to his beloved Radio 4, but the station had switched to Long Wave radio, so he began flicking through radio stations. He came across a Dutch radio station playing the soundtrack to the Stanley Baker/Juliet Prowse film, *Dingaka*.

Gabriel was mesmerised by the rhythm he heard, which he taped off the radio before eventually finding the soundtrack album from a specialist record store in London's Dean Street. It was the feel of the rhythm that truly captivated him. Gabriel had noted in his diary the death of student activist Steven Biko at the hands of the South African police in September 1977. His death, which had come after 22 hours of torture and then manacled transportation to a prison hospital, was subsequently explained by police as a result of a hunger strike. Like many white liberals with an awareness of events in South Africa, Gabriel was shocked by the brutality and the subsequent cover-up by police, and decided to capture his thoughts in song.

As Dorian Lynskey points out in his fabulously exhaustive book on the history of protest songs, *33 Revolutions Per Minute*, Gabriel was not the first musician to reference Steve Biko – in 1978 alone, he had been mentioned by Tom Paxton in 'The Death Of Stephen Biko', by Tappa Zukie on

'Tribute To Steve Biko', and Steel Pulse's 'Biko's Kindred Lament'. Perhaps closest to home was the reference by friend, associate, near-neighbour and fellow traveller Peter Hammill, who had cut the disturbing 'A Motor Bike In Afrika' on his *The Future Now* album, which contained the line "the bodies of Biko and the Soweto poor". But this was different – Gabriel was by far the most mainstream of these artists. Peter Hammill denies that 'A Motorbike In Afrika' would have influenced Gabriel. "I don't think so," Hammill told me. "Anyone who was awake at the time would have been aware of the issues. We just happened to be among the first articulating them into (near) mainstream song."

Gabriel was acutely aware of his shortcomings and lack of authenticity to become a champion of causes in far off countries, but that in no way blunted his passion and sincerity for the subject. He was unsure whether he should release it. It was ultimately his friend, Tom Robinson, who urged Gabriel on to release the song. Thankfully, it was one of the greatest decisions Gabriel made and it took him on a whole new course.

He told *Sounds* magazine in 1980: "It's a white, middle-class, ex-public schoolboy, domesticated, English person observing his own reactions from afar. It seemed impossible to me that the South Africans had let him be killed when there had been so much international publicity about his imprisonment. He was very intelligent, well reasoned and *not* full of hate. His writings seemed very solid in a way that polarised politics often doesn't."

"There had been a tremendous amount of shock about his arrest, but no-one was expecting him to be killed," Gabriel told Terry Wogan at the time of the later re-release of 'Biko' in 1987 to coincide with the biopic of Biko's life, *Cry Freedom*. "Had he been allowed to live he could have been a great African statesman, perhaps . . . crystallised the hopes of a lot of young people in the way that Kennedy did in America and I think it's tragic the way his life was cut short . . .Through the story . . . and suffering of one individual, it's easier for a lot of people to understand what is going on."

Gabriel knew exactly what he was doing in releasing the track: "I don't want all musicians preaching at me all the time, but I think . . . it's the first universal language all round the world, young people listen to rock music and to have that attention and that possibility for giving out information and not to use it for anything other than saying who you laid last night is, I think, a waste of time." Gabriel returned to the theme in 2012, celebrating 30 years of his WOMAD festival: "Whether anyone was ready to listen to a political song from an ex-public-school, middle-class prog-rocker was something I had doubts about."

All of this lyrical content would have meant nothing without the remarkable musical setting Gabriel and his team put together to support it. With its portentous opening drum rhythm and drone guitar played by Rhodes, two notes on open strings on his Fender Jazzmaster, this was clearly very different to anything Gabriel had recorded to date. It was probably the ultimate expression of the album's 'no middle ground' policy. "Peter had the basic poetry of the song in mind," Larry Fast recalls. "He had already discovered the African vocal underpinnings on shortwave radio as well as becoming more openly concerned about the injustices found in South Africa at the time . . . not to mention all over the globe. The organic thunderous beat and drone underpinnings mask what is a quite electronic track. It came together rather quickly because there wasn't that much needed to make it effective. Anything more would have made for sonic clutter."

What added to the song's escalating pathos was the mass chant at the end, recorded by Larry Fast in Bath: "That was done by nearly everybody who could be recruited at Ashcombe. I ran the tape machine and engineered for a few minutes while Steve and Hugh joined the chorus. I even climbed up on the roof of the mobile recording truck to take a picture of the vocalists who were singing outside on the driveway in the open air." David Stopps, a great admirer of the song, thinks that the mass vocal had its origins a decade previously. Proving that nothing ever went to waste, it bore a strong similarity with the chant that Gabriel extemporised on the night of a Genesis show at the British Legion, Princes Risborough during an equipment failure on October 6, 1970.

The one problematic synthesiser sound proved to be the bagpipes that gave the song its incredible texture. "The drone patch lent itself to transformation into an electronic bagpipes sound," Fast says. "We liked it purely as a musical element, but what possible connection could there be from this most Scottish sound to South Africa? A little pre-Internet historical research on the Boer War turned up that the First and Second Battalion Royal Scots were in numerous military actions played into battle by their traditional pipers. The underpinnings of apartheid had bagpipes. The historical accuracy was preserved and the sound became a sonic signature in the song."

'Biko' set him on a course that would see Peter Gabriel become of the most impassioned campaigners for Civil Rights in popular music. "That song was my calling card, a 'come and get me' for anyone who had a cause," Gabriel joked in 2011. "Then Bono rung up and asked me if I wanted to be part of the Amnesty tour – I was able to meet a lot of the people. I got more and more engaged." Phil Sutcliffe, writing in *Sounds* could see that Gabriel had truly found his voice. "'Biko' is so honest you might even risk calling it Truth. Probably Gabriel's finest moment – and an exact reflection of the man. It's a balance of his reticence and his openness, countervailing forces in harmony. Through 'Biko' there's Gabriel saying 'Here I am.'" With his third solo album, Gabriel had indeed arrived.

* * *

The album was finished. Whereas Gail Colson knew Charisma in the UK would welcome anything that Gabriel did with open arms, she was aware of the, at best, indifference to, and, at worst, hatred for, the work of John Kalodner. So she took the record personally to New York to play it for the Atlantic hierarchy. "I think the biggest mistake I made was by saying that I wanted to come over and play the album to Ahmet Ertegun and Jerry Greenberg myself," Colson says. "John Kalodner had already been over to the UK to listen to 'work in progress' and hadn't liked what he heard. He didn't like the choice of Steve Lillywhite as producer or the Town House and their toilet facilities, if my memory is correct. He had put the poison in by the time I arrived with the finished album." In a tense session at the Atlantic offices on the Avenue Of The Americas in New York, the two senior Atlantic team players listened to the album in its entirety, something they hadn't done with any of his other albums, including with Genesis. After a silence, "Ahmet suggested that Peter might have had some sort of a breakdown during the writing of it. After a lunch break, they came up with the suggestion that they would let us have this album back and then, when he had come to his senses, they would have the option for the next one! I told them exactly what they could do with that suggestion, so they dropped him."

Writing in 2001, Ahmet Ertegun said: "We made two terrific solo albums with Peter, but then he delivered an album which some people were not so crazy about. So Jerry Greenberg decided to let him go and we released him from his contract. In retrospect, that was a big mistake. Peter is a great, visionary artist." But great visionary artists releasing complex material in 1980 did not chime with Atlantic; especially for Greenberg, who had had great success with releases that came from disco.

Gabriel was bemused but sanguine. "I gather Ahmet Ertegun, the chairman, thought it was quite arty but the A&R department told him it was undesirable, too esoteric," Gabriel said in 1980. Peter Gabriel signed to Mercury in the States for the album. Although Gabriel wasn't overly keen on being signed to them, he felt they worked really hard and did a good job. In retrospect, it wasn't that much of departure, but what it was was modern. It was about the now. "Apart from the album having no cymbals, I didn't see that much of a change in direction," Gail Colson adds. "In fact, it has always been my favourite album of them all."

★ ★ ★

The self-titled album was released on May 30, 1980. For its distinctive sleeve, Hipgnosis worked with Gabriel for the fourth and final time, creating one of their and Gabriel's most enduring, distinctive and disturbing images. Hipgnosis founder Storm Thorgerson had arrived at this system called a 'charismagraph', which could manipulate the images from a Polaroid camera when the ink was still wet. It arrived at strange wayward and distorted images, just like the music contained inside the sleeve. Gabriel's face was melting in front of his audience, suggesting the lack of self-control that one of the album's songs spoke about.

Gabriel looked like a cross between a bizarre candle and a relief map of high ground; a stroke victim, perhaps, at once normal, at once deeply, irrevocably disturbed. His striped shirt and severe haircut made him resemble an inmate at a mental institution, or, indeed, a prisoner at a concentration camp. It spoke of mental turmoil, a nervous breakdown, a failure to keep it all together, disintegration, standing too close to the fire, perhaps even, like Icarus, flying too close to the sun. As a result, the album picked up its colloquial title, *Melt*. For a man who had spent most of his career behind masks, here he was, with new honesty and directness. The mask was slipping.

The no-middle ground approach had truly worked: "It made decision-making easier," Larry Fast said. "That is a pitfall in creating multitrack recordings. Decisions can be put off for the mix and it tends to dilute the vision of the production. The absolutes of no middle ground eliminated the options that didn't have an exceptional 'personality'. No 'twee' sounds unless intended to be so. Fewer sounds with exceptional impact set off by the silence of spaces made the defining sound of the album. Getting there was easier by ruthlessly exorcising middling options during the creative recording process."

"When he started getting in to these albums, his arrangement skills, his flair for getting the right instrument in the right place became absolutely obvious," adds Anthony Phillips. "I think by the end that was what he'd been trying to get Genesis to do and maybe got frustrated because the others weren't prepared to listen or couldn't see his vision. If some of his songs had been interpreted by Genesis, they would have been more rushed and heavier in the chord department, and they wouldn't have had that lean, gripping quality that they have."

In the main, the lean and gripping *Melt* was rapturously received; given it was a challenging listen. The album went to number one in the UK in June, where it remained for two weeks, giving Gabriel his first chart-topping album. Dave Marsh, writing in *Rolling Stone* on the album's eventual US release in September 1980, said: "Lucid and driven, Peter Gabriel's third solo album sticks in the mind like the haunted heroes of the best *film noirs*. With the obsessiveness of *The Big Sleep* (or, more aptly, Jean-Luc Godard's *Breathless*, since Gabriel is nothing if not self-conscious about his sources), the new LP's exhilaration derives from paranoia, yet its theme isn't fear so much as overwhelming guilt. If rock'n'roll is capable of comprehending original sin, then Peter Gabriel might be the man for the job." However not all critics were appreciative – although the review was largely onside, *Rolling Stone* continued, "His tribute to poet and black nationalist Steven (*sic*) Biko, who was apparently murdered by South African police, is a muddle. The melody and dynamics of 'Biko' are irresistible, yet what Gabriel has to say is mainly sentimental. He says he can't sleep at night because 'the man is dead'. *Why* can't he sleep?"

There is a fascinating critique of the album on an obscure website, *Heart Of A Punk, Soul Of A Rasta*: saying that another great shaper in the making of the album was his hanging out with and trying to assimilate with punks on his 1978 tour. It says from a 2010 perspective that, "He managed to cram all of punk's pet topics into *P3*: alienation, nihilism, introspection, protest, obsession and murder." It's absolutely true; of all of Gabriel's work, it is the one that always sounds fresh and surprising.

Brian James wrote on *Popmatters.com* at the time of the album's SACD release in 2003: "The majority of the tracks are character sketches of people on society's fringe: assassins, stalkers, and various stripes of the mentally ill. The accompanying music is so enjoyable that it raises the question as to whether the use of such themes exploits or glamorises human suffering, but on more than enough occasions, Gabriel hits the perfect notes to communicate his ingenuous empathy." Ingenuous empathy; that is absolutely the thing with *Melt*; the listener is completely taken along by Gabriel's meticulous attention to detail in his lyrics and characters. David Bowie biographer David Buckley believes that *Melt* sounds Bowie-esque; "'Start', with its saxophone, 'Intruder' has Bowie-type themes of the outsider, 'Games Without Frontiers' pre-dates the *Scary Monsters* style." For the first time in his career Gabriel was truly setting the sonic agenda.

* * *

For Dave Gregory, his contributions to 'I Don't Remember' and 'Family Snapshot' were the sum of his involvement on the album. He was asked if he could return for a further day's work on a track that Gabriel had in development. At this point XTC were finally achieving the commercial breakthrough they had waited two albums to achieve. The lead single from *Drums And Wires*, 'Making Plans For Nigel' was climbing the UK singles chart and his group had an opportunity to take part in *Top Of The Pops*, then the crown prince of UK mainstream television music shows. "I couldn't believe it," Gregory recalls. "A year previously I had been delivering parcels around Bristol, and now I had to make a decision to perform on *Top Of The Pops* or record again with Peter Gabriel." Gregory played on *Top Of the Pops* and it ushered in a three-year period where XTC became the UK's leading art-rock band. He was deeply disappointed when he realised working with Gabriel would have given him the opportunity to work with another of his heroes, Todd Rundgren. That was rectified in spectacular fashion when he produced XTC's *Skylarking* in 1985. Gabriel and Gregory's paths were to cross again. Gabriel came to XTC's pre-Christmas Swindon concert in 1979, and years later the two met again at Real World studios, although Gregory ruefully admitted that Gabriel "probably didn't remember who I was".

"*Melt* runs the gamut of all emotion," Dave Gregory concludes. "It begins with a burglary and ends with an anthem, with all human points in between." It is commonly seen by many as his best and most sustained work. "I was knocked out by the third album," Gabriel's future producer David Lord said. "It was one of the most interesting things I've ever heard soundwise: a knockout."

Gabriel took part in one of his most infamous interviews with *NME* writer Paul Morley, who in the style of the paper at the time, played up every tic and inconsistency of Gabriel's persona. Ruminating on middle class repression, he wondered if Gabriel felt that life was complicated, and wondered if he hid behind his music. Illustrated by severely lit pictures of him, it attempted to suggest that Gabriel was in some way damaged. "I think it's very important . . . in this business . . . to function . . . with dignity . . . and I don't always think that I'm clean and honest, but I like to think I'm trying," Gabriel said.

Gabriel had previewed some of the material from the album over five dates between May and August 1979, including performances at both Glastonbury and Reading Festivals. He returned on August 24, 1979 to Friars in Aylesbury, with Phil Collins as his drummer; the first time the pair had played there together since 1973. "Phil was going through one of his long beard phases," David Stopps remembers. "He joined Peter playing bongos which he wore around his neck. That was in 1979; he'd obviously developed his stagecraft and songwriting and everything else and then he took off in a very big way."

The full tour that supported the album got underway in February 1980: The *Tour Of China 1984* was a theatrical tour de force, with the band in striking jumpsuits and Gabriel appearing through the audience. The tour programme was a small pocket book designed as a replica of Mao-Tse Tung's 1966 *Little Red Book*. John Ellis from The Vibrators joined the band on guitar, with regulars Jerry Marotta, Larry Fast and Tony Levin. Writer David Buckley said Ellis told him that Gabriel "seemed very self aware that he was a posh boy who wanted to butch himself up a bit." And the performances were very masculine indeed.

"I saw Gabriel in 1980 in the Empire in Liverpool," Buckley notes. "They dimmed the lights and people walked in front of you with torches and people couldn't quite see what was going on, and then Gabriel just appeared as this clambering, Gollum-like creature from the back of the audience, and just crawled over everyone to get to the stage, as 'Intruder' was playing. I thought it was one of the best things I'd ever seen." It was if Gabriel was expressly suggesting that he was the same as his audience, breaking down the showbusiness fourth wall and challenging the conventions of a rock concert.

* * *

When 'Games Without Frontiers' became Gabriel's biggest hit in Britain, Atlantic tried to buy the album back, but Charisma declined. The recently formed Geffen label stepped in. David Geffen had been an industry mover and shaker in America for the best part of a decade, from initially working at the William Morris Agency to becoming the personal manager of Crosby, Stills & Nash. Ahmet Ertegun was sufficiently impressed with him to invite him to found the record label Asylum in 1970. In 1980, Geffen returned to the music industry and founded Geffen, with a roster that included Donna Summer and John Lennon's comeback album, *Double Fantasy*. Gabriel liked David Geffen's contracts, and attitude to artists. He loved the idea that the artist could get more involved. Geffen had enough power at Warner Brothers, the label's parent company, to have a degree of autonomy.

"I always found David Geffen very charming," Gail Colson recalls. "Apart from the courting and romancing of us and the negotiation of the deal, he was not hands on on a day-to-day basis and my main dealings were with the President of the company Eddie Rosenblatt." Ironically, one of the employees that Geffen siphoned off from Atlantic was John Kalodner. "He was at Geffen but had nothing to do with Peter and I; he did accompany us to the Grammys once, I remember but other than that, nothing." *Melt* would later be reissued on Geffen, and Gabriel's subsequent albums would appear on the imprint stateside.

* * *

Gabriel's willingness to experiment was underlined by another bizarre piece of side business. 'Animals Have More Fun' was produced by and co-written for Jimmy Pursey, the erudite south Londoner who had become an unwitting figurehead for the Oi! movement with his band

Sham 69. Sham 69 opened for Gabriel on the Belgian leg of his 1978 tour, and the two had hit it off. Pursey wanted Gabriel to produce him; this would indeed happen the following year, when he and Gabriel wrote the 'Animals Have More Fun' single together.

"I engineered that session with Jimmy Pursey at Crescent, in Bath." David Lord recalls. "He wanted a chorus on that. So he just walked out into Walcot Street and stopped mothers and little kids and got them to come into the studio. Pursey wouldn't work without a videotape of [then-recent Stanley Kubrick film] *The Shining* showing in the background. And we only had a rather old monitor, which had this high-pitch whistle on it, which to this day I don't know if you can hear it on the record, we couldn't get rid of it. He had it on with the sound down looped in the background – and then one morning he just completely disappeared; Peter found him on the platform of Bath Spa station. I think he seemed to be having a mini-breakdown."

Gabriel's work with Pursey shows his generosity of spirit and willingness to hep others, something he had done with countless support acts, and develop further as the Eighties progressed.

# 15: A New Age Of Electronic Skiffle: *Security*

*"I'm certain the third world is going to have an increasing influence on our culture, and in music, a very vigorous hybrid will be produced which is based on this non-European influence and new technology which is going to get very, very cheap and this facility will open up a new age of electronic skiffle."*

Peter Gabriel, 1982

*"Peter Gabriel has a new reputation as a thoughtful solo artist who takes immense care in writing and producing his own material. He's had big popular hits, but he has never turned his successes into formulas."*

Melvyn Bragg, *South Bank Show*, 1982

THERE is ample justification to suggest that 1982 was the most seismic year in Peter Gabriel's life. He began it as a solo performer embarking on his fourth record but by the end of the year his personal life would be in turmoil, he would have helped stage a groundbreaking musical festival that hemorrhaged money and culminated in death threats, and would ultimately headline a concert with his old band, Genesis. The album he was to deliver was one of his most musically complex and challenging and it split its audience straight down the middle.

Between the release of *Melt* and its clarion call, 'Biko' and what was to become his fourth solo album, *Security*, it hadn't just been Gabriel who had become increasingly interested in rhythms of the world. In November 1980, Talking Heads had released the Brian Eno-produced *Remain In Light*, a record so absorbed in African polyrhythms that it even came with a reading list of African fiction. Continuing on a similar theme, Talking Heads' leader David Byrne made an album with Eno comprising entirely of found sounds, played over drum loops and live rhythms. 1981's *My Life In The Bush Of Ghosts*, its title taken from a 1954 novel by Nigerian author Amos Tutuola, was a groundbreaking record, one that showed there was a different way of building music beyond a directly compositional approach.

Gabriel knew that his next album would absorb all of these new influences. In early 1980 he retreated to Bath and began work with producer David Lord, who had mixed the sound on the *Tour Of China 1984*. A considerable amount of money was spent on equipping the studio at Gabriel's home, Ashcombe House, which, according to Larry Fast, would soon become known as 'Shabby Road'. After initial recordings at Crescent Studios in Bath, including basic guide tracks on the Linn Drum, it was to be the first time that Gabriel worked entirely in his own space, and he wittily commented in 2007 that he knew then they had done something good, because "the cows would come and lick the windows". "Ashcombe was being rebuilt and we were trying to work around that," Lord said. "I bought a second-hand Neve desk which was being done up, and so we used an old desk and the Manor mobile for a while."

Bath had become something of a low-key art hub in the six years Gabriel had lived there. Getting on with the job was key in this beautiful city whose architecture, especially the famous Crescent and Roman Baths, attracts tourists in their droves. "I'd started to meet people locally in Bath," Gabriel's new producer, and Crescent Studios owner, David Lord said, "because I had this studio, the word got round. There wasn't really anything locally. I had famous people turning up and recording albums in my bedroom. People like John Renbourn, some guys from Judas Priest; all the local punk bands and stuff getting played by John Peel. This led to me meeting the guys from Stackridge, who became The Korgis and early recordings of Tears For Fears. Hugh Cornwell was around as well; it was quite a vibrant scene: and of course we had the live venue Moles, where lots of bands would come down and try out their new material. I was the only guy around with the tape machine. I was also doing a lot of things locally, conducting orchestras and choirs, and teaching at Bath University. Eventually I had to give that side of things up because the recording thing was taking up all of my time. In theory I'm really a composer – that's why I moved to Bath for a little peace and quiet, but that didn't happen."

"It was the reverse of the Soho years. For a start there's a kind of North/South Bath divide, strange as it may seem," Peter Hammill, a near-neighbour recalls. "And secondly, most of the people who gravitated here (or were born here, in Tears For Fears' case) are essentially pretty private. In our different ways all of us have just got on with the job."

Gabriel allowed cameras to capture his work in progress, though no one dreamed the album would take 16 months to complete. It would result in an appearance on the prestigious Melvyn Bragg-fronted UK arts programme *The South Bank Show* at the end of October, 1982. The show dealt in high-to-middlebrow arts, and its standard subject was Laurence Olivier, Tom Stoppard, and Woody Allen. Paul McCartney, Talking Heads and Elvis Costello had previously been featured from the world of pop music. The special on Gabriel was the third show in the arts magazine's sixth season, behind a two-part in-depth profile of Olivier.

A fascinating film, it charted the recording of what was to become *Security* and Gabriel's quest to find different influences and inspirations. He was listening to Afro-Caribbean and Aboriginal music and offered the telling statement, "I will steal certain key elements" as he assembled a whole suitcase full of cassettes from different sources, including taping music from the television programme *The World About Us*. "I wasn't surprised when he started getting into African rhythms," Mike Rutherford says. "Pete has always been a frustrated drummer and he was very rhythmically aware."

The atmosphere at Lord's Crescent Studio was relaxed and informal. Gabriel would often drop in to finish stuff, or remix. "When Peter recorded in Bath, he was incredibly open," Lord recalls. "The door to the control room opened out into the street, and we'd keep it open because it was often hot – people would walk in and not realise who Peter was. I recall Kate Bush coming through remixing something for her TV show; they were working on 'Another Day', the Roy Harper track they did."

On *The South Bank Show*, Gabriel came across as a passionate advocate for third world music, going as far as to say, "I'm certain the third world is going to have an increasing influence on our culture, and in music, a very vigorous hybrid will be produced which is based on this non-European influence and new technology which is going to get very very cheap and this facility will open up a new age of electronic skiffle." The documentary caught Gabriel's methodically painstaking processes on camera. It showed Gabriel building up his songs from rhythms, and how 'San Jacinto' was built up from an Ethiopian folk song. Gabriel and Lord are seen working at keyboards. Lord would work on the demo with Gabriel to produce an outline which the band would fill in.

* * *

David Lord had met Gabriel originally in 1977, when Gabriel asked him if he would transcribe some of the music of *Car* for the band to play live. A classically trained musician, Lord had set up Crescent Studios where a frequent visitor was Gabriel's old Charisma ally, Peter Hammill. "I'd just moved down to Bath," Lord said. "I wasn't involved at all in rock'n'roll. I'd been Head of Music at a contemporary dance college in London, the Laban. I got a knock at the door one day and it was Peter; he had a tape recorder with him and he wanted some tapes copied. And then he asked me to do some transcriptions for Genesis sheet music for publication. I used to tell my students that Mr Gabriel came to the door and they were all impressed. I honestly hadn't heard him then and I hadn't heard a note of Genesis. It was all a bit weird really."

Gabriel enjoyed the fact that Lord was completely outside of the rock 'n'roll world. As with the energising and challenging experience of working with new players for his albums and tours, he liked Lord's studied, methodical approach and the fact he knew little of his previous work. "I can remember being at a social evening at Peter's house one night, and we started playing charades. People were crawling around on all fours baa-ing and falling over and I had no idea what they were going on about; I'd never even heard the name *The Lamb Lies Down On Broadway*. Everybody was in fits of hysterics, and then in a while I ended up working with Peter, so it was all a bit strange."

Lord had joined Gabriel's 1980 tour as sound engineer, a role that the back-room man did not especially relish. "I'd never done live sound before on any level and all his crew and management were dead against it as you can imagine," Lord recalls. "We had some rehearsals at Shepperton; at the first warm up gig in Exeter, after one track all his support people came running up to me saying that it had never sounded so good and that it was the first time that they'd been able to hear the words so clearly, so it all seemed to go well. We were trying to get as close to the sound of the album as possible. I was using noise gates on individual drum mics, all of which is standard now, but it wasn't in those days; people were scoffing at this, but it all seemed to work. We used Pink Floyd's sound system, which they used for *The Wall* shows that summer, which had these huge sub-bass systems which you could put in at climatic moments, especially if Larry was doing a big keyboard solo. It would sound fantastic. People couldn't believe we made that sound system sound so good. I'd obviously made a success of the live stuff, and that's why Peter asked me to produce the album."

Not that Lord, as a producer, brought any particularly radical approach in with him: "The let-Peter-be-Peter approach that Steve Lillywhite had taken on *Melt* had worked very well," Larry Fast, who returned for his fourth album with Gabriel, recalls. "Hugh Padgham's engineering and emerging production sensibilities set the stage for the next project." Also present as the album progressed were Tony Levin, who by now had joined a reformed King Crimson with Robert Fripp, Jerry Marotta, David Rhodes and percussionist Morris Pert.

"I had never really produced anybody before," Lord continues. "I was really in at the deep end; I wasn't really sure how much to stick my oar in. The vast bulk of my contribution was before I got into the studio; I'd spent months at his house with him and a piano and a tape recorder – we had all these ideas and we were basically trying to piece songs together out of them. It was a lot of time."

The documentary also contains one of the first glimpses of the Fairlight CMI that Gabriel had used since 1979, and had begun to be popularised in music on Kate Bush's *Never For Ever*. It had made its debut on *Melt*. Gabriel almost mirrors exactly what broadcaster Kieran Prendeville had done on BBC TV's *Tomorrow's World* a couple of years earlier, selecting samples with the electronic pen on the screen. Gabriel is having great fun, smashing car windscreens and televisions and capturing the sound of them on tape.

Jerry Marotta was one of the first musicians to arrive at Ashcombe House in summer 1981 to get the recordings from demos to finished material. Marotta emphasised the need for the human element in the rhythm: "a machine is a machine – it's very hard to program emotion into a machine . . . it's important for me – you can feel that emotion – the machine and I split the work 50/50. We both work very hard."

*The South Bank Show* also offered insight into Gabriel's leisurely pace: "He's a slow worker and he likes to keep every possible option open for as long as he can." Lord said. "Peter moves at his own speed," Tony Levin said on the show. "I'm around to play croquet when he wants to play croquet," as Gabriel would often break for a game on the lawn. Gail Colson would drop by from time to time, but kept her presence to a minimum: "I used to visit him in the studio when I was invited but, to be honest, I prefer not to because if you are aware of exactly how much time they have spent on one particular track it makes you feel really bad when you have to tell them that the vocal should be more up in the mix." Colson acted as the contact with the outside world: "Gail would be cracking the whip most of the time; she was wonderful," Lord said. "I thought the world of her."

What Lord and Gabriel were left with at this early stage were 27 sixteen-minute tapes, and over seven hours of material. Different versions of 18 separate songs, several of which were running at over 10 minutes in length. "We chewed over ideas and tried things every day," Lord says. "The tapes were running the whole time, doing 16 hour days." Gabriel, Lord and Fast then spent three further months piecing everything together. Then, in the spring of 1982, the lyrics were added. The film-makers, although unobtrusive, found they had a great deal of time to put everything together: "They ran out of time basically because we were taking so long," Lord laughs. "We had to concoct the end of it in London pretending we were still recording."

"On the fourth album, Peter was able to use the Fairlight sounds during his creative writing stage so pieces such as 'The Rhythm of the Heat' and 'San Jacinto' were constructed around the sampled sounds and digital loops the Fairlight was capable of," Larry Fast says.

It was a painstaking, detailed approach. Ideas were constantly being worked out; Gabriel was at last in his own Christmas Cottage, endlessly working through new material with Lord. "It did wonders for my studio career," Lord says. "I was never out of my depth, but if anything there was a lack of confidence." "Peter had loose song structures and drum patterns ready for cutting the rhythm tracks by the third album," Fast adds. "Some of the tracks did end up with extended free-form explorations at this stage – jams in a sense. Doing that was helpful for working out the best bass patterns or drum parts; finding the focus of the rhythm track. These extended bits were not polished and were often edited out of the songs as they later developed. As a rule, though, the Peter Gabriel Band was not a jam band in any sense." Gabriel coined the phrase 'Gabrielese' for the vocal extemporisations he would do to get the melody together.

Gabriel's method was thorough. "I did get frustrated with him at times," David Lord said. "There was stuff we did that I would have been more than happy keeping that Peter wanted to re-work. Peter was the boss, and he was looking for someone to bounce ideas off. He wants to keep absolutely every possible option open for as long as he can, which is quite easy these days, but in those days we had mountains of two-inch tapes with every idea of it and every possible take of everything on every instrument."

The crucial point came down to the vocals, or at least the delivery of them and the lyrics: "I can't remember his vocals actually taking that long; we did a lot in the control room with monitors going. We would do these charts, he may do sixteen takes of the vocal then we would go through each line and then every word, every syllable would be given a mark out of ten and it was never like three or nine, it was always six and a half, or six and three quarters. We would then compile a vocal from the best bits, start again and carry on; that was pretty labour intensive. And for someone who can sing really well, it just seemed unnecessary; all the vocals were compiled from different takes, and I remember the painstaking detail when we were compiling. Peter was scared of hearing his voice *au natural*, he always had a harmoniser on his vocals, that was his sound. We ditched a lot of that and he became more confident hearing how he sounded."

"Oh, lyrics, was always his thing," David Lord said. "It was a major hurdle. He sang in 'Gabrielese', his vowel sounds when he was writing the vocal – there was never any vocals to start with. His great desire always was to work out the songs, do a live tour and then go and do the album. But you can't do that now, economically; because the tour has to promote the album. But that was all he wanted to do." At the end of it, Lord was satisfied, although the lens of 30 years means his view has shifted a little. "We were always getting loaned the latest reverbs and I thought we'd put too much on it but when I listen to it now, it sounds completely dry: I don't know what I was thinking of. It's quite grey and dry compared to a lot of things."

By September 1982, *Peter Gabriel*, *Peter Gabriel IV* or simply *Security* as it was titled in the States at the request of his new label boss David Geffen, was ready for release. Ironically, John Kalodner had urged Geffen to sign Phil Collins. Geffen wanted Gabriel and got his way. Initially, it seemed like a difficult decision, as Collins was immediately popular, and Gabriel was more of a slowburn. *Security* was a dense album that was not immediately accessible, but of all his work, arguably the one that has the greatest long term rewards.

'The Rhythm Of The Heat', originally known as 'Jung in Africa', was one of the first ideas that Gabriel brought into the sessions. Having read Carl Jung's book *Symbols And The Interpretation Of Dreams*, Gabriel knew that while studying the Collective Unconscious the Swiss psychologist had joined a group of drummers and dancers in Africa and became overwhelmed with fear. Worried that he would go mad as the drummers and dancers let the music control them, Jung became so terrified that he stopped the dance, and sent the dancers away. Gabriel was absolutely fascinated by this. In the song's frantic, escalating, hypnotic rhythms, Gabriel attempts to capture this accelerating panic.

Gabriel said in 2011: "I love the idea of this guy who shaped a lot of the way we think in the West, who lives in his head and in his dreams suddenly getting sucked into this thing that he can't avoid where he has to let go of control completely and feels that he has become possessed in a way, not by a devil but by this thing which is bigger than him." "'Rhythm Of The Heat' started life as a little loop, something he'd recorded off the radio," Lord says. "I think it was my idea to get Ekome to come in on the track, because I had worked with them at Crescent." Based in the St Paul's area of Bristol, the Ekome Dance Company blended African rhythms and drumming with dance. The chaotic Ghanian percussion climax is one of the most powerful moments on record in Gabriel's career.

'San Jacinto' looked at the clash of the culture around the San Jacinto American Indian and the relationship with the world in which they live – the protagonist wants to hold on to his roots, and not be seduced into the modern world. "We were in the Midwest somewhere on tour," Gabriel recalled in 2011. "We used to drive ourselves and we'd just checked into a motel after a gig. I got chatting to the porter who turned out to be Apache. He said, 'I'm sorry, my mind isn't really on the job tonight because someone phoned and told me that my apartment's burning down. I don't really care about it but my cat's in there.' I said, 'Why aren't you there?' He said he was working and didn't have any means of getting there, so I drove him. And true enough, when we got there he wasn't bothered about any of his things, just his cat, which really impressed me. His neighbour had his pet, so that was OK. So then we sat up most of the night and he told me about the initiation into being an Apache brave." It was from this exchange that Gabriel examined how the American Indian land and their pure rituals had been corrupted and bulldozed out of existence by American imperialists. 'San Jacinto' has a slow-burning emotional punch looking at how this noble tradition can continue amid a world of discos and steakhouses.

'I Have The Touch' put Gabriel back on more familiar territory and was the first track that seemed in any way commercial. *Sounds* said that it was "Fast and funky with loads of programmed synths – a technological contradiction if it takes so much hardware to convey a primitive feel? – it comes closest to the Talking Heads style of sheer marketability in funk." 'The Family And The Fishing Net' is a pitch black, difficult listen that compares the ritual of a wedding to voodoo. "His lyrics are quite to the point," David Lord notes. "I didn't know him emotionally enough to know what those songs were about at that point." *Sounds* questioned this track in their review of the album: "Evil and mysterious, throbbing sex, voodoo and death suggested in pseudo-poetic hints and shivers. What does it really all mean? Art?"

'Shock The Monkey' sounds positively hit parade after all of this. And indeed, it gave Gabriel his first US Top 40 single propelled by its strange, otherworldly video, directed by then-hot video director Brian Grant. The record had an incessant synthesiser riff, which sounds quite unlike anything else around at the time. Although various meanings have been ascribed to the song, Gabriel described it as a simple love song, exploring jealousy – how the monkey itself can be seen as a metaphor for suspicion in a relationship. And musically, it takes Tamla Motown as a reference, with its incessant beat. Gabriel's most danceable track to date, it showed him the potential of marrying a message to a groove and gaining commercial success.

Peter Hammill added backing vocals to the track, marking the first time that the pair had formally been on record together, despite all those early years at Charisma. By now, Hammill had long since disbanded Van Der Graaf and was working with a small band, making edgy, noisy solo albums, with flashes of pure, sweet sonic brilliance. He had also moved to Bath, and the two were near neighbours. Despite their friendship, there had never been any talk of formal collaboration: "No, I think we both like to be the ones in control." Hammill says. "Happy to work for somebody else on 'their' project of course, as hired gun . . . But I think we're both either solo artist in charge or group member, however (I speak for myself here) bombastic, egotistical, power-crazed."

There had been rivalry over the years: "Between VDGG and Genesis? Yes." says Hammill. "Between PG and PH, no. We've occupied different worlds and had, I think, different goals. What we share is the Great Gail Colson as manager! And, actually, a common aesthetic of come on, let's get it done properly." The 'let's get it done properly' approach extended to Hammill gladly assisting with backing vocals on the album. "Peter and David wanted some different vocal timbre in there," Hammill recalls. "I was happy to oblige and no, it took hardly any time. Us old school guys can go in there and do it in a couple of takes you know! I also did the German versions a bit later of course."

"As we were out at Ashcombe, Jill would join in as well," Lord recalls. "We all sang on everybody's else's albums in those days – with Bath being so small, if you wanted somebody to do something you just got somebody to come along. They'd be there in five moments – it was all very informal."

'Lay Your Hands On Me' was to become one of the live centrepieces from the album; after a slow build, with an almost Ian Dury-like rap from Gabriel to introduce the verses, it gives way to the impassioned plea for intimacy; whether it be sexual, religious or spiritual. Evoking a dream-like rapture, the beautiful ambiguity of the lyric is bolstered by the 'Biko'-like drumming onslaught and mass vocals. Again, it could be read as a plea by Gabriel to return to a secret childhood place to carry out some clandestine past time; a theme he would return to on *Us*, a decade later. Some criticised its messianic tendencies, but it was written with performance in mind; this song is much about Gabriel's relationship with his audience. There is one revealing lyric, however: 'there are no accidents round here' is a telling line that reflects this new approach: beautifully methodically crafted layers of work, with little room for spontaneity.

'Wallflower' is one of Gabriel's most beautiful and overlooked ballads, one of the few songs on the album that makes the listener wonder how it would have sounded with a Bob Ezrin production. Allegedly inspired by the arrest of Lech Walesa, the Polish Solidarity union leader, its message of 'holding on' and retaining individual spirit is universal. It holds a message for all detainees held for reasons beyond their control, with its final refrains ensuring the institutionalised person is not forgotten, while the narrator will do 'what I can do'. It is tender and unadorned, and contains one of Gabriel's most affecting vocals.

'Kiss Of Life' closed the album in a suitably dramatic style; featuring an up-tempo barrage of percussion, the infectious Brazilian rhythm offers huge relief and closure. Gabriel offered its meaning to Spencer Bright, about a "large Brazilian woman with abundant life-force raising a man from the dead." A distant cousin of Talking Heads' 'The Great Curve', the rapturous celebration of dance and the irresistible power of the female offers hope and sunlight after the album's more dramatic moments.

The whole process went right to the wire. There would be occasional work in progress listens for executives from Geffen, where Lord and Gabriel would sit in the corridor outside the studio, too embarrassed to listen with them, yet bursting in at static moments to distract listeners when they knew a bad edit was coming. "A common studio technique," Lord laughs. But the recording took an emotional toll on all concerned. "At a certain point I came close to a nervous breakdown because we were taking so long," Lord continues, his mood darkening. "The pressure from the management was huge. Literally the last mix we did through the night and Peter took off in a taxi with the tapes to Heathrow straight to America with the album. It was the fact we had lots of technical problems with my desk not being ready and there were a few times when we had the hire desk delivered and the normal things you'd expect just didn't work; things you'd normally do in a studio just couldn't be done, it was incredibly, incredibly stressful."

* * *

And then, something completely unexpected happened. "I got involved with Peter's wife," says David Lord. Being around for virtually every day for 18 months made him very accessible and he carried less baggage than the boy she had been with since she was 14 years old. "It was completely out of the blue, something I never dreamt would happen. That was extremely difficult because Peter and I had become very close. It wasn't a flippant thing; it was quite an intense affair. At a certain point she didn't know if she was going to stay with Peter. It was all very strange. It started the day he went to America, that morning. We had worked all through the night. I went home and crashed out, I woke up and there was a note through my door, asking to give her a ring. We were both emotionally shattered at the end of that long album, and she didn't know what to do, and I was the closest person to it all."

# 16: As Excited As We Were: WOMAD

*"Only a Genesis audience can make a Pakamac look like a kaftan."*

Tony Stratton-Smith, 1982

*"Ambition got ahead of reality. We went in there with evangelical fervour and we thought everyone else was going to be as excited as we were."*

Peter Gabriel, *The Guardian*, 2012

THE year continued for Peter Gabriel in its strange, bewildering fashion.

It is ironic that his new album was called *Security*, as his personal life was anything but secure. From today's viewpoint, it clearly appears that there were several young, attractive and creative people in a febrile emotional state. The album, so close to Gabriel's heart had taken so very long to make, and had resulted in an emotional trauma quite foreign to him. As he finally delivered the album, there was one further complicated commitment in which he was totally immersed. In a year full of strange events, the WOMAD (World Of Music And Dance) festival was probably one of the most strange, brave, big and bold music events ever staged: an attempt to educate an audience instead of simply mollifying them with music they expected.

The idea for WOMAD came to Peter Gabriel in 1980 when he was on a "long boring train journey in Germany, I was sitting around fantasising about some sort of event that might bring together ethnic musicians and some of the rock people who'd begun picking up – or to use a less polite word – stealing from this music." Gabriel's idea to do something more than simply record and write albums had had its genesis at least a decade earlier. His conversations with *Melody Maker* as far back as 1972 had talked of some kind of experiential park where people could be involved with a degree of multi-media experiences. WOMAD would be the first steps towards this dream.

Paul Conroy was unsurprised that Gabriel got so heavily into world music: "He was very bright. He had a lot of time for Bowie, and the way that Bowie was a chameleon and moved with the times, and he always listened to lots of music. I think the most surprising thing was when world music started, he was driven by all that, but then you think about the way he made some of his albums by making tape loops and banging bits of metal together, that's how he got into that sort of area."

The making and impending release of *Security* chimes perfectly with the intertwining activities of WOMAD. The original WOMAD festival introduced UK rock audiences to the likes of L. Shankar, Nusrat Fateh Ali Khan and, although deeply fashionable because of the then-current Adam Ant connection, the Master Drummers Of Burundi. Gabriel's interest in world music was brought through discovering the soundtrack to the 1965 drama *Dingaka*, which led directly to 'Biko'. Anthony Moore from Slapp Happy playing him Dollar Brand added further to this.

The festival and movement started to become reality when he met Thomas Brooman and Bob Hooton, who along with Alan James, ran a quarterly music magazine called *The Bristol Recorder*. It was while recording tracks at David Lord's Crescent Studios in Bath for their second compilation LP that Lord introduced them to Gabriel, who offered the trio a pair of his own live tracks for inclusion on their next *Recorder* release. A friendship blossomed and their mutual passion for exotic African rhythms dovetailed when the idea was mooted to stage a local festival, featuring a mix of mainstream acts and artists from across the world, with Gabriel headlining. After trying to get the festival off the ground for 1981, a date was set for the weekend of July 16–18 at the 240-acre Royal Bath and Wells Showground in Shepton Mallet. The showground had something of a pedigree for hosting similar events, not least the fabled Bath Festival of Blues and Progressive Music 12 years earlier, which had featured landmark performances by Led Zeppelin and Pink Floyd.

A committee was formed including Brooman, Hooton and Gabriel for the non-profit making organisation, with Brooman appointed Festival Director. Gabriel and the team went on a search to find the right people to play and to sponsor the festival, and while often bewildered by the amount of bureaucracy, he sought assistance from embassies, musicologists, and owners of record shops that stocked folk and world music. Prospective funding from the Arts Council was turned down. The BBC were interested in filming and broadcasting the show. Alongside performances, there would be many events that are now accepted as standard at rock festivals: films, spoken word performances, workshops and food from around the world. Gabriel was particularly delighted with the idea of a kids' day at the festival, breaking down the barriers of festivals as adult-only affairs. The original idea was to stage a six-day festival, but logistics soon suggested that it should be scaled down to three.

WOMAD was an enormous, ambitious undertaking. The idea was novel and far reaching but the logistics were terrifying. Ever practical, Gail Colson had advised Gabriel against it. "I am not sure that I was against it from the start, I think I was more worried about the people he was surrounding himself with and who he was leaving to organise it," she says. "I had nothing against them personally but they had no experience of running a festival at all. I had been very friendly with the Pendletons and the rest of the people who ran the Reading Festival and owned the Marquee Club and the original Jazz & Blues Festivals and felt that he should use them more."

Matters weren't helped when the supporting album, *Music And Rhythm*, due to come out in plenty of time for the festival, was severely delayed, as was the sizeable advance from WEA for the album which was to provide the organisation with revenue to fund the festival. The album featured a fabulous selection of artists playing at the festival and fellow supportive travelers: David Byrne supplied 'His Wife Refused' from his *Catherine Wheel* album, while Peter Hammill added 'The Ritual Mask', a track from his experimental album, *Loops And Reels* and Gabriel donated a version of the yet-to-be released 'San Jacinto'.

There was also the logistic issue of Gabriel's live performance that was to close the show – he hadn't played live since October 1980, and the band had yet to play the songs live that they had been slaving over for the past 18 months.

For the band it was stressful."We only had a few days to turn the complex studio pieces on *PG4* into a concert performance," says Larry Fast. "My panicked reaction was how the heck am I going to make all of these new digital sounds come alive. It was hard enough the old ways with Moog synthesisers. The revelation as I constructed the keyboard setups was that the new Fairlight CMI digital synthesiser, which we'd be using live for the first time, took so much of the burden of sound setup off of me by being able to store complex sounds on its disk drives during pre-show production, that WOMAD became the first 'modern' live show for me. In about four days I programmed and learned the songs that would make up the backbone of the 1982 and 1983 tours recorded on the *Plays Live* set."

Musicians from all over the world descended on the west country that July weekend to make a memorable festival; from the UK Simple Minds, Echo & The Bunnymen and Peter Hammill joined artists like Sasono Mulyo from Indonesia and Tian Jin from China. The Master Drummers Of Burundi were at the top of Brooman and Gabriel's wish list, and Ashcombe House was used as their rehearsal venue: "One memory that sticks out is the Drummers Of Burundi rehearsing on the croquet lawn in front of Ashcombe House," Fast recalls. "Amazing sound. I videotaped that on VHS using Peter's new colour video camera."

The festival was an artistic triumph, a display that naïveté can force through the grandest idea. "The people who were there proved that audiences needn't be as moronic as the industry treats them," Gabriel said. "The way people were prepared to give most of the stuff an open attitude was great." The open-mindedness of audiences was something that Gabriel would return to frequently, and how a rock audience would readily welcome overseas performers – "normally those groups are kept in a fairly academic environment but we were able to give them the space and opportunity."

And it was a financial catastrophe. The BBC pulled out soon before the festival; air fares for musicians to fly in from around the world were barely covered by the advance from the album. To top that, ticket sales were not robust. The local authorities, fearful of a repeat of the overcrowding from the 1970 Bath Festival, said that the popular UK headliners could only play in the Showering Pavilion venue in Shepton Mallet, which only had a capacity of 4,000. There was little 'walk-up' on the days. It was clear the festival was heading into a financial mire days before it began. The organising committee had to make some quick decisions. "We had to resign very quickly a couple of days before otherwise we would all have been due for that huge debt," said David Lord. This was the era before festivals came of age, when the idea of travelling half way across the UK to enjoy a festival was not common currency among those with money to spare, and when festivals like WOMAD – unlike the heavy metal romps at Reading and Donington – were the preserve of hippies or the recent phenomenon, New Age Travellers.

Gail Colson realised something was very wrong before she even arrived at the festival. "My vivid memory is of saying to my PA while we were driving to Shepton Mallet was that there was something wrong. She, having never been to a festival before, asked me why and my reply was that we were the only car on the road and that we should have been in a traffic jam! When we arrived there seemed to be more people walking about with laminates than there were audience. I think I spent most of the time in the box office, collecting whatever cash there was and prioritising who should be paid immediately and who could wait. The Drummers Of Burundi – pay; the Chinese delegation – pay."

The weather was not fantastic, there was a rail strike and the festival did not sell out. "It was a wonderful festival but obviously the weather played havoc with the finances," said Peter Hammill. "Artistically it was well on the spot, particularly the last night headline band of PG, Rhodes, Shankar, Larry Fast, Stuart Copeland and myself. Very wild. But also very stressful for Peter with all the flak flying. I have fond memories of the event . . ." Amid all this, Gabriel put on a shimmering performance. The new album, bar 'Wallflower', was previewed. Most potent was the version of 'The Rhythm Of The Heat', which featured live drumming by the Ekome Dance Company, and then a closing tumultuous 'Biko'.

And then, the flak really did start to fly. People wanted paying. "Ambition got ahead of reality," Gabriel told *The Guardian* in 2012. "We went in there with evangelical fervour and we thought everyone else was going to be as excited as we were. It became a nightmare experience when we realised there was no way we were getting the tickets to cover our costs. The debts were way above what I could manage but people saw me as the only fat cat worth squeezing so I got a lot of nasty phone calls and a death threat."

"I was hearing about the death threats," David Lord said. "It was horrendous. There were coaches full of Chinese orchestras stuck on the M4 because the coach company hadn't been paid for taking them back to Heathrow. On the surface at the time, the whole atmosphere was terrific."

"We naively assumed that we had an event with more appeal than it actually had," Gabriel said. "I'm very hopeful that even if we can't continue, the idea is going to be pushed through by some others because if

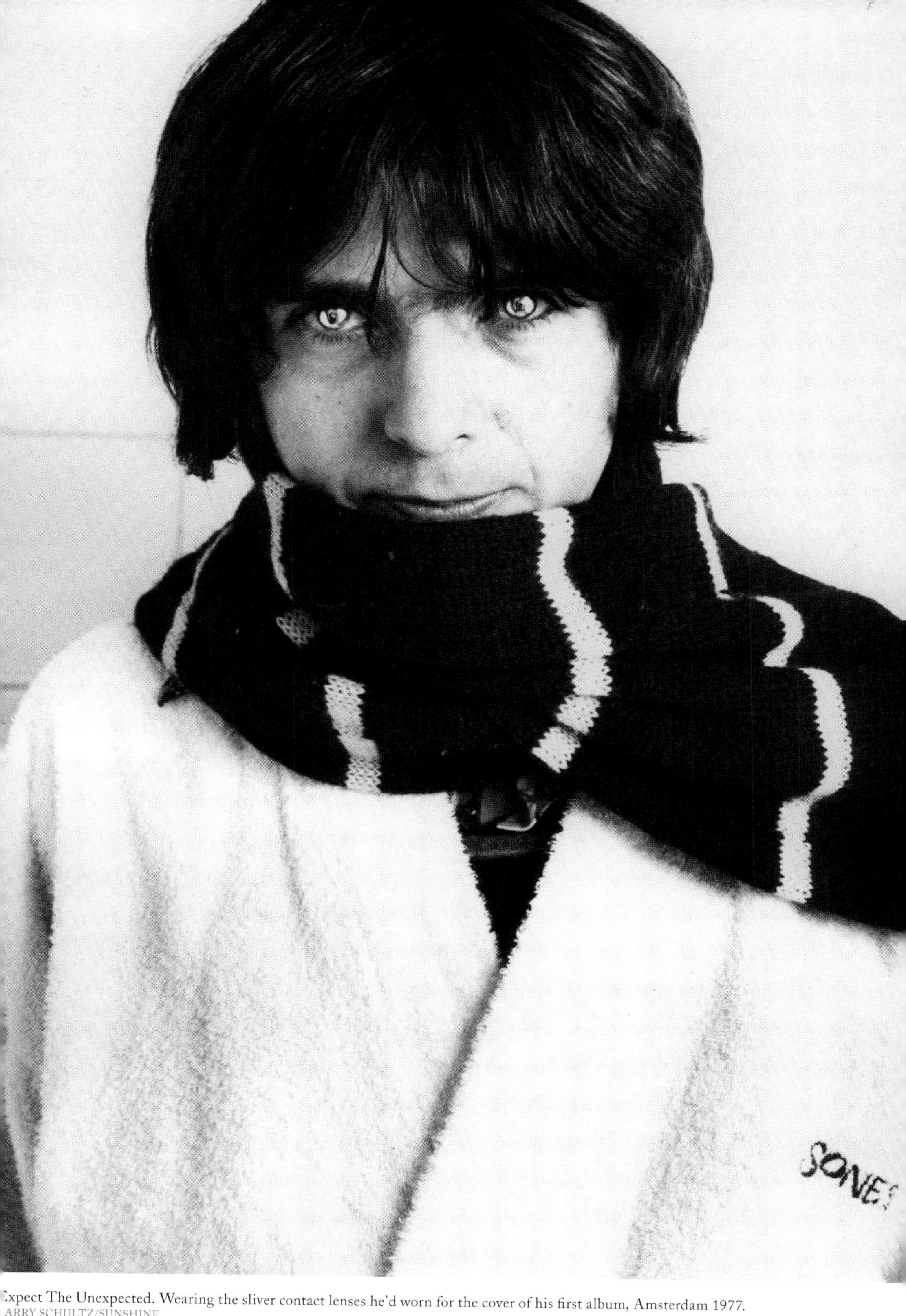

:xpect The Unexpected. Wearing the sliver contact lenses he'd worn for the cover of his first album, Amsterdam 1977.
ARRY SCHULTZ/SUNSHINE

The two Genesis vocalists and drummers in action. Gabriel understandably stopped wanting to over-manage the group's drummers when Collins arrived in 1970. Their friendship has endured. ELLEN POPPINGA - K & K/REDFERNS

Gabriel thrived on collaboration in the latter half of the seventies. After he and Tom Robinson began a deep friendship, Robinson was to encourage Gabriel to release 'Biko'. EBET ROBERTS/REDFERNS

Rob & Gab's Xmas Show, Christmas Eve, 1978. With Elton John on piano. DENIS O'REGAN/GETTY IMAGES

The 'Excuse Me' barbershop quartet in action, 1977; L to R: Phil Aaberg, PG, Tony Levin and Jimmy Maelen. BARRY PLUMMER

Two views of Knebworth, 1978. The panda became an indispensible prop for Gabriel's most complete return to childhood, 'Me And My Teddy Bear'. BARRY PLUMMER

David Jackson, of old *Ten-Bob Tour* compadres Van Der Graaf Generator would join Gabriel on his short 1979 tour. BARRY PLUMMER

At the Hit Factory, New York, 1978. The working relationship between Gabriel and Robert Fripp was incredibly fertile over a short period of time. LISA TANNER

No hard feelings. Collins and Gabriel clowning for the press, New York, 1976. CHUCK PULIN/SPLASH NEWS/CORBIS

Stripped clean, a symbolic shaving of the lamb: Gabriel's grade one, 1978. SUNSHINE/RETNA PICTURES

To promote 'Me And My Teddy Bear' and the Knebworth and Battersea Park gigs, Gabriel took to the London underground with photographer Fin Costello. FIN COSTELLO/REDFERNS

The Tour Of China, Gabriel's first solo shows began to challenge the conventions of a rock gig, ironically at the Convention Hall, Asbury Park, July 9, 1980. BOB LEAFE/FRANK WHITE PHOTO AGENCY

Two of the best. Rutherford and Gabriel onstage at Milton Keynes Bowl, October 1982. PETER STILL/REDFERNS

At home. Gabriel with Jill, Anna Marie and Melanie, late seventies. REX/NIKKI ENGLISH/ASSOCIATED NEWSPAPERS

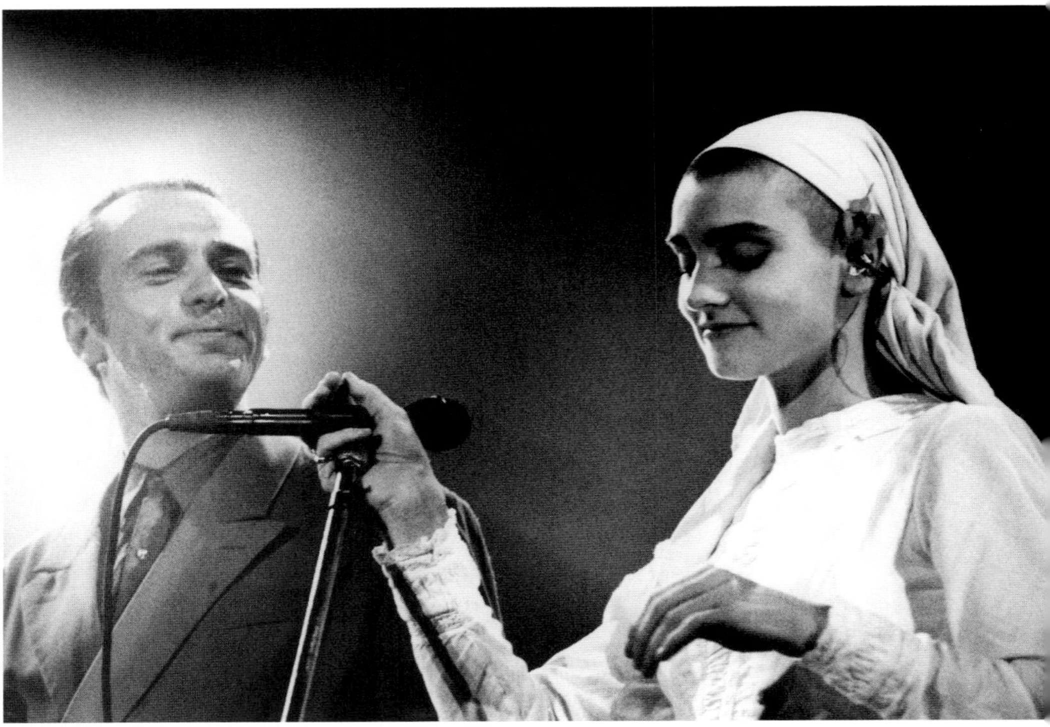

With Sinead O'Connor, at the Simple Truth Concert, The Hague, Holland, May 1991. MICHEL LINSSEN/REDFERNS

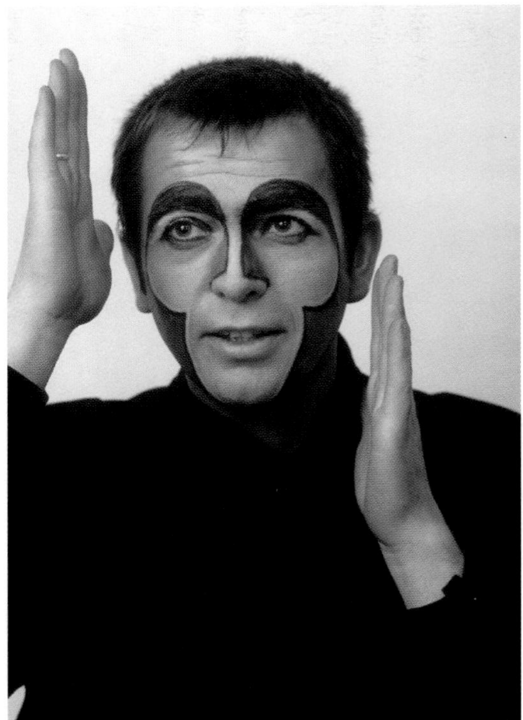

Rome 1982. Gabriel in his 'Shock The Monkey' facepaint, his last major dalliance with make-up. LUCIANO VITI

With great fan and friend Jim Kerr at the Mandela Day concert, Wembley, April 1990. ADRIAN BOOT/URBANIMAGE

nothing else we showed that a rock audience could give a standing ovation to a 50-year-old Chinese horn player – and that was great."

His old friends rallied round to help him out. Tony Smith, who still owned a 50 per cent stake in Gabriel's management, was the manager of Genesis and told them of their former singer's plight. The thought of their old friend going bankrupt was too much to bear for them. Conveniently, they were nearing the end of their *Three Sides Live* tour, so their massive touring machine was up and running. It was suggested that in order to recoup the debts that WOMAD had amassed Gabriel would rejoin Genesis for one massive outdoor concert at the Milton Keynes Bowl, a recently opened purpose built venue in Buckinghamshire, Saturday October 2.

"People had wanted us to do some kind of reunion," says Tony Banks. "And it gave us a good excuse to do it. Peter had got himself into trouble with WOMAD, and it seemed such an easy thing to do."

"It seemed a pretty obvious thing to do," adds Mike Rutherford. "The problem was logistics, as we were in the middle of a big tour and we hit it rather unrehearsed."

Gabriel had little option but to accept: "The motivation is to pay off the WOMAD debts," he told *NME* the week before. "For me, um . . . I think I will enjoy it but having tried for seven years to get away from the image of being ex-Genesis there's obviously a certain amount of stepping back. I don't think they would choose at this point to work with me or I with them but as they've offered, it's very generous. I'm very grateful and I'm intending to enjoy myself. Melodies, sounds, rhythms. I don't know. Their approach has sustained them. No, I haven't listened to their recent records very much. Just this last week or so because of this gig."

* * *

As posters and tickets were being printed for this momentous, life-saving concert, Gabriel's fourth solo album was released on September 10, 1982. It's an album that remains easy to admire but difficult to love, yet the one that arguably holds the greatest reward when the listeners get through the frontiers imposed by its digital modernism. "The fourth album was the third album with no restraints on it," Larry Fast said in 2012. "So, it went on and on for months and months and things never got finished the way they maybe should have. There was more money for toys and tech tools.

Sometimes, too much of something in that field can actually be detrimental because it can get in the way of creativity." It's a pitch-perfect exercise in exploration and boundary pushing, but the unmistakable melodies that weaved through the third album for all its strangeness seemed elsewhere.

As it was so pioneering in its use of Fairlight, it sounds at times like a museum piece for the then-latest available technology. "It was Fairlight days; the technology made the record as Peter would get off on certain sounds and rhythmic loops and things," Lord said. "It never got in the way. The other thing that people in Peter's camp regretted was that because the album took so long, by the time it came out, *everyone* was using Fairlight. At that stage we had the only one in the country and Peter was the sole agent for it and we didn't really capitalise on that." Had the album come out at the tail end of 1981, it would have beaten records like Trevor's Horn's very a la mode production of *The Lexicon Of Love* by ABC.

Reviews were mixed. *NME*'s Gavin Martin wrote "What is it that makes Gabriel and his ilk think that to address misery and depression the artist must sound miserable and depressed? Even when he uses The Ekome Dance Company – who, I'm sure, use music as a buoyant and uplifting release in their native environment, his music sounds like he's serving penance for the impurity and decay of the entire western world. What are we going to do with these arthouse bores?"

Sandy Robertson in *Sounds* said: "On 'Lay Your Hands On Me', Pete does his old talkalong, nearly-gonna-cry-into-the-bank-statement bit but it might reveal something. Amid the drum bursts he seems to be longing for passion and mystery while hanging out in an urban playground of perfect stainless steel nothingness. That's what the whole album seems to be about, in fact. The joke is twofold, I'd say, both parts on PG. Wonder is everywhere; you don't need to have primitive mindscapes to find it! And this record itself is a symptom of the spiritual paucity of modern life! What could be more naff than a big beat synth rock LP?"

Yet Richard Cook as part of his *NME* interview with Gabriel at the time said: "Flawed and difficult though it is, [it] has a rare quota of courage and experiment in it. Ugly and overstretched as it often appears, it takes breath in the forgotten resonance of the epic. It is Gabriel's first step at repositioning the heroic pretensions of rock."

It was understandable in some respects that reviews were mixed. "Part of it, I know is a straight reaction to the music, and I'm not dodging that, I think there is a lot to do with fashion," Gabriel said on *The South Bank Show*. "One of the real satisfactions for me with this record is that I'm getting played by black stations in America, even though in the white press I got some fair slaggings this time. I had a very good review in *Black Music* magazine, and even though I don't think my music has much in common with main black music, it's still great for me to feel that the rhythm content is strong enough to get through to black people. I want to continue this hybrid between hi-tech and non-European influence." His cultural magpieism was something he felt passionate about, and explained to *NME* in 1982: "I think theft of all types is very important to any music that is alive. A few rhythmic workhorses have carried rock for so long. If I hear original rhythm patterns from elsewhere that motivate me, that I wouldn't have come across in rock music, then I'll make use of them."

However, it was an album that withstood repeated listens and revealed its charms slowly and gracefully. *Rolling Stone* were most enthusiastic about the album retrospectively: "*Security* elaborates on its predecessor's approach by adding world music elements into the mix. Granted, Gabriel made moves in this direction on 'Biko' . . . but that's nowhere near as dramatic as his use of the Ekome Dance Company in 'The Rhythm Of The Heat'. Yet it isn't simply exoticism that makes the song so intriguing; it's the way Gabriel incorporates such touches into his melodic structures, generating a kind of magic that's as applicable to the boisterously tuneful 'Shock The Monkey' as the moody, mysterious 'I Have The Touch'."

The album certainly struck a chord in America, which was less obsessed with Gabriel's past than the UK. *Trouser Press* said: "Gabriel delivers his examinations of fear and disaster with an oddly paradoxical new emphasis on hope and restraint, displaying his usual fine craft and quality." It continued saying that several of the tunes were "among the best things he's ever done, combining all of his strengths – lyrical, melodic, structural and experimental – into bracingly original pop music with a solid footing."

*Record Mirror* went as far as saying: "Gabriel walks a fine line between brilliance and churning out a load of old cobblers." David Lord is amused by this line in 2013. "I wouldn't go as far as saying it was a load of old cobblers. But it must have been a very strange time for him, because the commercial pressures were enormous and he was not marketing himself at all to be commercial. It had a very mixed response, and we were very surprised at that. We weren't in any way trying to be commercial, we were just doing what Peter was into; 'Shock The Monkey' was the only commercial thing."

"I thought that the fourth album was absolutely wonderful," says old friend Anthony Phillips. "I was less keen on the one with the aggressive stuff that came before that, I felt that was more pandering to some of the things that were going on at the time; it was good but it wasn't really my kind of thing. He came into his own. Even back at Christmas Cottage, his ideas for arrangements were always quite well ahead of the rest of us. We were big block chords and we filled up too much space." Tony Banks agrees with Phillips: "The third album was brilliant, and I thought the fourth album was probably slightly better. In terms of composition it was wonderful. 'San Jacinto' is probably my favourite of Pete's tracks. I would have been a big fan of Pete's even if I hadn't known him."

Following the success of the German version of *Melt* that Gabriel made in 1980, he released a sister version of *Security*, titled as the previous release, *Ein Deutshes Album*. However, while the previous album had been merely Gabriel overdubbing his vocals into German, here he went the whole hog and re-recorded and remixed huge swathes of the album, including getting Peter Hammill back in to sing backing vocals in German. It was a great achievement to remix and re-record some of the work, with different effects and vocal lines. It demonstrated that this had been Gabriel's masterwork to date in that he had exercised a level of control over the recording that he hadn't been able to before, the building-up-from-the-ground approach suited him perfectly and would be the method he would use on all further recordings.

* * *

To avoid any legal issues, the October 2 show at the National Bowl in Milton Keynes was billed as being by 'Six Of The Best' – a reference to the term used for caning that was so prevalent in public schools, a neat little allusion to Charterhouse. But everyone knew exactly what it was – seven years after last appearing onstage with them, Peter Gabriel was rejoining Genesis. On all the publicity, the purpose of the concert was clear: underneath the title it said simply and unequivocally, 'A Benefit For WOMAD.'

Genesis, now with live regulars guitarist Daryl Stuermer and drummer

Chester Thompson, had culminated their tour with some smaller, back-to-basics gigs. Gabriel caught their concert at the Showering Pavilion, Shepton Mallet on September 19 and discussed final logistics, before the six of them convened at Hammersmith Odeon on September 28 for three afternoons of rehearsals. The rehearsals were photographed on the 29th for inclusion in the souvenir programme for the show.

The group were a little rusty – by now their shows only included 'The Lamb Lies Down On Broadway', 'In The Cage' and, on occasion, 'Supper's Ready' from the Gabriel era. "We were very under-rehearsed because we only spent a couple of afternoons working at it," Collins said in 2007. "But I guess it must have fallen back into place quite easily, otherwise we would have been in trouble." The band were amazed at how little they remembered of material they used to play so frequently. Rutherford, for one, had completely forgotten a whole four-minute section in the middle of 'The Musical Box'. Gabriel was nothing less than honest in all of his communications about the show: he wrote in the programme, "I'm sure that, as with anyone reliving their youth, I'm going to feel a lot of nostalgia about the gig although in terms of career moves, it's probably not a very good idea for them or for me. But financially, it's going to be very useful for the WOMAD festival and I'm certainly going to enjoy it."

The show was memorable, and not always for the right reasons. It was an absolute quagmire at Milton Keynes. The National Bowl, a former disused clay pit had been converted in 1979 into an outdoor venue that could hold 65,000 people. Queen had played there that summer, and it was now the main venue for one-off gigs outside London. The bill of the concert, which ran between 2pm and 8pm, included industry veterans The Blues Band, John Martyn and surprisingly, Talk Talk, who although going on to be one of the greatest art-rock bands the UK has ever produced, at that time were still peddling a sort of Duran Duran-lite. They were booed and bottled throughout their set by the rain-soaked crowd.

To further the Charterhouse references, the group was introduced by their original mentor and old Carthusian Jonathan King, who was quick to point out how he gave them their name. The show started with Gabriel being carried onstage in a coffin – a late example of his determination to spring surprises on his fellow bandmates. Sensing that the idea would be quashed during the band's fabled democratic process that he had been free of for six years, he went ahead and performed his, as he later called it, 'typically humble gesture'. Safely onstage, he sprang out of the box, resplendent in Rael's leather jacket to sing 'Back In NYC'. "We all smiled when the coffin came on," Rutherford remembers. "It was like 'that's our Pete'."

For two hours, the band cantered somewhat raggedly through the highlights of their pre-1975 catalogue: 'Carpet Crawlers', 'The Musical Box' and 'Supper's Ready' were all present and correct. It was incredibly touching to hear 65,000 souls singing along, terrace-style to the opening of 'Dancing With The Moon Knight'. Before 'Firth Of Fifth', Gabriel spoke to explain the situation with WOMAD and thank the audience and band for supporting him – "In return for your cash, we will try and give you what we think you would like from this combination." The only nods to the preceding seven years were Genesis' stab at 'Solsbury Hill', and Gabriel playing drums while Collins sang Genesis' 1980 superhit, 'Turn It On Again'.

Gabriel had a teleprompter onstage so he could remember the words. By the time he launched into his spiel about croquet before 'The Musical Box', it mattered not a jot about the strength and length of the rain or the under-rehearsed nature of the band. This was Genesis, back together, 11 years since the song had been played around the student unions of the home counties.

"It was filthy weather," Gabriel said on *The Old Grey Whistle Test*, the week after. "It started at about 6am and went on to 2am, solid rain. The day before was perfect, and the day after was perfect. The audience was amazing, they waited out for about six hours in the rain. In return for us getting our fingers in their pockets, we tried to give them what we thought they'd want from the six of us – and we had a bonus with Steve Hackett coming back for the last numbers." The group was also bolstered by the addition of Hackett for the encores of 'I Know What I Like (In Your Wardrobe)' and 'The Knife'.

Since leaving Genesis in 1977, Hackett had been enjoying a successful solo career. He had been on tour in South America, and rushed back for the event: "I got on a plane immediately and joined them just in time for the two encores," he told *Classic Rock* in 2012. "There was a lot of talent on that stage and it was very emotional." Hackett added to me: "It was wonderful to work with everyone again, especially to help Pete and WOMAD, an auspicious moment at the birth of World Music. There was a fabulous audience reaction."

"It was a weird one," Tony Banks added. "I was wearing a tracksuit that had 'kamikaze' written on it which underlined my attitude. It was odd, and not as good musically as we had been used to. There were moments when Pete went on to the second drum kit for 'Turn It On Again' but he couldn't keep time because he didn't realise that there was an extra beat in it. It was quite amusing really." "I was very strong on not filming it," Rutherford adds. "It felt good. It was my birthday and pissing with rain."

Larry Fast was back in America and missed the show, but recalls watching it on VHS in the front room at Ashcombe House, which lays to rest the oft-repeated myth that the show was not filmed.

With all seven of them, the entire line-up of all versions of the band since December 1970 onstage, it was certainly a momentous occasion. It may not have been the most polished performance, but a fitting tribute to one of the greatest live acts of the Seventies. Gabriel found the experience strange, and needed all the help he could get: "I was never good at remembering words, but this time I had to watch the lips of the front row very closely."

Tony Stratton-Smith's words he wrote on the day of the concert capture a man proud and delighted. "Tonight I looked at one aspect of my work these last 12 years and, Pepys-style, 'found it pleasing'. The reunion for this one night of Genesis, Peter Gabriel and Steve Hackett, was a happy success, and the members of the band revealed more emotion than one thought they possessed. It was Mike's birthday, which gave additional excuses for much hugging and reminiscence. This was but the continuation of a party spirit effervescing earlier from 60,000 people enduring six hours of incessant rain, and maybe they deserved the biggest hug of all. Only a Genesis audience can make a Pakamac look like a kaftan." With his characteristic élan and turn of phrase, Stratton-Smith had been transported back to the early days of his charges: "One of the truly great radical groups of the last 12 years, something not often said since the golden days of Chris Welch reviews. Equal with The Who, and the two of them inferior to the Only Begetter Of Us All here in Britain, The Beatles."

Gabriel's debt of gratitude to his old band was immense. Although they had maintained their stiff-upper-lip relationship over the past seven years, the press had sought to exaggerate any quotation that may have meant bad blood, but in coming to his aid, they showed how deep the old friendships went. After all, he and Banks had been friends for almost 20 years by this point. Gabriel was very quick to dampen talk that Genesis' assistance had been anything other than altruistic. "There was one or two suggestions saying that Genesis got some money out of this, and although they are often portrayed as very unhip, exploitative capitalist men of the rock world, it's entirely down to them now that the WOMAD movement can move or struggle or crawl forward and they didn't get anything out of it." With tickets £9 in advance, or £10 on the day, the concert made more than half a million pounds, and once overheads were deducted the debt was wiped out in one fell swoop.

One single concert meant that WOMAD was able to settle all their debts, and tentatively look towards the future. Although damaged by the experience, his love and admiration for other cultures and musics meant that Gabriel wanted WOMAD to continue. He told Mark Ellen and David Hepworth on *The Old Grey Whistle Test:* "I'd like to try it again. Except with someone else footing the bill. We hoped for a commercial sponsor because it could have been really viable. There's still room for a lot more types of music to make a place in 'youth culture'."

The Milton Keynes Bowl show was significant for Gabriel in one other aspect. The Italian music writer and Genesis biographer Armando Gallo had brought along his friends from the group Toto, whose keyboard player Steve Porcaro was accompanied by his girlfriend Rosanna Arquette.

In the course of the afternoon Arquette was introduced to Gabriel, and the actress – who would soon make her name starring alongside Madonna in *Desperately Seeking Susan* – turned his already complicated personal life upside down.

# 17: Watch The *Birdy*

*"In my whole career I've never sought out an artist, or indeed tracked anyone down. He is the only one."*

Nile Rodgers, 2013

RELIEVED that the *Six Of The Best* concert was now out of the way and that WOMAD's balance sheet had gained some semblance of normality, it was suddenly and swiftly back to business as usual for Gabriel: promoting *Security*. Emotionally, however, he was about to go on a rollercoaster ride that would inform his work for the remainder of the decade. Smitten by Rosanna Arquette at their initial meeting after *Six Of The Best*, a chain of events would drive him into her arms intermittently, and bring about the closure of the relationship he'd had with Jill since they were teenagers.

Returning from a European promotional tour for *Security* he went home to Jill and, stressed from all that had happened during this tumultuous year, confessed that he'd committed an indiscretion on tour. But she had something to tell him, too. "I can tell you what actually happened the night he found out," Lord said. "He blurted it out to Jill. She was shocked, so she told him that she'd been having an affair with me. He couldn't believe it. He came straight round and Jill followed him about 10 minutes later. I'd never seen him angry; but then it calmed down a bit and we were talking fairly rationally about it, and we were talking into the middle of the night. He decided to go home, and he asked Jill to go with him. She refused. That made it even worse. It was all very tragic."

Jill Gabriel took the children and moved up to the Lake District, to a cottage without a telephone, while both men agreed to leave her in relative peace to assess the situation. "Peter and I were both making trips up there, unbeknown to each other," says Lord. "Peter and I were civil to each other, but it clearly ruled out working together any more and I hated the deception. I didn't know what to do."

It was a strange time. Gabriel had found a like-minded partner in Lord, and the fact that he was on the doorstep in Bath made it all the more attractive. Now, clearly, the work that they had done together was completely undermined. A period of estrangement followed, and while Jill and Gabriel were apart, he met up with Arquette again and commenced a relationship with her.

* * *

The tour to support *Security* was large, and helped build and secure Gabriel's fan base in the States. Characteristically cryptic, the shows were entitled *Playtime 1988*, and they finally found the balance between his extreme rejection of his Genesis persona on his early tours, and greater theatricality. "When I got the reputation for being a clothes-prop with Genesis I wanted to drop theatrical presentation altogether," he told *NME* in 1982. "There's always a danger of using theatre concepts where musical concepts aren't strong enough. But there's things I've enjoyed doing and been most moved by using that approach – and if I can do that and get closer to it in performance then I think I should do it."

Jeffrey Callen, in his extended essay *I Need Contact – Rock'n'Roll Ritual: Peter Gabriel*'s Security *Tour 1982–83*, says that the tour "synthesised the theatricality of his work with Genesis (minus its props and elaborate staging) and the minimalism of his prior tours as a solo artist. Gabriel no longer had any interest in revisiting the 'mythology' that had characterised his work with Genesis, and chose instead to emphasise the use of 'ritual' as an element of his work."

The show was immense, engaging and melodramatic. Working with Tony Levin, David Rhodes, Larry Fast and Jerry Marotta, the band settled into the North American tour, riding on the wave of goodwill that the success of 'Shock The Monkey' had provided. The performances were warmly received and found Gabriel at ease with his persona. His performance back with Genesis at Milton Keynes had shown he could be comfortable with large crowds; the show had been cathartic, but above all, he was thrilled and proud with the direction his material had taken.

Gabriel sought to break down the fourth wall of performance, again initially appearing at the back of the concert hall and walking through the crowd. With the band all taking drums in a line for the opening 'The Rhythm Of The Heat' and Gabriel appearing in face paint for 'Shock The

Monkey', it was the material from *Security* that had the greatest impact and coherence onstage. The ritual element of his work was truly emphasised by the bond, sought and exploited by Gabriel, with his audience; for music so occasionally remote and spiky he was bringing out all of the emotion, underlined by the set's climax of 'Lay Your Hands On Me' where Gabriel would walk among the crowd touching their hands. As the tour progressed, he would go to the lip of the stage, facing the band and fall backwards into his audience. The throng would hold him aloft and carry him across the auditorium with his arms outstretched, cementing the bond between audience and performer. The ultimate trust exercise, and a long way from when Gabriel launched himself into the crowd at Friars over a decade previously.

Phil Collins attended the first leg of the tour on December 15 at the Universal Amphitheater in Los Angeles and met Gabriel backstage. Collins had become an enormously successful solo performer with a career running in tandem with Genesis, who, unlike their response when Gabriel needed time during *The Lamb Lies Down On Broadway* sessions, gave Collins time to commence a separate career productively while remaining in the band. His debut album, *Face Value* had become a runaway success, its blend of soul, pop and prog confections had tapped a world-wide nerve and he was doing his first world tour to promote its follow-up, *Hello I Must Be Going*. Gabriel's tour ended in San Jose on December 19. The concerts had proved life-affirming for Gabriel, the beginning of the next phase of his career, alongside Geffen's promotion of the album which had seen 'Shock The Monkey' climb into the US Top 30.

As most of the concerts had been recorded, it was decided to release a live double album of the shows, especially useful in America, as Geffen could use the opportunity to promote it as a collection of Gabriel's hits to further increase his audience. The resultant album, *Peter Gabriel Plays Live* was released in June 1983, and was recorded over four dates in Illinois and Kansas in early December 1982. It carried the telling disclaimer "some additional recording took place not a thousand miles away from the home of the artist. The generic term of this process is known as 'cheating'. Care has been taken to keep the essence of the gigs intact, including 'human imperfection'. As a mark of Gabriel's popularity, 'I Go Swimming', which had been in his live sets since 1980 and not on any other album, was released as a single in the US and made the *Billboard* Mainstream Rock Charts.

The super, poppy new wave of the track sounded like the perfect addition to the US power synth pop market currently seeing mainstream success for previously leftfield Devo and the latest reinvention of LA art-rockers Sparks. 'I Go Swimming' showed that no matter how intense his work could be at times, Gabriel was still, after all these years, happy to play daft. David Fricke in *Rolling Stone* said: "As live albums go, *Plays Live* is an inspiring introduction to Gabriel's extraordinary solo ambitions. If it isn't the next best thing to being there, it's certainly enough to make you want to go." An inspiring introduction was exactly what the album set out to be.

When not reeling from his emotional situation, Gabriel spent the early part of 1983 recording and trying out song ideas. Spurred on by *Six Of The Best*, he returned the favour to members of his old band and turned up for Steve Hackett's encores when he played the Civic Hall in Guildford on January 28 that year. With Mike Rutherford also onstage he sung 'Solsbury Hill' and 'Here Comes The Flood'. He delighted the crowd by displaying his Motown roots and singing an impassioned verse on the Four Tops classic, 'Reach Out (I'll Be There)', which had been a UK number one in October 1966, one of the records he played on his Dansette in Charterhouse. In February he played the San Remo Song festival in Italy and in June spent time in California with long time friend and writer/ photographer Armando Gallo.

The tour, re-titled *Plays Live*, reconvened at the end of June 1983 and played through until the end of October. Gabriel supported David Bowie on his *Serious Moonlight* tour at two stadium gigs in Canada that August. Bowie had reinvented himself with the assistance of Nile Rodgers, the urbane guitarist from CHIC, who had enjoyed a world-conquering run of single success at the end of the Seventies. Bowie was now stripped of all his personas and appeared as a clean cut, healthy and tanned showman, who had just delivered the most successful album of his career, *Let's Dance*.

Bowie had won an Italian TV award, the *Telegatto*, Song Of The Year for the single 'Let's Dance', a trophy that Gabriel had won the previous year for 'Shock The Monkey'. In a backstage photograph, taken by Denis O'Regan, Gabriel hands the Award, a golden cat, to Bowie. Gabriel's face is painted, ready to take to the stage; Bowie is in his civvies, hours before showtime. Both smile for the camera. It was a long way since the Atomic Sunrise Festival at the Roundhouse, 13 years previously. "Gabriel's smiling and Bowie's looking to camera, but I think Gabriel looks a bit silly," David Buckley says. "It was almost as if Bowie is saying, 'Come on now, we did all of this in the Seventies.'" It was to be the final tour on which Gabriel hid behind any mask or make-up: within two years, Peter Saville would be supervising clean-cut photoshoots for him.

* * *

As ever, on the 1983 tour Gabriel again showed his unerring support for new artists when he arranged for David Stopps' protégé, Howard Jones, to support him at a show in Brussels. Jones was a veteran of Genesis' shows at Friars in the Seventies and was managed by none other than Stopps, who, in turn, had been signed to Warners by Paul Conroy. Jones had broken through with his debut single, 'New Song', which bore a passing resemblance to 'Solsbury Hill' to the extent that BBC Radio One DJ Mike Read refused to play it, suggesting it was simply too similar. "I spoke to Peter about this afterwards. He said he didn't think there was any similarity whatsoever," Stopps says. "Peter played a big part in Howard's career. We'd just signed to Warners through Gail Colson. Peter needed a support for his Forest Nationale stadium show in Belgium, so he asked Howard. It was his first ever time we'd ever done anything abroad. We had no talkback between stage and mixing desk, it was incredibly thrown together – but Peter came out and announced Howard. That is the sort of person Peter is. It was very kind of him to do that."

The tour ended on October 28, 1983 at the Hall de Penfeld, Brest. It was to be the final live show that Gabriel performed with stalwarts Jerry Marotta and Larry Fast in the line up. "I'm never quite sure why Peter changed from using Jerry and Larry; he was looking for different feels," David Lord said. "Jerry was that classic laid back American rock drummer; the timing and way he hit the drums was terrific; it was a joy to try and use those sounds on the PA. But, it was Peter's show. What he said went, but he was never didactic. Life with Peter was all very low-key."

In the background of Gabriel's life for the next few years were prolonged attempts at a reconciliation with Jill, while he spent time with Arquette in America. In between his work schedule, Jill and Gabriel attended family therapy sessions. David Lord knew that deep down Peter and Jill would remain together, at least in the mid-term. "Peter would take the family off on holiday, and I'd stay at her house, looking after it and doing the garden and stuff until they came back. I decided to back out, ultimately, assuming that they would always stay together. I was quite surprised when they didn't but then everything had moved on. I was with somebody by then." By the end of 1984, Jill and Gabriel were back together for the time being.

★ ★ ★

Film remained a large part of Gabriel's reference, and he often thought back to when he turned down the opportunity to go to the London School of Film Technique in 1968, and his disappointment that the William Friedkin opportunity and *The Lamb Lies Down On Broadway* film had both come to nothing. Gabriel was therefore delighted to be approached by legendary New York-based director Martin Scorsese as early as 1983 to consider scoring the soundtrack to his proposed film *The Last Temptation Of Christ* for Paramount. However, a film such as this was forever going to be mired in controversy. Funding fell through, and the film was, for the meanwhile, shelved.

Nevertheless, for the next few years film took up a considerable part of Gabriel's time and provided a diversion from the business of creating more albums. In late 1983, he had agreed to contribute a song to the soundtrack of the forthcoming Taylor Hackford-directed romantic thriller *Against All Odds*. Tony Smith was the film's music coordinator, proposing artists that Hackford might use for the soundtrack and, naturally, he looked to his own. Amid the specifically-composed Larry Carlton score, the film and album contained work by Stevie Nicks and Kid Creole & The Coconuts. It also contained new and exclusive material from Mike Rutherford, Phil Collins and Gabriel himself. Gabriel's track, 'Walk Through The Fire', had actually been started at the time of and considered for inclusion on *Melt*. Gabriel completed it and it was included on the album and in the film. When Charisma wished to release it as a single, it was felt that it needed a little more beef to it. Nile Rodgers, who had recently so enlivened the work of David Bowie and was then very much the go-to remixer and producer, was brought in to assist.

Rodgers had been an admirer of Gabriel for a considerable time. Although aware of his work with Genesis, it was hearing the drum sound on 'Intruder' that made him seek Gabriel out for potential collaboration. "I got to know Peter after he did 'Intruder'," Rodgers says. "I had never heard that drum sound before; it was like 'wow, I've got to meet this dude'. Now, in my whole career I've never sought out an artist, or indeed tracked anyone down. He is the only one. He was kind enough to agree a meeting. We met at a Japanese restaurant and we talked, I said I'd listened to that album and was so impressed, and asked him how he came up with that sound. He gave me some really artistic, almost Bowie-esque kind of an answer. There is 'artist logic' and 'real logic' – it made all the sense in the world to him, but you explain it to someone else and they go – 'uh?' So when he explained it to me, we just bonded."

Gabriel called on Rodgers to assist with the single version of the track: "'Walk Through The Fire' is one of my favourite things ever; I just love that song," Rodgers says. "At that time, I thought it was going to be a smash, but it wasn't. We didn't get that record. Phil Collins was the man, and he had a great record." Indeed, Collins was the man – his career lift-off seemed unassailable at that juncture. Gabriel's track, although possessing a jaunty rhythm, was more of a groove rather than a song, ideal for incidental music, whereas Collins' 'Against All Odds (Take A Look At Me Now)' was a fully fledged power ballad that topped the US charts.

However, 'Walk Through The Fire' led to a further collaboration between Gabriel and Rodgers: "That was a remix, and it was through that, we started to date, if you will," Rodgers laughs. "I met him, we talked, there was a meeting of the minds, and it was like, hey, we can do this right now. For us, artistically, it was wonderful – if he was happy, I was happy, and then, of course, *Gremlins* and then the work with Laurie Anderson."

The pair took their relationships into *Gremlins*, working on a track entitled, 'Out, Out'. *Gremlins* was a dark and comical film directed by Joe Dante and produced by Steven Spielberg, a macabre flipside to the feel-good family classic *ET* that Spielberg had recently directed. "We were working on *Gremlins* and I was getting Peter's vocal sound. I'd listened to a whole bunch of his records before we did it, and I was doing the typical record producer thing that we call 'the press conference', setting up every great microphone and see which one is the most flattering for the singer. Peter said look, let's just use that one and put all this shit on it. That's pretty much how I do it." Rodgers admired Gabriel's candour and worked on the track with his usual Power Station crowd to record the track. Gabriel and Rodgers were pleased with the results, a seven-minute groove that continued the funk elements of *Security*.

'Out, Out' was a slight track slotted into the film. Available only as a promotional 12″ in the Netherlands, it wasn't selected for single release but on the soundtrack album. Rodgers was disappointed it didn't make a bigger ripple. "I always say to Peter that's one thing in my life I'm so sad about that I wasn't able to give him a hit; and he replied, 'I didn't write a song good enough for you to have the hit.' I mean, wow, who takes that attitude in rock'n'roll – it's always the producer's fault when you don't get a hit and it's always the artist's responsibility when you do." And the songs, although diverting, were simply not good enough.

* * *

However, there was a major film project that was to take up a considerable amount of Gabriel's time, enough to delay recording his new studio album. British director Alan Parker had risen through television adverts and had enjoyed significant success with his films *Bugsy Malone*, *Fame* and *Midnight Express*. He approached Gabriel with a view to scoring his new project, *Birdy*, and composing the soundtrack was to prove a marvellously liberating experience for Gabriel. Parker had recently worked with Pink Floyd's Roger Waters on the troubled filming of *The Wall*, and was initially sceptical about rushing headlong into working with a musician again. Gabriel loved the fact that Parker was a true craftsman and felt passionately about the music that he worked with. The feeling was mutual: "He's a very different person," Parker told Spencer Bright in 1988, recounting his experience with Waters. "He doesn't have any of the hang-ups or the unpleasantness of that particular business. We got on so well, he's such a sweet man, it was a refreshing change." Parker had already earmarked some songs that he wished Gabriel to use from his recent catalogue to soundtrack his film.

*Birdy* was based on the novel by William Wharton and concerned two friends (Matthew Modine and Nicholas Cage) who arrive back from Vietnam, scarred in different ways. One has physical injuries; the other has mental problems that make him yearn to be a bird. Gabriel looked at his work to date and began to assemble and reimagine portions of existing tracks to fit the mood of the film. In fact, although *Birdy* is often seen as a stop-gap for Gabriel, it is one of the most important albums of his career, as it offered the first opportunity for him to think truly outside the conventions and structure of popular music. He had been heading this way for years with differences in recording techniques and layering sound, but now he could experiment fully. By remixing, editing, and adding to as needed, Gabriel stripped away all vocals, and added newly recorded pieces – it became about texture and feel and manipulating musical ideas. "We worked for a couple of weeks with unorthodox explorations of some of the sounds, rhythms and themes of existing tracks," Gabriel wrote in 2002. "This provided many moods but I felt some new material was needed as well." The combination of both approaches created a stunning, atmospheric and discrete work.

The most significant aspect of the project was that it marked the start of Gabriel working with Daniel Lanois, who would significantly shape his sound over this album and two further album releases. David Rhodes had introduced Gabriel to the multi-instrumentalist Canadian producer, who had worked in studios since the age of 17, with bands such as Martha & The Muffins. When Lanois set up Grant Avenue Studios in Hamilton with bandmate Bob Doidge the studio attained its good reputation. It was here that Lanois met Brian Eno, and the pair would establish a fruitful partnership, working first on the collaborative album *Apollo: Atmospheres and Soundtracks* in 1983 with Eno's brother Roger and then the beautiful piano-based ambience of *The Pearl*, with Harold Budd. "Eno, we always have done very beautiful and innovative work together," Lanois said in 2006. "So I think about him all the time . . . In the early Eighties we did a bunch of ambient records and those values were a great part of my bedrock and have been with me ever since. Small toolbox, a lot of dedication and becoming a master of a few ways of doing things. I still do that now. Don't embrace too much at one time, only embrace what you are excited about." This chimed exactly with Gabriel's thinking.

Primarily a musician, Lanois had a great sense of humour, was prepared to experiment and possessed boundless patience. It was these four qualities as well as his dedication and 'small toolbox' that immediately drew him to Gabriel. Also, he had no previous baggage in tow; they hadn't been to school together or lived near each other. They only had Brian Eno, one of Gabriel's most trusted and admired friends and inspirations, in common. And there could be no higher recommendation for Gabriel.

"I didn't know anything about him until I came to do the *Birdy* soundtrack, when one of my friends and musicians, David Rhodes, strongly recommended Danny for his work on the Harold Budd record," Gabriel said in 1986. "He thought Danny would be very good for the atmospheric pieces – as indeed he was. We got on well, and he has good instinctive reactions to my music." Lanois recounts in his autobiography, *Soul Mining: A Musical Life* first meeting Gabriel, and how he "felt I had met him before. He had the eyes of a relative . . . when I saw Peter I trusted my feelings. And accepted I was working with a relative. We didn't know what we were about to do, but I knew Peter was made of good. That was enough for me to go on."

Recording the *Birdy* soundtrack at Ashcombe House between October and December 1984, Gabriel used tapes of material recorded over the past four years. The album was credited as being 'written and performed by Peter Gabriel', with 'special musical contributions from Jon Hassell, the Drummers of Ekome, Larry Fast, Tony Levin, Jerry Marotta, David Rhodes, with additional material performed by Manny Elias, Morris Pert and John Giblin'. Around half of the material had its roots in other Gabriel recordings – 'Close Up' utilised the keyboards from 'Family Snapshot' and 'The Heat' took Gabriel's beloved Ghanaian drumming of the Ekome Dance Company from *Security* and built up a climactic, chaotic piece of rhythm: 'Birdy's Flight' was based on 'Not One Of Us'; 'Under Lock And Key' came from 'Wallflower' and 'Powerhouse At The Foot Of The Mountain' from 'San Jacinto'. The remaining seven tracks were all new material. Gabriel thought highly of the album: 'I am pleased to have done this soundtrack for my first attempt at a score," Gabriel said at the time of its reissue. "*Birdy* is a special film."

'Slow Marimbas', which took Morris Pert's frantic marimba of 'No Self Control' and slowed it down to a crawl, was to feature in his live set for years to come. 'At Night' is properly atmospheric and fairly sinister. 'Sketch Pad For Trumpet And Voice' is just that, with Gabriel shouting out and Jon Hassell's distinctive trumpet that had graced so many Eno recordings. The Fairlight CMII plays an enormous role on the album, marshalling Gabriel's sounds. Borrowing heavily from the ambient world of Brian Eno on one hand, while completely reinventing the process on the other, *Music From The Film Birdy* is another tremor of the seismic shift in Gabriel's approach to recording that had begun with *Melt* in 1980.

*Music From The Film Birdy* was released on March 18, 1985, three months after the film's release. The film was well received critically and won the Jury's Special Grand Prix at the Cannes Film Festival in 1985.

However, it was not a great success at the box office, recouping less than a quarter of its original budget. It has gone on to become something of a cult film in both director Parker and star Cage's filmography.

The back cover of *Music From The Film Birdy* loudly pronounced a 'warning – This album contains re-cycled material and no lyrics'. Its chart performance suggested that Gabriel had secured his significant cult following – the album reached number 51 in the UK chart and number 162 in the US, still pretty impressive for what is essentially an album of sound collages. *Rolling Stone* said that the album emphasised "mood over melodic content". *Trouser Press Record Guide* opined: "Although it's uncommon to hear sustained instrumental work from someone so known for vocal music, the score is audibly identifiable, and provides a fascinating glimpse into his adaptational thinking. A strongly affecting work and a major challenge vanquished admirably with style and character."

★ ★ ★

In 1985, through discreet, upmarket entertainment estate agents, Pereds, Gabriel had acquired Box Mill, six miles outside of Bath with a view to turning it into a recording complex. Situated in over 4.8 acres, this historic building would prove the realisation of his dream, be somewhat less chaotic than Ashcombe and, most importantly, across its 20,000 square feet of space, house all of his operations under one roof. The property came with planning permission for 'the expansion of small scale employment in existing premises' and suggested uses were 'high tech, office campus/headquarters, residential training centre or hotel and conference centre'. Ironically, what was to happen there became a mixture of all of those suggested uses. However, for his next album, Gabriel recorded at the barn in Ashcombe House, offering him time and space to make his dreams reality.

In June 1985, a major tie with the past was cut: Tony Stratton-Smith, now increasingly involved in the world of horse racing and film and screenwriting, sold out his remaining shares in Charisma Records to Richard Branson of Virgin Records. Virgin had been distributing Charisma since August 1983 and now subsumed the label. When it first started, Branson's Virgin had been modelled almost entirely on Charisma, so although both founders had moved increasingly further away from their original hands-on approaches, the label was in safe hands. "Genesis made

Charisma a valuable commodity which is why Strat got a huge sum of money when Branson bought him out," writer Chris Charlesworth recalls. "They made the Charisma catalogue valuable, they were probably worth more than everyone else on Charisma ten times over. He picked one big winner and that's all you need." Stratton-Smith remained a consultant for the label, and in a letter to Gail Colson, said that all of the existing team and newcomers "will make this label sing in the very personal and unique way that it has always done".

Gabriel's next release would make the legacy of the label sing loud and clear. The album repaid all the patience, money spent and flights of fancy that Charisma had had to weather over the years. It would provide Gabriel with something he had never before enjoyed: *bona fide* transatlantic success. Peter Gabriel was heading for the 'Big Time'.

# 18: The Tremble In The Hips: *So*

*"Peter Gabriel is made of good, he's made of dreams."*

Daniel Lanois, 2010

IT was inevitable that major success would eventually come Peter Gabriel's way. His next album, *So*, released in May 1986 was to change everything. The world was shifting and there seemed little room for the left-field experimenter in mid-Eighties pop music. The underground had truly gone overground. This was typified in remarkable terms by the man who had just a decade-and-a-half ago swum in Gabriel's parents' swimming pool while other drummers were being auditioned. With the release of *No Jacket Required*, in January 1985, Phil Collins rose from being a big selling chart-topping artist, to become a global megastar, topping the charts in nine countries and spawning two US number one singles. The album was to go 12x platinum in the US alone. Gabriel himself had added backing vocals to one of the tracks on the album that was to be used as a single, 'Take Me Home'.

Although there was no pressure at all for Gabriel to deliver an album of similar magnitude, there surely must have been something subliminal at work. The man who was the intelligent avatar of prog-soul had to have his moment in the sun as well. Certainly it would repay the faith and patience that Charisma had shown him across the years, and it would also prove to Geffen, who had been so supportive of his work, that he was able to deliver one enormous, creative and commercial success. To achieve that level of popularity he might have to forfeit some of the artistic freedom he so relished but at the same time he would attain the financial freedom to pursue whatever path he wanted.

Gabriel was in tune with the times. Inadvertently, he had helped introduce one of the production crazes of the Eighties, thanks to the sound of 'Intruder' from *Melt*. Nile Rodgers and his partner in CHIC, producer

Bernard Edwards, were using that record's drum sound freely in their chart-making productions, among many others. Rodgers recalled: "It's funny that the thing that brought me to Peter was the thing that Bernard ended up defining with The Power Station, when he did 'Some Like It Hot'." The record, with Tony Thompson's thudding drums, was a transatlantic hit in 1985. "It had that gated room drum sound. The engineer who was working with me at the time was Jason Corsaro, who ended up working with Bernard. So we [both] experimented with it after we'd listened to Peter Gabriel, but they finally got it right with The Power Station. It's funny how we are all tied together."

Gabriel had considered working with Rodgers for the album. "The problem is because I was living and breathing all of that air around Peter at the time," Rodgers recalls. "Just from a fan's point of view, I just wanted to know what was in his brain. So if he talked about something like producing his album, maybe I would have heard it, but I was more interested in him as an artist. You know a person is a star when you are interested in what they ate for breakfast." However, Gabriel was delighted with the relationship that he had cultivated with Lanois.

"I'd actually been thinking of other people for this album, such as Nile Rodgers and Bill Laswell," Gabriel told *Musician* magazine in 1986. "But as everything was working out so well with *Birdy*, we carried on. Besides, he [Lanois] likes to create an environment where live performances can happen, and he makes sure they don't get lost once they're recorded. He and David Rhodes were my other ears during these sessions."

It was about working with trusted hands, unafraid to experiment. In the interim between *Birdy* and Gabriel's next album, Daniel Lanois had become very much in demand thanks to his production, in partnership with Brian Eno, on U2's album *The Unforgettable Fire*. Initially released in September 1984, it had established the Irish band at the very forefront of stadium rock, and was unusual in that it was essentially an intimate, quiet and introspective album, despite the anthemic ballads and mass-market appeal.

As always with Gabriel, the ultimate success of the album that he was about to record was that blend of determined hard work and a degree of happy accident that was to make it one of the most highly regarded and enormously commercially viable records of the Eighties. However, experimentation was very much the order of the day once again.

*Security* had been the dress rehearsal. Gabriel was by now used to working for himself, away from the clock-ticking pressure of by-the-hour London studios. He could set his agenda, and importantly, save every morsel of the process to tape. One of Daniel Lanois' abiding memories of the album was standing in the control room at Ashcombe up to his waist in two-inch tape while piecing the album together. It was going to be a long hard slog; but here Gabriel was obsessed with the tune, whereas on *Security* he had seemed obsessed with the process. It was going to be something very different.

Work on the album began in May 1985, and it was fundamentally Lanois, Gabriel and Rhodes sitting in the studio rehearsing. Gabriel had prepared rhythms to use, and, in some cases, a simple set of chord structures for Lanois and Rhodes to improvise around. "We had a nice starting point," Lanois said in *Behind The Glass, Volume II: Top Record Producers Tell How They Craft the Hits*. "In that kind of scenario, it's not a good idea to have a lot of people around because you get nervous that you're wasting people's time while the song is getting written. But by having just the three of us, we had this 'turning up for work' kind of humour: we'd wear these construction worker hard hats." With the three of them, approaches could be quickly changed, and by not involving other musicians immediately, Gabriel, in theory, could head down fewer cul-de-sacs.

Lanois recalls in his autobiography that he, Rhodes and Gabriel called themselves the Three Stooges, after the black-and-white Hollywood comedy troupe. They built up a close, humour-rich rapport. Lanois was working with great focus, and recalls, "the intricate details covering every nuance of song arrangements border on forensic. The planned psychological manoeuvres to steer Peter in a certain direction . . . I saw every problem as a personal obstacle to knock down." It was if, after working with him on the *Birdy* soundtrack, and aware of Gabriel's love of a distraction, he had got the measure of him and sought to keep him on track.

Although hardly a democracy, necessary changes were likely to be identified sooner, and Lanois likened it, due to the lack of extraneous musicians present initially, to changing the course of a canoe rather than a supertanker. Lanois lived in the room above the studio, and was ready to leap to the construction site whenever Gabriel demanded it. It took "A year to finish," Lanois was later to say. "And I was told it was the fastest record Peter ever made." It was a spiritual experience for Lanois, who is on record as saying that he loved Gabriel as a brother.

The early work that the three captured had, according to Lanois, "The feel and soul like breadcrumbs on a path" but if they strayed too far from their path of improvisation, they could always find their way back to the source. With engineer Kevin Killen, they were able to capture the spirit of these ideas, and flesh them out.

As the album grew, Gabriel relied on an accomplished team of players old and new to support him: Tony Levin, one of his most trusted lieutenants was there, of course; so, fleetingly, was Jerry Marotta. One of Gabriel's greatest finds was Ivorian-French drummer Manu Katché, who added remarkable restraint and texture to some of the album's greatest tracks. Stewart Copeland of The Police added percussion; L Shankar, whom Gabriel had encountered through the first WOMAD festival, played violin. Laurie Anderson and Nile Rodgers dropped in on 'This Is The Picture'.

The material was rich and varied. 'Red Rain' underlined that this was a new Gabriel – as if to demonstrate clearly the break with the past, the first sound that is heard is Copeland's busy, fussy, hi-hat and cymbals. The 'no metals' rule, which had lasted five years, was clearly now out. Gabriel's desire for the album to 'crash open at the front' was plainly acheived.

'Red Rain', along with 'That Voice Again', were perhaps the final excerpts of what was to have been Gabriel's Mozo 'wandering stranger' concept that had featured briefly on *Car* and *Scratch* back in the Seventies. "Mozo is set in this fishing village, which is very upmarket, not quite Mediterranean, but something of that ilk," Gabriel told his biographer Spencer Bright. "There is this volcanic sand which gives the sea a red colour. Everything is focused on the sea, which is very rough, and the great macho fear is to cross the water, which no one had done."

The song came from a dream that Gabriel had of a big, red sea being divided, and glass bottles shaped like humans filling up with blood. Although it was new, fully of shiny Eighties modernism, it all seemed as if Gabriel from 1974 was talking rather than the new, lean, handsome heart-throb he had become. It was a brooding opening to the album, and to reflect two very current Eighties obsessions: AIDS and nuclear fallout. The fears of the day were infection beneath the skin and nuclear catastrophe after the Chernobyl disaster in the Ukraine in 1985. Yet 'Red Rain' was a song of hope, of the shared lifeblood.

However, it was the album's next track and first single, 'Sledgehammer', that was really to change the course of Gabriel's career. It presented him as a child in a sweetshop, dabbling in all manner of sexual innuendo, some implicit, some frankly rather explicit. Speaking at the time, Gabriel saw 'Sledgehammer' as an "attempt to recreate some of the spirit and style of the music that most excited me as teenager – Sixties soul. The lyrics of many of those songs were full of playful sexual innuendo and this is my contribution to that tradition. It is also about the use of sex as a means of getting through a breakdown in communication."

And thanks to the events of the past few years, Gabriel knew a lot about the breakdown in communications. The song was a slinky, superb calling card that was as different to the album opener as possible. The song itself was, unbelievably, an afterthought. With recording of the album nearing completion, Gabriel was tinkering with a groove, and considered it with a view to a future project. Its title, according to Lanois, arose from the construction worker language that the three of them used, hitting problems with a sledgehammer. Built up from rhythm box, Gabriel quickly got Levin and Katché to add texture. Lanois' guitar playing was invaluable to the mix. When the initial recording was finished, Lanois and Gabriel ran round the studio jumping up and down. It was that special.

The song took on an extra dimension when it was being mixed and overdubs were added at New York's Power Station studios. Gabriel hit on the idea of contacting Wayne Jackson, one of the original players in the Memphis Horns who had played with Otis Redding the night that the young Gabriel had seen them in Brixton. Gabriel thought if he could put together a horn section, it would add added authenticity to the track. Jackson duly obliged. "It was partly homage and we tried to find whoever was left of the Memphis horns," Gabriel told NPR in 2012. "Wayne Jackson put a group together. And part of the excitement of that session was hearing all these Otis Redding stories." When Gabriel started extemporising his refrains that went into the end of the song, Lanois was astounded. He wrote, "Were we not meant to be making a profound, mystical, West country record? Peter, Rhodes and I surrendered to this ride: an all-encompassing dance party, a kind of new craze . . . a celebration of life."

It was a riot of a track, a celebration of life that stunned the listener on first hearing. For once, Gabriel had produced a straight-out-of-the-box, unbelievably catchy hit single. Its commercialism made even 'Solsbury Hill', Gabriel's most radio-friendly hit to date, seem positively *difficult*. The best thing about 'Sledgehammer' is its wonderful false beginning, where the E-mu Emulator II shakuhachi bamboo flute sound (that seemingly was then placed on virtually every record that followed it) drops away, and sets up the dirtiest, greasiest horn break. It completely confounded expectations. There was a palpable sense of relief when 'Sledgehammer' was first heard. After the dense, complex sounds of *Security*, Gabriel had truly, publicly and loudly got his groove back in a way he never had before. And although it seemed to be the fascination for every white boy to add a horn section and go funky in the early to mid-Eighties, here Gabriel was doing it with the Memphis Horns.

Through its extremely retro styling, the song sounded like the future, a time capsule of the most zinging, up-to-date production available in 1986. "Karl Bartos told me that when Kraftwerk were making *Electric Cafe* they went into the Power Station where Gabriel was doing overdubs on *So* and 'Sledgehammer' was put on," Kraftwerk biographer David Buckley said. "They were knocked back by how fantastic it sounded. They felt their record was puny sonically by comparison, even though it's a completely different genre of music."

The following track continued this incredible quality control. An evocative ballad, 'Don't Give Up' was partially inspired by the startlingly evocative Dorothea Lange pictures of Americans during the Great Depression. Written as a duet, Gabriel initially envisioned Dolly Parton, one of the greatest American bluegrass vocalists of her generation, to sing the song but that fell through. Instead he turned to his great friend, Kate Bush, who was then enjoying huge commercial success in the wake of her 1985 album, *Hounds Of Love*, to add the impassioned female vocal part. Bush's album can be seen in some ways as a sister album of *So*. Both he and Bush had released difficult, complex albums in 1982 that had not chimed as resonantly with the public as earlier records had done. With *Hounds Of Love*, like *So*, Bush had kept all of her inherent strangeness, yet sweetened it with some of the most commercially accessible singles of her career. Like an actor playing a part, she delivered her lines with conviction and sincerity. Over the gentle swell of Richard Tee's gospel influenced piano part, the song was a masterpiece of understatement that was in step with the straightened times lurking beneath the shiny veneer of the Eighties.

'Don't Give Up' is arguably Gabriel's most powerful statement. By the mid-Eighties, the Conservative Prime Minister Margaret Thatcher's government was shredding society with its defiant selfishness, handing down edicts to an unemployment-ridden populace with a superior and self-satisfied approach. In response to the inner-city rioting that had bedevilled the country in 1981, Thatcher's Employment Secretary Norman Tebbit infamously used an analogy about his father being out of work in the Thirties, and instead of rioting, he got on his bike and looked for work. This became interpreted popularly as telling the unemployed to 'get on their bike' to get a job. The way that Gabriel picks up the tale of a dispirited man at the end of his tether looking for work touched a raw nerve with millions of listeners in the UK, and latterly, the world.

Channelling the emotion of his set-piece numbers such as 'Wallflower', he presents this simple, personal tale, which made a remarkable connection. Designed as a conversation between a man and a woman, it seeks to emphasise the power of a bond between a couple that can defeat all obstacles. With two attempts at her vocal, Bush added the requisite warmth and vulnerability to the song. It became, as Bush biographer Graeme Thomson notes, for many people in the US their "first point of reference" for her.

The song, with Gabriel's despair in the verses and Bush's words of hope in the chorus, has gone on to be arguably Gabriel's most loved composition. Cover versions have been recorded by Bono and Alicia Keys, P!nk and John Legend, Willie Nelson and Sinead O'Connor and Maire Brennan and Michael McDonald. Pop sensation Lady Gaga covered it with Canadian rockers, Midway State so "that young people would hear and learn something about Kate Bush".

Gabriel has stated that a well-known rock star and a comedian both said that the song had stopped them from committing suicide. "You don't know how some of the songs are going to hit people . . . you realise that it's like a tool box full of emotional tools when you put out music and you put some real feeling into it. I'm a bit more conscious of that . . . I thought of what I was trying to do."

DJ and author Mark Radcliffe writes with genuine affection in his book

*Reelin' In The Years* when he says, "It is beautiful and not without hope. The song is a duet between the battered jobseeker and his loving, protective, faithful, embattled wife. In essence, as the title suggests, she says that things might look grim but whatever happens, they'll be together." "The sentiment of this song is not very rock'n'roll, but it might just outlive rock'n'roll," writes Daniel Lanois in his book.

After such high drama, 'That Voice Again' is a beautiful, Byrds-like pop song that often gets overlooked amid the album's plentiful highlights. Unusually co-written lyrically with David Rhodes, it looked at Gabriel's attempts to become less judgemental, and was written in the wake of his first discussions about *The Last Temptation Of Christ* with Martin Scorsese. Originally entitled 'First Stone', it sounds almost as if Gabriel had taped one of the therapy sessions that he had been going through. Musically, it is relatively simplistic, with Rhodes playing jangling Rickenbacker over the rhythm section of Katché and Levin.

'Mercy Street' was another of the album's more touching numbers. Gabriel had been reading the work of American poet Anne Sexton after having become interested in her work through the book, *To Bedlam And Part Way Back*. Sexton had committed suicide at the age of 45 in 1974, leaving a slender yet highly confessional body of work, and the gentle, lilting rhythm of Gabriel's song supports lyrics that allude to this. Its title was taken from one of her plays, *Mercy Street* and one of her posthumous collections, *45 Mercy Street*, concerning her search for a father figure. Percussion for the track was recorded by Gabriel in Rio De Janeiro by seasoned player Djalma Correa. The track also utilises the marvellous bass work of Larry Klein. With its deeply reflective tone and affecting vocal, 'Mercy Street' became one of Gabriel's most popular numbers and a staple of his live set. The song leant itself to being covered, becoming one of Gabriel's most lucrative copyrights as artists such as Black Uhuru and Al Di Meola have recorded versions. One of the greatest and tenderest versions was by Herbie Hancock, who recorded it on his *The New Standard* album in 1995.

'Big Time', the sister track to 'Sledgehammer', was another splendid romp through Gabriel's soulful side, a sardonic reflection on the music business. It has the opposite viewpoint of the Jacob character in 'I Know What I Like (In Your Wardrobe)'; it was time after all, to try for that future in the fire escape trade. Gabriel wrote the lyrics examining the dichotomy of his character, and perhaps realising it was fame he craved after all. The story of the man breaking out of the small town with his big words and widest smile, could be read as humorously autobiographical. With fantastic support from the horn section and female vocalists led by PP Arnold, the track was an obvious choice for a later single from the album in the UK, and the second single in the US, where it reached number eight. Clean cut and funky, this was clearly how the States liked their Gabriel.

'We Do What We're Told (Milgram's 37)' had been around for a considerable period, originally recorded as far back as *Melt* and seriously in the running for *Security*. As it is, it sounds like the last link with that era on the album; strange, undercooked and difficult, it is the album's 'Lead A Normal Life'. It was about Professor Stanley Milgram's social psychology experiment from 1961: volunteers assessing how far they would be prepared to follow an authority figure, even if it was in complete opposition to their conscience or their views. Gabriel looked at how people are conditioned to believe in dictators and support war. With its patter of Marotta's processed drums and Shankar's squalls of violin, and two overdubbed guitar tracks by Rhodes, it is a disquieting interlude, proving to all Gabriel's new found audience that it was still within his power to unsettle and disquiet.

'This Is The Picture (Excellent Birds)' was adapted from the track that Gabriel had written with Laurie Anderson for her *Mister Heartbreak* album. On it, he worked again with Nile Rodgers. "I recorded my part in New York," Rodgers recalled. "In those days of course I was gigging, and that was the height of my life. Sometimes it's hard for me to remember what studio, what work, where I was. Like Winwood, 'Higher Love' – how long did that take? 20 minutes or something – maybe a little longer but not much." Rodgers' speedy contribution added a fabulous rhythmic, melodic density to the groove. "I loved that sound that Daniel got. It was also when my partying and drugging was going on. I almost partied like it was a job. That was the period of my life where my brain was flooded with information and one day is not really that much more important than the next – the fact my heart stopped eight times but I'd walk out of the hospital was just one line of conversation. It was then, what do you guys want to do tonight?" What Gabriel wanted Rodgers to do was to add his remarkable, rhythmical guitar playing to another skeletal idea, and one that had been inspired by the Korean video artist Nam June Paik, who used to make TV shows. He had asked Laurie Anderson and Peter Gabriel if they would like to collaborate, and they worked quickly to produce this groove.

The album closed with another of Gabriel's most loved songs, written from inside the Gabriel-Arquette-Gabriel triangle, and ostensibly a love song for Rosanna. 'In Your Eyes', originally titled 'Sagrada Familia' and inspired by the cathedral in Barcelona, had been around for a considerable period of time. Also alluding to Antoni Gaudi and rifle heiress Sarah Winchester, the song was multi-layered and deeply affecting. The power of the track was made real by the stunning guest vocal performance from Youssou N'Dour, who sings in his native language, Ouoloff. Gabriel, by now very accustomed to having guests on his recordings, was apprehensive about working with N'Dour, whom he'd first seen play live in Paris in 1983. "I got really worked up about him coming to Bath to record the vocals for 'In Your Eyes'," he told John Doran for the *So 25* notes, "You have to remember that where he was from in Dakar, Senegal, he was treated like Elvis Presley." He went on to explain that when he first saw him live, it "blew my mind – his voice was like liquid gold pouring from the sky." Gabriel need not have worried; the two became firm friends. The song was multi-layered, and also featured Simple Minds leader and lifelong Gabriel fan, Jim Kerr on backing vocals.

'In Your Eyes' was featured dramatically in the Cameron Crowe film, *Say Anything* in a sequence when protagonist Lloyd Dobler (John Cusack) plays it loudly from a ghetto blaster above his head. Although not a huge success in the UK, the film is somewhat totemic in the United States, and has given the record a long afterlife, being equally as popular as 'Sledgehammer.' It reached number 26 in the US charts.

*So*, of course, went to the wire with Gabriel's customary reticence in providing final lyrics for the album, much to the frustration of Lanois. Like Bob Ezrin gaffer-taping him to a pillar to get the best vocal performance, in order for Gabriel to finish the record, Lanois actually nailed him inside the barn at his house to complete the words. "I wouldn't have dared do that," David Lord laughed. "Of course, Peter can be deeply frustrating to work with," Richard Macphail says. "I don't think songs come with great difficulty to Peter – he loves to start with a rhythm, some harmonies, the song comes, but what is agonising is the lyrics; he works really hard on them and they are bloody good. His lyrics are fantastic. Always whenever he's supposed to have another album coming out – he's got 20 songs and the lyrics aren't done."

Gabriel obsessed with the sequencing of the album, putting track beginnings and ends together on cassette, to hear how the songs would blend. On the original vinyl, 'In Your Eyes' had to start the second side, while 'This Is The Picture (Excellent Birds)' was put as a track on the CD only. By the end of the recording period, the album cost £200,000 to make and was finally finished in February 1986. Lanois stayed on at Ashcombe to continue working on the Robbie Robertson album on which Gabriel, Eno and U2 all lent a hand, which would come out the following year. Gabriel's voice on 'Fallen Angel' is one of the standouts of Robertson's self-titled debut solo album.

*So* looked as if it would be something special. There would be no anxious meetings with record company executives.

* * *

While overdubs were being recorded for *So* at New York's Power Station studios, Gabriel assisted the former E-Street Band guitarist, Little Steven (Steven Van Zandt) in the recording of his anti-apartheid 'Sun City' project, which in turn had been inspired by Gabriel's own 'Biko'. Sun City was a resort in Bophuthatswana, an independent state set up by the Apartheid government of South Africa. Van Zandt wrote on the sleeve-notes to his *Sun City* album a thanks to Gabriel, for the "profound inspiration of his song 'Biko', which is where my journey to Africa began." Gabriel contributed to the title track, which featured a veritable who's who of left-leaning rock and soul musicians under the umbrella of Artists Against Apartheid, including Bruce Springsteen, Gil Scott-Heron, David Ruffin, Eddie Kendricks, Bono, Bobby Womack, Run-DMC, old friend and debut tour support Nona Hendryx and Bob Dylan. He also made a cameo appearance in the song's video. As Gabriel began contributing musically to the track 'Sun City', he produced seven minutes' worth of material, playing with violinist L Shankar, who was currently working with him on *So*. Van Zandt was sufficiently impressed with the material that he decided to use the largely instrumental track, complete with chanting, on the single's parent album. 'No More Apartheid' is a loose, clattering jam, which highlights the amazing ability Gabriel has to work quickly if he really has to.

PART THREE

# . . . To Revelation: 1986–2013

# 19: Life Is One Big Adventure: *So* And Its Aftermath

*"A man works for however long – decades even – to get to a point where it all comes to an apex and that was Peter's moment."*

Gerry Gersch, Geffen Records, 2012

SO was a remarkable update of Peter Gabriel's music for the mid-Eighties, especially given the fact that aside from the hit singles, it was fundamentally exactly the same album as *Security*. It slotted in well with the pattern of similar acts of a Seventies vintage all having haircuts, embracing technology and exposing their soul roots.

'Sledgehammer' was released as *So*'s lead single in April 1986. The record on its own would have been an enormous hit, but what propelled it even further into the wider public consciousness was its accompanying video, made with Bristol-based Aardman Animations and directed by Stephen R. Johnson, whose work Gabriel admired. Johnson had worked on the promotional film for Talking Heads' 'Road To Nowhere' from the previous year.

Gabriel had understood the power of video from its inception, and his early promos all have an arty, naïve charm. He had noted the impact that the video for 'Shock The Monkey' had had on the US market. It had been perfect for MTV, which had come into being in August 1981. As British acts tended to have more ornate, story-led promos, the channel was eager to run them and it heralded a wave of success for British bands in the US, notably Duran Duran and Culture Club. With the success of 'Shock The Monkey' in mind, Gabriel wanted something as big, brash and innovative as his new track sounded to accompany it. By now, the happy arty accidents of his early videos had to be left behind – promos had become increasingly expensive and grandiose. For example, Duran Duran were creating huge subterranean underworlds, Frankie Goes to Hollywood had world leaders grappling in wrestling rings and of course Michael Jackson was enlisting Hollywood directors to make full-on short films for him.

Johnson introduced Gabriel to the Brothers Quay, who were leaders in their field, the technique known as stop-motion, and Gabriel in turn introduced Johnson to Bristol-based Aardman Animations. All parties began to storyboard an extremely literal interpretation of the song. The green light for the video, which would clearly be expensive, was given by Tessa Watts at Virgin Records. It was a huge gamble investing over £100,000 in an artist usually confined to the art-rock margins.

Ironically, techniques that took so long to employ on the video can today be done in a matter of seconds on a mobile phone. In 1986, the shoot took over 100 hours of filming between April 7 and 15. "It was really exciting, creative brainstorming," Gabriel said in the *So Classic Albums* documentary. "[It's] one of the most exciting things that I do, working with people smarter than me from different backgrounds." These smarter people created an incredible, innovative world, unlike anything that had been hitherto seen in the world of the simple pop promo. Whereas Gabriel had to dress and constantly repeat his characterisations of his songs night after night onstage with Genesis, here he had to do it once, and then be seen countless times in homes all around the world. Gabriel had to pose 25 times for each frame to create the quirky, unfinished effect of it all.

Shot at Aardman Studios and the Wickham University Theatre in Bristol, the video starts with a close-up of sperm entering a womb, we then see Gabriel's eye, ear, mouth, and his finger tapping his face in close-up, before he commences singing in stop-motion. As the steam train is mentioned, a toy train track appears around his head with an engine circling his face; a paper plane then flies round his head, before his face is painted blue with clouds scudding across it.

Gabriel sings into a megaphone before sitting in front of a chalkboard drawing of a rollercoaster, his hair going wild to emphasise the movement of the big dipper in the song going up and down and around the bends. Plasticine dodgems hit his face; his hair turns into candy floss. It looks as if he is having the time of his life, laughing and smiling, two things he did often in his real life, but seldom in his stage persona. His head is created in ice which is subsequently sledgehammered away; fish appear and Gabriel holds cabbages – a neat reference to what he had previously left the music business to grow, and all manner of fruit dance around him. A wooden workbench is constructed over his face, with various tools scuttling across – his father Ralph's workshop, perhaps?

His face is then animated in plasticine as his fists turn to hammers, smashing his head. One of the more memorable sequences is an egg hatching to reveal two chicken carcasses dancing on a vaudeville stage – this section was animated by Nick Park, who would go on to find fame as the creator and animator of Aardman's best-known export, *Wallace And Gromit*. Gabriel then appears in stop-motion dancing as backing vocalists join him. His daughters Anna and Melanie appear briefly as he dances frenetically around them, crowds of people join, as ultimately does a whole heap of furniture. It finally ends with Gabriel going through a door to the universe in a suit of lights. It was a huge, time-intensive labour of love – at one point Gabriel had to stay in the same position for six hours for ten seconds of train track footage.

The video was finished on the Sunday, and by Thursday it was being broadcast on the BBC's flagship music programme, *Top Of The Pops*. Its appearance was the start of the seismic change in Gabriel's commercial fortunes. "I think the song would have fared okay, because it did seem to work well on the radio," he told *Rolling Stone*. "But I'm not sure that it would have been as big a hit, and I certainly don't think the album would have been opened up to as many people without the video." And it's true the video was everything not associated with Peter Gabriel; out there, in-your-face, charming and fun. "I was seen as a fairly intense, eccentric Englishman," he added. Not now. With his dashing image, sharp suit and impeccably coiffured hair, Gabriel strode out as a hunky everyman who liked a laugh. And through this disarming sense of humour, a new audience was prepared to listen when he sang about Anne Sexton or experiment with Laurie Anderson, just as long as he packed a hit single in tow.

Old friend and fan Kris Needs was in America when 'Sledgehammer' came out: "I do remember the effect his 'Sledgehammer' video had on MTV when I was in New York around that time. It defined the music channel and almost vindicated what it was trying to do."

Gail Colson had lived with the album on and off for a year. "I heard most of the tracks in many stages before the final mixes so I can't say that there was one time when I first heard the album," she said. "I knew that it was more accessible than the other albums but I think it was when I first saw the video for 'Sledgehammer' that I knew we had a massive hit on our hands but I don't think that any of us realised quite how successful it would become."

"It's always a song that elevates you. 'Sledgehammer' really was the one," David Stopps, at this time hugely successful as Howard Jones' manager, recalls. "I was in America, I was told by the people at Elektra to hear the song. It had just gone into the stratosphere."

Of course, many disparagingly commented that with 'Sledgehammer' Gabriel was following Phil Collins in his pursuit of the commercial shilling. Gabriel commented to *Musician* magazine in 1986: "I consider my approach to be very similar to Sixties soul, whereas I think Phil's style is more contemporary. In any case, I was definitely trying to borrow the style of that period, and it is no coincidence that the man leading the brass section is Wayne Jackson, who is one of the Memphis Horns . . . With regard to Phil – I respect his music and I would like my own to reach as large an audience as possible, but I would strongly refute the suggestion that I'm just trying to copy him. That pisses me off, because about the time of my third album there were considerable stylistic changes in Phil's music, and I feel that my influence on him hasn't been fairly acknowledged." The drum sound for 'Intruder' has many fathers; and the sparseness of *Melt* certainly was an influence on Collins' first album, *Face Value*. Both Collins and Gabriel were steeped in the history of African–American music, and both would pay homage to it in their own way; the two were also great friends.

* * *

*So* was released on May 19, 1986. Writing in 2012, Gabriel said: "When I first heard *So*, I was really pleased. It wasn't as rich with texture and sonic experiment as my earlier albums, but it had a very strong spirit. It wasn't like I was an obscure artist. I'd had hits with 'Shock The Monkey', 'Games Without Frontiers' and 'Solsbury Hill' but after each of them I'd purposefully retreated partially back into the shadows. With *So* this was the end of the idea of me being a sort of cult artist at the fringes of the mainstream, especially in America. There wasn't an option to go and hide in the shadows any more." There were no shadows to hide in; Gabriel was in the full glare of the spotlight, and for the first time in his life, it shone really very brightly indeed.

The most striking aspect for many was the look of the album and its outward normality. With a beautiful portrait of Gabriel by Trevor Key – the man who photographed the bell on the front of Mike Oldfield's legendary *Tubular Bells* album – the album was all clean lines, framed in white. Designed by Peter Saville, with Brett Wickens, it was direct and simple, especially given the density and strangeness of the look of his preceding four studio albums. Saville had designed all of the Factory label's artwork from 1979 onwards, and his sparse, modern look gave the record a sense of immediacy as appealing as its musical content. It was possibly Gabriel's only real concession on the album to commercialism. *And* it had a title. Gabriel was questioned by *Rolling Stone* as to why he had bitten the bullet and given his album a title after so long resisting: "The new record has a universal title so that people won't end up buying the same record twice. I'm quite happy that that's happened, because there's a little change in style – I wanted the album to be elemental, alive, unselfconscious."

Geffen were delighted, as it became one of the label's biggest selling albums, staying on the American charts for 93 weeks, lodged at number two, while it reached number one in seven countries worldwide. It gave him his second UK chart topper, going straight in at the top spot and remaining there for two weeks. It received, in the main, warm and generous reviews: *Rolling Stone* said: "The songs are astonishingly wide ranging, drawing upon everything from Shona mbira themes to Senegalese mbalax singing. What makes them pop isn't their concessions (if any) to the marketplace, but the sheer ingenuity of Gabriel's songcraft."

The album's success was prolonged by the release of 'Don't Give Up' as its second single – Gabriel had provided us with the floor filler, now he was giving us the slow dance. Released in October 1986, it reached number nine in the UK chart, and although a much lower 72 in the US, it acted as a remarkable postcard for the album. The video, which as Daniel Lanois says features "Peter and Kate slowly spinning like two wedding cake figurines", touched a nerve. Its simplicity was as stunning as the intricacy of 'Sledgehammer'. Directed by Kevin Godley and Lol Creme, who had gone on to be the UK's leading video directors after they defected from pop group 10cc in 1976, it captured in one, long shot, Gabriel and Bush locked in a passionate embrace while the camera span around them, giving the impression they were indeed revolving, clinging on to each other as life dealt them its blows.

Gabriel also used interviews around the album to talk about his latest obsession, a desire to create a theme park: "My current preoccupation, besides music, is the planning of an amusement park . . . a kind of real world alternative to Disneyland. It's long been a fantasy of mine, but there's an architect in Australia with a two-acre site in Sydney who heard about my idea, and he's asked me to put forward a proposal." The thought of a 'real world' where participants could learn and partake in sensory experiences delighted Gabriel's inquisitive mind, and would compliment the multi-media aspects of his work. He continued: "The ideology and aesthetics of the amusement park were established in the Forties and Fifties, and I strongly believe that the creative minds of today could come up with much more interesting experiences than has usually been the case. And with contemporary interactive technology, you could have events and experiences that would respond to the visitor, so it would be a truly participatory process." Gabriel had initially investigated a site in Sydney and talked to artists and planners to assess whether it could become a reality. The plan was to go through many twists and turns, but one thing remained a constant throughout, its title – Real World.

* * *

Gabriel realised that he was now much in-demand and knew that his time would not be his own for the foreseeable future. True to his beliefs, he decided to use this newfound platform of mass success to channel his energy towards causes that were dear to his heart. While *So* was being painstakingly assembled in Bath, the Live Aid concert had happened in Wembley and Philadelphia. The brainchild of Boomtown Rat Bob Geldof, for people of a certain age it was as if the world stopped dead in its tracks on July 13, 1985. Aside from the wonder of its altruism, for the music industry the Live Aid concerts came just at the right time and acted as a world-wide shop-window for its recently developed innovation, the compact disc.

There had, of course, been big charity fundraisers before. Charity concerts welded the feel-good vibe of the 1969 Woodstock Festival with the often-genuine belief that given such an enormous platform to act upon megastars should *do something*. Former Beatle George Harrison asked some heavy friends to turn up and play at New York's Madison Square Garden in August 1971 for the flood-ravaged former East Pakistan, then in the throes of a civil war to gain autonomy as Bangladesh. Rumours of a Beatles reunion beforehand and Bob Dylan turning up made it a memorable event. The concert was filmed and a commemorative album was released, with funds, through UNICEF, going to aid schemes.

Thereafter Paul McCartney was the leading light in The Concert For Kampuchea at London's Hammersmith Odeon and in America, Bruce Springsteen et al went *No Nukes* in 1980, a concert in reaction to the Three Mile Island radiation leak, and for disarmament, at New York's Madison Square Garden. Live Aid, however, topped the lot and had it been a year later, Gabriel would have certainly been on the bill.

It was the charismatic singer of U2, Bono, who contacted Gabriel just under a year after Live Aid, with the idea of a short American stadium tour, *A Conspiracy Of Hope*, that was intended to celebrate the 25th Anniversary of the global charity organisation, Amnesty International. U2 had always supported political causes right from their first album, *Boy*, in 1980, and, aside from Queen, U2 had created most impact at Live Aid.

An independent, democratic and self-governing body, Amnesty International, had been founded in 1961 following the publication of an article, 'The Forgotten Prisoners' by lawyer Peter Benenson in *The Observer*, about two Portuguese students imprisoned for drinking a toast to liberty. Benenson suggested that prisoners of conscience might be released if people wrote letters to governments. The organisation – which took the 1948 Universal Declaration Of Human Rights as its credo – had a simple objective: "To conduct research and generate action to prevent and end grave abuses of human rights and to demand justice for those whose rights have been violated." Since that point, it had made stands on prisoners of conscience, the right to fair trials and the abolition of the death penalty.

Amnesty International had long connections with the arts and music, but their events had been confined to comedy and acoustic music in London, with the *Secret Policeman's Ball* series of shows. These had provided a very necessary wake-up call to artists and musicians. Bob Geldof appeared at *The Secret Policeman's Other Ball* in September 1981 which had pricked his social conscience, leading indirectly to his groundbreaking and historic work with Live Aid.

Bono, then too lowly a pop star to join the others onstage, had been in the audience at *The Secret Policeman's Other Ball* in 1981. Jack Healy, the director of Amnesty's American division, had seen U2 in concert in 1984 at

New York's Radio City Music Hall, and was so taken with them he asked if the group would support the cause at some juncture in the future, and Bono and group manager Paul McGuinness gave him an IOU for a week of the group's time. After the success of Live Aid and with the 25th Anniversary of the organisation, it seemed the perfect moment to call in that IOU.

Bono and a small number of staff at McGuinness' office went through a long list of everyone they knew, and took to the telephones, badgering artists to take part in a short stadium tour of America. Gabriel was the first to commit. Scheduled to run for two weeks in June 1986, it would mean that he would have to reschedule an all-important promotional tour in Europe for *So*, which by now looked as if it was going to be bigger than *Security*.

"I had Bono hustling me on the phone saying that the song 'Biko' had been what had first opened him up to Africa – and saying that I had to be there," Gabriel said in 2012. "I wasn't sure about it because it was quite a time commitment and there was obviously no money in it, but afterwards I was so glad that I did it." It was difficult for Gabriel to refuse, and an opportunity to put his money – of which, for the first time in his career, it seemed there may well be a surfeit – where his mouth was. It also effectively meant that the shows he would take out to support his new work would immediately be stadium-sized. With all his years of stagecraft and performance ability, he knew that he could truly seize the moment and, if he wanted to, become a superstar in that handful of dates.

Gabriel quickly assembled a band for these shows. Live and studio regular David Rhodes was joined by *So* contributor Larry Klein on bass, as Tony Levin was otherwise engaged with King Crimson. Manu Katché – on his first tour outside France – came in on drums, and Bath associate, Ian Stanley, who played with Tears For Fears, provided keyboards. They had four days to rehearse for the tour. Working with a small, tight unit sharpened Gabriel.

The line-up of *A Conspiracy Of Hope* – which would be joined by special guests at every venue – was remarkable, and significant for the fact that all the artists halted their work to go on tour. U2, Sting, The Police, Joan Baez, Lou Reed, the Neville Brothers and Bryan Adams were the tour's regulars. Guest performers were also hugely important and included Bob Dylan, Tom Petty, Jackson Browne, Miles Davis, Little Steven and Bob Geldof. Joni Mitchell guested because Klein, Gabriel's bassist and her then-husband, had said what a wonderful experience he had been having on the tour. Robin Williams did some stadium-size stand-up in Chicago, while Madonna and her then-husband Sean Penn introduced Bryan Adams at Cow Palace. The players on *A Conspiracy Of Hope* criss-crossed America, travelling in a charter plane, which, according to U2's bass player Adam Clayton, felt like "something that happened in the Sixties". He added, "I think they were very clear as to why they were on the tour. It's hard to have an ego when you are dealing with prisoners of conscience."

Aside from the various collaborations, each act performed a short set – and Gabriel honed his very best and most commercial material for the occasion. It translated perfectly to the stadium. Whereas most artists would have embarked immediately on their own tour to sell their album, Gabriel was able to showcase the hits from *So*, which was scaling the charts at this point, with a smattering of his catalogue. He performed a convincing 30-minute set that opened with 'Red Rain' and contained 'Sledgehammer', dipped back to 'Family Snapshot' from *Melt*, 'San Jacinto' and, importantly, his biggest Stateside hit to that point, 'Shock The Monkey', and, of course, to close the set, 'Biko'.

Before each show, there would be a press conference, which would begin with Aaron Neville singing 'Amazing Grace' *a capella*, and then Jack Healey would underline the intent of Amnesty. It created a huge impact. The tour opened at the 12,000-capacity Cow Palace in Daly City, California, before visiting Inglewood, Denver, Atlanta, Chicago, and culminating in an enormous performance at the 76,000-capacity Giants Stadium in New Jersey on June 15. The Giants Stadium show was televised by MTV and its final three hours were also broadcast on Viacom.

Gabriel said the following morning on NBC's *Today Show* with Bryant Gumbel – "It was the best tour I've ever been on, there was a real spirit between all the artists . . . A lot of people were new to the work of Amnesty and a lot of people were coming in for the music, but I'm sure there are a lot more letter writers and a lot more active people as a result of this tour. If only 10 per cent of people who saw us on this tour become letter writers, then that is thousands of people who are spared torture and maybe get out of jail."

The decision to take a place on the tour was one of the most significant in Gabriel's life. It provided a springboard and facilitated a sharpening of his political views that had begun to harden around the time of 'Biko'. Most importantly, it set him on the course to founding his own political organisation WITNESS in 1992, and become renowned as an international man of peace. "I started meeting people involved in the human rights world for the very first time," Gabriel was later to say, "meeting people who had been tortured – and suddenly this whole area of the world that I'd seen from a distance in newspapers or TV reports became real." That reality would deeply affect his work right up to the present day. Gabriel was the real surprise of the tour, for many had never seen him before, or even heard his work. And the 15 years of rehearsals paid off. Charismatic, handsome and able to transform a stadium into an intimate space of ritual, Gabriel won over the crowds.

Bono was effusive in his praise for Gabriel's work on *A Conspiracy Of Hope*: "The person whose spirit lit up the place every night was Peter Gabriel, in my opinion," he wrote in 2006. "His generosity as a man, his humour, his spirit as a performer. He was right up there. His song 'Biko' was the most articulate on the subject of Amnesty . . . the song became an anthem for that tour."

Guitarist David Rhodes, who had travelled a long way with Gabriel from the sodden studio in Bath to the world's biggest stages in a short space of time, initially felt out of place with such superstars but soon overcame any nerves. He recalled on his website, aside from watching U2 every night and commenting that Bryan Adams was the least starry, that after the Giants stadium concert, "I was very emotional after hearing so many people join in with 'Biko', that I dashed off to have a teary shower. 'Sledgehammer' went to number one the following week."

The performances and US-wide exposure did Gabriel's career no harm whatsoever. 'Sledgehammer' had been climbing the charts since its release in April, but after the coverage of the shows on live television, the record sped into the top five and, on July 26, 1986, it topped the US Chart, replacing 'Invisible Touch' by Genesis. It was a sweetly significant moment. Genesis had long become a commercial behemoth since the explosion of Phil Collins' solo career and the release of their 1983 album, *Genesis*. Their recent pop-oriented sound had translated perfectly to the American market.

In fact, the American charts of June 1986 demonstrated quite how successful Genesis had been. An amazing *seven* records out of the *Billboard* Hot 100 involved all five members of the classic 1971–1975 line up. The group themselves were there with 'Invisible Touch', and 'Sledgehammer' was just about to enter the Top 10. Collins' unstoppable solo career was also represented. He was in the chart with his former number one, 'Take Me Home', and also as the producer of Howard Jones' (Aylesbury Friars' David Stopps' protégé, lest we forget) 'No One Is To Blame'. Mike Rutherford's offshoot group Mike + The Mechanics had *two* records in the chart – 'Taken In' and 'All I Need Is A Miracle', while even Steve Hackett, in his short-lived GTR project with Yes guitarist Steve Howe, had a big brash Top 30 hit 'When The Heart Rules The Mind'. It would have been put down as one of Tony Stratton-Smith's wilder, wine-fuelled fantasies if he had suggested this US chart supremacy to them when the group were shuffling around Charisma's offices in Soho waiting for their cheques 15 years previously. "It was the Genesis mafia!" Tony Banks laughs. "We thought we'd finally made it when 'Invisible Touch' topped the American charts. And then it was, 'Oh, right Pete's got there, too'. We never had enormous hit singles in the UK, because people would always wait for the albums."

Gabriel was delighted with the single reaching the top spot in the US. The most affectionate homage to the music that originated from deep within America, here was almost the ultimate tribute. An introverted white boy from a privileged British background convincingly interpreting the music of the impoverished segregated south of America. And somehow, it not only worked, it absolutely nailed it.

It was an once-in-a-lifetime moment when the planets aligned. As Gerry Gersch, Gabriel's supporter at his US label, Geffen was to note in the *So* Super Deluxe edition – "A man works for however long – decades even – to get to a point where it all comes to an apex and that was Peter's moment. It doesn't mean it was his best work, but it was the moment that the perfect storm hit: the man and the public and the record and the tour – everything came together . . . It was not what anyone was expecting to happen, but it's exactly what should have happened."

At the end of June, Gabriel appeared at the Artists Against Apartheid concert on London's Clapham Common on a bill will Elvis Costello, Sting, Hugh Masekela and Boy George. It proved again that now superstardom beckoned, he was going to use the platform to get his message across to the widest audience.

* * *

And *So* kept on selling. It was a perfect example of the sort of album that worked so well on CD, the new format introduced by the music industry in 1982. Although *Security*, *Plays Live* and *Birdy* had all had releases on CD, *So* was the first one to be released in the white heat of the explosion of hardware and the desire by consumers to replace existing vinyl albums with CD. It was a field day for the music industry: Live Aid encouraged the thirst for what was soon disparagingly labelled 'heritage rock': aided and abetted by popular publishing. In 1986, EMAP, the company that had been known for publishing *Smash Hits*, launched a new magazine, centred around alumni of *Smash Hits*, *The Face* and *New Musical Express*. The mysteriously titled Q Magazine focussed on this new CD generation and began to spend pages and ages on artists who were too old for *Smash Hits* and *NME*. The audience was there – they'd grown up with those magazines and that music. *So*, just funky enough, just obscure enough, just nostalgic enough, fitted perfectly with the magazine's readership profile. And now, with people buying CDs, the divisions that had been put in place when punk broke in the UK, meant that men in their thirties could go out and buy again those Genesis albums they had binned in 1977. When Q launched, the first edition had a free booklet, *Key CDs*, recommending all that was best on CD – and *So* was in there: "This is consummate modern pop, as inventive and tasteful as Talking Heads at their best but infinitely more direct and in some cases, better to dance to."

The social change facilitated by the world's credit-fuelled leap out of recession in the early Eighties meant that CD players were well within the remit of the new yuppie class, and Gabriel began to attract a new breed of listener that welcomed him as a 'new artist'. This was to prove liberating (there were more girls at his concerts, as Tony Levin noted and fewer calls for obscure Genesis numbers) but would ultimately prove constraining. Although a super-slick short single had always been part of Gabriel's oeuvre, how willing would this new audience be when he was experimenting?

* * *

Gabriel's proper, fully fledged tour to support *So*, the *This Way Up* tour, began on November 7, 1986, in Rochester, upstate New York. Working with Levin, Rhodes, Katché and, maintaining his connection with the E-Street Band, keyboard player David Sancious, the group's original keyboard player before Roy Bittan. With a set that contained over half of *So*, and a breathtaking overview of Gabriel's career to date, the first American leg went through until December 16, where the tour finished in Los Angeles. Venues were bigger and the crowd, many of whom were now watching him for the first time, were amazed by his showmanship. The set would begin with 'This Is The Picture (Excellent Birds)' with the band playing standing in a line and before the rousing finale of 'Biko', would end with Gabriel performing his ritualistic tumble into the crowd for 'Lay your Hands On Me'.

One unusual piece of business cropped up to close the first leg of the tour. Headquartered in Costa Rica, the United Nations-mandated University for Peace was established in December 1980 as a Treaty Organisation by the UN General Assembly. It needed an injection of funds to develop. As benefit concerts had become the currency of the day, Gabriel decided to put on a performance to assist, to be called Hurricane Irene.

"He'd met a nun somewhere, a Mother Teresa-type character who he knew and had tremendous respect for and she said to him on her deathbed to organise a big concert and raise money for the university," David Stopps recalls. "So he wanted to put together this big concert for her memory. He approached Harvey Goldsmith and he went to New York and we had a meeting at the United Nations and he invited Lou Reed, Bono, Jackson Browne, Steve Van Zandt, Howard and I. Gail Colson was there, too. I remember sitting around this huge table with him talking about what he wanted to do at this event. Bono said, 'This doesn't sound like a train that's moving,' and U2 declined to take part. We said we would take part."

The concert, held at Meiji Jingu baseball Stadium, Tokyo on December 20 and 21, 1986, was to raise funds for a global computer system for the university. It became known as *Japan Aid: Hurricane Irene* and was named after Irene, the Greek goddess of peace. Gabriel and co-organiser Hart Perry (who had shot the 'Sun City' video) turned down millions of pounds of sponsorship and world television broadcast rights, because they didn't want to lose control of the project. They wanted the revenue to come in through ticket sales and the rights to video sales. In many ways, it could have been as large scale an event as Live Aid, but it was, if anything, an underground multi-artist benefit in front of around 120,000 people across both nights.

"It was Tokyo in winter and it was cold," Stopps continues. "The promoter handed out chemical hand warmers to everyone in the audience. Lou Reed had to come off because it was so cold and his fingers wouldn't work anymore. It was a very interesting experience. There was this running order with Peter on late and Howard on very early. I said that Howard should be further up the bill: the next day the promoter raised him, realising that Howard had sold more albums in Japan than anyone else. Everyone was a bit shocked of how well he'd done – no tension, but Howard went up bill. But, it was too cold for an outside concert." Nona Hendryx, whose paths crossed with Gabriel many times, performed. "We all came together for that," she said. "We were there for that purpose, we made a unique performance. Each time with Peter has been a unique experience in my life." She also recalls Gabriel taking part in offstage 'silliness' with her band members Steve Scales and Steve Jordan.

* * *

1987 began with Gabriel's standing at the highest it had been in his career. In early February, he found himself at the epicentre of the UK music industry by winning the Best British Male Artist (from a field that contained Billy Ocean, Chris de Burgh, Robert Palmer and Phil Collins) and Best British Music Video (for 'Sledgehammer') at the Sixth Annual BRIT Awards at London's Grosvenor House Hotel. Gabriel's speeches were his charismatic mixture of awkwardness, understatement and effusiveness. He was pictured both with Jill, and, making a rare public appearance, his friend Kate Bush, who won Best British Female Artist and presented Gabriel with his Best Male Award. Gabriel said he would place his awards among his garden gnomes. In April 'Don't Give Up' was named Best Song Musically And Lyrically at the 32nd Annual Ivor Novello Awards.

But the potency of the collaboration of Gabriel, Stephen Johnson, the Brothers Quay and Aardman was written large at the MTV Video Award held in Universal City. 'Sledgehammer' won nine awards that night, plus a special 'Video Vanguard' award for Gabriel. Ten trophies in one night is a feat still unequalled in the MTV Awards history, and Gabriel, with some subsequent awards in following years, is unbelievably the second most garlanded artist in the awards history, second only to Madonna.

The *This Way Up* tour recommenced in June the following year playing Europe, with a brief return to America and closing in Greece in October

1987. The tour illustrated how hot a property Gabriel now was: with his capable and supportive players, the group played 93 dates. Tightly choreographed, musically slick and frequently thrilling, the show delivered exactly what audiences would expect from the newly minted megastar. David Stallbaumer, Gabriel's former assistant, who had been with him on previous tours, noted the change. Speaking in 2012, he said: "Everything catapulted; we went from playing 3,000 to 10,000 venues to stadiums. Instead of seeing 5,000 die-hard student fans in a college town somewhere, you were seeing 40,000 people who knew every word to *So*. It became a very different environment: 20,000 to 40,000 people was a regular concert after that."

There was a sense of validation when Gabriel returned for the British leg of the tour. Aside from stints at Glasgow's SECC and the National Exhibition Centre in Birmingham, he performed a four-night residency at the 19,000-capacity Earls Court in West London in June 1987. On June 28, Kate Bush joined him onstage for her only ever live performance of 'Don't Give Up'. According to Graeme Thomson in his superlative Bush biography, *Under The Ivy*: "The thunderous ovation prompted by her unexpected arrival onstage spoke more eloquently about the genuine love and warmth with which she is regarded than a thousand words ever could." Even *Smash Hits*, the then-pop bible of the UK teens wrote in their July edition of the concert: ". . . before you start thinking that a Peter Gabriel concert is one long yawn, let's set the record straight . . . everyone goes completely bonkers, even though most of them are somewhat elderly types who probably used to go and see Peter Gabriel when he was still the singer in Genesis and wore a lawnmower on his head." *NME*, then in its archest, hippest, era said of his Earls Court show: "As a result it sometimes seemed his audience – cig-lighter wielding hippies to rockin' pre-pubes to baggy-trousered philanderers – just wanted to sing along, consciences barely jogged, to such as 'Games Without Frontiers' and 'No Self Control'; some would gladly have crucified their cats just to go *"boom boom boom"* throughout 'Solsbury Hill'."

By the time the tour concluded at the Lycabettus Amphitheatre in Athens in October, the performances had been honed into a feat of pure showmanship. The footage of the nights show a band working together as one, enthralling the crowd with an appropriate balance of social conscience and showbusiness. Five players completely at ease with each other, and effortless guest appearances from Youssou N'Dour and Les Super Etoiles de Dakar.

On June 5, 1988, Gabriel demonstrated arguably for the final time how far he had relocated into the mainstream by performing at The Prince's Trust Concert in London's Royal Albert Hall. The shows, which had been established by the charity founded by the Prince Of Wales in 1976, had become regular fixtures on the annual rock music calendar. They showed quite how readily rock and royalty were prepared to get into bed with one another in the Eighties, thanks largely to Diana, the Princess of Wales, who early on in her ill-fated relationship with Prince Charles had declared her interest in groups such as Duran Duran and Dire Straits.

Since 1982, a whole host of artists had performed for the charity at fundraisers in London. Gabriel was there alongside the established cream of pop royalty – The Bee Gees, Eric Clapton, Joe Cocker, Elton John, and Phil Collins – and more recent acts who were enjoying their moment in the sun – Colin Vearncombe from Black, tea-boy turned heart-throb Rick Astley and Glaswegian faux-soul band Wet Wet Wet. After The Bee Gees had finished, Gabriel came on and completely owned the stage in his powder blue jacket, romping through 'Sledgehammer'. Only David Rhodes was present from his normal band – behind him were Midge Ure's All-Stars; Howard Jones on keyboards, Mick Karn from Japan on bass, Brian May on guitar, and playing alongside Big Country's Mark Brzezicki on drums, Phil Collins.

The performance, complete with Rhodes, Ure and Gabriel doing the Shadows-esque high-stepping at its climax, offers a glimpse into the parallel career path that Gabriel could so easily have taken at this juncture. A world of easy commercial route-ones, milking his hits and releasing albums that all sounded rather like *So*. However, during the day, Gabriel was working on what would become one of the most significant projects of his career, *Passion: Music From The Last Temptation Of Christ*. No matter how many times his future work echoed elements of *So*, he would never go back there.

★ ★ ★

In April 1987, Tony Stratton-Smith fell ill on a visit to see his old friend Vera Bampton in Jersey and subsequently died. Gabriel, like all of the

Charisma family, was distraught. He attended the memorial service for Stratton-Smith at St Martin's In The Fields on May 6, where Keith Emerson, his first big star in The Nice, played the piano, with Michael Wale and Python Graham Chapman providing eulogies. Fellow Python Michael Palin was to note in his diaries: "Wale talks from the enormously high pulpit about Strat's fondness for public houses, though, of course, no-one mentions that it was 'the lotion' that did him in." The after party was at, where else – the Marquee. The next day, after his old compadre, Marquee manager Jack Barrie had scattered Strat's ashes over the final fence at Newbury, one of his horses, Sergeant Smoke, came in at 20/1.

Although Van Der Graaf were always Strat's favourites, Gabriel and Genesis held a strong place in his affections. "They were never one of the lads," he would say. "Genesis had dignity."

Gabriel contributed to his obituary in *The Daily Telegraph:* "His favourite occupations he listed as 'writing, talking and drinking' and, in each, he could compete with the best. Strat earned himself a unique place in the worlds of entertainment and sport, a big man with a big heart. I will miss him."

"Strat was one of these people, he was very emotional," Tony Banks says. "We were still in debt when Peter left the group. It wasn't until 1978 that we broke even. You'd be hard-pushed today to find people who would support you through that length of time."

Tony Stratton-Smith was a true one-off.

★ ★ ★

There was a final piece of *So*-related business to attend to: the closing of the cycle that had begun four years earlier. The apogee of the work that Gabriel had done on the album, and the *Conspiracy Of Hope* outing was the *Human Rights Now!* tour for Amnesty International which coincided with the 40th Anniversary of The Universal Declaration Of Human Rights. Although he had begun recording *Passion*, Gabriel joined a tour that made the *Conspiracy Of Hope* look the trailer for the main feature for 20 dates in 19 cities between the start of September and mid-October 1988.

The tour centred on five headline acts. U2 had gone truly global now with their *The Joshua Tree* album and could no longer afford to give up time, especially as they were committed to a touring schedule that would earn them their status as 'the world's biggest band'. Even without Bono's charisma, the line-up was amazing – Bruce Springsteen and the E-Street Band, Gabriel, Sting, newcomer Tracy Chapman, whose debut album had been a recent sensation, and Senegalese singer and Gabriel collaborator, Youssou N'Dour.

*Human Rights Now!* started at Wembley Stadium on September 2, 1988. Wembley, since the Live Aid concert in 1985, had become something of a spiritual home for the charity festival, staging the Nelson Mandela 70th Birthday concert there, on June 11 – which was broadcast around the world to 67 countries.

*Human Rights Now!* began with an all-cast performance of Bob Marley and the Wailers' 'Get Up, Stand Up' and ended with a similar performance by the amassed artists performing Bob Dylan's 'I Shall Be Released'. Gabriel performed a nine-song set, which opened with the instrumental 'Of These, Hope' from the *Passion* project on which he was currently working. 'Games Without Frontiers', 'Red Rain', 'Shock The Monkey', 'No Self Control', 'Don't Give Up', 'Sledgehammer', 'In Your Eyes' and of course, 'Biko', made up the rest. Youssou N'Dour would reprise his performance on 'In Your Eyes', while Chapman would stand in for Kate Bush on 'Don't Give Up'.

The shows weaved a course playing fairly non-traditional venues at a time when established stadiums were becoming the norm. There was a resolute desire to play off the beaten track. Aside from conventional arenas such as the Nou Camp in Barcelona, the JFK Stadium in Philadelphia, and the Olympic Stadium in Montreal, the tour took music to the places in which Amnesty had campaigned long and hard for advances in Human Rights – Zimbabwe, the Ivory Coast, Delhi, Sao Paolo and Mendoza and Buenos Aires in Argentina.

To the untrained eye it appeared that Gabriel was becoming another rich pop star with a conscience, joining the hordes of Geldof, Bono and Little Steven wannabes that seemed to populate pop at the end of the Eighties. Questioned about his adoption of causes in the *NME* in 1989 and responding to suggestions that he should look closer to home for some of his causes rather than casting his net so wide, he explained: "I care a lot about Central America because there's so much misinformation in the papers. I feel much less an Englishman, much more someone who lives on this planet. I meet so many people who say, 'What about the poor, the unemployed and the homeless in this country?', but once you visit these other countries and you see the horrors of their lives it's very hard to walk away and shut your eyes."

It was around this time that Gabriel and Gail Colson, ever his fiercely supportive champion, parted company. As Peter Hammill ruminated when Colson retired in 2011, along the way: "PG was always the more likely, more destined, more driven one out of the two of us to head for genuine Star status and of course eventually this did come along. Shortly thereafter . . . actually, not so shortly, there were quite a few bumps along the way . . . Gail and PG parted company."

"I was quite shocked when I heard he'd split with Gail, because I thought they were really, really tight," said her friend Chris Charlesworth. "I thought that was a partnership that would go on for a long time."

Gabriel's charity work left him open to criticism, and an indirect remark from one of his heroes, Pete Townshend, in July 1989 must have stung. While crafting a charity event for the Texas Special Olympics, Townshend told *The Washington Post*, "It seems that charity in the music business has come to consist of the same half a dozen people – me and Peter Gabriel and Sting and Phil Collins and a few others – calling each other on the phone and saying, 'You owe me a favour'. And I've had enough of that bullshit."

Also in 1988, Jimmy Maelen, the man who had brought so much to Gabriel's first album, died. "Losing him was a terrible tragedy," Bob Ezrin said. "It broke everybody's heart. One of the little known facts is that Peter and I paid for Jimmy Maelen's daughter's education. We contacted his wife and put in some Gabriel money."

Peter Gabriel was now on a big platform, yet he continued to care locally as well as globally.

# 20: Unquestionably Rhubarb

*"There's lots of successful pop which doesn't have much soul to it but I'm drawn to music which does have a passionate spirit. Historically, religion and music have been very close. Ours is probably one of the first cultures to separate the two."*

Peter Gabriel, *NME*, 1989

PETER Gabriel was astute in realising the full possibilities that the success of *So* offered him, not least the financial freedom it brought. Although its sales would inevitably dwindle to a steady trickle across the years, songs such as 'Sledgehammer', 'Don't Give Up', 'Big Time' and 'In Your Eyes' were copper-bottomed copyrights that would continue as radio staples for a long time into the future.

The thing that Gabriel wanted most to do was realise his dreams and establish his Real World: the working name for his proposed theme park. The first stage would be to establish a studio and record label of the same name, to offer a place where he and those artists he admired could record: "The royalties from *So* gave me a basis from which to work," he told *NME* in 1989. "But that's gone almost exclusively into the studio. It's provided a foundation in that we can make records of really good quality without being killed by budget. We have as much light and space as we can – if a studio cannot provide the situation for a great performance then it's failing as a studio."

Since gaining his autonomy from the London-based studio system with his move to the increasingly inadequate Ashcombe House studio in 1979, Gabriel had bought the 200-year-old Box Mill. He had set to work getting the picturesque gaggle of buildings into a live and studio complex, complete with residential space for artists, a room in which to write and a big control room, filled with natural light.

The idea for Peter to invest in a studio came originally from Gail Colson, who was by now coming to the end of her time as his manager.

Colson, who had been straight and true, yet also unafraid to question him deeply as an artist, was about to move on. "I suggested that Peter invest in his own studio because of the time he spent in commercial studios. I mentioned a budget but, needless to say he far exceeded that." Of course he would, driven by the dreams of his father inventing in his shed, Gabriel was about to do the same; and timescales and budgets were something to which his visionary nature paid scant regard.

Gabriel had been considering the idea of a studio and performance space for the best part of a decade, but his original partner in the idea was the by now persona non grata David Lord. "Real World would have been Peter and me," Lord says. "Before the Jill thing, we were looking round properties in Bath to turn into a studio. We were going to join forces and be *the* studio around here. We looked at The Forum, what is now the main concert hall in Bath; we were going to do half a studio and half a live room, but they wouldn't sell it to us. It was a Christian church, art centre and cinema and used for most of the classical concerts in Bath. It was the only possibility apart from the idea of building a completely new place." Gabriel and Lord had made enquiries to purchase in the early Eighties, but their application was turned down. "Things could have gone down a completely different route, really," Lord says.

Real World Studios was established in Box, Wiltshire. Set in land near a watermill, the inspirational nature of its surroundings, reflecting light and water, were captured inside the studio, too. Though its inception was fraught with issues, it was a very beautiful location, and would provide a great deal of peace and karma for the artists that were to record there.

Julian Huntly, Gabriel's international Label Manager at Virgin Records, said: "It was rural and peaceful. I was told that all the pipe-work in the studio was made of earthenware rather than metal to improve the ambience and that part of the studio is constructed over water, which led to untold costs in soundproofing. I may well have been having my leg pulled." But he wasn't; everything had been painstakingly constructed, and beautifully crafted: however, the meeting of dreams and reality was to come into sharp focus. Being surrounded by water meant there would be a permanent risk of flooding, and the main London to Bristol train line passed nearby. Real World meets the real world.

"Peter built that studio but then realised that the railway line would have an effect on it," says Paul Conroy, by now at Warners but still in touch with Peter through Gail Colson. "They would have to rebuild it again on a floating platform to stop the vibrations. He put lots of the advances from Geffen into Box and the entourage that worked there. I don't think Peter has much idea about money, but his advisors Mike Large and Mike Thomas have kept him afloat for all these years. Peter's become some sort of arts figure – he was on some sort of pedestal by then."

Mike Large would play a significant part in Gabriel's future. Installed as the General Manager of Real World, he would later become Gabriel's *de facto* manager in tandem with solicitor Mike Thomas from Sheridan's, the leading entertainment legal firm. Large had worked at the BBC and then at Solid State Logic, where he and Gabriel had met. A methodical, personable and astute businessman, in 1986 he came across to head up the Project Management for the Real World enterprise. In 1990 he would become the Director Of Operations for Real World and remains in that position, carefully and thoughtfully expanding Gabriel's empire.

The studio had great impact: "I've never been to Real World, but because of the photos of it, it changed everybody's concept of what a record studio could and should be like," said Nile Rodgers. "Before Real World, every recording studio had blacked out windows or no windows at all. You couldn't see outside, you weren't supposed to keep track of time, which made the environment so special – time stood still, but at Real World you could see outside. A different perspective, getting inspired by nature – that's a perfect example of how Peter thinks. It was exactly the opposite of what we had known in the recording business. And now, you come to my studio, it's the first thing people say, oh god, it's so great here, look at this panoramic view. And now I would never think of having a studio where you didn't know the difference between night and day." Gabriel was moving out of the dark, into the light.

John Metcalfe, who was to work with Gabriel on his 2010 album, *Scratch My Back* says: "It's rather like how I imagine the old writing houses for publishers used to be. There's a huge amount always going on there, which creates an extraordinary atmosphere of creativity. You meet such a variety of other musicians from all over the world, which helps to give you energy and ideas for your own work. Added to which Jerome's food is fantastic." The food reflected the global nature of the musicians that Gabriel would encourage to record there. With fabulous food, good accommodation and three airy recording spaces, everything helped to encourage the best performances possible from visiting artists. And Gabriel himself had somewhere to ensure he could make his painstaking dreams reality. "In Peter's writing room and in the big room there is lots of natural light which is such a bonus when you are spending long days in front of computers and monitors," Metcalfe adds. "It's increasingly rare to find a place like that."

"I think it's the Unreal World," says Bob Ezrin. "I think it's fantasy land, it's such a beautiful place. Its setting could not be more gorgeous and conducive to creativity and sensitivity. There's just magic in the air from the time you pull through the gates. Peter did a fabulous job technically on the studio. Acoustically, the rooms all sound good and I love the big control room – that's how I work now, drums outside – everybody in the room."

Ezrin had been a studio owner for many years, and was all too aware of the pitfalls of ownership. It was understandable that Gabriel did not ask his advice, as he would most probably have advised him against, and that was something Gabriel did not want to hear. "Having been a studio owner, it's such a dream. They rarely make money unless you operate them purely commercially and I knew Peter would do, in his inimitable style. There would be a bit of everything; every kind of music and every sort of client and collaborator working there – I may have said no, so I'm very glad he didn't ask me."

* * *

The next part of Gabriel's dream was to establish his own record label, that would be distributed by Virgin, and would release his own records, as well as building a roster of artists from around the world. He wanted to capture the spirit of WOMAD on disc, placing it, as its website says, "at the heart of a peaceful revolution in the music business".

In one of her final acts as Gabriel's manager, Gail Colson negotiated a deal with Virgin for Real World for a certain amount of money per album, and within a matter of years Gabriel had created a thriving niche label, introducing western listeners to a range of African, Middle Eastern and 'world' talent. Names such as Papa Wemba, Nusrat Fateh Ali Khan, the Musicians Of The Nile and S.E. Rogie would gain wider exposure through Gabriel's patronage. "I negotiated their deal with Virgin but didn't have any more involvement than that," Colson said. "I was aware that Peter didn't want me to manage him any more for quite some time before we actually stopped working together in December 1989. He had told me about 18 months before so, apart from all the *So* touring, promotion and Amnesty International tour, I started getting involved with other artists and distanced myself from all his other interests as he began to build a new team of people around him."

The new team of people was initially led by Steve Hedges, who had been Gabriel's booking agent for years, now taking over as his manager. Before finally retiring in 2012, Colson continued to manage Peter Hammill, and latterly, a reformed Van Der Graaf Generator, Chrissie Hynde, Jesus Jones, Alison Moyet, and briefly, Morrissey. She remains on good terms with Gabriel and all of the ex-members of Genesis.

Real World releases came in a distinctive house style, a series identity, provided by designer Garry Mouat, with a nine-colour bar on each spine, emphasising the label's title, and high-art covers by Malcolm Garret's team at Assorted Images. Understandably, the label took a while to establish itself: "The idea of the world music brand with colour co-ordinated sleeves, large CD booklets that consumers would collect was hard to say the least," Virgin executive Jon Webster recalls. "Labels like Island and Virgin in their early years particularly had followers who would basically investigate anything that they released but that was hard earned." This became the case with Real World, and its product authority and Gabriel's good taste would ensure that audiences would experience artists that they had hitherto unheard.

"The reason that Real World did so well was that they got a sum per album and that was down to [Virgin executives] Simon Draper and Ken Berry, because they loved Peter so much, gave him that opportunity to develop all those acts," said Paul Conroy. "Some of those records were not an easy sell at all. It's taken a long time for Peter to see any money back, but I don't think he cared about that – because of his background he could never say, 'I've got another 10 million in the bank'. He definitely saw it as ploughing back into the business of what he did and what he believed in."

Among the label's best sellers were the soundtrack from *Passion: Music For The Last Temptation Of Christ* and records by Papa Wemba and Nusrat Fateh Ali Khan.

★ ★ ★

*Passion: Music For The Last Temptation Of Christ,* with music by Gabriel, was to be the first release on Real World in June 1989, almost a year after the film's release. With the catalogue number of RW LP/CD/MC 1, it showcased Real World's distinctive 'colour bar' logo. Gabriel wrote a note for the album and CD's inner bag. "Real World is developing new ways for artists of all sorts to work together with technologists. Whatever the music, whatever the technology, great records come from great performances. Our studios have been designed for the artist, to provide a place for great work around which we hope to build the label." The final words sounded not unlike the sort of note that Tony Barrow or Derek Taylor would have written on a Beatles sleeve note of the early Sixties: "I hope you get as much enjoyment from these records as we have had in making them."

*Passion: Music For The Last Temptation Of Christ* became one of Peter Gabriel's favourite releases. Now one of the best-selling world music albums of all time, it became the must-have accessory for the CD generation to demonstrate their breadth and range of taste. Released too as a double vinyl album, it shows the range and depth of Gabriel's experimentation, as well as his ability to collaborate.

Recording the film's soundtrack, Gabriel worked with many international musicians; some captured at Real World Studios, some on the film's location in North Africa, and others sought out from archives. Martin Scorsese had initially approached Gabriel in 1983 to score his film, *The Last Temptation Of Christ* and had been trying to get the film off the ground ever since. It finally opened amid great controversy in April 1988. Gabriel wrote in the album's sleeve notes and after outlining Scorsese's initial approach, he said that he (Scorsese) "wanted to present the struggle between the humanity and divinity of Christ in a powerful and original way, and I was convinced by his commitment to the spiritual content and message. He is an excellent and very musical director and working with him has been a great experience."

For those awaiting a follow-up to *So*, this was most resolutely *not* it. The 21 excerpts from the soundtrack to Scorsese's controversial *The Last Temptation Of Christ* and additional in-mood pieces by Gabriel were striking in their scope and ambience. For the first time in his career, Gabriel produced alone. Daniel Lanois was, by now, one of the world's most sought-after record producers after his work on *So* and U2's The *Joshua Tree*. He was also recording his own album, *Acadie*.

The drum-heavy introduction, 'This Feeling Begins', a collaboration with old associate, ex-Tears For Fears drummer Manny Elias, who had earned his spurs in Bath band Interview, set the tone for this remarkably atmospheric release. As journalist Chris Jones was to write for the BBC, the release allowed "the public school polymath to disseminate a burgeoning global village culture to a mass audience. With this and the WOMAD festivals he succeeded admirably."

'Zaar' came from an Egyptian rhythm that was supposed to fend off evil spirits. It certainly was one of the tracks that had the greatest commercial potential on the album. A surreal, stunning video was made by German artist Stefan Roloff which featured animated paintings coming to life. 'With This Love' borrowed heavily from Bach. Robin Canter's oboe and cor anglais were the centre of this track, which presented English chamber music amid the range of styles offered by the album. David Sancious played beautifully sympathetic keyboards that added to the remarkable texture of the track. The gorgeous, sedate and painterly music of 'With This Love' was rather spectacular, making a case for Gabriel as a modern classical composer. With Shankar on violin, parts of the melody would later resurface in Gabriel's beautiful 'Washing Of The Water'.

If Gabriel had released a pop album at this point, it could have been huge. Not all at his label were pleased. Jon Webster, the Head of International at Virgin, recalls thinking, "[it was] a great record but how on earth are we going to sell this?" Julian Huntly, his International Label Manager at Virgin, said: "Initially I know we were disappointed when the album was delivered, well after the movie had peaked and disappeared. The fact that it didn't have his name or title on the cover and that it was instrumental did not exactly make the marketing easy. Having said that, for us in Spain it was a much bigger commercial success than we had ever hoped for. Personally I love it, nothing better to lie by a pool and listen to."

It did indeed provide a serious updating of Brian Eno's ambient music for a new era. These were serious times; and this was serious music to accompany them. The yuppie generation and Q magazine were elevating the realm of popular music to something with greater gravity. Those who populated the common rooms of 1973, smoking their first furtive joints to 'Supper's Ready', were now the publishers and editors of the rock publications. *Passion: Music For The Last Temptation Of Christ* was a grown-up, expansive album that revealed its gifts slowly and passionately. Gabriel was absolutely thrilled with it. In 2007 he told *Uncut* magazine: "I think *Passion* may be the best one I've ever done. I wasn't working with a producer, and as I was serving someone else's vision, that gave me freedom in a strange way. Some of the 'Sledgehammer' fans wouldn't be into it – a bit too 'out there' for them."

He was echoing exactly what he had said contemporaneously. "I think it's some of the best work I've done," he told *NME*, "but I know it's not going to reach a very large audience. I still want to continue writing songs and lyrics; this is instrumental music which is just as important but certainly not commercial. I was trying to mix various elements, although historically inaccurate, so as to establish a living world within the film, they could taste and see. Because normally Christ is sanitised with this halo and you don't actually have a sense of humanity. Scorsese was determined to portray Christ's struggle between humanity and divinity."

There were frequent accusations levelled at Gabriel that he was simply stealing African rhythms in order to inspire his career. He told *Musician* magazine: "I'm not trying to deliver African pastiches. I'm using the influences as tools to take me to somewhere else within my own music. There are plenty of precedents for that process; for instance, in his painting *Les Desmoiselles d'Avignon,* Picasso took the African mask and totally transformed his own style of painting . . . Theft, if you like, is the lifeblood of all art."

*Passion . . .* received a Golden Globe Award nomination for Best Original Score – Motion Picture in 1988 and it won the Grammy Award in 1990 for Best New Age Album. On many ways Paul Simon's *Graceland* album had paved the way for the acceptance of a full world music album, and *Passion . . .*'s relatively handsome commercial performance gave Gabriel the green light to continue.

It's indicative of the era that Gabriel had to appear on a TV show like *Star Test* to promote such a difficult work. Devised as a programme that would highlight the latest stars in a semi-intelligent environment, *Star Test* was a short-lived Channel 4 show in which a disembodied computer voice asked stars questions they pretended to select from a screen. After being asked trivial questions like "which do you prefer, pineapple or rhubarb?" ("Unquestionably rhubarb," Gabriel drolly replied) and "if you met God what would you ask her?" ("For her phone number"), it went in deep with sucker punch type questions: "What's the one thing in your life that you most would like but don't have?" "Right now?" Gabriel stared into the computer screen. "A happy family."

Gabriel talked about the impact of the *Human Rights Now* tour on him. "It's very important as the world begins to shrink we get a sense of how what we do in our country has an effect on other countries. Suddenly these people are not just newsprint, they are really people; you are meeting them and you're finding out about family members that have been killed or the very real problems that are facing them. It's very hard to walk away and say this is where I come from and I just function in this little place." When asked what he would fight for, he replied, "I believe in non-violence – I think maybe that's a cause I'd fight for." Gabriel had to sum himself up in five words. He chose 'wicked, open, creative, humorous and kind.'

Gabriel wanted his audience to know and understand his influences. He took the unparalleled step of releasing, simultaneously, a supplementary album of bonus material from which his album was derived, *Passion: Sources*. It contained material by various musicians who had inspired him while composing the soundtrack, or had been sampled by him for the work. The 46-minute, 14-track *Passion: Sources* offered the opportunity to hear the artists in their own right. Q Magazine was to say: "These inspirational items are full of musicological interest and show team members such as Shankar and Baaba Maal going through some impressive paces."

* * *

One project that didn't come off during this period was another opportunity to work with Todd Rundgren, whom Gabriel had remained in intermittent contact with since the Seventies. Rundgren approached him to duet on the song 'The Want Of A Nail' for the album, *Nearly Human*. "I thought that that would be a fun thing to do," Rundgren told biographer Mike Myers. "But at that point, for whatever reason, Peter just couldn't make it happen. Might have been scheduling, or maybe he just didn't feel comfortable with the tune." In the end Bobby Womack sang with Rundgren on this incredible piece of faux-soul. It remains one of the most intriguing 'what-ifs' of Gabriel's career.

* * *

In February 1990, Nelson Mandela was freed from prison after 27 years. It was remarkable and surprising news and, with 'Biko', Peter Gabriel had played a small yet significant part in the events leading up to his release. In the spirit of the post-Geldof age, a concert was hastily arranged at Wembley Stadium, a combination of a celebration of his release and his 70th birthday. Mandela himself travelled to Britain to take part.

Gabriel had wanted to play after Mandela's speech, but the speech had been brought forward at the request of the police. Steve Hedges then proposed that Gabriel close the show and Gabriel asked Simple Minds to cut their set from four songs to two. Kerr acquiesced, not without some rancour. "I couldn't believe myself," Kerr said in 1991. "I'm looking at my hero and what I'm saying is, 'You've got a fucking cheek!' "

"I've put it down to nerves on Peter's part," Kerr continued diplomatically. "We're still talking. The last time I spoke to him he was telling me he's trying to devise a way of recording in the car, because he gets all these great ideas when he's driving. Imagine doing an overdub on the motorway! That's Peter, I guess he doesn't work like other people."

Peter doesn't indeed work like other people. In time for Christmas 1990, with a marketplace hungry for new material, Gabriel acquiesced to Virgin's wishes and released a greatest hits compilation album. However, it came with a twist. Tracks were remixed, and it took its title from the Youssou N'Dour collaboration he had worked on the previous year, *Shaking The Tree*. With a beautiful Robert Mapplethorpe portrait of Gabriel on its cover, he has his eyes closed, as if to absent himself from this commercial process. To add to the sardonic nature of the enterprise, he added the title 'Sixteen Golden Greats' after *Shaking The Tree*, a parody of the TV albums that had been a staple of the world record industry for so long. The album reached number 11 in the UK charts and number 48 in the US. All that was really wanted, however, was a proper, bona fide follow up to *So*.

# 21: Dark And Sticky

*"*Us *is, first and foremost, start to finish, a truly wonderful blast."*
Robert Sandall, Q Magazine, 1992

WHAT a difference a decade makes. Whereas 1982 saw Peter Gabriel tussling with creditors, delivering a complex album and involved in a bizarre love triangle, by 1992 here he was with a successful festival, the best-selling album of his career and his own studio and record label with a roster of exciting and vibrant artists.

In 1992, WOMAD came into the Real World umbrella after years of joint partnership between Gabriel and the festival organisers. Since its rocky beginnings in 1982, WOMAD, run by Thomas Brooman, had established itself as a fabulous boutique festival, fulfilling all the aims of Gabriel's original dream. Gabriel was still actively involved, but left the day-to-day running to the festival team.

In 1992 a book with a forward by Gabriel, *10 Years Of WOMAD,* was published. It had an understated yet valiant tone – the festival had, thanks to the shot in the arm provided by *Six Of The Best,* been able to realise its aims and ambitions; and by initially playing smaller spaces had been able to build quietly and effectively. It held performances at the Institute Of Contemporary Arts on the Mall in London over 17 nights in 1983, with acts such as Peter Hammill and Misty in Roots. By 1985, it had returned to a three-day festival on Mersea Island in Essex in July with acts such as The Fall (whose mercurial frontman, Mark E. Smith, sneered 'We're from the first world' when they played), New Order and The Pogues. By now a formula was struck, to book cult British bands, and play to a receptive audience that would be delighted with music from around the world they had never heard before.

In 1988 WOMAD took an offering of acts to the Roskilde festival in Denmark, and thereafter began its incredible overseas expansion – by 1992

WOMAD festivals had visited Italy, Canada, Spain, Finland, Germany and Sweden. In the next decade it would continue as one of the world's most successful music and culture festivals, providing over 160 festivals in 27 countries.

★ ★ ★

Gabriel's domestic situation, although far from settled, had been explored through years of therapy. He and Jill had split finally in 1987. Due to *EST* training, it was important for family friend Richard Macphail to remain cordial with both parties: "One of the things that was very important to me was that when Peter and Jill split up, I was determined to keep my relationship with both of them; to a degree I failed. Some time later Peter felt that I'd gone to Jill's side. It was really only that I could see her any time I wanted, but I couldn't with Peter, because he was just too busy. I never did take sides. We're over that now. My only issue is that I don't see him enough – but I think there are a lot of people that would say the same thing."

Gabriel's relationship with Rosanna Arquette had been on and off. She had been briefly married to the American composer James Newton Howard, who'd once played in Elton John's band, while Gabriel was linked to various women. He remained a doting father, supportive of and loving to his daughters as they progressed through their teenage years. He was about to make use of all this experience as the subject matter for *Us*, his song-based follow-up to *So*.

Made with over 50 musicians and recorded between October 1989 and June 1992 at Real World, and in New Orleans and Dakar, *Us* was released on September 28, 1992. Daniel Lanois returned as producer. "I let my emotions go in this album," Gabriel told *The Independent*. "They're very evident." To leave the listener with no doubt about the album's content, Gabriel wrote this soul-baring sleevenote: "Much of this record is about relationships. I am dedicating it to all those who have taught me about loving and being loved. Especially to my parents, Ralph and Irene. To Jill, for giving me so much in all the time we were growing up together. To Rosanna for all her love and support that I didn't properly acknowlege. And to my daughters Anna and Melanie, my pride and joy."

It also acknowledged that Gabriel had spent time in therapy, by thanking 'the group', and providing their first names. Admitting freely in interviews that he had been in therapy for five years, he said: "I feel a lot of anger, unexpressed anger. I have a tendency to deaden the emotion. It's got to go out or reflect back in and start eating away. Part of my struggle is to break out of that box, which I feel that at least I have the capacity to do and the means and knowledge to do now." As a result, *Us* was a complex, strange and fascinating album.

Gabriel discussed his therapy at some length in *NME* in 1989: "Since my marital problems I started going to, initially, a couple's group therapy, but now I do a group on my own. I wish people wouldn't see therapy as something that happens when you're sick, you could avoid a lot of sickness. A lot of people seem to think therapy's some sort of self-indulgent American fad, but I'm sure it'll be part of everyday life in the next century . . . As soon as you go in there and see the people you're doing it with you don't feel in the presence of a company of nutters."

"You don't need to be a psychiatrist to interpret *Us*," Richard Macphail says. "It's all laid out. He put it right up there. It's his version of [John Lennon's] Primal Scream album. A lot of artists do it, but when it's not a painting or a sculpture, it's all the more balder. Peter gets more and more direct and he finds it very freeing. It works, it's a catharsis – he wouldn't be being true to himself if he didn't do it that way – he is compelled to follow that path – which is another reason why he defended its difficult-to-write lyrics, because they don't come easy, because he has to be completely honest to himself."

Dark and sticky, fractured and at times inaccessible, *Us* was a bold follow up to *So*. The first commercial Peter Gabriel album made truly for the CD age, it contained one more track than *So* and was 12 minutes longer overall. With almost every song clocking in at over five minutes, it was as if Gabriel was so locked in to his groove he didn't wish to be disturbed from his ruminations. Its detractors could suggest it was sluggish, and even, at times, tune-free. But to believe this would be to miss the point entirely.

The first piece of family business appeared on album opener 'Come Talk To Me', where he addressed the gulf in communication between himself and his youngest daughter Melanie. Since the split with Jill, Melanie evidently felt he had become distant. Emerging from a drone of guitar feedback, the track was based around a tape of African percussionists the Babacar Faye Drummers; as layers of bagpipes and doudouk amass, Gabriel's beautifully impassioned vocals build and swell. The chorus vocal was emboldened by Sinead O'Connor, whom Gabriel greatly admired and with whom he had been romantically linked. "Sinead sung from the gut which was a powerful thing for me," Gabriel said in 2002. The song manages to combine the textural feel of 'Biko', with the emotional pull of 'Wallflower'.

In a 1993 UK Channel 4 documentary about his work, Daniel Lanois spoke of his time with Gabriel and said that 'Come Talk To Me' was "a very simple song about one of his daughters, but it has quite a huge production around it, so a little message to one person can be interpreted as a universal message." The documentary showed Gabriel recording at Box with long hair, as long as his Genesis heyday.

Lanois had an innate sense of where a record's peak should be, and strove to bring the record in on that peak. Fortunately, he was able to ensure that the album stayed exactly on point. 'Come Talk To Me' seems to fade out sharply and then take an age to actually disappear. Whether intentional or not, it gives the idea that the conversation is continuing in a permanent loop, going on long after the listener has been allowed to eavesdrop.

The low jet groove of 'Love To Be Loved' was a bold examination of Gabriel's condition of the heart. Exploring his naked emotion after therapy, it seemed to suggest that his desire to be desired was so strong, mourning relationships that had passed, holding on to emotions, but facing the ultimate challenge of letting go. Again, like its predecessor, it seems unfinished, or at least ends before it actually gets started, and far from a gang-busting start for the follow-up to a multi-platinum album.

'Blood Of Eden' is where everything really begins. Another duet with Sinead O'Connor, it was, sonically, a sweet, sensual follow-up to 'Don't Give Up'. An early version of the track had been given to Wim Wenders for his 1991 film *Until The End Of The World*. Gabriel again presents himself as a man who 'cannot get insurance any more' and doubts his faith, wondering whether what he sees is a dagger or a crucifix. In the increasing distance between the man and the woman in the song, Gabriel presents himself as child-like, back to Adam in the Garden of Eden faltering with a relationship. The song's touching restraint underlined quite how accomplished he had become as a writer and arranger. The musical support from Tony Levin's lilting bass, Levon Minnasian's use of the Armenian wind instrument the doudouk and David Rhodes' atmospheric 12-string, is remarkable.

Melvyn Bragg's assertion in 1982 that Gabriel had had big popular hits but has never turned his successes into formulas was challenged somewhat by 'Steam'. Although it is a truly tremendous romp, it is almost a note for note reassembling of 'Sledgehammer', crashing in on a wave of guitar-led, horn-driven energy, finally giving the casual listener something to cling onto. Big and daft, it was another hot and wet paean to relationships and indeed the sexual act. Gabriel is courting a woman who clearly knows more about life than he, but knows little about herself. Featuring Leon Nocentelli from The Meters on guitar, it's brisk and joyous and resists lapsing into parody. Released as the album's second single, it benefited from one of Gabriel's funniest and most surreal videos, reuniting him with Stephen R Johnson.

Gabriel appears as a velvet-suited megastar in an enormous limousine, in an animated jungle and with his head superimposed onto the body of a dancer in a thong, a reference to the Chippendales dance troupe, while women clamour to put dollars into his trunks and start ripping off his limbs, thus implying that everybody wanted a piece of him now that he was 'famous'. Sexual politics abound through a variety of images until the video charts Gabriel's growth from baby in the womb to old age, complete with an amusing parody of him with long hair from the *Nursery Cryme* era. It showed Gabriel's sense of humour and self-awareness, and gained him a Top 10 single on both sides of the Atlantic as a result.

With backing vocals from Kenyan singer Ayub Ogada, 'Only Us' was the meat of the matter, another exploration of Gabriel's relationship with the women in his life. A beautiful mesh of sound that spends its time arriving without ever truly getting there, its message of 'the further one gets the less one knows', is based on Sanskrit teaching that George Harrison had interpreted with The Beatles in 'The Inner Light' in 1968. When it moves into a full-on swing, it is actually one of the most breathtaking moments in Gabriel's catalogue.

'Washing Of The Water' epitomises the album's emotional heart. Effectively a nursery rhyme or a hymn, it revisits Gabriel back down on the farm, and is one of his very best songs. When the bridge kicks in with Reggie Houston and Tim Green's horns, arranged by Malcolm Burn, it echoes Gabriel's desire for amelioration from the predicament in which he has found himself.

The album's dark and difficult lead single, 'Digging In The Dirt', emanated directly from Gabriel's experiences in therapy. It was a bold first single from the album – in the way that 'Shock The Monkey' was too far ahead for British audiences who'd just 'got' 'Games Without Frontiers'. Built around Rhodes and Nocentelli's funky, fuzzy guitar riffs and interplay, it was a trip into the psychiatrist's chair, with Gabriel aided by his long-term friend and near neighbour Peter Hammill on backing vocals. "Peter rang me one evening and asked if I could do some BVs," Hammill said. "Of course I said, 'Sure, when?' and he said, 'Now'. So I said, 'Well, I'm looking after our daughters tonight, I'll have to bring them over as well.' So a couple of sleepy heads sat in the back of the Real World control room as we did the vocals. The super low voices you can hear as it plays out is my suggestion, with my dulcet tones."

Richard Macphail also contributed vocals to the track. He had left the music world at the turn of the Eighties, working in the field of alternative energy. However, he and Gabriel remained as close as ever. "Peter was visiting us in Notting Hill, and we were talking about the death of the Liberal Democrat MP for Truro, David Penhaligon, who had been killed in a car accident. For an MP, he was someone I really liked, smiley, funny, who said a lot of sensible things. I started crying at the sadness of it, Peter asked me if there was another regret that this linked into; I'm crying about a guy I never met. I expressed some regret about not having done more with my singing. He made it possible for my wife, Maggie, and I to go down to Real World and record three songs. One was the slow version of 'Breaking Up Is Hard To Do', 'My Girl' and 'Still'. On 'My Girl', he used the 'Sledgehammer' brass to do a solo on it – it was a great thing to do, and a very nice gesture. As a result of that, he was then making *Us*, and he invited me down to sing on 'Digging In The Dirt'."

Many were unprepared for the stark emotional depth of the song. "'Digging In The Dirt' is about uncovering the unconscious and anger," Macphail adds. "Not unlike many of us, people have an anger issue with our mothers. Hence the line 'shut up and drive the car'. Peter is so unlike that when you meet him, he's still very shy and hesitant. He's this extraordinary combination. Deep down, he knows exactly what he wants. You can push him and he will allow himself to show disharmony and discord and be angry about things, which was something he previously found difficult."

'Digging In The Dirt' won Gabriel a Grammy for best video. Directed by John Downer, it was a remarkable piece of time-lapse filmmaking.

Centring around a young boy having flashbacks to his youth, spurring on unwarranted bursts of anger, Gabriel acts as the narrator and protagonist. It was, to use therapy-speak, a heavy scene, and as a result, only reached number 24 in the UK, 22 places lower than 'Sledgehammer'. With its lowly placing, at a time when the singles chart (in the UK especially), was so based on hype, it seemed to vanish without a trace. In the US, Gabriel's key market especially since *So*, it only reached number 52 on the Hot 100. Although it topped the *Billboard* Hot Modern Rock track chart and the Hot Mainstream Rock Tracks, it did little to herald the arrival of a new Gabriel product.

"Peter Gabriel addresses sex directly and uniquely among his contemporaries," says writer David Buckley. "I think he's sort of repulsed by intimacy; as a very young man at Charterhouse he was obviously quite repressed, and then he went a bit wild and bonkers in the Eighties, dating beautiful actresses. The line 'I feel it in my sex' seems an archetypal Freudian or Jungian way of regarding one's personality. I don't know where my sex is, I can't put my finger on it."

'Fourteen Black Paintings' was the dark heart of the album, sounding not unlike something that Gabriel would have cut for *Passion.* Over a bubbling cauldron of Assane Thaim's talking drum, John Paul Jones' surdo and Babacar Faye's djembe, Gabriel intones the song's 31 words. It was inspired by a visit to the Rothko Chapel in Houston, Texas, which contained 14 of artist Mark Rothko's 'black' paintings, an experience Gabriel found both moving and spiritual. Rothko, who was to take his own life in 1970, had been commissioned by art patrons John and Dominique de Menil to create a meditative space in a non-denominational chapel. Opening in 1971, the chapel took on a role to promote greater understanding of Human and Civil Rights issues. Although Gabriel was initially reluctant to visit, David Rhodes encouraged him and the result, 'Fourteen Black Paintings', is a plea for the power of collective strength. It is a suitably moving addition to *Us*, and chimed perfectly with the impassioned work Gabriel had been carrying out with Amnesty.

'Kiss That Frog' sees a return to the boudoir, an idea Gabriel developed from reading *The Uses Of Enchantment: The Meaning And Importance Of Fairy Tales,* a 1976 book by psychologist Bruno Bettelheim that looked at legends through the lens of Freudian psychology. A glance at the sexual metaphor behind the Brothers Grimm tale, *The Frog Prince,* musically it was another search for the elusive 'Sledgehammer' moment. Based on a rhythm track Gabriel had first worked with while recording *Music From The Film Birdy*, it was enlivened by Gabriel's joyful treated organ and, making a rare appearance, his harmonica playing. With Marilyn McFarlane's upbeat chorus vocal, and Gabriel's passionate, emotional delivery, it is one of his most soulful, direct moments on the whole album. Released as a single in the UK to compliment the Secret World Live tour the following year, it reached number 46.

And then, it appears. It is almost as if the whole album, as stunning and as melodramatic as it has been, is a prolonged overture for the track 'Secret World', possibly the greatest thing he has ever written and certainly on a par with his most notable successes. Gabriel said that the song was "About the private world that two people occupy and the private worlds that they occupy as individuals within that space, and the overlap of their dreams and desires." Written after the final collapse of his marriage and his tumultuous relationship with Arquette, musically and lyrically the song feels like an enormous purging of Gabriel's soul.

The leisurely way the music unfolds marks it out somewhere between his friend and one-time hero Bruce Springsteen's 'Thunder Road' and 'Tinseltown In The Rain' by The Blue Nile. It is suitably dramatic. By detailing the minutiae of stolen time between lovers and the search for rekindled passion in a dying relationship, it is one of his most powerful moments. By cataloguing the differences between 'putting on' and 'receiving' and examining all the places love is hidden, the song turns aggressive with an astonishing bass run by Tony Levin. Lanois builds the sound and the volume slowly and painterly throughout. Here, in this secret world of the lovers, their own rules could be set. Adam and Eve are referenced, as with 'Blood Of Eden', it is as if everything returns to that first relationship.

And then the song suddenly stops, and Gabriel urges his audience, almost in a stage whisper, to 'listen'. The groove turns nagging, insistent, and then, ultimately, begins to fade. What does he want us to listen to? The album again? His heart? Our instinct. After seven minutes it disappears, and you want it back. Lanois' unmistakable guitar figure locking with Rhodes, sounding like hi-life guitar players crossed with James Brown and Funkadelic guitarist 'Catfish' Collins make this a standout. Gabriel was pleased too. *Rolling Stone* suggested that the song arrives at sober grief, posing the wrenching, solitary question "In all the places we were hiding love/What was it we were thinking of?" and finds no answer but only the response: "With no guilt and no shame, no sorrow or blame/ Whatever it is, we are all the same."

With the music finished, Gabriel painstakingly assembled the album's sleeve. Working with photographer David Shineman, in the distorted image of Gabriel trying to hold another, also distorted person, this sense of searching for the unknown, communicating and not communicating simultaneously was made clear. For each of the tracks, Gabriel commissioned different artists to interpret his work for the CD booklet. Scottish sculptor David Mach interpreted 'Come Talk To Me' as a screaming head of Gabriel; French-Ethiopian Mickael Bethe-Selassie took on 'Only Us', saying his picture "represents a goddess of love. Besides, we have two couples which are coloured. This represents multi-ethnic persons." Barcelona-based painter Zush painted 'Digging In The Dirt' as a cave-painting. German installation artist Rebecca Horn interpreted 'Secret World' as an open suitcase, empty but for a flower-like brooch that could be interpreted as a butterfly or a bow-tie: "It's a story about a secret world Peter developed. It's like a private little museum and you can open it and it's your little secret world you carry with you."

Gabriel felt as passionately about art as he did about music, and was all for breaking down barriers: "Just as a white rock band has a much better chance of reaching the media than an Indonesian, Chinese or African group,' he told Dalya Alberge of *The Independent* in January 1993, 'the same is true of the art world, which still tends to be very dismissive of artists of other cultures. A little less so now, but it's still a European and North American focus . . . Those barriers need to be totally destroyed."

The paintings accompanied Gabriel on a promotional tour for the album's release. "On the *Us* promo tour of Spain, Peter insisted that in each city he visited we set up an exhibition where the art used for the album artwork would be displayed," Julian Huntley says. "They were not small paintings and there were about eight of them. We duly set up a show at the end of the trip in a nightclub and invited along the press and TV. We were due to start at seven and finish at half past eight, but as with all things in Madrid, everyone turned up late. I remember right in the middle of the exhibition Peter, me and the other guys from the label had to grab all the artwork and pile into three cabs and a limo to get out to the airport for his flight, which was thankfully a private jet . . . I am told the party carried on for some time after we left, with empty easels and walls."

In the end, the paintings were shown officially at the London Business Centre in Islington in January 1993 and at the Landmark Tower, Yokohama, Japan later the same year.

* * *

Gabriel said in 2007: "*Us* was all about relationships and the crap that goes with them. And the joy." It made number two in both the US and UK albums chart, topping the chart in Germany. Ironically, the MD of Virgin Records was now Paul Conroy, who had worked subsequently at Stiff, Warners and Chrysalis since leaving Charisma in 1974. "We picked up straight away. As Tony Banks says, 'You were there at the beginning, you'll be there at the end'. We have that sort of relationship. We did go through a lot of stuff together." Conroy was acutely aware of Gabriel's situation after having produced such a huge album as *So*. "My neck was always on the line to make things more commercial," Conroy adds. "By the time *Us* came out, people knew that Peter was his own man, and you weren't going to tell him to add accessible tracks, it didn't quite work that way."

His international marketing manager at Virgin, Julian Huntley, recalls: "I think it would be fair to say that both Geffen and Virgin exerted pressure on him to deliver another *So*, as to whether Peter took any notice of that pressure or in any way changed his schedule of work or his pace of work I couldn't say, he didn't appear to. From where I was standing I couldn't see it."

It was a "dense piece of art", as Jon Webster adds. "Everything was late. Sleeve. Videos. I thought often of the Douglas Adams quote about deadlines flashing by. I became a point person trying to deal with the logical questions. We were also faced with an artist who, as usual, wanted their baby unleashed on the world as soon as it was finished."

But *Us* was a special baby. *Q* magazine said: "The worst thing that can be said about . . . *Us*, is that its formula is as expected: a cross between *Passion* and Gabriel's last proper (i.e. vocal) solo effort, 1986's five-million seller, *So*. The stately and pleading melodies are pure, timeless Gabriel but they've been extended and overlaid on this occasion with all manner of doudouks, ney flutes, djembes, sabar drums, wailing vocals and a heavy quotient of unidentifiable ambient noise, presumably courtesy of co-producer Daniel Lanois. So disregard all suggestions that this is an 'adult' album, designed for sensitive, musicologically correct, vaguely troubled fortysomethings. *Us* is, first and foremost, start to finish, a truly wonderful blast."

"For the record company, *Us* was always going to be compared to *So*, which is one of the great albums of all time," Julian Huntley says. "In my opinion *Us*, is not as good as *So*, but then very few albums by anybody are. Having said that *Us* is still very good, showing off all the skill, creativity and musical experience of a great artist. The songs stand up to time, and live they worked incredibly well."

As ever, Gabriel was painstakingly concerned about giving his audience a close set of cross-references for his work. Released in May 1993, *Plus From Us* was the supporting document to *Us*. As Gabriel explained in his sleeve note, the positive feedback from *Passion Sources* had encouraged him to produce a 15-track sampler of the musicians who were involved on *Us*: "I have an extraordinary band who provides the foundation of my records, and at the same time I am very lucky to be able to work with musicians from all over the world. They make an enormous contribution to the sound of my work and this is an opportunity to hear some of the other music that these remarkable musicians have created."

Again, it showed Gabriel to be the arbiter of excellent taste, with numbers from old friends Peter Hammill, Daniel Lanois, Tony Levin, Brian Eno and David Rhodes, to Kenyan Ayub Ogada, Kudsi Erguner from Turkey, Doudou N'Diaye Rose from Senegal among others. Unbelievably, it was the thirty-third release on the Real World label in just over three years. The label had built up an impressive roster of talent that showcased music from around the globe and did so with great integrity.

In November 1992, a strange bit of US-only business came out entitled *Peter Gabriel Revisited*, an Atlantic compilation of material from the first two albums. Pointless in the extreme, it looked as if Atlantic were still kicking themselves 12 years later for letting Gabriel go.

# 22: See It. Film It. Change *it*.

*"Like most of the things Gabriel does, it has taken far longer than it should have, gone way over budget and left many around him in a state of nervous exhaustion. But it is, as usual, worth the wait."*

Robert Sandall, Q Magazine, 1993

*"There's a lot of hippy ideals in there I think. My hippy past is not that secret – I mean, somebody who dressed as a flower . . ."*

Peter Gabriel, 2000

WHEN Gabriel was on *Star Test* in 1989, he talked more about the Real World Experience Park, his high-concept idea for adventures for everyone. The Sydney scheme had fallen through, and he had been costing for a park in Cologne, Germany, in disused railway sidings. In the early Nineties, working again with maverick British architect Will Alsop, Gabriel looked at another opportunity for the theme park. With a proposed cost of £150 million, Gabriel's thoughts had turned to space afforded in the wake of the Barcelona Olympics.

Julian Huntley would translate for Gabriel with selected Spanish journalists and media when he visited Barcelona on the promotional tour for *Us*: "You could tell pretty quickly that he wants things his way and knows exactly what he wants," Huntley says. "He is a very intelligent, quick-witted man, bright, clever and can be very funny and charming. I think that beneath that gentlemanly 'ummer and ah-er' outside is a core of steel. He knows the game and is a professional and promotion is part of the process. We worked hard and he definitely took the opportunity to use the Spanish interviews to push his own agenda, the Real World theme park in Barcelona. And this somehow managed to come up in every interview. He was interesting and professional but also engaged and interested in the team from the label. I think as so often happens with artists, if they are asked serious questions about Nelson Mandela, for example, they give serious answers and then that is what gets printed and that is the image they have."

Friends, collaborators and performers Brian Eno and Laurie Anderson were also linked to Gabriel's idea, as was Richard Branson. As Eno's biographer David Sheppard notes, the main problem with Gabriel's scheme for the 'alternative Disneyland' was that it lacked two principal elements: "finance and an authoritative, definitive plan". Le Vall d'Hebron had been selected, a former Olympic site on the outskirts of Barcelona. Ex-Monty Python film director and animator Terry Gilliam, French interior designer Phillipe Starck and pioneering Argentinian architect, Emilio Ambasz, a leading proponent in green architecture, were all linked to the project at one point or another. But it seemed to remain a pipe dream: he had established his studios and label, built a now lucrative career, but the theme park was simply a step too far.

★ ★ ★

*Us* did not win the accolades bestowed on *So*, but everyone agreed it sounded wonderful. Gabriel won Best Producer at the BRIT Awards in February 1993 at London's Alexandra Palace. To see Gabriel standing at a podium made from a shield and trident to resemble Britannia, after whom the awards were named, seemed an ironic throwback to how he had dressed onstage 20 years previously. He also performed a version of 'Steam', which helped the record reach the UK Top 10. A remarkable performance, Gabriel appeared as the fedora-hatted, velvet-suited pimp of the song's video, carried into the arena on a chair. As flunkies dance around him, they rip off his jacket to reveal a muscle-bound rubber torso, and Gabriel performs the rest of the song bare (prosthetic) chested with just his bow-tie, continuing the parody of the then-current popularity of the Chippendales. Flunkies swarm around him throughout. During that year's award season, the John Downer-directed promo for 'Digging In The Dirt' won a Grammy for Best Short Form Video at the 35th Award ceremony. Gabriel again performed 'Steam', this time in a show-stopping performance with the *Cirque Du Soleil* performers.

*Us* suffered mainly because it was not *So*. One of the most accomplished albums to bear his name, because the tracks were long and appeared occasionally to emulate too closely its predecessor, it sort of came and went. There was a feeling somewhere, however suppressed, that it came from the long line of 'rock star makes a fortune and then moans about his life' school of recording. However, it was also a brilliant, shining album, and probably his greatest update of progressive rock, the genre that he had helped define with Genesis yet with which he remained an uneasy bedfellow. It sold a million copies in the US alone and four million worldwide. It would be the last time Gabriel would hold such universal appeal. It was understandable that with an album as good as this he would want to take it on the road and offer something spectacular, in contrast to the relatively stripped-down performances he had delivered on the *This Way Up* tour that promoted *So*. It was time, metaphorically, to dig out his masks again. Gabriel wanted a show that was truly multi-media in its ambition and contacted Canadian director, actor and playwright Robert Lepage to help him make his dream a reality. "I think Robert is his generation's Peter Brooke," he told *Q*. "He does very simple things, which are almost gags, but which have a real emotional starkness to them."

With money and ambition in spades, they came up with a set with two stages to represent male and female, bridged by a corridor through the audience that housed a moving walkway. As the record had been about relationships, so the tour looked at wider relationships – town/country, synthetic/organic, male/female, represented by square and round stages – Gabriel joked that when Lepage suggested a phone box to represent the male and tree for the female he was "reminded of *Spinal Tap* for a moment when Stonehenge arrived". He had envisioned a grand tree, but as it had to appear on risers through the stage, it had to be smaller.

"I wanted to break some new ground with this show," Gabriel told *Q* in 1993. "I was originally planning an all-out video assault, with flying screens and stuff, but then I saw the U2 *Zoo TV* tour in America – I saw it five times, actually – and the visual intelligence there was so strong that I thought maybe I shouldn't be trying a video spectacular, I should be trying something else."

The *Secret World* tour took Gabriel's statement "Everything seems still and calm on the surface and then you detect a little disturbance and you know for sure that underneath the surface lies some other Secret World" as its ethos. After rehearsals in Los Angeles, it opened at the 16,000-capacity Globe Arena in Stockholm, Sweden, on April 13, 1993, seven months after the release of *Us*. Gabriel had played a handful of dates in 1992, including a performance at the Glastonbury Festival and had played at one of WOMAD's most successful sister festivals WOMADelaide in Australia in February 1993.

The *Secret World* Tour was originally budgeted in the region of £3million, but final estimates came in as double that. As writer Robert Sandall pointed out, "If it sells out across Europe and North America, it should break even. If the crew are still on their feet thereafter it might yield a tiny profit in Australia and Japan, as long as the production is slimmed down." Gabriel emphasised the point to him: "You want a piece of wood to solve a particular problem and you think it'll cost £10 but by the time you've flown it round the world, it's cost you £10,000." It was the biggest visual thing he had done since *The Lamb Lies Down On Broadway*. Slimmed down and sporting a goatee beard for most of the show, Gabriel looked beautiful.

Transition and transformation were the keys to the show, and it looked remarkable. The tour was a true event, a spectacle. Gabriel took a band of trusted regulars and newcomers for the performance: Manu Katché, Tony Levin and David Rhodes, Shankar, who had played with Gabriel for over a decade joined on violin, French Martinique musician Jean Claude Naimro, who had played with Miriam Makeba and had been recommended to Gabriel by Youssou N'Dour, was on keyboards. Levon Minassian, whose sound was so central to *Us*, joined on doudouk and US vocalist Paula Cole, who had been introduced to Gabriel by engineer Kevin Killen, added the Bush/O'Connor vocal parts.

The opening 'Come Talk To Me' set the tone for the spectacular. A red British telephone box rose from the ground, another symbol of the disappearing Britain that Gabriel had first catalogued on *Selling England By The Pound* 20 years previously. He emerged on the phone singing – the receiver is on a long cable that as Gabriel tries to move away from the box, pulls him back repeatedly. The band moved between stages in 'Across The River' while Gabriel held a rain stick as some great oarsman, and the band followed him on conveyor belts from the male to the female stage. Gabriel wore a headcam for 'Digging In The Dirt', showing a distorted close up of his head. The anger and rage in the song should not be pretty, Gabriel thought. For 'Kiss That Frog' Levin, Rhodes and Gabriel looked down into a trap door in the stage which concealed a square of water. They were filmed through the water, to make them look like they were staring down through a pool.

Gabriel had not forgotten how to entertain. During 'Secret World' a parade of luggage came down the conveyor belt, turning the stadium into an airport carousel; secrets within luggage, nomadic lifestyles, moving out; all the things that Gabriel had encountered over ten turbulent years were, at once, turned into spectacular theatre. The show ended with Gabriel taking the largest suitcase down the walkway, opening it as all the band disappeared down the trap door leaving just Gabriel alone to carry the case as a huge semi-circular blue dome came down over the female part of the stage. It was pure theatre that frankly could have looked awful and pretentious in the wrong hands. For the encore, the dome lifted to reveal the band again for 'Don't Give Up' and finally 'In Your Eyes' joined by WOMAD and Real World stalwarts, Papa Wemba.

"I left Genesis after *The Lamb Lies Down On Broadway* which was the first attempt by a rock artist to do a multi-media thing, and I've always, always wanted to do that," Gabriel told Robert Sandall. "But I was very aware at the time that my reputation as an artist was more as a wearer of flowers than as a musician. So I decided to spend some years in a visual wilderness to get the musical foundation sorted out." Sandall noted that "Like most of the things Gabriel does, it has taken far longer than it should have, gone way over budget and left many around him in a state of nervous exhaustion. But it is, as usual, worth the wait."

In June 1993 the tour came to Britain before heading out to America. As the Secret World Tour progressed Gabriel headlined a 13-date travelling festival tour to introduce WOMAD fully to North America and Canada. The *Chicago Reader* said, "The event is sort of a more studied, less narrowly cast Lollapalooza; it posits the existence of a Generation Z, say, that's interested in ethnicity beyond rap, a technological future that goes beyond smart drinks, and a definition of the word 'alternative' that suggests something more than Primus. I have to say I'm rooting for it."

On Sunday September 19, 1993, Gabriel played the largest ever WOMAD festival to date at Golden Gate Park, San Francisco, in front of a reported 98,000 people, the largest ticketed event in the world that year. Sponsored by hippy ice cream makers Ben And Jerry, it seemed a perfect capture of the festival's original intentions; the crowd were presented with Remmy Ongala, Geoffrey Oryema, Sheila Chandra and the Drummers of Burundi, alongside South London rappers, Stereo MCs, Gabriel and Crowded House among many others. WOMAD workshops, global village and 'future zone', which looked at all the interactive latest technology with which Gabriel was obsessed, were all present.

It was Gabriel's intention to film and record *Secret World* and two nights of the show were recorded in Modena, Italy. The tour continued through the following year, playing dates in America and the Middle East. 1994 was characteristically busy; aside from preparing the live album and video, he provided the track 'Love Town' for Jonathan Demme's Oscar-winning film, *Philadelphia*. He also won another Grammy for Best Short Form Video for 'Steam' at New York's Radio City Music Hall. Gabriel maintained his high profile in the US, guesting with Angelique Kidjo at the Africa Fete in Central Park in July, appearing on *The Late Show With David Letterman* in August and turning up with old friend Lou Reed at New York's Beacon Theatre. The 'Kiss That Frog' video won Best Special Effects Award at the 11th Annual MTV Music Video Awards at Radio City Music Hall. The Secret World Tour finally ended with a performance at the Woodstock 25 concert on August 14, 1994.

★ ★ ★

To support the tour and album Gabriel, in conjunction with software developers Brilliant Media, released the CD-ROM X-Plora on Real World. For Mac initially in 1993, it went to Windows the following year and finally came out as a CD-i in 1995. The game, which was full of puzzles and scavenger hunts that highlighted Gabriel's career to date in a fun and informative manner, was well-received and won the Best Musical category at the inaugural Cybermania: The Ultimate Gamer Awards in Los Angeles in October 1994. Looking back in 2012, the *Adventure Classic Gaming Site* suggested, "Typical of Gabriel, the game is at times bizarre and feels like a purchase from a modern art museum store instead of a computer or record store. Rather than giving you a quest (or even a story), this is the kind of game meant to be played with more than played (or explored, as the game itself calls it), which is a double-edged sword. Despite its age, the talent and care invested in its production is evident, and it looks younger than it is."

He had a fellow traveller in software development in old friend and first album producer Bob Ezrin. "We kept in close touch," Ezrin says. "When we did the Grand Scientific Musical Theatre as part of Comdex (the Computer Dealer's Convention) in Las Vegas in 1992, we put on a huge multi-media circus effectively to raise a flag and saw we are getting into this world. There were basically 15,000 propellerheads in the arena and we said that we saw them and we were excited and that we were coming to play too. Peter was my guest." He and Ezrin visited *Cirque Du Soleil* together and looked at ways their CD-ROM explorations could assist each other. A further CD-ROM, *Eve*, followed in 1996.

The Real World studio itself went from strength to strength. Old friend Brian Eno turned up with engineer Markus Dravs to produce Manchester band James across summer 1993 there, recording the albums *Laid* and *Wah Wah*. The label, which operated on the basis of proportionate advances being negotiated no matter who the artist, gave artistic freedom and Gabriel thoroughly enjoyed his role as label owner and A&R chief, taking his responsibility very seriously. Although at times he may have had little day-to-day involvement, all releases and artists had some direct involvement from him, and he especially enjoyed the work of the label's first American artist, Joseph Arthur. It became the go-to studio and not just for world artists; New Order created mayhem when they recorded their *Technique* album there; Van Morrison was a frequent visitor, as was, surprisingly, David Lord. "We all helped each other out," he said. "I've been to Real World many times. My engineer Neil Perry was heavily involved in its set up. We'd lend microphones and we always had a team at their annual boules contest. We've always been relatively friendly."

One of the things that really marked out the difference at Real World was their 'Real World Week Of Recording', which began in August 1991, and offered an opportunity for musicians, writers and producers to get together and see what would come out of a week creatively writing and jamming. Some 75 artists from 20 countries came down for the project in association with WOMAD. Music in performance was the keynote of the week, with many artists recording what were essentially live albums. Another followed in 1992, and a third and final one happened in 1995. With a sympathetic, music-focused recording team like Richard Evans and Richard 'Dickie' Chappell, artists such as Dave Ball and Richard Norris, aka The Grid flourished there. They had worked with Evans on the 1987 single 'Jack The Tab', with Genesis P-Orridge, then of Psychic TV. When The Grid signed to Virgin, they were invited down to the first recording week by Evans.

"It was an amazing, life affirming week," says Richard Norris. "We were given one of Peter's enormous storage hangers as a makeshift studio, and recorded musicians from Spain, Mozambique, New York and more. Everyone involved in the week had a mighty time, recording, getting involved in nightly gigs as performers or audience, hanging out in Lulu's cafe. Peter was a fantastic host."

The event was completely in keeping with the marvel and majesty of Real World. "One week in the middle of summer this craziness exploded in our Real World Studios," Gabriel was later to say. "We had this week of invited guests, people from all around the world, fed by music and a 24-hour café. It was a giant playpen, a bring your own studio party." Studios were set up in the garage, on the lawn; people would compose and then meet in the café to discuss. "It was like a dating agency, then they'd disappear into the darkness and make noises – and we'd be there to record it."

The following year, when the next Real World recording week was announced, The Grid didn't have their own production room. "Alex Gifford, who engineered for us during the first week and subsequently joined The Grid, invited me down anyway," Norris says. "I felt like a bit of a gatecrasher, but Peter put my mind to rest by saying of course it was fine that I was there, I was part of the Real World family, which was very generous."

There was an interesting visitor that week. Joe Strummer, then in something of a creative wilderness since The Clash had disbanded in 1986, had heard about the happening over at the mill and pitched up. "One sunny afternoon I was sitting on the grass outside the mill and what looked like a travelling circus drove into the car park. It was Joe, accompanied by flags, children, his partner and a gang he'd hooked up with at the WOMAD festival," Norris laughs. "They looked like a bunch of fun and a bunch of trouble. Mike Large, the Real World studio manager, wasn't keen to let them in, probably recalling the recent New Order session in the studio where a Manchester busload came down and had a bit of a party, breaking toilets and generally trashing the place. However, Peter came out and talked to Joe, curious he was there, welcoming him in. Peter diffused the situation pretty quickly." The Clash had been at the vanguard of the punk explosion that was supposed to wash away the old timers like Gabriel and Genesis. The two hit it off; Strummer was only two years Gabriel's junior, and he too had been brought up middle-class, though this tended to be brushed under the carpet during The Clash's heyday. "I got to know Joe in later years when he became interested in world music," Gabriel told *Uncut* in 2007. "We'd have recording weeks in the studio and set up 'Strummerville' for Joe. He was a delightful man."

"As I was sitting watching this unfold Joe said 'Can anyone programme this drum machine?' so I offered my services," Norris remembers. "He said 'I want that real techno sound, you know, Boom Boom BOOM . . .' "

This kind of thing highlighted the spirit of openness and adventure that Gabriel was keen to foster and what made the studios so very special. Many bands were surprised that Gabriel would often join them for lunch or breakfast. It was his home, after all. When The Grid produced World Of Twist at Real World for their one and only album, *Quality Street*, Gabriel presided over a long and drawn out table tennis competition, and presented the cup himself. World Of Twist (and future Earl Brutus) members Nick Sanderson and Gordon King were serious Gabriel fans, and Sanderson, when a schoolboy, had gone on a pilgrimage to Ashcombe House to see where Gabriel lived.

"My main memory is of Peter's generosity and spirit of possibility," Norris says. "I was just some punk kid who'd made an acid house record, but he gave me as much time of day as he did anyone else. Many other rock musicians in his position would be content to sit counting their money in a country pile, but with the Real World recording weeks Peter genuinely made something happen."

Heavyweight friends such as Phil Ramone came out (he produced the *La Candela Viva* by Colombian singer Toto La Momposina for Real World) and Bob Ezrin arrived to lend a hand. "I made some friends there," Ezrin says. "It was spectacular. Nobody gets a chance to do that sort of stuff anymore. Every city had its scene; there were areas like Haight-Ashbury or Greenwich village or Camden Market. People would live and play there and they'd know each other so they'd end up in people's flats or in clubs jamming and having fun, and cross-pollinated ideas. We don't have that now, it's been rendered economically unviable and all those places dried up. Now it's a series of separate clubs with their own economy and people live within them and the only time people see each other is when they go to somebody's show. There's no hanging out anymore and that's a shame. I think that's why everything sounds bland and repetitive these days."

The Recording Weeks clearly tried to regain a little of that spirit. By the time of the final one to date in July 1995, 80 musicians attended, and Karl Wallinger from World Party was given the task of putting the best recordings of the weeks together for a possible release.

* * *

With everything developing at such a pace and his recording and touring cycle about to step up, Gabriel turned again to activism by co-founding WITNESS with the Lawyers Committee for Human Rights and the Reebok Human Rights Foundation. It was intended as an international non-profit organisation that could harness the power of video and storytelling to open the eyes of the world to human rights abuses.

The leaked video footage of the Los Angeles Police Department beating Rodney King in March 1991, taken by George Halliday from his apartment balcony, was beamed around the world, marking an important milestone for justice. Before, equipment that could have captured such footage would have been solely in the hands of the media, or clumsy home movie cameras. Now, thanks to the explosion of cheap technology, the world saw this flagrant example of police brutality and racism. Now, *anybody* could capture moments like this and, as a result, an event that would have gone unnoticed was broadcast around the world. Gabriel was absolutely intrigued. He had taken his recently acquired HandyCam on the *Human Rights Now*! tour to detail meetings with activists in countries to keep a diary of their stories; now human rights abuses could be filmed directly and beamed across the world.

The message of WITNESS ('See it. Film it. Change it.') was simple: to empower human rights defenders to use video to fight injustice, as well as "to transform personal stories of abuse into powerful tools that can pressure those in power or with power to act. By bringing often unseen images and seldom heard stories to the attention of key decision makers, the media, and the public. WITNESS catalyses grassroots activism, political engagement, and lasting change."

It was a powerful idea that could have huge ramifications. By harnessing the explosion of cheap video technology, people could bypass traditional systems of authority to get their message heard. "We bridge the worlds of human rights, media and technology by incorporating cutting-edge innovations into traditional approaches to advocacy," the mission statement continued. "WITNESS' unique contribution to the human rights community is to serve as a global authority on best practices in the use of video for human rights purposes and a frontline resource for training and expertise."

Gabriel attended the annual Reebok Human Rights in Action ceremony at Boston's northeastern University in December 1994 to further promote the cause, and the following December, he co-hosted an event with Michael Stipe from R.E.M. in Los Angeles to keep its presence felt. WITNESS was destined to start small, but with the changes in technology, and the widespread availability of recording devices, it could be a potent method for change.

★ ★ ★

Gabriel refused to let the grass grow under his feet. As the *Secret World* tour concluded, he and producer Peter Walsh put together a double album souvenir of the shows entitled *Secret World Live*. Released in September 1994 it was, unusually for many live albums, an instant critical success. *Rolling Stone* commented: "The result is tantamount to a religious rite, merging grandeur with the intimacy of feeling, the public with the secret. More than Gabriel's *Plays Live* (1983), this album maintains a powerful continuity that loses neither pace nor momentum; more than the studio originals, these versions elaborate on the dramatic potential inherent in them – the heat and magnitude of rhythm, the human/animal ambiguity of an otherworldly cry."

It was successful in capturing the rapture of the tour, and demonstrated that the playing matched the spectacle. 'Secret World' and 'Digging In The Dirt' matched the power of their studio counterparts, and the album acted as an effective update of a greatest hits set.

Only *Entertainment Weekly* were critical: "Woodstock '94's closing act doesn't add much spice to the bland *Us* tunes. Listeners might find themselves hoping – even praying – for the audience to shout out for gems like 'Biko' or 'Shock The Monkey'." With its cover design co-ordinated by Martha Ladly, formerly of Martha & The Muffins, who was working at Real World at the time, the album reached number 22 in the US and 10 in the UK.

The accompanying VHS, released simultaneously, was spectacular and portrayed the shows inventively. It was directed by French-Canadian director Francois Girard, who had made the award-winning film *Thirty Two Short Films About Glenn Gould*. Ten cameras captured the concert and audiences saw the hard work and exhilaration of the performance, as well as the full, dizzying effect of Lepage and Gabriel's concept for the show. Gabriel's sense of fun is evident and it demonstrated that beneath all the machinery and special effects, here was a vibrant band enjoying their work. It was broadcast on UK television, and understandably won a Grammy in 1996 for Best Long Form Music Video.

With the tour finished, Peter Gabriel would not release another album under his own name until 2000. Not that he was idle. In fact, he began recording material right away for his next project. Recording would continue intermittently at Real World and locations across the world for the next six years. Being so close to his studio meant that any idea could be captured quickly and it was rumoured that by the end of the decade he had stockpiled around 100 songs. In the meantime, he was involved in a bewildering array of projects; donating material to film soundtracks, curating Real World's output and campaigning on behalf of WITNESS.

★ ★ ★

In 1996, Phil Collins, who for a decade and a half had been running a hugely successful solo career, left Genesis. Tony Banks and Mike Rutherford had soldiered on, recruiting former Stiltskin vocalist Ray Wilson to become the band's third vocalist and frontman. Unfortunately, their amazing ability for reinvention based around the Charterhouse core could not weave its magic again, and the resulting album, *Calling All Stations,* was panned in the press, and despite reaching number two on its release in the UK, it only reached number 54 in the US, fifty places lower than the group's last studio album, *We Can't Dance,* in 1991. Although the album was a success in Europe, the proposed US tour was cancelled. Banks and Rutherford quietly decided that the group should be laid to rest, at least for the time being.

With all of this going on, Peter Gabriel also found time to be pulled back into the Genesis fold, to help approve and take part in a series of reissues. In June 1998, the first of two proposed historic Genesis box sets, *Archive 1967–75*, was released. It was a beautifully assembled, painstaking affair that brought together a wealth of unreleased material from his time in the group. With the full participation of the entire band, including as many of their early drummers as they could find, the four-CD set began the critical rehabilitation of the group, who had been in a wilderness since their hit-making period in the eighties.

*Archive 1967–75* offered a glimpse into their old working practices, and it contained many highlights and long sought-after tracks. Presented in reverse chronological order, the first two discs contained a complete *The Lamb Lies Down On Broadway* live from the Shrine Auditorium in Los Angeles in January 1975. Gabriel had agreed to overdub some of the vocals, as occasionally they had been lost, most notably during the ridiculous stagecraft needed to wear the Slipperman outfit, and Steve Hackett added some new guitar parts. "It was really like stepping back in time 25 years," he told Sylvie Simmons in 2000. "Not just the music, the relationships. It's just like you never left. It's the same sort of thing like when you go back home and your mum and dad start treating you the same way they did when you were four or five. It's very hard to break out of that mental bubble."

The most exciting item, almost hidden in plain sight at the time, was that the band actually reunited to re-record '*it*' from *The Lamb Lies Down On Broadway* in its entirety, as the tapes ran out during the original performance. It was the first time that the five members had been in the studio since 1974 together. It is a beautiful version, with Gabriel's added maturity giving the song extra gravity.

The third disc tidied up further live recordings, mainly the 1973 live show, which finally presented Gabriel singing 'Supper's Ready' live, as well as 'Twilight Alehouse', 'Happy The Man' and the single mix of 'Watcher Of The Skies'. The final disc was, for many, the real revelation: BBC sessions, mixes and the very earliest demos, recorded for and before *From Genesis To Revelation.* Hearing a 17-year-old Gabriel in his transformative year playing tentative drums to 'Patricia' and singing with his youthful, sweet and soulful voice on the Bee Gees-esque 'Try A Little Sadness', was a lovely glimpse into the simplicity of his style. It made the listener wish that, in all Gabriel's quest for studio perfection, he would at some point experiment again with such a straightforward approach.

Mark Radcliffe, writing in *The Guardian,* stated: "Gabriel-period Genesis remain lodged in my heart forever. There's a moment in Bret Easton Ellis's novel *American Psycho* where the anti-hero Bateman states that the band got much better after Gabriel left. It's at that point you know that guy is trouble."

The set contained essays by Tony Banks, Chris Welch, Richard Macphail, Ed Goodgold, Jonathan King and David Stopps. All members of the band had approval on the words. Gabriel at this point was in Senegal, recording material for the follow-up to *Us*. "I remember phoning Peter who said there's only one thing wrong," David Stopps recalls, wondering if he had written something that might have offended him. "And then he disappeared off the line for about ten minutes. Peter then said, 'You're never going to believe it, but they've just brought my air conditioning.' He was so relieved. And then he told the mistake. I'd spelled 'Mellotron' wrong. That was the only comment he had!"

To promote the release, on May 11, 1998, a press conference was called at Heathrow Airport. For the first time since Tony Banks' wedding to Margaret in July 1972, not only was the classic five-piece all in the same room, but they were joined, too, by Jonathan Silver and Anthony Phillips. It was a jolly, upbeat meeting to promote the set, and photographs reveal a group of people absolutely delighted to be in each other's company. Phillips stands in the middle of the shot as if to acknowledge that, without him, the band may never have happened in the first place.

"Pete suggested we all had dinner together which was a really nice idea," said Hackett, and afterwards the group sat and reminisced, marking the moment when Genesis became a heritage act as opposed to an ongoing concern releasing new material. But heritage rock was now an exceptionally lucrative industry, as reflected in the number of old fans who waited in the rain at *Six Of The Best* and, like the members of the group, happily relived their pasts while clamouring for reissued material.

The final commercial act for the Genesis industry in the 20th century was the release of a CD single-disc hits collection. Although *Turn It On Again: The Hits* contained only one track from the Gabriel era, 'I Know What I Like (In Your Wardrobe)' and the majority from the three-piece commercial years, it contained the fascinating curio, 'The Carpet Crawlers 1999'.

Produced and stitched together by Trevor Horn, this was a re-recording of one of the songs closest to Gabriel's heart, featuring both him and Collins singing, with Hackett back on guitar. It is very much of the moment – with late Nineties production techniques abounding; random noise splashes and effects. Gabriel sings the first verses and then Collins continues. A video was made, intercutting vintage footage of the group with a Rael-like character crawling through tunnels. It remains, at the time of writing, the last new material recorded by Genesis. Although flawed, it presents a fitting tribute to the Charterhouse dreams of those young schoolboys.

★ ★ ★

In 1997, Gabriel was thrilled to be asked by his long-term hero Randy Newman to sing on 'That'll Do', a track Newman had written for the film *Babe 2: Pig In The City*, the follow-up to the hugely successful 1995 film, *Babe*.

"We really enjoyed that," Bob Ezrin said. "It was interesting because when we were making *Car*, I turned Peter on to Randy Newman as a writer and an artist – Peter's first exposure to Randy was through me at Nimbus. Lo and behold, we were asked if we would do it. Harry Garfield, the music exec on the film *Babe 2* made the call. I thought that was poetic. I called Peter. He was naturally excited. It was exciting that the three of us could get together in the same room, it was a mutual admiration society between those two guys. As far as I know, that was the first time they'd met." Recorded at Air Lyndhurst with the Black Dyke Mills Band and Paddy Moloney from The Chieftains, it was a sweet and affecting song that reflected the phrase said by Farmer Hoggett (James Cromwell) to Babe, the animated pig of the film's title. Although the film did not equal the success of the original, the song was nominated for an Academy Award, Gabriel's first nomination.

They performed the song at the 71st Academy Awards ceremony on March 21 at the Dorothy Chandler Pavilion in Los Angeles. Introduced by *Friends* star Lisa Kudrow, it was a moving performance, highlighting Gabriel's newly-shaven head with Newman looking on, all avuncular at the piano. The Black Dyke Mills Band added the air of northern Britain to the glamorous veneer of the star-studded Los Angeles evening. Unfortunately the song lost out to the Stephen Schwartz-written 'When You Believe' from *The Prince Of Egypt*. The Mariah Carey and Whitney Houston duet seemed so much more Oscar material than Newman's beautiful, down-home, sentimental song complete with brass band.

Gabriel's work sprang up in various places throughout the remainder of the decade. It appeared on the soundtrack to *Virtuosity*, and he recorded a version of 'Suzanne' for the Leonard Cohen tribute album, *Tower Of Song*. He contributed 'In The Sun', a cover of Real World artist Joseph Arthur's haunting track for the album *Diana, Princess Of Wales: A Tribute*, the proceeds of which went to the recently deceased Princess' memorial trust fund. Another great loss to Gabriel personally was the passing of Nusrat Fateh Ali Khan, the Qawwli devotional singer who had been one of Real World's biggest stars, and had first worked with Gabriel on *Passion*. They had most recently collaborated on the track 'Taboo' that featured in Oliver Stone's controversial road movie, *Natural Born Killers*.

* * *

As the Nineties progressed, the dawning of the new century seemingly became the single preoccupation of the British news media and a year-long event was planned to celebrate this new era. The Millennium Dome, situated on a bend of the River Thames on the North Greenwich Peninsula in South East London had first been mooted in February 1996 by Conservative Deputy Prime Minister Michael Heseltine, as part of the Thames regeneration programme. When a tumultuous majority returned the Labour Government to power in May 1997, there was every opportunity for the new government to halt the proposals for the Dome, which had already been deemed a white elephant by the media, and undertake something far more vital to the country with the money instead. Labour Minister Without Portfolio Peter Mandelson was put in charge of the project.

With a nod to the Dome Of Discovery from the Festival Of Britain, the structure, the largest of its kind in the world, resembled a huge marquee, distinguished by its twelve 100m high yellow support towers, chosen to represent the 12 months of the year and each hour of the day, emphasising the worldwide significance of Greenwich Mean Time. The building was 365 metres in diameter, for the days of the year.

In late 1997, Gabriel was approached by Mark Fisher to assist in the creation of a multi-media music and video experience for the dome that would run for all of the year 2000. A government research paper, published in February 1998, announced to parliament that Gabriel and Fisher would be responsible for the central performance. For the next 12 months, the pair sketched out concepts and ideas. The performance would become known as *OVO*, and could best be described as 'an audiovisual show designed to tell a story'. It used some of the material that Gabriel had been writing since *Us* and brought in a stellar cast of friends and musicians.

Given the frequent thwarting of Gabriel's theme park idea, his being involved in the Dome seemed to evoke the dream he'd talked about since 1972: the "cross between Disneyland and an art gallery where the visitor goes through a tremendous amount of first hand experiences which would completely upturn his points of relativity and put him through a series of changes." Barbara Charone, writing in *NME* in 1973, signposted that "Gabriel believes that one day film, music and theatre will merge." The initial concept for the Millennium Dome was to be something like that.

As Gabriel said in the *OVO* booklet, "We were asked to do something that reflects a bit of the past, the present and the future, so I suggested we develop the plot around the struggles of three generations of a family." Gabriel came up with three acts, the first looking at nature and prehistoric times, the second the industrial period, and the third, moving towards the future, looking at the integration of nature and technology.

For the music for the project, Gabriel worked with his trusted team at Real World: Richard Evans, Richard 'Dickie' Chappell and Meabh Flynn. Gabriel selected the singers personally and painstakingly, to reflect some of the best voices from around the world: Elizabeth Fraser, who after leaving the Cocteau Twins had sung on Massive Attack's ethereal 'Teardrop'; Blue Nile leader Paul Buchanan, whose distinctive, emotional vocal style suggested that he was permanently on the verge of tears; Alison Goldfrapp, yet to become the UK 00s glam rock noir diva, who had sung with Tricky and her musical partner Will Gregory; Real World recording artist and sometimes Afro-Celt Soundsystem collaborators Iarla O'Lionaird; and the remarkable vocal talents of Richie Havens, who sang on 'The Time Of The Turning', all came together for Gabriel.

The most remarkable track was 'Father, Son', a beautiful tribute to his dear father Ralph, who was, by now, in his late Eighties. "My dad is getting old now, and I felt I hadn't really bonded with him as much as I had wanted," Gabriel said. "So, since he's been into yoga for 40 years I thought we could get a yoga teacher and go off to a hotel for a week together. It took a lot of courage internally for me to organise that, but he was very up for it. And we had a big breakthrough at one point so I thought, 'I'll put this into a song.' And it seemed to touch people. I think when you've provided an emotional tool for yourself in a song, you're more likely to provide it for other people too." Gabriel's beautiful baldness with emotions shines through on this simple, effective piano ballad, away from all the machines and programming of the rest of *OVO*.

The Dome seemed doomed from the outset. Although Tony Blair called it, "a triumph of confidence over cynicism, boldness over blandness, excellence over mediocrity", it seemed to bring out all the British reserve of gallows humour and cynicism. It began amid confusion: a muddled opening night tested transport infrastructure and led to Mandelson sacking Jennie Page, who had been put in charge of the overall project. Images of dignitaries waiting on the platform at Stratford Underground station for transport to the venue was not the greatest message to send out to the world, and the project struggled with sufficient visitor numbers.

The show, which featured 160 dancers, was performed 999 times before closing on December 31, 2000. Their performances covered a real range of emotions that brought the *OVO* family to life. It was remarkable, a clear spot in a confused, over-educational experience that seemed ultimately to be Arthur nor Martha. The half-hour long show was also dogged with sound problems, frequently drowned out by the noise of the sideshows and attractions outside the performance space, while having to battle with complaints from older audiences that it was, indeed, too loud for them.

"Everyone always said it was the best thing of the dome," Richard Macphail says. "And I loved the album." It was indeed a lot of spectacle. It did succeed in introducing audiences to Fraser and Buchanan, neither of whom were artists with particularly high profiles, as their main groups were not even distant memories for younger audiences. "Clearly the Dome has been the most unpopular project in the country, probably in my lifetime," Gabriel told Sylvie Simmons in 2000. "But in a way that was also, perversely, an attraction. What I find interesting in art is the struggle between two potentially opposing forces."

The accompanying album was released in June 2000. Gabriel worked hard with his cast of collaborators to ensure the album was a faithful reflection of the music that people had enjoyed at the show. "As well as drawing on many references within our own folk traditions, the music also draws on the cultural origins of the many peoples that now comprise contemporary British culture," Gabriel wrote. "It layers Asian, African, Middle

Eastern, Australian and European elements against a mostly contemporary British backdrop. From 12th century hurdy gurdy to didgeridoo, from the pulsing rhythms of the Dhol Foundation and the nostalgic brass of the Black Dyke Band, from Arab laments over drum and bass to meditative moments with string section – the soundtrack is a really eclectic mix." Chris Welch wrote: "This album of music for the show provided a welcome souvenir of an otherwise controversial event."

"The songs and the sound on Peter's later albums are absolutely brilliant," says Anthony Phillips. "The songs are so well presented in a very original way. Some of those sounds are strange – George Martin would be a good cross reference, as some of the sounds on *Sgt Pepper* are very strange; these things took a lot of work and a lot of time. It's slow but very sure. It takes as long as it takes with that kind of music. Sometimes you have to go down blind alleys because it is about experimentation. It's different if you're working with an orchestra, but if you are starting off with an open palette, you can spend a whole day on something." *Pitchfork Media* suggested: "The Tower That Ate People' is Gabriel's funkiest track since 'Sledgehammer', with growling verse vocals, phased guitars, overdriven organ, and a gorgeously haunting bridge melody. But the best track by far arrives just before the ending. 'Downside-Up' is, melodically, one of the best songs in Gabriel's entire catalogue."

*Allmusic*, however, was not kind: "*OVO* sounds laboured, choppy, and pasted together, like it is the soundtrack to a visual installation, and feels incomplete without it."

Musically, *OVO* was one of those projects that ends up being labelled for 'hardcore fans only', but to dismiss it as that would be to do it a complete injustice. There was an edginess present that pleased traditional fans and confused those looking for another *So*. It had been 12 years since *Passion*: people had forgotten that Gabriel could also make collaborative, exciting music like this. It reached number 24 in the UK albums chart.

It is not too far a stretch of the imagination to suggest that the piece of theatre that was staged at the Millennium Dome, although flawed, was a direct predecessor of the incredible show that Danny Boyle and Frank Cottrell Boyce presented for the opening ceremony of the London Olympic Games in 2012. Through all the controversy and debacle of the Millennium Dome, Gabriel emerged relatively unscathed. The reputed £800 million it cost UK tax payers could simply have been better spent. "I would have done something different with that money," Gabriel told Sylvie Simmons in *Aloha* Magazine. "I would have had the Millennium Tower as an alternative health centre that changed health care from curative to preventative and changed the perception of hospitals, which for the most part are places you go to when you're sick to get sicker. It would have not only the latest and best equipment available, but health restaurants, health club, anything to do with health."

⋆ ⋆ ⋆

In the same year that Shawn Fanning launched the highly illegal and copyright infringing Napster in November 1999, Gabriel helped start OD2, the acronym for On Demand Distribution, again illustrating that he was far ahead of the curve. Working with Charles Grimsdale, the original purpose of the enterprise was to provide the technology to allow music distribution infrastructure and rights management on the Internet for unsigned bands. With the success of the management system, bigger organisations got on board. Gabriel, although no businessman, was able to get the best talent and to look forward and be receptive to ideas. Peter Gabriel was, not for the first time in his career, exploring another frontier.

# 23: A General Feeling Of Beautiful Dread – *Up*

*"Speed is not my strength: diversions are."*

Peter Gabriel, 2002

*"I think sometimes when you stare mortality in the face, life is lived a little bit more fully."*

Peter Gabriel, 2002

PETER Gabriel continued to work at a steady pace, although it wasn't always obvious as his releases seemed so sporadic. With the great wealth of material he had amassed since the mid-Nineties, it became a case of ring-fencing where each separate track could be put; one for a solo album, one for a soundtrack project, one for the many requests for his material for charity work. Add into this his studio, label, WITNESS, interests in technology *and* his family, it was with little wonder his releases were sporadic. "It's just now I own more stuff and I've got more possibilities for diversions and displacement activity," he told Sylvie Simmons in 2000. "I think it's also that I've just wanted a life too. I don't work weekends now, except on a couple of occasions. I still work till midnight or 1 am most nights, which is just stupid, but I've been doing other projects – some stuff with Real World Records and some of the Net things, and these I also really enjoy, and I'm also trying to do a cabaret thing with Robert Lepage. That and the Experience Park; I get great conversations with people that I think are smarter than I am and I just get fed by that. It's like garbage in, garbage out – I'm more concerned by getting quality input than being strapped down to an album-tour-album-tour life. That's a sad life."

In 1997, Gabriel, a man whose heart could best be described as restless, fell in love with Meabh Flynn, the Limerick-born engineer and pianist who had been working at Real World since the mid-Nineties. She was 22 years younger than him but he felt strongly attracted to her and it took a while for him to make an approach, given his previous form. Unlike most of Gabriel's previous relationships, Flynn had working class roots, and her no-nonsense practicality struck a chord with him. A romance blossomed, and on September 27, 2001, she gave birth to their son Isaac Ralph. Gabriel was delighted.

Gabriel was still on good terms with Jill, now working as a counsellor and psychotherapist in Bath, and doted on his daughters, Anna, now a filmmaker, and Melanie, who sang with him, but like many rock stars who became fathers while they were on the album-tour-album treadmill, he regretted missing large chunks of their childhood. As a result he was determined to give Isaac as conventional a family life as his profession would allow. "You don't get panicked by all the neurosis you felt as a young parent – you know, will this kill them?" he told Sylvie Simmons. "It's the first time for her, but I think I'm definitely more relaxed about things, so that's an advantage. You have a different perspective. It's a wonderful gift." With his parents, Ralph and Irene, still very much alive, Gabriel was now more settled emotionally than he had been at any point in his life.

In 2001, Gabriel bought a small private hotel, Li Capanni between the two villages of Cannigione and Palau set in 12 acres of its own land in one of the most beautiful parts of Northern Sardinia. Described as a hidden treasure, with its private gardens and its own secluded beach, it offered peace, tranquility and a place to unwind. "I never wanted to be a hotelier, but when I heard that my favourite hotel was about to be bought and destroyed by developers, I thought it was time to give it a go," he told the *Daily Mail* in 2004. "The other option was to lose it forever, which would have been heartbreaking. It was time to call the bank manager." It was here on June 9, 2002, that he and Flynn were married. Scottish harpist Savourna Stevenson performed, while passages of Kahlil Gibran's *The Prophet* were read aloud. Phil Collins was his best man, and with Rutherford and Banks in attendance, there was an impromptu Genesis reunion that evening. Influential DJ Gilles Peterson played, but his serious set was cut short by Flynn's working-class Irish family who had put a cassette of their favourite tracks through the sound system.

However, the two releases that accompanied this breakthrough in his private life were not joyous celebrations of love. Some of the material he had been recording since *Us* that hadn't been used on *OVO* was split

Gabriel photographed in his natural milieu, the Real World studios. Tony Banks: "Music is fundamental to his reputation and he keeps a consistently high standard. It couldn't happen to a nicer guy." PHOTOSHOT/GETTY IMAGES

The Conspiracy of Hope Tour was timed like a perfect storm just as 'Sledgehammer' was breaking into the American charts; L to R: Joan Baez, Jackson Browne, Bono, PG. BOB LEAFE/FRANK WHITE PHOTO AGENCY

From Conspiracy of Hope to Clapham Common. Artists Against Apartheid, June 1986; L to R: Boy George, Sting, Sade, PG. REX/ANDRE CSILLAG

The Human Rights Now Tour 1: Gabriel singing 'In Your Eyes' with Youssou N'Dour. NEAL PRESTON/CORBIS

The Human Rights Now Tour 2: PG, Tracy Chapman, Youssou N'Dour, Sting, Joan Baez and Bruce Springsteen perform in Philadephia. NEAL PRESTON/CORBIS

Two images from the Brit Awards, 1993: Gabriel in pumped up body suit for 'Steam', and then receiving the award for Best Producer. The event's trophy, and stage set of Britannia, offered comparisons with Gabriel's own performance as her 20 years previously.
ALL ACTION/EMPICS ENTERTAINMENT

From Amnesty To Greenpeace: Brinsley Forde, David Byrne, The Edge and PG in Red Square, Moscow 1989. ADRIAN BOOT

With Rosanna Arquette, late eighties. REX FEATURES

With Kate Bush, Brit Awards, Grosvenor House Hotel, February 1987. REX FEATURES

At his pride and joy, Real World Studios, in the nineties. CHRISTOPHER PILLITZ/ALAMY

Gabriel at Robben Island, November 29, 1993, photographing Nelson Mandela's speech before playing the 46664 concert later that day. LOUISE GUBB/CORBIS

Gail Colson: "A wonderful songwriter, musician and performer. He is challenging and always comes up with something thought provoking, a true artist." STEVE TRAGER/FRANK WHITE PHOTO AGENCY

The Elders together, Johannesburg, July 2007: L to R: Graca Machel, PG, Nelson Mandela, Richard Branson and Jimmy Carter. AP PHOTO/JEROME DELAY

Headlining the Open Air Stage during the WOMAD Festival at Charlton Park, Wiltshire, July 25, 2009. EMPICS ENTERTAINMENT

With Meabh at the 81st Academy Awards Sunday, February 22, 2009. AP PHOTO/CHRIS PIZZELLO

With daughter Anna Marie at the 2013 Ivor Novello awards at the Grosvenor House Hotel. PA WIRE/PRESS ASSOCIATION IMAGES

Peter Gabriel in 1983. It had been a tumultuous 12 months. DEBORAH FEINGOLD/CORBIS

between *two* releases: the soundtrack to the film *Rabbit Proof Fence*, and for his first 'proper' solo album since *Us*, to be called *Up*.

Given that he had enjoyed the experience of working on *Passion* and *OVO* so much Gabriel was enthused by the offer to work on another film, again a distraction from the business of releasing the proper follow-up to *Us*. Directed by *Dead Calm* and *Clear And Present Danger* director Phillip Noyce, *Rabbit Proof Fence* was based on the Australian book *Follow The Rabbit Proof Fence* by Doris Pilkington Garimara, first published in 1996. The film looked at the controversial topic of the 'Stolen Generation', the removal of Aboriginal children from their families by the Australian church and state for their own protection to be trained as domestic workers for white society.

It was based on the true story of the author's then 14-year-old mother, Molly Craig (Evelyn Sampi), an eight-year-old friend, Daisy Kadibil (Tianna Sansbury) and 10-year-old cousin, Gracie Fields (Laura Monaghan) who escaped from the Moore River Native Settlement in Perth to journey back to their Aboriginal settlement at Jigalong in 1931. The film centred on the 1,500 mile journey that they make along the country's 'rabbit-proof fence' to get back home, pursued by A.O. Neville (Kenneth Branagh), the self-styled protector of Western Australian Aborigines, and Moodoo (David Gulpill), an Aboriginal tracker.

Released just ahead of *Up* in April 2002, *Long Walk Home: Music From Rabbit Proof Fence* did not stir quite as much interest as Gabriel's previous *Passion* album. The music, recorded at Real World with the London Session Orchestra, the Electra Strings and the Dhol Foundation, complemented the haunting, downbeat film perfectly. It also featured his trusted team of David Rhodes, Richard Evans, Shankar and drummer Ged Lynch. 'Gracie's Recapture' was a beautiful piece of music which, like 'Ngankarrparni', used some of the instrumental from 'The Nest That Sailed The Sky' from *OVO* and added the haunting Aboriginal voices of actors Ningali and Myarn Lawford. It featured the mournful refrain from the as-yet unreleased 'Sky Blue', amongst the most lilting music Gabriel had ever recorded. Still to be heard at the time of the album's release in its proper form, it featured the Blind Boys of Alabama – Clarence Fountain, Jimmy Carter, Eric McKinnie, Joey Williams and Fred Rice, the group who had been together in some form since 1939. Gabriel was more than willing to champion them, and the vocal refrain he had written for them, which again featured in 'Cloudless', the main theme from the film, was a remarkable piece of work.

*Long Walk Home: Music From Rabbit Proof Fence* was always going to be a low-key release, and was generally reviewed warmly. *E! Online* said: "Walk's mellow mood sidesteps the usual overly melodramatic soundtrack hoo-ha for a journey that works as well on the stereo as it does on the screen." Perhaps it was *Billboard*'s review that was the most apposite: "*Long Walk Home* passes the ultimate soundtrack test: it stands alone beautifully, capably supporting the work of director Phillip Noyce while at the same time feeling like a natural and fluid extension of Gabriel's own distinctive artistic vision." Q Magazine was not quite as kind: "The synthesised tropical shimmers, buzzings of insects and blat of helicopter blades largely lack the momentum to sustain interest outside the cinema."

Chris Jones, always the most eloquent of writers on the subject of Gabriel, said in his BBC review, "Undoubtedly *Long Walk Home* will never have the profile of Gabriel's song-based releases, but for a man who has continually eschewed the standard ephemeral rock star's dalliances this is a real shame. The album is a beautiful addition to his back catalogue and deserves to be judged as a complete statement in its own right. Who knows? Maybe in twenty years' time the film music of Peter Gabriel will be the work by which he is most fondly remembered." *Long Walk Home: Music From Rabbit Proof Fence* was soon joined two months later by the reissue of all of Gabriel's solo albums to date (bar *Secret World Live*). They were packaged in 'vinyl-replica' CD digi-packs, remastered with rare photographs and pictures of the mastertapes. The catalogue was reviewed extensively, showing that there was great goodwill for Gabriel and that he had built an incredibly beautiful, discrete body of work in his 25 years as a solo performer.

* * *

Gabriel's continued affair with innovation ran and ran: "There's an incredibly close tie between Ralph as an inventor and his technical wizardry and what Peter took and where he went with it," Richard Macphail says. "You can see the progression." The possibilities of the Internet were now Gabriel's keen passion. In the late Nineties, he had registered the domain name www.petergabriel.com which had first appeared on the sleeve of *OVO*.

Gabriel was an early adopter of communication directly with his audience and, through his website, understood the potency of having a ready-made database of fans to sell to directly. To coincide with the release of *Long Walk Home: Music From Rabbit Proof Fence* and to ready audiences for *Up*, his first solo album in 10 years, he established the Full Moon Club, to which he would release snippets of his new music, and send filmed messages to his audience (his 'lunatics') via the web at the time of each full moon. The Full Moon Club and the *Up* countdown seemed to pale in comparison with another project he was involved with – how to communicate with and record music with Bonobos, the great apes who, as members of the chimpanzee family, are one of the closest mammals to man. There is only .6 per cent of difference between these apes and man. Gabriel turned this profoundly affecting experience into the song 'Animal Nation', which was featured in the tour that supported his next album.

Gabriel had been exploring the language abilities of the apes and, noting that the Language Research Centre at Georgia State University was also working in this area, asked if he could look at the possibility of making music with them. The University was delighted to have him along. Gabriel captured the results on film, showing a female ape playing the keyboard. Richard Evans and Tony Levin were present at the blues-jam with the ape respectably if clumsily playing two-handed keyboard. "No-one has ever shown her what an octave is, so she's discovered this entirely on her own," Gabriel told Sylvie Simmons. "It was an extraordinary experience."*

★ ★ ★

Heralded by a press announcement that explained his Full Moon activities and his work with the Bonobos, Peter Gabriel's *Up* was released on September 24, 2002. Basic tracks had been recorded as early as 1995 at Real World, with sessions continuing at Youssou N'Dour's studio in Senegal and at Meribel in France. Made from over 150 compositional fragments that Gabriel had amassed in that time, he explained to the press why it had

* Amusingly, five years later Cadbury's ran an advert for their chocolate featuring a gorilla playing the drums. It was to 'In The Air Tonight' by Phil Collins, which went high in the UK charts again as a result. Although Collins had had little to do with the advert, again his old drummer had seemed to follow Gabriel to huge commercial success.

taken so long with the throwaway line, "old men take more time."

"It started off in an ambling way, and then I'd take a little bit of equipment out to Senegal," Gabriel told Sylvie Simmons. "We didn't have air conditioning so I'd be sitting with a towel on my head full of ice cubes, water dripping down my back, trying to stay cool, because I can't think properly when my brain gets too hot. Then we went to the snow in France. We were snowboarding in the afternoon and working in the morning, one extreme to the other."

Richard 'Dickie' Chappell explained to *Sound-On-Sound* their routine at Meribel in the French Alps: "We achieved a lot there because there were no distractions," he said. "We did a lot of writing, and a lot of snowboarding. It's a dream way of working, up in the mountains every day. It was very inspiring and made Peter very happy. We generally worked at night time, which was tiring, because we'd be exhausted from jumping around and running around the mountain by day."

And if that wasn't enough, before recording got fully underway at Box, Gabriel and Flynn did some recording in Brazil. "I was going down the Amazon on this amazing boat," he continued to Simmons, "which had a fully equipped 48-track studio on board, just playing away and suddenly you would look up and there would be this amazing vegetation and insect life. That's part of the reason why I didn't discipline myself and say, 'Right, I've got 30 ideas here, I should finish them off', but just kept on generating new ideas. I was enjoying it."

The majority of *Up* was recorded in the Writing Room at Real World, away from the production room: Chappell kept Gabriel's keyboards and microphone live, so whenever Gabriel was ready, he could get straight down to work. Some of these ideas fed into *OVO* and *The Long Walk Home*. Working with the core of Levin, Rhodes and Katché, Gabriel added legendary bassist Danny Thompson, Fleetwood Mac guitarist Peter Green, the Five Blind Boys Of Alabama, and using vocals recorded in 1996 before his death, Nusrat Fateh Ali Khan.

Sifting through the material took a lot of time. Gabriel enlisted engineer Tchad Blake: "I think Tchad Blake did a remarkable job on the mixing and that provides some cohesion," he told Simmons. "But yes, it has been a long, slow process and maybe the palette of sounds that we've had available helped bring it together."

The long slow process meant that the title of the album, which Gabriel had arrived at early in the process, had already been used for many other releases. ABC and fleeting sensations Right Said Fred had used it. It had been used again by R.E.M., Shania Twain and Ani Di Franco. "The title *Up* came first, before a lot of the songs," Gabriel said. "Which is why I'm still using it, even though other people have used it . . . it's been tried and tested. And now I've got a whole lot of songs about death – but in a way I think there is a positive edge to this stuff . . . out of death comes life. I think sometimes when you stare mortality in the face, life is lived a little bit more fully." The death of his brother-in-law from cancer, the passing of friends, the ageing of his parents, and the birth of Isaac all fed into the process. As a result, *Up* is the most difficult of all of Gabriel's work.

Originally entitled 'House In Woods', 'Darkness' was the album's blackest track and the decision to put it as the first track was a warning signal to all of those casual listeners who were expecting *So II*. "It is one of the first tracks that we finished, and it was one of the easiest we worked on, to get it right," said Richard Chappell. "It just has so much muscle and it seemed like a fun idea to have the quiet intro and then the loud assault. Some people have actually broken their hi-fi because of it." Gabriel was adamant that this uncomfortable track should open the album. It's a musical version of a fairy tale – getting lost in a dense forest of tangled thoughts before coming to clearings, where fear is confronted, and the music reflects this. After 30 seconds of deliberately quiet synthesised bleeps, a sonic assault of David Rhodes' squawking guitar makes it resemble a death metal record. It nods to King Crimson's '21st Century Schizoid Man', the track that had so motivated Gabriel at Christmas Cottage right back in 1969. Gabriel emerges as a troubled man, drowning in emotion, the tiniest thing stirring up the past. However, when he actually confronts the fears, all the monsters in his head are really small, like a 'baby boy', which makes him cry until he laughs.

"It's very uncompromising and he pushes the envelope," says old friend David Stopps. "It's almost unbearable to listen to. You can't listen to that, you have to turn it right down before you start or otherwise you just jump out of your skin when that comes in – it's not easy listening, but that's typical Peter."

'Growing Up' illustrates how gifted a lyricist Gabriel is. There is not a word spare in this deceptively straightforward song about the brevity of the cycle of life, culminating in him feeling so strange about his final departure when it feels as if he has only just arrived. With its great, lilting groove, part funk-workout, part-Bond theme, Gabriel plays keyboard bass and performs a stunning vocal arrangement; the album's de facto title track became the title of the tour as well.

'Sky Blue', however, was the album's pure standout. The oldest track, its central riff was something that Gabriel had been toying with since the mid-Eighties. "It was something that I always liked and felt had good emotion in it," Gabriel said at the time of the album's release. "As a teenager I was very influenced by soul and blues and it was my starting point for a lot of music. I think this was definitely an influence on that track." Gabriel was thrilled to have the original Fleetwood Mac guitarist Peter Green playing on 'Sky Blue', and although he wanted him to solo on the track, Green instead added rhythm and texture to the song. But it is all about the finale, where the Blind Boys Of Alabama add their remarkable church-hued soul vocals. *Popmatters* said: "The haunting chants . . . lift 'Sky Blue' into the same pop-gospel terrain occupied by 'Don't Give Up' off Gabriel's masterpiece, 1986's *So*." Nature courses through the work, whether getting lost in it, or showing how insignificant man is when compared to its scope.

'No Way Out' emerged from the early sessions for the album. Originally boasting a Latin feel, it became somewhat buried under the layers of production. Its rhythm was programmed by Chris Hughes using a Supercolider, a Mac freeware programme which broke everything into little pieces and then reassembled them. "It has this strange mysterious percussive quality to it," said Gabriel. "I was thinking a little more Roy Orbison when I was doing some of the singing and I think there is that influence as well as the computer-mangled ethnic rhythm element." It deals with the emotions and shock brought on by a near-death incident and the memories triggered at that point. With Danny Thompson's fluid upright bass playing with Levin and Rhodes over Steve Gadd's drums, it is another affecting number.

However, any optimism offered by 'No Way Out' is snuffed out in 'I Grieve', an explicit song about loss that sets inextinguishable grief against the onward march of life with a lilting, lullaby-like melody packed with portent. As the bereaved becomes more accustomed to the passing, the song turns into a jaunty pop-lope, before ending on a keening question mark, suggesting that grief will last forever. An early version had appeared on the 1998 soundtrack to the Brad Siberling film, *City Of Angels*, but Gabriel had reworked some of it after the terrible world changing events of 9/11, when both Anna and Melanie were in New York and he was unable to contact them.

Arguably the only wrong-foot on *Up* is 'The Barry Williams Show', a satire on the growth of confessional television programmes, which seems out-of-step with the first person emotion of the rest of the album. The closing refrain over the synthesised bangs and crashes of 'come on down' echoed the famous *The Price Is Right* game show catchphrase. The track was chosen as a wholly unrepresentative first single from the album, and missed the charts, despite a humourous Sean Penn-directed video, which featured *Happy Gilmore* actor Christopher McDonald as Williams.

'My Head Sounds Like That' evokes a nervous collapse. Gabriel said: "Some chords in there are very old, but the mood was something I liked. And then there was this moment in Africa when one of the echo machines jammed and started malfunctioning and I liked the sound of that." What brought the song alive was the wonderful brass arrangement by none other than his old and dear friend, Bob Ezrin: "We worked together with Ed Schurmer on the brass at Air Lyndhurst where we did the *Babe* session. We kept the Black Dyke Mills Band over after 'That'll Do', and we recorded the brass for that song. I'm very pleased with it; I thought it came out well."

'More Than This', a darkly commercial number with Gabriel's sampled guitar at its outset, was taken as the album's second single. The basic track had been around for some considerable time. "I was mucking around with guitars and Daniel Lanois had left his beautiful Telecaster," Gabriel said. "I can't play guitar to save my life, but I can make noises on it. The first sound that you hear on this track is me manipulating my guitar samples on the keyboard."

'Signal To Noise' was one of the oldest recordings on the project, taking the vocals from the performance with Nusrat Fateh Ali Khan that he and Gabriel had recorded at the *VH1 Honors Awards* in 1996. Khan, a dear friend of Gabriel's and one of Real World's most lucrative artists, had died in August 1997. Its near eight minutes of sound collage was a fabulous showcase for the keening emotional tones of Khan over the London String Orchestra's arrangement, arranged by Gabriel and Will Gregory. With Dhol drums and increasing pathos, it was a fitting stirring tribute to Khan.

When the orchestra erupts six minutes in, it is particularly affecting.

'The Drop' ends the album on a suitably introspective note. Effectively a solo track with Gabriel on Bosendorfer piano, with atmospheric programming by Richard 'Dickie' Chappell, it finds Gabriel flying high above the clouds looking down on the earth and trying to imagine the make up of the world. Its timing, a year after 9/11 and talk of fuselage and people falling stirs up striking images of the disaster. In closing the album with it, Gabriel added more pathos at just the right time.

Like *Security*, *Up* was an album that was easy to admire but somehow difficult to love. What it did beg was repeated listening, and by 2002 this was something that seemed difficult to commit to. With commissioned photographs to illustrate all of the tracks as opposed to paintings, *Up* featured 10 long tracks that took time to live with in order for their beauty to emerge. At the time of release someone quipped that the album was "probably the first to have its own archaeology department".

If ever an album needed a *So*-like picture on its front to sell it, it was *Up*. Designed by Gabriel's favoured designer, Marc Bessant, the cover was entitled *The Observer And The Observed: Peter*. It had Gabriel's face manipulated into five drops of water by English photographic artist Susan Derges. And given that Gabriel was now shaven-headed with a long, grey goatee beard, he could hardly create the appearance of the matinee idol of *So*. The album didn't fit entirely in with the profile of Virgin Records' current roster, which was as Blue Nile author Allan Brown notes, "of accessible, well-crafted pop of the kind that's played at postgraduate dinner parties."

It was as if with every successive release Gabriel was trying to lose the audience he had gained with *So*. And, because it was presented as a part of the range of activities in which Gabriel was involved, it had little feel of the event or resonance of his previous releases. It is a great shame that the album was ultimately overlooked as it is the sound of an artist resolutely doing what he wants to do. Had 'Sky Blue' been taken as a first single, it may have been different.

Reviews were largely favourable. *Launch.com* said: "Full of the obscure and deranged moods that made *Security* alternately delightful and demented, this album revels in craggy vocals, thumping beats, esoteric instrumental sounds and a general feeling of beautiful dread." *Entertainment Weekly* said, "Those who value the emotional nakedness of his best work will find much to treasure here." *E! Online* suggested "This is an eerie meditation on ageing, death and the corruption of popular culture." Andy Herrman, writing for *popmatters*, said that "*Up* surpasses even the extraordinary richness of *Passion*, Gabriel's soundtrack to *The Last Temptation of Christ*. It's the most sophisticated record he's ever made; songs like 'Darkness' and 'Sky Blue' really sound like they took ten years to make, breathing with dense, thoughtful instrumentation and taking more startling twists and turns than a David Mamet thriller."

Gabriel was proud of the album, and in a happy place. *Up* was dedicated to Meabh, his children, his mother and father and to his sister, Anne, who had lost her husband to cancer during the making of the album.

*Up* reached number 11 in the UK charts where it spent four weeks, his shortest run ever for one of his 'proper albums'. In the US, it went into the Top 10, reaching number nine. "*Up* was darker, and maybe had more connection with my third and fourth albums," Gabriel said in 2007. "It didn't do very well, but I felt it had some of my best work. The older you get, the easier it is to learn and accept who you are, what you do and how you do it. Whatever stuff is there, just let it come out – regardless of whether it's commercially attractive." And, like it or not, stuff kept coming out.

# 24: Man Of Peace

*"In our part of the world, we would give him our highest accolade and say, 'He has* ubuntu.' *It is that marvelous quality that speaks of compassion and generosity, about sharing, about hospitality."*

Desmond Tutu, *Time* magazine, 2008

GIVEN the range and diversification of his interests in the new millennium, it was little wonder that the next new Peter Gabriel album would not be released until 2010. Music became one element of his portfolio but that didn't stop Gabriel being full of optimism for a follow-up, tentatively titled *I/O*. "The way I view it is with *OVO,* with *Long Walk Home: Music From Rabbit Proof Fence* and this other one I'm hoping to have out within two years," Peter Gabriel told Sylvie Simmons in 2002. "There would then have been four records out of the ten years, and that doesn't seem so bad." But as always, there were many other distractions that vied for Gabriel's time, not least his family and the business of touring *Up*.

The tour to support *Up* was amazing and complex. Its first leg started in New York in September 2002, through to December that year, with the European leg starting in April 2003 and going through to November. Gabriel was joined by stalwarts Tony Levin and David Rhodes, ex-Ruthless Rap Assassin and Icicle Works drummer Ged Lynch, whom Gabriel had met through Real World, faithful studio assistant Richard Evans on guitars, respected jazz pianist Rachel Z, and his daughter Melanie on vocals. It was the first time that Lynch, Evans and his daughter had played arena shows. The set reflected the breadth of his career and contained six out of the ten songs from *Up*.

The show, again designed by Gabriel and Robert Lepage, equalled their previous collaboration, *Secret World*. Performed in the round and with a circular projection screen above the players, it opened with a solo rendition of 'Here Comes The Flood' just like his very earliest solo performances had done in 1977. But whereas audiences then were unsure of what to expect, here he was, beautifully delivering his early masterpiece to a receptive crowd. The circular stage allowed Gabriel to patrol its lip like a sinister showman, especially on 'Darkness'. It looked initially as if there would be little spectacle, but amazingly during the *OVO* centre-piece, 'Downside Up', the projection screen opened to reveal a secondary stage – by the end of the song, father and daughter are suspended upside down from it, running around, delivering their words.

A huge screen emerged for 'The Barry Williams Show', which presented Gabriel as a cameraman filming his own chat show, with crew members coming on aping the floor staff on shows like *Jerry Springer*. An enormous flower bulb in the middle of the stage gave way to an ovoid. Perhaps most effective of all was Gabriel singing 'Growing Up' from within a Zorb, the transparent inflatable sphere based on a hamster ball. Here Gabriel had finally been completely ensconced by the casing, his latest mask. It was amazing to see Gabriel bouncing in time to the music and chasing Levin around the stage.

The tour highlighted the as-yet-unrecorded song 'Animal Nation', inspired by his Bonobo adventure, singing about the wonder of the experience. For all of the trickery one of the most affecting pieces of stagecraft was Gabriel getting on a bicycle and cycling around the stage while singing 'Solsbury Hill'. The show ended in simplicity with Gabriel alone, back at his piano, singing 'Father, Son'. The tightness was certainly there in the band and certainly between Levin, Rhodes and Gabriel: "It's always fun, and always has been. I think we all enjoy showing off, to varying degrees, and we're all quite shameless," Rhodes said in 2004. "I suppose through years of working together we don't really bother thinking about it too much. If we have any staging problems or thoughts we share them, and try to make things work as best we can. The staging of Peter's shows has always been a hybrid of seriousness and playfulness." The evening opened with the Blind Boys Of Alabama who had recently gained the world's attention. Their Real World album, *Spirit Of The Century* was a near-perfect capture of the work they had been performing in various forms since the Forties.

Gabriel recorded every show from the *Growing Up* tour and made them available for sale on CD at the end of the night, and subsequently through Real World. This embracing of technology and desire to beat the bootleggers – *and* circumvent the record company – meant that fans could now, like Genesis used to do in the tour bus back in Italy, paw over every second of the concert, then and there.

★ ★ ★

Gabriel was in the British press for two varying reasons during 2003. His activism had not faltered as the years progressed. The atrocity of 9/11 had manifested in a ridiculous war against Iraq led by the America of George W. Bush and, in tow, the Labour Government of Great Britain, led by Tony Blair. Gabriel had been a vociferous and generous supporter of the Labour party in the Nineties, and by working on the project for the Millennium Dome had effectively been in their pay. Now it was very different: in March 2003, Gabriel issued a public statement backing the *Daily Mirror*'s call to find a solution to the crisis in Iraq without resorting to war.

He said, "This is a fundamental issue of life and death and I very much think the Prime Minister is in the wrong. I'm also sure George Bush is an affable bloke but he's highly dangerous and I wish America was in the hands of someone else. To put oil interests ahead of human life is appalling. War is always terrible but unjustified war is obscene and on present evidence that is what we are facing . . . I think the consequences of this war would be the biggest threat to world peace in my lifetime. Blair has got to get it right. To take action without UN backing would be inviting disaster by setting the Muslim world against the West. If we are taking a moral position why did we arm Iraq when they were killing the Kurds?"

He concluded: "I'd like to see a reinforced UN weapons inspection team in Iraq and disarmament much more in line with the French and German proposals. There is a slogan, which says: 'Peace is what happens when you respect the rights of others'. Iraqis have rights too." Unfortunately his and many other opponents' comments fell on deaf ears. On March 19 2003, troops from the US, UK, Australia and Poland began a 21-day combat operation that heralded the start of the Iraq War which was to continue for the next eight years.

On a far more trivial note, The *Daily Mail* reported that there were issues with the property Gabriel and Meabh had bought in Notting Hill for the times they were in London. In one of the paper's typical foaming-at-the-mouth pieces of scorn and judgement on rock stars whose agenda didn't conform to their right-of-centre views, the paper berated the singer for not having moved into his house and for the ongoing building work. The building firm was up in arms at the continual alterations Gabriel was making to the plans.

Resembling a mid-period Genesis lyric, the paper quoted his neighbours, saying "He is obsessed with detail and apparently the house is full of curves and arches and in some way resembles a cave." Another said: "He is doing it in a piecemeal sort of way. It has been a building site for years but to be fair to him he has done his best to keep us happy. He is an affable sort of bloke and sent letters round explaining the delays and interruptions." Yet another added: "If it was a record he would be doing it much quicker." His neighbours obviously were not aware of his release history.

* * *

Gabriel maintained his high profile with a series of releases to close 2003. In November came *Hit*: *The Definitive Two-CD Collection*, which was a summation of his career to date, featuring material from every album bar *Birdy*. A double-disc set, one disc was entitled 'Hit' and was a pretty comprehensive selection of Gabriel's work, and the other, 'Miss' an overview of his deeper catalogue, with slight variants between the UK and US editions. A new track, 'Burn You Up, Burn You Down', co-written with World Party's Karl Wallinger and Neil Sparkes from Transglobal Underground, was a product of the 1991 Real World recording weeks, and had been on early promotional copies of the *Up* CD. As upbeat as *Up* was downbeat, it, among many others, featured Jah Wobble on bass and Billy Cobham on drums. 'Cloudless' was there from *Rabbit Proof Fence*, 'A Different Drum' from *Passion*, 'Father, Son' and 'The Tower That Ate People' from *OVO*, 'Love Town' from the *Philadelphia* soundtrack as well as a live version of 'Downside Up' from the *Growing Up* Tour.

With great, career-spanning iconic photographs and a CD-ROM element containing a game based around 'The Tower That Ate People', it was assembled by Richard 'Dickie' Chappell at Real World. *Hit* was released in time for the Christmas market and reached number 29 in the UK charts. To complement his rare mood of retrospection, a year later, Gabriel released an anthology of 23 of his videos on DVD, entitled *Play The Videos*. It was a remarkable demonstration of how he had mastered the form in his 27 years as a solo performer. With new surround sound mixes by Daniel Lanois and Richard Chappell and restoration work done at Real

World, the videos looked beautiful and showed collectively how groundbreaking his work had been from the early innovation with 'Shock The Monkey' through to the pioneering 'Sledgehammer' and then the subsequent attempts to emulate its success. Possibly the most effective was the Anna Gabriel-shot 'Father, Son', a simple capture of Gabriel at the grand piano with footage of Ralph and Peter together.

A DVD of the tour, *Growing Up: Live* was released in November 2003 to coincide with the release of *Hit*. Recorded in Milan in May of that year, it captured the serious artist Gabriel had become, yet still with an enormous sense of play. Directed by Hamish Hamilton, who had produced long-form performance films for Madonna and U2, the film captured the warmth, and despite its arena setting, the intimacy of the show. The most touching moment is when Gabriel introduces the band to lots of chanting Italians. This was an audience that had a very strong bond with Gabriel, some going all the way back to 1972 on the first visit of Genesis. It is especially touching when he introduces Melanie Gabriel as "someone I have known all her life, that you don't know so well, she makes me very proud", and he heralds Tony Levin as "the king of the bottom end, the emperor of the bass guitar" and Ged Lynch as "a small castle of explosive fireworks". Gabriel's daughter, Anna directed an emotional document of the tour, *Growing Up: A Family Portrait*, which was released separately, highlighting the closeness of the Gabriel family unit at the heart of the tour.

The band played some scaled down British dates in November before taking part in the *46664* charity concert played in honour of Nelson Mandela to support AIDS charities at Green Point Stadium, Cape Town. "It was very special to perform 'Biko' down there," David Rhodes said on his website. "There are obviously huge problems with the population being ravaged by HIV, so it was good to help bring attention to those, and also refer back to the troubled times that have been overcome." The concert was filmed and broadcast, and put Gabriel among artists such as Beyoncé, Bob Geldof, Robert Plant and Jimmy Cliff and raised millions of pounds for AIDS charities. Gabriel became an active supporter of *46664* and supported the concerts again in Malmo in June 2005 and again in Johannesburg in December 2007. It also reinforced the relationship that Gabriel had with Mandela.

Gabriel thoroughly enjoyed touring again, especially as he was travelling with Meabh, Isaac and Melanie: he was truly combining business with pleasure at last. He put together a further leg in 2004, entitled *Still Growing Up*, which began in Austria in May 2004 and closed in Germany in July. These were more intimate, conventional performances, which only contained five of the numbers from the previous tour. It came out as a sister DVD, *Still Growing Up: Live And Unwrapped*, again directed by Hamish Hamilton in November 2005. There was more tentative talk of *I/O* and tracks such as 'Baby Man' which had been played on tour, and 'Curtains', 'Wild' and 'Silver Screen' were mooted for possible inclusion, yet in April 2005, a fire broke out in Real World and interrupted the work process and talk in the meantime of a new album was laid to rest.

⋆ ⋆ ⋆

In 2004 OD2, Gabriel's digital content solution service, was making a significant loss. Bloomberg noted that: "For a time, OD2 was Europe's leading online music company with clients like Nokia, MSN, Virgin, and HMV." It had been slightly ahead of the game and then Apple's iTunes had come on to the scene and rather superseded all that had been before it in the music download business. OD2 was bought by US company Loudeye for $40m, with Gabriel allegedly trousering $11m of the profits for the sale. "I did not vote to sell it," Gabriel said. "Apple does what it does very well. But I thought it would just be a phase." Apple's supremacy was not a phase, and it has yet to receive any significant challenge to its supremacy. "I think he had the right idea but it tried to do too much too soon," Jon Webster, who had worked with Gabriel when he was at Virgin, says. "OD2 was well conceived but the exit had to come – world wide scale was needed."

However, from the enterprise, Gabriel became interested in 'recommendation technology', an on line business that provided the mechanism that suggested other items for you based on what you have already purchased. The Filter came into being. Devised by Gabriel with Rhett Ryder and Martin Hopkins, the service recommended what you needed to hear or watch based on the algorithms of what you had previously listened to or purchased online. Hopkins had developed it from a system he had to manage his personal music collection. Although Mike Large was his representative on the board, Gabriel would attend planning and strategy sessions. By 2009, they had modified the programme to license the recommendation engine solely to other businesses such as NBC and Sony. It has remained successful, and is arguably the most flourishing to date of all Gabriel's digital start-ups.

Webster, who had worked with Gabriel at Virgin and afterwards as a consultant, saw Gabriel's pioneering spirit. "I think he was ahead of his time with MUDDA which I worked on." Gabriel put MUDDA (Magnificent Union of Digitally Downloading Artists) together with Brian Eno in 2004. "We are now witnessing the most fundamental transformation of the selling of music since records were first invented," Gabriel said at its launch. "The economic restraints of the traditional business model have for all these years dictated what music can be made and when and how it can be sold. If artists are willing to act together, there are extraordinary opportunities both creatively and commercially."

MUDDA published a manifesto that, if not strictly challenging the supremacy of the major record companies, realised that with the rise of digital downloading, labels had to ensure that revenues gained from downloads were paid promptly to the artist themselves.

It was a fascinating and labyrinthine area in which to get involved, and although ultimately the organisation was little more than a talking shop, it planted the seeds of Gabriel's next digital venture. But Gabriel was still much-loved and respected within the music industry itself for his visionary spirit. Because he was seen as a trusted insider, his more wayward ideas would always be listened to. On November 1, 2004 he was awarded a Music Industry Trust Award for his contribution to music in front of an audience of friends and peers at the Grosvenor House Hotel in London. Previous award winners had been George Martin, Ahmet Ertegun and Elton John and Bernie Taupin.

* * *

In late 2004, there was a rare moment of looking backwards for Gabriel. He got in touch with Tony Smith as he'd heard rumours of a Genesis reunion. Gabriel remained fascinated with the afterlife of his old band. The archive set had sold well, and there was demand for another deeper delve into their catalogue. A burgeoning cottage industry in Genesis tribute bands had developed, led by the British Re-Genesis and Canadians the Musical Box, who went to painstaking lengths to recreate the sound of the group's 1970–1975 era. Gabriel had actually gone to see one such band in Bristol with Melanie and Anna. "The musicians worked really hard to reproduce it as accurately as possible," he told *The Guardian* in 2002. "Some of it seemed naff to me now, some of it had a certain charm and some of it I was surprised still to feel some emotion from it."

Gabriel was considering doing some live shows around *The Lamb Lies Down On Broadway*. Tony Banks, Mike Rutherford, Steve Hackett and Phil Collins were all interested too. The only date when all five of them could get together was in November 2004 when Collins brought his *First Final Farewell* Tour to Glasgow.

Gabriel attended a meeting with Mike Large and the group and Tony Smith. However, although the others felt that the meeting could be a formality to discuss logistics, Gabriel went on a more existential roam, wondering if the reunion should be done at all. As Collins noted: "For the first two or three hours we were together in Glasgow, everybody assumed their old positions." "We also discussed the possibility of doing it as a musical," Steve Hackett told *Classic Rock* in 2012. "The idea was rejected – I'm not going to name names, but one person employed the power of veto. I think Pete lost interest right there and then. The idea of coming together and doing that was killed stone dead at that point."

"It reminded us how easily Phil, Tony and myself decide things," Mike Rutherford laughs. "After a two-hour meeting with Peter and Steve we were getting nowhere. They left, we thought it's probably unlikely it's going to come to anything, and if it does it's three years away. In the meantime, let's go and do a tour. It took three minutes to say that."

Peter Gabriel did not rejoin Genesis. In the end it came to nothing. Although Gabriel kept his options open, Banks, Collins and Rutherford decided to tour together, and in 2007, had one last decisive hurrah, working again with Chester Thompson and Daryl Stuermer. When the group booked rehearsal space in New York in 2006, there was still a vague possibility that Gabriel may have joined. But it wasn't to be; the world had turned too far, too fast. On December 10, 2007, Gabriel went to the 02 Arena in South East London, where he had orchestrated his Millennium show in 2000, and saw his friend Robert Plant reunite with Led Zeppelin for the final time. If any thoughts crossed his mind to attempt similar with Genesis, he firmly kept them to himself.

* * *

On July 2, 2005, almost 20 years to the day after Live Aid, Bob Geldof reprised that concert's ethos with a string of events around the world that would tie in with the meeting of world leaders at the G8 summit in Gleneagles, Scotland. With money raised going to support the Make Poverty History campaign to increase government aid to Africa and cancel debt, the Live 8 concert would centre on Hyde Park and be broadcast live around the world.

Geldof announced the concert at the end of May, featuring a host of well-known megastars on the ten stages around the world. However, the event came in for criticism almost immediately for the fact that bar Youssou N'Dour, there was very little African musical presence. Gabriel sprang into action, and looked at the possibility of arranging a concert featuring the best of African music to support the cause. He contacted Tim Smit and a concert line-up was assembled for Smit's Eden Project in Cornwall. It was imperative that Africa was also shown as a creative hub with many wonderful artists and not just a continent that needed western support.

"I did speak to 'Chairman Bob' at some length about what would have been our preferred way of doing this," Gabriel told Reuters. "His belief is that any artist unfamiliar to an audience in remote regions of the Arctic, China, or wherever they come from, is going to channel hop. I fully understand that, but I don't agree with it. We asked for Bob's blessing, which he freely gave; that was in his role as Pope. I'm a big fan of what he and Live 8 are trying to do."

Set amid the stunning bio-domes of the Eden Project in a formerly disused quarry near St Austell, Gabriel acted as MC for the event, which sold out immediately and artists such as Angelique Kidjo, Thomas Mapfumo, Kanda Bongo Man, Emmanuel Jal and Daara J demonstrated that they were equal in stature to artists on the main stage in London: Madonna, U2, Paul McCartney, and the headline news of the day, the reformed Pink Floyd.

"It was wonderful that so many African musicians were willing to join us at such short notice," Gabriel told Reuters. "The artists felt that it was really important that Live 8 had a strong African musical presence." Gabriel had showed again, that if given a tight deadline, he *could* work to it.

Two years later, Gabriel would play a set to commemorate the 25th anniversary of WOMAD. It was now a quarter of a century since the first noble steps to establishing the festival with Thomas Brooman. By now, it was a global enterprise. "It has been wonderful to see what has happened with WOMAD over the last 25 years," Gabriel said at the time. "It is different from any other festival I've ever been to, and although I usually get to enjoy it from the audience rather than the stage, I am delighted to come back as a performer for this 25th anniversary." The experiment had paid off.

* * *

Like his father offering dial-up television in the early Seventies, Gabriel was, if anything, a bit too previous about his idea to offer digital exclusives through a streaming content-based service. A company was quickly assembled, poaching some of the best talents in the UK music industry to look at offering a subscription service system to get music out to audiences with artists to receive suitable recompense.

We7 was originally founded in 2006 by John Taysom, with CEO Steve Purdham and Gabriel becoming founder investors in early 2007. We7 aimed to offer an advertising supported streaming service, all tracks came with adverts at the start of them, with the option to download an ad-free version after a certain number of listens. It made tentative inroads into streaming but was wholeheartedly railroaded out of the scene by the UK arrival of the eventually all-conquering Spotify in 2008. At first, We7 didn't have the support of major labels, but Gabriel was undeterred. "We7 provides artists, even across the more experimental or minority genres," Gabriel said, "with the opportunity to build a new source of income from their music."

"WE7?," Jon Webster says. "The Internet is full of singularities. Google. Amazon. i-Tunes. e-bay. It was hard to compete. A brave try." With the arrival of Spotify, We7 concentrated on becoming a personal DJ service, presenting playlists based on its audience's preferences. It maintained a small presence as a content deliverer, but its sophisticated technology was sought after. In June 2012, Tesco acquired We7 for £10.8 million to incorporate the technology into its already existing digital products.

Gabriel had not lost his interest in recording technology either. Right back from co-founding Syco systems in order to import and distribute the Fairlight in the early Eighties, Gabriel bought a stake in his favoured recording console. In 2005, he acquired Solid State Logic (SSL) with US Broadcast technology entrepreneur Dave Engelke. Gabriel had had a long association with the company, going right back to when the first SSL desk had been installed in the Townhouse in West London, when Hugh Padgham, Phil Collins and he arrived at the gated reverb drum sound for 'Intruder'. The premier studio desk, Gabriel maintained an active interest in its development. It was a wonder he had any time at all for making music.

★ ★ ★

Aside from his business interests, Peter Gabriel became more and more statesman-like as the new millennium progressed. In 2002, he established, with Mike Large and Michael Thomas, The Peter Gabriel Foundation, which quietly looked at bringing together all of Gabriel's charitable activities under one umbrella; primarily concerned with education and training, prevention and relief of poverty and overseas aid and famine relief, with money from donations being distributed to organisations such as WITNESS.

Gabriel was awarded the 2006 Man Of Peace award during the seventh World Summit of Nobel Peace Laureates on November 17, 2006 for his "commitment to human rights and for his outspoken rejection of war as a means to solve conflicts". The Award was "for the men or women of peace chosen from personalities from the world of culture and entertainment who have stood up for human rights and for the spread of the principles of Peace and Solidarity in the world, [and] made an outstanding contribution to international social justice and peace". Gabriel was deeply honoured and was presented with the Award by Lech Walesa with the Award's founder, Mikhail Gorbachev in attendance. It was all a very long way away from wearing a flower on his head.

As Gabriel said, "I was getting more and more interested in my life getting older." The closeness of his new family unit seemed to give him the freedom and confidence to merge all of his interests. Yet, even with WITNESS and his work with Amnesty, few would have expected the scope of his next enterprise; to assemble together in one organisation some of the world's most powerful people.

Originating from a conversation with his friend and former label owner Richard Branson, Gabriel and Branson hit upon the idea of founding the Elders – a private alliance of senior global figures to launch diplomatic assaults on the globe's most intractable problems; working on the belief that 'a global village needs global elders'.

Part-funded by The Peter Gabriel Trust, the criteria for membership was that these figures would no longer be in public office, so could move freely between the world's trouble spots and advise accordingly. Gabriel and Branson assembled Kofi Annan, Jimmy Carter, Nelson Mandela, Mary Robinson and Desmond Tutu, with an empty chair for Aung San Suu Kyi, who was then under house arrest: "Richard and I had this child-like fantasy of a group of superheroes coming to sort things out," Gabriel said. Both felt that it was important that Mandela be the group's founder and spiritual figurehead. The group could advise on mediating conflict; heal wounds where conflict has been and inspire positive social change.

"Now we sit in the room with these extraordinary people as they have conversations about what they're going to work on," Gabriel said. "For someone who did a little politics and economics at school it's an amazing thing." The Elders operate quietly and discreetly in the background, exactly how it should be. "No one really knows about the Elders," Richard Macphail says. "It's unbelievable what they do and part of it is that they *don't* stick their heads up that way, that's not what they do. But what they do behind the scenes is incredible. If Mary Robinson or Jimmy Carter rings up the President of Sudan or wherever, they'll take the call."

To compliment his Man Of Peace Award, Gabriel was honoured by Amnesty by being asked to become their 2008 Ambassador Of Conscience. Previous holders of the title had been Nelson Mandela, Vaclav Havel, Hilda Gonzalez and Mary Robinson. Gabriel was again humbled and delighted: "It was through the tours for Amnesty International that I first met many people around the world engaged in human rights work. It was these people and their extraordinary stories of suffering and courage that I found impossible to walk away from, so the Ambassador of Conscience Award means a great deal to me."

Most amazingly, Gabriel was voted one of *Time* magazine's most influential people in 2008; the annual list was divided into categories; leaders, thinkers, heroes, artists, scientists and more. One hundred people from around the world were selected. Gabriel did not fall into the 'Artists and Entertainers' category, alongside Bruce Springsteen and Herbie Hancock: he was listed under 'Heroes and Pioneers' alongside Aung San Suu Kyi and US Senator George Mitchell. Desmond Tutu wrote a eulogy for him:

"What is his secret? He has a heart – in our part of the world, we would give him our highest accolade and say, "He has *ubuntu.*" It is that marvellous quality that speaks of compassion and generosity, about sharing, about hospitality."

To complete a remarkable 2008 for Gabriel, Meabh gave birth to their second child, Luc, on July 5. Gabriel posted on his website: "Big brother Isaac reports that mother, father and baby brother are all doing well, and requests that any congratulatory flowers people may contemplate sending be left to grow in the ground for all to enjoy."

* * *

There was also, unbelievably, some time for a new album; or, rather, a new old album: *Big Blue Ball*, the product of the Real World Recording Weeks. Its 18-year gestation period was a spectacular length of time, even by Gabriel's standards.

Taking its title from the astronauts' description of Earth from space, it was an incredible concept album pieced together by Gabriel and Karl Wallinger of World Party. Gabriel appears on five of the album's 10 tracks: aside from the already released 'Burn You Up, Burn You Down', there was 'Whole Thing', a beautifully diverse soulful melody with Tim Finn and Francis Bebey on ndewhoo flute, 'Exit Through You', which Gabriel wrote with Joseph Arthur, 'Everything Comes From You', a haunting song recorded by Sinead O'Connor, and 'altus silva', a collaboration between Arthur, Vernon Reid from Living Colour and Eric Mouquet and Michel Sanchez, French techno duo Deep Forest.

*Big Blue Ball* was launched on June 24, 2008 and was funded by a venture capital trust initiative, allowing Gabriel to release it away from conventional record companies. "After all these years, it's a fine wine ready to be drunk," says Peter Gabriel, "It was the most fun music making I've ever had."

Also in 2008, Gabriel collaborated with Thomas Newman for Andrew Stanton's PIXAR motion picture, *WALL – E.* Stanton wanted to use Gabriel as he was one of his favourite artists. 'Down To Earth' was one of the most sweetly straightforward songs that Gabriel had been involved with for many years. Gabriel contributed lyrics and musical ideas to Newman's melody and it was sung with the Soweto Gospel Choir. Recorded in LA and Real World with Richard Chappell and mixed by

Tchad Blake, the haunting, uplifting number won the Grammy for Best Song Written For A Motion Picture, Television or Other Visual Media in 2009, after being nominated and losing out for both the Academy Awards and the Golden Globes.

'Down To Earth' was one of three songs that were nominated for Best Original Song category at the Academy Awards, yet Gabriel was affronted that he could only perform a 65-second snippet of the track. "We were originally hoping to perform," he said. "We'd assumed, as there are only three nominees, that the songs would be performed in full. But the producers came in to revamp it as audience figures were falling off," Gabriel said. "So I've now decided to withdraw from the ceremony, but I'll still go along." John Legend performed the song instead at the ceremony on February 22, 2009. 'Down To Earth' lost out to 'Jai Ho' from *Slumdog Millionaire*.

One minute pop singer, the next peace campaigner, technological pioneer, Academy Award nominee, Nobel Award winner: "It's a pretty big route to take. But that's Peter Gabriel, and that's what's cool about him," Nile Rodgers says. "He is that guy. I don't know anyone else in rock'n' roll like him; he's a unique individual. And he's always the same. Charming, gentlemanly, soft-spoken, and introspective. If we've ever had something we've disagreed on, it sure didn't feel like it. He is always open to ideas."

The very variety of Gabriel's work makes him difficult to tame. "That's what makes Peter unmanageable, because he's just got so many things going on and it is utterly remarkable what he has achieved," Richard Macphail says. "At the same time, as a friend, my only frustration is that I don't get to see him enough because he's so busy. To try and get him and Meabh for dinner – we have managed it, once, here. From that point of view as a friend, it's frustrating I know I'm just one of a very large group of people who'd like to see him more but just don't, I know I'm not singled out for special treatment. It's unbelievable what he does."

# 25: That Sort Of Light-Footedness I Enjoy Now: *Scratch My Back*

*"The worst brief for an artist is to be told they can do anything."*

Peter Gabriel, 2010

IN 2008, Peter Gabriel was briefly catapulted to the cutting edge of indie-pop culture, somewhere he hadn't been for years, by Vampire Weekend, an interesting, preppy-rock group from New York. They married the look and sound of The Feelies, early Talking Heads and Jonathan Richman, complete with a liberal dose of *Graceland*-era Paul Simon. Fronted by Ezra Koenig, their album included the track 'Cape Cod Kwassa Kwassa' on their self-titled debut album. In its breakdown, it included the mysterious repeated line "and it feels so unnatural, Peter Gabriel too". Gabriel was alerted to the generous reference by XL, Vampire Weekend's record company. The group joked that it would be great if Gabriel was to cut a version of it himself. He told BBC 6Music in June 2008: "I actually do like that song a lot and they've asked me to sing a version of it now which I may well do." However, he had some issues about singing his own name: "I haven't quite worked that out whether I should be doing that or substituting it with a name that might be appropriate to me. I think playing with yourself makes you go blind after a while." Almost as a joke, he set about recording a cover version with London-based electronic group Hot Chip but after singing his name for the first time, he added. "It feels so unnatural to sing your own name." It was a spirited release, which was briefly made available as an iTunes single.

As Gabriel returned to the recording process in 2008, he was looking for a new direction. Still tinkering with the thought of releasing *I/O*, he hit on the idea of working outside his comfort zone, on a totally different project and decided to make a purely orchestral album of cover versions. *Scratch My Back* was to become a bleak-yet-beautiful, introspective record, complete with its Arvo Part-inspired orchestrations, all strings scything.

The genesis of the work had come in 2008. Gabriel explained in the sleeve notes: "Song writing is what drew me into music. The craft and the process of putting together a good song seemed both exciting and magical. I have also wanted to record some of my favourite songs for a long time." However, it was important, as with all things Gabriel, to add a new and decisive spin on the proceedings. Rather than make a traditional covers record, Gabriel "thought it would be much more fun to create a new type of project in which artists communicated with each other and swapped a song for a song, i.e. you do one of mine and I'll do one of yours, hence the titles – *Scratch My Back* and *I'll Scratch Yours*."

The idea of working solely with an orchestra, according to David Lord, had been around for over 20 years: "I tried to put more of a classical influence into what we were doing. I was conducting the Bath Youth Orchestra at the time, and we were going to do a classical concert with Peter. I would have loved to do that with him. It's all very common now, but at the time, the idea of someone doing that with a classical orchestra would have seemed pretty bizarre." Time and circumstance brought them, of course, apart, but the kernel of the idea had been planted. It had simply been a matter of selecting the appropriate time.

In September 2008, Gabriel began to assemble and review material for possible inclusion on the project. Around 100 songs were discussed. He met up with neighbourhood friend and music industry grandee Dave Bates (his website proclaims: "He has seen more hits than the Internet; Bates is almost a brand in himself"), who in his days in A&R at Phonogram had signed or been responsible for the careers of acts such as Def Leppard, The Teardrop Explodes, Tears For Fears and Texas. Bates assisted Gabriel with song choices as did Gabriel's daughters Anna and Melanie and Real World engineer Richard 'Dickie' Chappell. Gabriel said: "The list was pruned several times, and nearly all of the writers I ended up choosing for this first *Scratch*, wanted to get involved. Sometimes we'd have an exchange about which song to choose and how to do it, and sometimes it would be hands off. The intention was that we would each do the songs in our own idiosyncratic ways."

The biggest challenge that faced Gabriel was what approach to take: the cover album had become a familiar standby in an artist's catalogue, and by now, many of his peers, including Bryan Ferry and Rod Stewart, had returned to classic songbooks, some with conventional arrangements, some leaping outside the box.

An early idea was to use home-made instruments. However that came to nothing when Gabriel realised, like several others had before him, that he couldn't find "the range of tone and expression that was clearly available in existing instruments that had been developed over time, with years and years of improvements." Gabriel toyed too with using choral groups.

The project gathered momentum when he was introduced to composer and arranger John Metcalfe, who had been working at Real World studios. A viola player by training, the New Zealand-born Metcalfe had studied at the Royal Northern College Of Music and the Hochschule in Berlin. He had helped Tony Wilson form the short-lived Factory Classical imprint, and had played alongside Vini Reilly in The Durutti Column. He worked as part of the contemporary classical outfit, The Duke Quartet, who aside from performing their own work, developed a lucrative sideline playing on pop albums by artists such as Blur and Simple Minds.

"In late 2008 I was involved with a live composing project with the Bays, the Heritage Orchestra and a fellow composer/arranger called Simon Hale," Metcalfe recalls. "Dickie Chappell plus some other Real World bods came to a show we were doing in Bristol. At the time my work was already known to Real World but it was around that time that Peter was looking for collaborators for his covers project. Dickie heard something in what I was doing (my band were also playing that night) that he liked and thought it would be good for Peter and I to meet. We met before Christmas 2008 and I got four initial vocal tracks to work on."

Metcalfe had been an admirer of Gabriel's work since the mid-Eighties: "Like a lot of people, I came to Peter's music through *So* and didn't know any of his previous solo albums. When I was getting into music as a teenager, I was into Kraftwerk and emerging bands of the early Eighties. When *So* came out I did love it for all sorts of reasons – I was intrigued by the sounds and production particularly."

Metcalfe had a fresh and innovative approach, looking at classical music as if it were pop, resolutely avoiding cliché. He began working with Gabriel on versions of David Bowie's '"Heroes"', Talking Heads' 'Listening Wind', Radiohead's 'Street Spirit' and Bon Iver's 'Flume'. "Peter spent a lot of time choosing the songs," Metcalfe continues. "When I got involved Peter had already spent some time recording vocals so had key and tempo for the song. Most crucially of course what he wanted to create for the song in terms of emotion and mood, was implicit in his vocal so the arrangements stemmed from there. I always drafted the arrangement first then we'd work from that point on."

Gabriel was delighted. In the introduction to the album, he said: "I really liked his scores, which seemed original, soulful and fresh. When [Metcalfe and Gabriel] met, I felt we also had enough of an overlap of taste around such composers as Steve Reich, Arvo Part, Stravinsky etc. I asked John to keep the arrangements simple, stark but always emotional, so the songs could be really heard and felt." Metcalfe adds: "We were careful that the arrangements should always serve the vocal and lyric. Where this idea did apply was to only use sounds/instruments/ideas where necessary, not to add things simply for bombast or pointless musical gestures."

Gabriel felt that the biggest change in direction should be the removal of his conventional tools-of-the-trade. He went one further than his banishing of metals in the early Eighties, by going the whole way and abandoning drums all together. Considering his well-known passion for percussion and his status as a frustrated drummer, this was an enormous departure. Secondly, as someone who had worked with guitarists the calibre of Steve Hackett, Robert Fripp, Nile Rodgers and David Rhodes, he decided as well to remove guitars from the project, and look at ways the voice could be explored as if it were the principal instrument. He explained, "The worst brief for an artist is to be told they can do anything. I have always believed that artists are a lot more creative if you tell them what they can't do. It's easier to find holes in a wall than it is trying to build out of nothing. The rules applied in this case were no drums and guitars. I also wanted to make the vocals as personal as possible, with much less tracking than I usually do."

Metcalfe was not phased by Gabriel's desire to abandon the conventional tools of the trade. "I wasn't surprised. Why would I be? It's Peter Gabriel!" he laughs. "The question could imply that orchestras have no rhythm which is, of course, wrong. Without drums you have to create pulse in different ways. The great thing about the orchestra is you can do it using a multitude of methods."

In December 2008, Metcalfe presented Gabriel with the first four demos. As things began to spiral, and orchestras were booked, Gabriel enlisted his old friend Bob Ezrin to come in and oversee the album.

Gabriel knew he would be perfect to oversee the orchestration. He wrote in the album's sleeve notes that "He would come in like a SWAT team for short periods, offering his feedback and suggestions, giving us a great deal of help with the orchestral recordings."

"I learned a huge amount in a very short space of time," Metcalfe says. "Bob is very focussed on getting the best out of recording sessions and the people he is working with but keeping it cool and happy! I picked up lots of stuff about recording, arranging, problem solving – you name it. He cares profoundly about the music he is involved with." Care was the absolute order of the day with the project.

For Ezrin, hooking up with his old friend was "a bit of a lifesaver". Ezrin's eldest son, David, a musician, had died aged 42 in December 2008. "I lost interest in almost everything," Ezrin says. "I didn't know what to do, I was working in something of a fog. Peter and I had talked about working together and all that came along and interrupted and I never followed up with him." In January 2009, around a month after his son's passing, Ezrin awoke and felt, "I need music and I really need it to be good. So I called Peter and said look I know the bus left the station, but if it's not too late, is there a seat for me. He said absolutely, come over. He was so kind and supportive. I got on a plane shortly thereafter – I flew to London and drove to Bath and found Peter in his writing room: he gave me a big hug, Dickie gave me a big hug. I met John for the first time and we jumped right in."

That night, they were due to record a version of Randy Newman's 'Baltimore'. "I said we have to do 'I Think It's Going To Rain Today' instead," Ezrin says. "Nobody really knew it. We pulled it up online, Peter heard it and right off the bat said that's fabulous, we've got to do it. We did it right then and there. I conducted a little to give Peter a sense of the phrasing. That vocal is the one we cut that first night. On the bridge, there was a little break in his voice. I was looking at him and we were both in tears, each for our own reasons. We never got it better than that; it was a magical, brilliant, wonderful moment so that was the kick off for me to the project."

Ezrin's presence added to the overall magic of the recording, and Gabriel's support was exactly what he needed. "I had a brilliant time – I needed music, but I needed to be with my friends, I had to be with someone that I love, making music with them that had to be emotional and deep and all of those criteria were met and then some in this project. I love Peter with all my heart, and I've known him a long time and I consider him to be one of the finest people that I know and to do it with him was lifesaving. After that I came back to life, got enthusiastic again and I got very happy."

Recording went on in Bath throughout 2009, and in the end the mixdown was overseen by Tchad Blake and Richard 'Dickie' Chappell with Metcalfe. The orchestra, who would go on to work with Gabriel on-and-off for the next two years, were remarkable players: "All of the musicians knew each other already and came from chamber ensembles or from the London session world where you have to be able to work with click and play great all the time," Metcalfe says. "There is a big element of chamber music in the arrangements so it was important to have players who were experienced in that area. I knew most of them so just picked up the phone and got suggestions where there were gaps. It does take a while. They are all busy most of the time so to find suitable space was quite a job. The orchestra was one of the key reasons why this project went so well. They are extraordinary musicians and were great to work with. No attitude, just bionic playing."

What was important was blocking out any ideas of the originals while recording. Metcalfe, who knew the originals of about half of the songs, said: "I tried to block out my memory of the originals as much as I could to allow more freedom in the arranging." Of the tracks, "Heroes" is absolutely fascinating and sets the tone for the album. It is one of David Bowie's most-loved standards, recorded in Berlin in 1977. The original featured Robert Fripp's guitar solo, and was recorded between his work on *Car* and *Scratch*. It was a bold track with which to open the project considering it was so closely linked to Bowie. 'The Boy In the Bubble' sees the afro-jump of Paul Simon's original replaced with a plaintive piano, and Gabriel bringing out the song's curious mixture of hope and dread.

Elbow, the Manchester group saved by the belief of their new record company in 2008, were long-time Peter Gabriel fans, and wasted no time in expressing their admiration for him. Their work often carried a heavy solemnity akin to Gabriel's, but, just like him, they were not afraid to cut life-affirming pop songs. Their song 'Mirrorball' was beautifully delivered, as was Bon Iver's 'Flume'. 'Listening Wind', from Talking Heads' ground-breaking and much loved 1980 album, *Remain In Light*, was one of the album's two ethereal, dirge-like pieces that closed the second side of the original album.

Inspired by the Vietnam War and several other insurgencies that had broken out since the end of the Second World War, Byrne delivered the song as a dispassionate storyteller, but Gabriel's version loaded the song with even greater gravitas and, certainly, post 9/11 gave 'Listening Wind' a darker edge. David Byrne was impressed. He commented in June 2010 that Gabriel's version was "lovely. It brings out the incantation in the song. What a choice at this time politically though! One could get waterboarded for singing that song in the wrong place!"

One of the most successful songs on the album was 'The Power Of The Heart', a relatively unheard Lou Reed song from 2008. Gabriel and Reed had been friends for a long time, and the version of the song that Reed had written as a marriage proposal for his girlfriend, Gabriel collaborator Laurie Anderson, was delivered with a touching sensitivity. 'My Body Is A Cage' was originally by Canadians Arcade Fire, who had moved from being critics' darlings to being art-rock superstars very quickly. The version that Gabriel performed featured the Choir Of Christ Church Cathedral, Oxford.

The only track not to be orchestrated by Metcalfe was the Magnetic Fields' 'The Book Of Love', on which experienced arranger and orchestrator Nick Ingman assisted Gabriel. It offered some light relief, before the emotion of 'I Think It's Going To Rain Today'. Regina Spektor's 'Apres-Moi' (selected by Anna Gabriel) and Neil Young's 'Philadelphia' showed that Gabriel could work with artists' material old and new and offer similar gravity. 'Street Spirit (Fade Out)', the final track on Radiohead's groundbreaking *OK Computer*, was the final track here, and it makes the Radiohead original sound like bubblegum pop. Gabriel and Metcalfe slow it down, extracting every scrap of pathos from the original. Gabriel told *The Quietus*: "It felt to me that there was a reconciliation and sense of acceptance in that last line of lyric, 'immerse yourself in love' that takes the song out of despair. A great and natural end." *Scratch My Back* was a challenging listen.

The album was released in February 2010 and its reception was split right down the middle. Will Dean, writing for the BBC, said: "The pop world has finally caught up with the WOMAD-founder's open-minded approach to music from near and far and, as such, it's surprising, fitting and pleasing that one of the most essential albums of early 2010 is his. Wonderful." Q magazine said: "As a covers album, this is about as good as it gets." *Mojo* said: "An album to make you happy feeling sad, *Scratch My Back* gets better with each play; it might just turn out to be the best surprise present of the year." Alexis Petridis wrote in *The Guardian*: "He slows the songs' tempos and sets them to string arrangements that range from filmic and lush to something approaching the icy screech essayed by John Cale on Nico's *Marble Index*."

*The LA Times* wondered if it was all a little opportunistic – linking his material with that of the greats such as Bowie and Neil Young, while also courting younger audiences with the selection of Bon Iver and Arcade Fire, but surmised: "By turning these songs into Shakespearean soliloquies, he argues for their complexity and depth, their right to be considered as art songs." The review concluded with a view that was held by many: "Yet it's impossible to not pine for some rhythm here and a chance for this outstanding ballad singer to also show off his intact talent for soulful whooping and wailing." Neil Spencer in *The Observer* suggested that "the ghost of Genesis is never far away" throughout his versions of the Elbow and the Bon Iver tracks. However, not all were keen: *Rolling Stone* said that the album was "a cool idea that turns into a stone bore".

Everyone was wrong and right at the same time; it was a pitch dark listen that reached number 12 in the UK and number 26 in the US. It topped the charts in Belgium and the Czech Republic, and made the top three in Germany, Italy, Poland and Switzerland. Gail Colson, who had kept an eye on Gabriel's career in the 20 years since she managed him, considered the album to be one of his very best works.

* * *

As *Scratch My Back* was released, a further inevitable flurry of questions was asked about the possibility of a Genesis reunion. "I did talk to those guys about it . . ." Gabriel told *Rolling Stone*. "I just didn't want to lose that sort of light-footedness that I enjoy now. And I don't know what the others would want to do. Phil [Collins] has had a lot of physical troubles recently, back problems that have restricted his drum playing, so there may be other reasons that would make it difficult now. So I assume we won't lose any sleep if we don't do more. You know, we had a great run." It was ironic that Collins, the ultimate 'can-do' man and pacifier in so many a situation, was ultimately the one to kibosh any thoughts of a get-together. In September 2009, he issued a statement declaring his performing days were over.

In February 2010, Peter Gabriel turned 60 and had a get-together at Li Capanni. Tony Banks was among the guests, and the two soon reverted to playground rivalries: "Every time we meet there is something there that is unique between us," he says. "Peter and I always do that and go back to that friendly rivalry. We were playing table tennis in wind. He played 'wind against' and won, and he wanted to end it there. I said we had to play the other way round, so fortunately we left it as a draw, which was very good. His mother was wonderful, she was on the sidelines gunning for him, going 'come on Pete, come on Pete.' "

Later, the pair repaired to the tennis courts, to play a game of doubles with a couple of friends: "Peter's always got great shots. We were 1-5 down and then suddenly my wife comes out and tells Peter that he was foot-faulting, and then he kind of lost it. We psyched them out and beat them 7-5. It was such a wonderful moment for me. After all these years of rivalry, *I actually beat him*. He keeps talking about a return."

* * *

In May 2010, Gabriel spoke out about plans to develop the Woolley Valley, right by Solsbury Hill, where he had lived at Ashcombe House. A farming company, Golden Valley Paddocks, had bought 55 acres of land from TV presenter Jonathan Dimbleby and planned to intensively farm chickens. Gabriel joined the Save Woolley Valley Action Group to halt future development.

"I lived in Woolley for seven or eight years and spent a total of 13 years in the Woolley Valley area," Gabriel told *The Telegraph*. ". . . I was somewhat disturbed when I heard these developers are so deliberately flouting the planning laws and that there has been so little reaction from the council. If developers are allowed to do this here then it sets a precedent for any other area that this is an acceptable way of bypassing planning laws."

The response of the farm company could not have been wider of the mark: they tried to denigrate Gabriel as a 'rock star' from Los Angeles, simply because that's where he made his contribution to the campaign from. Nothing could have been further from the truth.

# 26: Happy Family Snapshot

*"I do take some of my work seriously, but I try to avoid pretensions, and I still see it as entertainment more than anything else."*

Peter Gabriel, 1986

As Peter Gabriel was about to embark on one of the most interesting phases of his career, Genesis were honoured at the Rock and Roll Hall Of Fame on March 12, 2010. Tony Banks, Phil Collins and Mike Rutherford, were joined on the night by their 1971–1977 guitarist Steve Hackett. Trey Anastasio from US cult rock group, Phish, introduced them as the "quiet rebels", and said that in their work, "Every musical rule and boundary was questioned and broken. It's impossible to overstate what impact this band and its musical philosophy had on me as a young musician. I'm forever in their debt." Gabriel was not there. Rutherford spoke for Gabriel. "Peter has a very legitimate, genuine excuse, he's starting a tour, him and an orchestra, but he sends his love and thanks." The introductory footage for the band, a clever archival montage, had new and vintage interviews with Peter incorporated. "If you are the front man for a band you get to be the main spokesman and that tends to create a lot of resentment," Gabriel said on the film. Collins added that they were determined to show people that Genesis was a band, and that they weren't simply "Pete's backing band". Yes, 35 years after his departure from the group, Genesis were *still* emphasising that they were no longer 'Pete's backing band.'

* * *

The *New Blood* Tour, which supported *Scratch My Back* began in France in March 2010 and continued in short installments through to July 2012. In early 2010, in the UK, an O2 gig was announced for March 27, seeing Gabriel return to the place where his *OVO* show was seen as one of the few triumphs of the Millennium Dome. As fans rushed to order tickets a set of adverts came out stating: 'no drums. No guitars – just a 54-piece orchestra'. It sounded intriguing, and such a radical departure for an artist who had been so pioneering with rhythm.

The shows were a fantastical two-and-a-half hour-voyage through the album and then a hand-chosen selection of Gabriel classics. They were, in the main, warmly received. If there was a downside, it was simply that the venue was too cavernous. Ideal possibly for a full-on Gabriel show with band, the quiet intimacy of the music was all but lost in the hall.

The show was meticulously rehearsed: "You can't really have 50 people onstage being too spontaneous or it's soup," said John Metcalfe. "Peter is fairly known for taking time with projects but with good reason. We were understandably a bit apprehensive as to how the audiences would react. It was a risk. People turning up expecting to dance to 'Sledgehammer' and instead, getting a very sparse arrangement of 'The Boy In The Bubble' with bass clarinet, piano and a couple of violas. Not very rock'n'roll. But they were amazing – really listening but enjoying themselves when the surf was up in the big numbers." When the surf was up, it was thrilling. The menace and intimacy and raw emotion that Gabriel conveyed was simply exhilarating, as he prowled the stage, delivering *Scratch My Back* in order and then returning with a selection of his own material from across the years.

Metcalfe continued, "You can't simply rattle something off and hope it will be OK on the night. Everything has to work and be right. Where there is room for variety from show to show with a smaller band you don't have that luxury with 50 players onstage. You are doing something different with great songs and that difference has to have reason and integrity and move people. It can't be a very expensive gimmick."

Gabriel had originally intended the *I'll Scratch Yours* project to be the follow-up to *Scratch My Back*, with artists returning the favour and recording one of Gabriel's songs. Although it was still the idea to complete the project, only six of the 12 tracks were completed. Neil Young, Arcade Fire, Radiohead and David Bowie, for a variety of reasons, declined to return the favour. "I've sort of given up waiting for the others," he told *Rolling Stone* in October 2011. "But we have six excellent tracks with Bon Iver, Paul Simon, Lou Reed, David Byrne, Stephen Merritt and Elbow. So now I think that I might try to find three or four other people to cover my stuff so that I can make an album out of that, and then get that out next year in some form." He met with Win Butler and Régine Chassagne from

Arcade Fire at the Montreal premiere of *New Blood Live In London*, but recognised the fact that they had had "fantastic success and they just got swamped".

As a result, the six *I'll Scratch Yours* tracks were released digitally, as part of his Full Moon Club. Elbow recorded a beautiful version of 'Mercy Street'; Paul Simon made a spirited 'Biko', Lou Reed a noisy 'Solsbury Hill'. Stephen Merritt of Magnetic Fields ran through 'Not One Of Us' while David Byrne re-imagined 'I Don't Remember' as a dance number, which made the song actually sound like an outtake from *Remain in Light*. The former Talking Head was looking to cover something more obscure, but Gabriel suggested that he cover the *Melt* standout. Byrne expanded on his choice of song for the Real World website: "I realised that the tempo, the groove and the catchy chorus might be perfect for an uplifting clubby treatment – which would give a nice spin on the lyrics." The relentless groove indeed suggested the temporary mind-shift offered by club drugs.

It was rumoured that Byrne's former collaborator and Gabriel's old friend, Brian Eno, was going to take David Bowie's place. Bowie had become something of a recluse after his tour in 2003, living in New York with his wife Iman and daughter Lexi, determined to be with his child in the way that he resolutely hadn't been with his eldest son Zowie back in the Seventies. Eno was going to tackle 'In Your Eyes', then the B-side of 'Sledgehammer', 'Don't Break This Rhythm', and then 'Mother of Violence'. To date, nothing has happened, although John Metcalfe firmly believes that the full project will see the light of day at some point in the not too distant future.

But Gabriel wanted to undertake more work. Now he had amassed the orchestra and found such an excellent foil in Metcalfe, he wanted to expand the project. Gabriel thought about experimenting with home-made instruments, but he and Metcalfe began to flesh out the ideas explored on the *Scratch My Back* tour. "As the work went on other ideas would come up spontaneously," Metcalfe adds, and, accordingly, *New Blood* – orchestral reworkings of 13 tracks from his previous catalogue – Gabriel' s ninth studio album evolved out of *Scratch My Back*.

* * *

Gabriel took to the stage at London's Hammersmith Apollo on March 23, 2011, for a two-night residency almost exactly a year after debuting *Scratch*

*My Back* live at the 02. With the purpose of filming the show for a forthcoming 3D live DVD, Gabriel replicated his 2010 *Scratch My Back* show with the New Blood orchestra. Still resolutely without drums or guitar, Gabriel modified the previous year's show making it punchier, and if anything, more moving.

The show was conducted by Ben Foster, who had worked on *Scratch My Back*, while Metcalfe acted as MD. "Ben got it straightaway," Metcalfe says. "He is a very experienced conductor and gave great performances. Audiences loved him and he was an important part of the show. He would bring up points about the scores – such as dynamics and phrasing. We would discuss those points quite a lot. As MD, I was running around a lot sorting different issues out so he would get on with rehearsing and I was happy to leave him to it." It made for a thrilling, compelling view.

The visuals were, of course, stunning, and Gabriel was all over every micro-millimetre of this show, exuding warmth and humility onstage. It was an emotional *tour de force*, especially during 'Biko', newly added to the set, which closed the first half. A wag kept shouting for 'Harold The Barrel'. He got it all wrong and perhaps all right at the same time. Gabriel had left that world long ago but must be the only significant figure in popular music who hasn't extensively mined his previous group's oeuvre. Although 'Carpet Crawlers' would probably have sounded wonderful in this format, the shows proved, more than ever, that Gabriel simply didn't need to go that far back. Allegedly Gabriel had considered 'Supper's Ready' for inclusion in the project, a claim that Metcalfe denies. "I thought *New Blood* was such a brilliant show. I was a little apprehensive as it didn't have conventional instrumentation, but I absolutely loved it. It was a really inspired thing to do," says Dave Gregory.

With the DVD slated for release in Autumn 2011, Gabriel returned to the studio and finished *New Blood*. Gabriel clearly thrived on the orchestral approach. Again without the guitar, drums and bass ('the traditional weapons of the rock armoury'), he felt a liberation that he hadn't felt in years. Although the original idea of getting the artists he covered to return the favour had been lost along the way, his live shows, integrating his catalogue with the covers, were a remarkable accomplishment.

Gabriel reinvented 13 selections from his career on *New Blood*. Metcalfe and Foster realised his dreams and made an incredible if somewhat uneasy album. All the songs presented their own issues.

"We tried one or two things and they seemed to go okay, 'Rhythm Of The Heat' particularly," Gabriel told John Doran in 2011. "We had this idea of taking the drums from the end of the original and translating them to orchestral music . . . We really felt as if we'd come up with something that we hadn't heard before." *Us* standout, 'Digging In the Dirt' proved problematic: "[It] took a long time. I just couldn't get the groove to sit. I made the rule 'no drum kit, no guitar', so this sort of funk generation of machinery was missing. It took a while to get the orchestral players to sit in the pocket." But sit in the pocket they did. The song, which had so energised the live *Scratch My Back* performances, was the nearest the album would get to funky.

The impenetrability of 'The Rhythm Of The Heat' is made denser, darker. Gabriel was understandably excited by what he had created, and in Metcalfe, he had someone who could recognise his dreams. 'Intruder' is as weird and claustrophobic as it ever was, but with Gabriel now sounding like an old master criminal as opposed to the young offender of the 1980 original. A joyous 'In Your Eyes' and the five minutes of ambient noise recorded by Richard Chappell on top of Solsbury Hill before the song itself, make *New Blood* a rather memorable experience. However, there was much debate whether to include his first solo hit: "There has to be a musical reason for including anything on an album," John Metcalfe said. "Peter may have been initially unsure that the song lent itself completely to his overall vision for the record. He had to know that it worked artistically rather than lump it in there just because it's one of his hits."

*New Blood* is the ultimate souvenir of Gabriel's orchestral experiment. Released on October 10, 2011, it showed that if anything was tentative about *Scratch My Back*, it was now triumphant. It brought the two years of the New Blood Orchestra to a close and clearly rejuvenated Gabriel. He had been able to further his art without having to write a single note of new music or spend an age toiling over lyrics. The album was well reviewed; the BBC suggested: "Arranger John Metcalfe realises Gabriel's ambitions throughout, whether it's on the comparatively jaunty 'Solsbury Hill' or the sweeping power of 'Red Rain'. And they can shuffle 'In Your Eyes' all they like, but its chorus remains stoically hooky and uplifting." "I was determined that it shouldn't be just a sort of 'hits goes to the orchestra'," Gabriel explained to John Doran.

The DVD of the live show came out simultaneously – it was, as UK magazine *Record Collector* noted: "An intense and engaging transfusion." Seen in 3D, *New Blood: Live In London* is a work of art. Directed by Blue Leach, the performance captures all the intensity of the Hammersmith shows; and like the gigs themselves, it refused to conform to any cliché. Leach's filming demonstrates how the most minute detail can make the greatest difference. The panning shots of the serried rows of microphone stands above the 60-piece orchestra suggest some sort of intense cultural building site, with work constantly in progress. Throughout, Gabriel is captured clearly having a whale of a time. He hovers, studied, intoning his lyrics with extreme gravity, supported vocally by his daughter Melanie and Swedish singer Ane Brun. Gabriel dons his headcam, and shines a torch on the audience in 'San Jacinto'; by the time of 'Solsbury Hill', his merry dance acts as a respite from the claustrophobia.

Although shorn of his funkier tendencies, what remains is passionate and soulful. *New Blood: Live In London* gains the intimacy that was occasionally lost at the concerts themselves. *Record Collector* concluded: "In years to come it will be talked about in the same breath as *Stop Making Sense*, it's that good." In various ways, it drew many similarities with Jonathan Demme's mould-breaking 1984 concert film of Talking Heads. This dense, theatrical experience had its premiere in September 2011 to journalists and the music industry at the Electric Cinema in Notting Hill Gate, just round the corner from Gabriel's London residence.

On June 29, 2012, Gabriel headlined promoter Vince Power's no-nonsense, back to basics festival, the Hop Farm in Paddock Wood, Kent. Playing a truncated, seven-song set that distilled the whole *Scratch My Back/ New Blood* project down to one biteable chunk, *The Independent* said: 'Friday's happily challenging headliner Peter Gabriel conjures 'Biko''s prophetic, apartheid-licking flames, and Jung's struggle with self-consciousness in 'The Rhythm Of The Heat'." Local paper *Kent News* summed up the feelings of many, and for some, the views on the entire *New Blood* project: "Gabriel's dazzling display of lights and video screens providing a sumptuous treat for the eyes, with the power of a full orchestra supporting him making it something of a spectacular." For the casual observer his performance was perhaps best summed up by one audience member who quipped: "It was all right if you like Peter Gabriel", while others left early, having expected the hits.

Closing in July 2012, the tour had been an exhilarating experience. John Metcalfe recalls his memories: "Hollywood Bowl, Radio City, conducting the orchestra in front of 10,000 French people with Peter and Youssou N'Dour singing 'In Your Eyes', flying over the Andes, the Canadian audience response to the cover of Arcade Fire's 'My Body Is A Cage', listening to the orchestra on the *Scratch* recording sessions. The only real logistical challenge was trying to arrange 'Secret World' while on tour. The odd 22 hour day . . ."

Gabriel had met and worked with another on-side collaborator; the two have subsequently worked on some soundtrack material, yet it is unlikely they will ever work quite as closely as they did on this recording.

* * *

2012 also marked the 30th Anniversary of the WOMAD festival. "Pure enthusiasm for music from around the world led us to the idea of WOMAD in 1980 and thus to the first WOMAD festival in 1982," Gabriel said. "The festivals have always been wonderful and unique occasions and have succeeded in introducing an international audience to many talented artists. Equally important, the festivals have also allowed many different audiences to gain an insight into cultures other than their own through the enjoyment of music. Music is a universal language, it draws people together and proves, as well as anything, the stupidity of racism." The events had garnered a fabulous reputation, a million miles removed from the chaos and controversy that surrounded the inaugural event in 1982.

Gabriel's old friend, Nile Rodgers played the festival with CHIC in England in 2008 and in Australia in 2012. "The whole place went crazy. When we played England the cops and the security guys, the whole staff stopped working and came and watched us. To look down and see my hero Peter Gabriel standing there watching our whole show, and the entire security went to pieces. I thought, 'Aren't they supposed to be protecting people and directing traffic?' Both experiences were incredible. In Australia we played with a lot of African musicians. When we were in England it was more bands that I had known before. It's a wonderful vibe, beautiful setting, I don't know how he thought of it, but what I do know is that this is great."

* * *

In 2012, Peter Gabriel announced that he was going to take a year off to be with his family, running roughly October 2012 – October 2013. In typical Gabriel fashion, he gave it a name: The Year Of Interesting Things. Just before Christmas 2011, he became a grandfather for the first time when Melanie gave birth to a baby boy, Ira Thomas, with her partner, Wave Machines frontman Tim Bruzon.

There was one final piece of business to attend to before Gabriel took his very necessary sabbatical. He had been working on a box-set reissue of *So* for longer than he had worked on the original. The success of the *New Blood* project meant that the deadline for the album passed.

The perfectionism that courses through Gabriel's work was borne out by the 26th Anniversary edition of *So*, his 1986 commercial tour de force. It should, of course, have been ready for release to commemorate the album's silver jubilee in 2011, but with Gabriel's craftsmanlike care and attention to detail, and, coinciding with one of the busiest periods in his entire career, he was not to be rushed. So, 26 years and five months after its original release, the reissue appeared. It was worth the wait.

As the record industry began to collapse in the early 21st century, record company marketing departments had increasingly explored the multi-disc box set as a method of presenting fans with as much material as possible. Genesis had received the treatment to huge acclaim with the multiple CD box sets covering their various eras, alongside two vinyl box sets. The in-depth appraisal of a single album had begun in 2008 with Sony Legacy's amazing work with Miles Davis, starting with *A Kind Of Blue*. The lavish multi-disc set presents the fullest picture possible of *So*. If you hadn't heard the original for a while, the 2012 remaster added a discreet depth and brightness to Gabriel and Daniel Lanois' production.

It was, without doubt, the additional material on the lavish set that attracted the most attention. As Gabriel said in the accompanying 60-page hardcover booklet: "This was a time full of highs and lows, experiment and discovery, exhaustion and frustration, excitement and passion – and lots and lots of laughter." Of greatest interest was the specially assembled 'DNA' disc, where the listener became part of Gabriel's creative process, hearing sections of his original demos as they mutate into band work-throughs, offering a detailed insight into the writing and recording. The patchwork of sources is a compelling listen. 'Sledgehammer' begins as a minute-and-a-half of basic piano blues over a drum machine, complete with Gabriel's soulful scat vocals with snatches of phrasings from 'Don't

Give Up'; it then breaks into a moment of a later version, still with incomplete lyrics. *Classic Prog* said: "Listening to the disc is more than just like paying a visit into Gabriel's demo studio – it's like leafing through the pages of Gabriel's mind."

Alongside the heavyweight vinyl of the original album, there was a 12″ with three completely unreleased tracks – 'Sagrada', from which parts of 'In Your Eyes' were formed, the funky 'Courage' and a significantly different version of 'Don't Give Up'.

There were also two DVDs – the Eagle Rock *Classic Albums* documentary on *So*, which was also available separately, was now an integral part of the box. However, the real treat was the unearthing of the live show at the open-air theatre at Lycabettus in Athens in October 1987 on the final nights of the *So* world tour, parts of which had previously been seen on the VHS-era *POV* release. With props and theatricality at a bare minimum (although with a surfeit of in-era duster coats) it captures a band totally at ease with one another, performing freewheeling versions of *So* tracks and highlights from Gabriel's catalogue. Martin Scorsese, with whom Gabriel was about to work on *The Last Temptation Of Christ*, oversaw the production. Fully restored and pieced together from over 150 reels of original 35mm negatives and remixed in 5.1, and available for the first time on DVD, it is one of the best-ever captures of Gabriel live.

The album also came out in a single and a triple disc version but it really was all about the big box. It was impossible not to commend Gabriel and his working processes. The complexity of his writing, the skilful way the music was pieced together and the joyous manner in which it was celebrated in concert all captured perfectly in the package. It was the cradle to the grave of *So*.

Reviewers were quick to reappraise an album that had been held with so much affection and regard across the years. *Consequence of Sound* summed up: "*So* is that all-too-rare record that manages to have it both ways, earning its richly deserved critical and commercial respect without giving so much as an artistic inch." *Classic Prog* said: "Simply put, it's like all of a Gabriel devotee's Christmases arriving at once."

A final piece of business related to the album was the eventual release of the accompanying app, developed in conjunction with Music Tiles, which would allow fans to create remixes of songs and music from *So*. "I have always loved the idea that music and art should be fully open media from which no-one is excluded," Gabriel said. "They are languages that anyone can learn to speak and definitely not the exclusive province of the high priests armed with 'Talent'." Gabriel was still tinkering, inventing, modifying.

* * *

Energised by this rare spell of looking back, and also relieved to be so busy but with no pressure off to deliver new material, Gabriel decided to tour the reissue. In sharp contrast to the time and overheads of taking the New Blood Orchestra on the road, he contacted all the players of the touring band of *So* and enquired whether they would be amenable to touring it again. A short 16-date tour was scheduled, commencing September 16, 2012 in Quebec, taking in familiar venues such as the Red Rocks amphitheater in Colorado and the Hollywood Bowl. As a result, the *Back To Front* tour closed this hectic phase of Peter Gabriel's life.

On October 2, 2012, he visited Google's headquarters in Mountain View, California. In a webcast interview, he joked about his return to stage with the *Back To Front* tour: "I've never really done a retro tour before and was pretty resistant – I know Robert Plant quite well and we were chiding each other on who was going to succumb to the big money first. I went to see The Beach Boys do *Pet Sounds*, which I always used to love and that convinced me to see one of the records you enjoy from start to finish, was actually a good thing. And that coincided with some nice offers, so that was an easy decision." It would be a suitably grand overture to Gabriel's sabbatical year.

Gabriel put the band back together – Tony Levin, David Rhodes, Manu Katche, David Sancious and, replacing new mother Melanie, Jennie Abrahamson and Linnea Olsson, on backing vocals. The show started off with an unfinished song, looser 'unplugged' material, and then, as Gabriel said, "electric versions of things". He added: "If you can get through that you get your dessert, the complete version of *So*." He said at Google that working with such a familiar line-up was "a bit like family get-togethers; you end up with the same bunch of folk doing the same things that you always did, with all the pleasure and problems that went along the first time. It feels very familiar. I'm enjoying it a lot." The performances on the tour felt futuristic and retro simultaneously.

The tour ended in Fairfax, Virginia in the middle of October 2012.

Tony Levin, Gabriel's most loyal accompanist, wrote about the tour eloquently and enthusiastically on his *papabear* blog: 'Well, what can I say about this tour . . . it's been one of the most fun ever. Great music, great people, both in the band and production group, and the wonderful crew doing all the work for us." It certainly had a huge end-of-term feel to it, and after the studied perfection and detail of the *New Blood* shows, Gabriel actually seemed to let go and have fun – it was like a very long happy Friday afternoon before a fortnight's holiday.

Before his sabbatical Gabriel enjoyed the highest profile he had for several years. He hosted the 20th Anniversary Benefit Celebration for WITNESS on October 11, 2012 at the Roseland Theater in New York, flying in from his show at the Santa Barbara Bowl in California.

WITNESS was developing. With its slogan of 'See It, Film It, Change It', it had come a long way since it shipped the first 25 camcorders to Civil Rights groups around the world in 1993. In 20 years, video cameras had gone from bulky items in the hands of the privileged to being in everyone's pocket on their telephone. This had led, although it was still a small organisation, to WITNESS making considerable advances such as exposing the trafficking of women via the Russian mafia and exposing female oppression under Taliban rule in Afghanistan. With the arrival of YouTube in 2005 came the ability to share violations of human rights instantaneously with the world via the internet. This was also the year that Gabriel began to host a WITNESS fund-raising gala in New York. "This is his brainchild . . . he usually doesn't like to mix his art and his activism," Gillian Caldwell, the organisation's original vice-president, said that night. Hosted by actor Alan Cummings, Gabriel performed 'Don't Give Up' with Canadian singer, Feist. Former Irish President and Elder, Mary Robinson, was in attendance.

* * *

In October 2012 at the end of the *Back To Front* tour, it was announced that the tour would be coming to Europe, starting at the O2 in London in October 2013. And then, Gabriel disappeared, to embark on his Year Of Interesting Things. "It's the gap-year philosophy. I meant to do it when I was 50 so I'm only 12 years late," he said as he disappeared into the sunset.

Sadly, there was a delay to the adventure, and this time one completely out of Peter Gabriel's hands. At the start of his year off, his dear father,

Ralph Parton Gabriel, died aged 100 with his family around him at the home he'd lived in all his married life.

Mike Rutherford and his wife Angie had gone to visit the Gabriels a few months before, and sensed that Ralph was nearing his end. "We were sitting in that drawing room where we used to rehearse, where we auditioned Phil – and it hadn't changed. We were served tea on the same china. Irene didn't accept any help, she had to do it all herself. The time warp was amazing. With all the change that had gone on in that period of time, to be in the same house with the same people, the same china was rather charming. Ralph had had enough, though."

Gabriel placed an announcement in *The Daily Telegraph*, his father's favourite paper, stating that Gabriel senior was the "Beloved husband of Irene, father of Peter and Anne and adored by all his family. We will miss you so much." The funeral was held on November 16 at St Lawrence Church in Chobham. Gabriel posted the touching 'Father, Son' video from *OVO* as a tribute on his website. Gabriel had reached 62 years old with his father still alive. Ralph saw his four grandchildren from Gabriel and two from Anne, as well his first great-grandchild, and lovingly watched Gabriel's career, a career he had continued to inspire so greatly for so long.

Richard Macphail says that the service was, as one would expect, deeply moving. "It was fascinating to learn more about Ralph at the funeral, and Peter did this wonderful resume of his life. What an unbelievable lifespan. That particular 100 years, before the First World War – no century has seen so much change in the history of man. They were the first family in the village to have a motorcar. When Peter first played 'Father, Son' to his father, Ralph said he must sing it at his funeral, and so he did. There was a keyboard there and he honoured his father and sung it very beautifully, there was not a dry eye in the house."

"It was very moving," adds Banks. "I was amazed he was able to play 'Father, Son'."

And finally that was it; Gabriel, Meabh, Isaac and Luc disappeared for their year off. "He had suggested a year out to Jill when Anna and Mel were young," Richard Macphail says. "This is an idea that had been around for a long time. The pivotal moment was when Isaac's favourite teacher decided to go on a sabbatical – Peter thought we could link this up and they could all go on a sabbatical together, because Isaac loves her as a teacher, and she is tutoring them throughout the year. I imagine Meabh reacted better to the idea than Jill did at this time."

⋆ ⋆ ⋆

Gabriel seemed to be having the time of his life on the year out. In a career that had seemingly been without frontiers, he was finally communicating with space, the final frontier. He posted footage on his Twitter site on February 21, 2013 of his wife, boys and himself at Mission Control in Houston talking via satellite link to the astronauts on the International Space Station. Gabriel and his family were the guests of astronaut Ron Garan and spoke with Expedition 34 Commander Kevin Ford of NASA, Flight Engineer Tom Marshburn of NASA and Flight Engineer Chris Hadfield of the Canadian Space Agency.

Gabriel discussed life and work in orbit with the three crew members and was treated to a few chords of 'In Your Eyes' from Hadfield on his acoustic guitar. The family looked happy and relaxed, with the boys slightly overcome by the fact they were talking to outer space. It also showed that the 'Year of Interesting Things' was paying dividends. Luc sat happily on Gabriel's knee. All masks were off. At the end of the clip, holding his youngest child in his arms, the real Peter Gabriel stood up.

# Afterword

## PETER IS WHO PETER IS

*"I don't think I'm very smart or very talented, but I'm an obstinate bastard – I've seen other people at every stage of everything I've done who are smarter and better at them than I am, and that hasn't deterred me."*

Peter Gabriel, Al Jazeera, 2011

As I continued writing, *Without Frontiers* became a more and more apt title for a book about Peter Gabriel. He has an idea, and he makes it happen. Whether that is dealing in world peace, staging a tour, singing, writing or collaboration, there is absolutely no word for 'no' in his vocabulary. It may take a long time to come to fruition, but he makes it happen. Aside from his curious inability to maintain a stable relationship while so absorbed in his work in the middle stages of his career, the only grand scheme that has failed to bear fruit to date has been his much-discussed Real World Theme Park. Yet even elements of that have been incorporated into his other work. His joy in discussion and exploration is so much greater at times than the end result. *But what end results he has produced.*

However, it is problematic to assess how Gabriel's work and legacy will be valued as the years pass. Because he works so long and arduously on his material, the feeling that he has never fully embraced pop stardom has cost him his mainstream appeal. When interviewed by Al-Jazeera in 2011, Gabriel said that he now sees his time as a third music, a third technology and a third 'benefit project'. His sense of play is unparalleled and his restless mind means he is open to whatever challenges lie ahead. "New toys lead you into new directions," he said, "that childish sense of discovery, exploration and fun is what keeps it alive for you and your audience."

The sabbatical that Peter Gabriel has taken in 2013 signalled his first complete withdrawal from work since his departure from Genesis in 1975.

Although his Full Moon updates ceased, there was still social media traffic from him, which suggests he can never fully switch off.

There are still myriad loose ends. On a website somewhere, people are speculating that there should be a film of *The Lamb Lies Down On Broadway*, with suggestions that Tim Burton should direct and Jack Nicholson could play Doktor Diaper. *I/O* is still talked about as his next project and *I'll Scratch Yours* was finally released in September 2013. Gabriel told *Rolling Stone* in 2011 that he was considering "something lighter, rhythmic, more electronic maybe . . . With *I/O,* I was thinking of a particular batch of material, which is sort of half-finished. So if it becomes something else, I might look at it and see if it still seems relevant." When I met Gabriel in 2011, I mentioned how he would feel about a 'quick and dirty' soul album, a thought he welcomed. Speed is hardly in his make up. Everyone that I've spoken to, while listing his many good qualities, are all in agreement that he takes an inordinate length of time to complete *anything*.

The admiration for Gabriel as a person and for the quality of his work could not be any higher. "He's got a brilliant mind," Dave Gregory, who played on *Melt*, and is a lifelong fan, concludes. "And is a great musician. Everything he does is with whole-hearted conviction and a strong intelligence at work. With his genuinely strong social conscience, he is truly a good human being and a kind-hearted soul. One mustn't forget, too, that he is loaded with charisma. I go back to the first time I saw him on the cover of *Melody Maker* as a 20-year-old. He's always looked like a star, and he's been able to back it up." Whether he likes it or not, Gabriel is a star, brimming with the practicality inherited from his father, Ralph. It astonishes all who have worked with him from Anthony Phillips onwards.

Peter Hammill applauds Gabriel's qualities. Although Hammill was the star at Charisma when Genesis first appeared, Gabriel eclipsed Hammill commercially soon afterwards. "I have great admiration for Peter's man-management skills," Hammill says. "He's managed to cajole, enthuse, organise and motivate a whole motley crew of people and a whole slew of different activities over the years. I wouldn't have a clue how to go about all that. And all power to him for it, I say. And along the way he's made some wonderful music as well. We're both singers, front men, solo careerists. That makes us complicated within the work. But I think we've both done our best to be as normal and human as we can be away from the work. Not easy, actually, for either of us. But why should it be? We're privileged guys. And in the end our enthusiasm has made our own luck. When Peter and I meet socially we hardly ever speak about music or musicians. And that's just the way we like it, even after all these years!" When asked about reasons for Gabriel's longevity, Hammill merely quipped, "Because he's worth it."

"He is just an unstoppable force," says Richard Macphail. "Peter is unbelievably dogged, and it can make him very difficult. The reason I stopped working for him was that he would come up with two or three ideas daily that were potentially amazing, but not really what we were doing. Peter is unmanageable as he's such a force. He's just this fountain of ideas. He is such a visionary; he doesn't give up."

Gabriel's generosity of spirit is at once obvious; when Richard Norris talked about Joe Strummer's maverick appearance at Real World's Recording Weeks he noted their "mutual respect and intrigue. Peter let Joe in instantly, unreservedly. He welcomed him as part of the experiment, as he did everyone else."

Gabriel is blessed with a deep thought process. As his friend and occasional collaborator Nona Hendryx said, "He's a great thinker and he really considers what he is going to say before he says it. There will be these long silences, and before you get to know him you're really not very sure if he wants to talk to you or not. That said, I don't think people see his fun side. He can laugh at himself."

Nile Rodgers compared and contrasted two artists he had worked with. "You know, Madonna could call me with the most mundane subject and would have me riveted, and I'm thinking *why am I listening to this bullshit* – because it is interesting coming out of her mouth. But it's in a very different way to how Peter is interesting. Peter is interesting in the same way that if I had a chance to go back in time and talk to Mozart or Michelangelo. Madonna is riveting in the way a powerful personality is riveting. She is a personality and hyper, Peter is introspective and interesting on multi-levels. God knows how many discussions Peter and I have had. That's what was great about working with him; he speaks and he lives on that different plane that I actually hear. I don't know if there is anyone in rock'n'roll that I love more. My god, I've never met anyone like Peter. He's magical to me. His kindness – think of all the people in my universe who are kind and gentle and wonderful and a true gentleman, and as artists we have worked together on a number of projects and we've never gotten a hit and our stuff to me was really good."

"People are protective of Peter, because Peter is who Peter is," says Paul Conroy. "Peter always mixed in a different world and his interests were always much broader. He would be going off to see theatre, be less blinkered. He'd always have books and things on the go – he's a man of the people, his whole interests are so much broader."

"It was obvious from that very first gig that Peter wasn't your normal rock star type," Kris Needs says. "The rapid way he evolved through Genesis, both visually and musically, pointed at him both leaving the band soon and then never standing still when he embarked on a solo career. He's always looking for something new to tackle and has never rested on his laurels."

Gabriel has always thrived on collaboration; sometimes these have proved long-lasting, others have come and gone, but there is little doubting the absolute intensity of the moment. Aside from demos, Gabriel has never worked alone. His original collaborator Tony Banks always remains one of the most interesting and key relationships in Gabriel's life – as Gabriel said in 2007, tellingly: "We were best men at each other's weddings and best friends and worst enemies at the same time." Working with Banks seemed to give him a confidence to deal with people from Desmond Tutu to Bob Geldof to Bob Ezrin – if he can deal with that old fashioned playground relationship, then he can deal with anyone. "In the early days we were best friends, but also very close rivals," Tony Banks agrees. "We used to compete at everything. We used to play squash and tennis extremely badly, but at our own level we would really care. And anything we could compete in, we would. We really enjoyed that."

Gail Colson, who worked with Gabriel for 20 years, adds "Peter is a very caring human being, as it says/used to say in his passport, a Humanist. A true visionary who wants to make the world a better place and who will do anything he can to help make it happen. Needless to say a wonderful songwriter, musician and performer. He is challenging and always comes up with something thought provoking, a true artist. He has a very loyal following who have grown up with him."

Steve Hackett adds: "Peter has a great voice, he's a fabulous performer, an original thinker with a good head and heart. He also has the courage to put his ideas into practice. He's an example of someone who preferred to take the road less travelled. He's a great risk taker, and also influential. With his third album he helped to make Apartheid in South Africa unhip. World leaders have implemented his ideas. He's been a great influence for good on the planet and he's welcomed in musicians from all over the world. He's more than a musician and I'll always love him for it."

Recent collaborator John Metcalfe says: "Peter is constantly curious about all sorts of possibilities and that desire to stay engaged is certainly one of the components."

School friend and co-Genesis founder Anthony Phillips says simply: [He is a] very good songwriter; a brilliant lyricist. Excellent arrangements, excellent stage performance."

And then, there is Gabriel's singularity and procrastination: "He's trying to be more un-user friendly with every release," David Stopps says. "I have no idea what's going on his head. He likes to consider every possible angle of every possible note before coming to any sort of decision."

And Bob Ezrin, his friend and producer, adds: "He is never quite satisfied with his own work. As long as there is one pixel out of place on the screen, he'll go after it and try and correct it and often when you're dealing with things like great songs, and then you change something you are unhappy with, then that uncovers something else and it shines a light on something else, and before you know it, you're going round retracing your steps. Peter has a painstaking approach to a lot of things because he is a perfectionist and he gets distracted. Because he's got so many things going on in his life. Even back then [in 1976], there was the situation at home he had to contend with, launching a solo career from nothing, he'd never been out on his own before, there was just so many things for him to think about – there has always been that in his life. When he took on Real World suddenly he's got this enormous army of people, this huge facility and big machine that needed to be fed, lots of distractions. Things take Peter a while."

Mike Rutherford suggests that this doggedness is the reason for his prolonged success: "Pete will always ask *that* question; he'll never settle for something. There will always be something at the back of his head wondering if it should be like that. That's his strength. And his weakness, too."

"Peter is genuinely talented and has such a fantastic voice," Tony Banks concludes. "He's always been a very enquiring person, which is why he is into all this other stuff, such as his Human Rights work. He's very good at meeting people. Peter, regardless of anything, would retain a charm, which I didn't really have in the first place. With other people, he was always the easier one and I was the more brittle one. I was very shy. So was Peter, but his shyness came out in a very endearing, very haunting way, where I just tended to look fuming, serious and surly. Music is fundamental to his reputation and he keeps a consistently high standard. It couldn't happen to a nicer guy."

We close in the sometimes flippant world of music journalism. Neil Perry wrote in *Sounds* in 1987: "He seems like a man who would never compromise his art for anything, the sort who would exile himself to a desert island rather than be forced in a direction not of his choosing" and almost in that throwaway comment is the essence of Gabriel through and through. Many agree with Perry's assessment, but John Metcalfe adds, with great illumination, that: "Yes, but I don't think Peter would exile himself from anything. He'd probably want to engage in whatever the 'force' was to see if there's something creative to be gained from it. I felt he relished having restrictions placed on a process to bring about a new and potentially interesting set of results." And one thing Gabriel has consistently delivered has been an interesting set of results. Above all, Gabriel is a supportive and caring human being.

He has kept his friends close across the years: "He's fairly shambolic, tremendously supportive and enormously loyal. Even though he's been going through everything, his father dying, two young boys, his year out, he's still there as a friend," adds Richard Macphail. "His longevity? It's a combination of his vision and his cussedness – he won't take no for an answer."

Peter Gabriel is a visionary man, who has just happened to make some of the most interesting music of the past 40 years. All of his characters and personas have been good for business. He has created a body of work that is full of thoughts and questions. When it has been loveable and coincided with the needs of the mass markets such as his commercial high water marks, 'Solsbury Hill' and 'Sledgehammer', he has enjoyed global success. But any barrier or restriction is something that Gabriel will continually slough through. Peter Gabriel's work remains without frontiers, and with time, this most elusive of characters is unmasked.

# Peter Gabriel Uk Discography

## ALBUMS

**Peter Gabriel (*Car*)**
**Charisma CDS 4006, February 1977 (Uk No. 7)**
Moribund, The Burgermeister / Solsbury Hill / Modern Love / Excuse Me / Humdrum / Slowburn / Waiting For The Big One / Down The Dolce Vita / Here Comes The Flood

**Peter Gabriel (*Scratch*)**
**Charisma CDS 4013, June 1978 (Uk No. 7)**
On The Air / D.I.Y. / Mother Of Violence / A Wonderful Day In A One-Way World / White Shadow / Indigo / Animal Magic / Exposure / Flotsam and Jetsam / Perspective / Home Sweet Home

**Peter Gabriel (*Melt*)**
**Charisma CDS 4019, May 1980 (Uk No. 1)**
Intruder / No Self Control / Start / I Don't Remember / Family Snapshot / And Through The Wire / Games Without Frontiers / Not One Of Us / Lead A Normal Life / Biko

**Peter Gabriel (*Security*)**
**Charisma PG 4, 1982 (Uk No. 6)**
The Rhythm Of The Heat / San Jacinto / I Have The Touch / The Family And The Fishing Net / Shock The Monkey / Lay Your Hands On Me / Wallflower / Kiss Of Life

**So**
**Virgin PG5, 1986 (Uk No. 1)**
Red Rain / Sledgehammer/ Don't Give Up / That Voice Again / In Your Eyes / Mercy Street / Big Time / We Do What We're Told (Milgram's 37) / This Is The Picture (Excellent Birds)

**Us**
**Real World/Virgin PGCD7, September 1992 (Uk No. 2)**
Come Talk To Me / Love To Be Loved / Blood Of Eden / Steam / Only Us / Washing Of The Water / Digging In the Dirt / Fourteen Black Paintings / Kiss That Frog / Secret World

**Up**

**Real World/Virgin PGCD11, September 2002 (Uk No. 11)**

Darkness / Growing Up / Sky Blue / No Way Out / I Grieve / The Barry Williams Show / My Head Sounds Like That / More Than This / Signal To Noise / The Drop

**Scratch My Back**

**Real World/Virgin PGCDX12, 2010 (Uk No. 12)**

Heroes / The Boy In The Bubble / Mirrorball / Flume / Listening Wind / The Power Of The Heart / My Body Is A Cage / The Book Of Love / I Think It's Going To Rain Today / Apres Moi / Philadelphia / Street Spirit (Fade Out)

**New Blood**

**Real World/Virgin PGCD 13, October 2011 (Uk No. 22)**

The Rhythm Of The Heat / Downside Up / San Jacinto / Intruder / Wallflower / In Your Eyes / Mercy Street / Red Rain / Darkness / Don't Give Up / Digging In the Dirt / The Nest That Sailed The Sky / A Quiet Moment / Solsbury Hill

**Scratch My Back/I'll Scratch Yours**

**Real World/Virgin PGCD15, 2013**

Heroes / The Boy In The Bubble / Mirrorball / Flume / Listening Wind / The Power Of The Heart / My Body Is A Cage / The Book Of Love / I Think It's Going To Rain Today / Apres Moi / Philadelphia / Street Spirit (Fade Out)

I Don't Remember – David Byrne?/ Come Talk to Me – Bon Iver / Blood of Eden – Regina Spektor / Not One of Us – Stephen Merritt / Shock the Monkey – Joseph Arthur / Big Time – Randy Newman / Games Without Frontiers – Arcade Fire / Mercy Street – Elbow / Mother of Violence – Brian Eno / Don't Give Up – Feist ft. Timber Timbre? / Solsbury Hill – Lou Reed / Biko – Paul Simon

## LIVE ALBUMS

**Peter Gabriel Plays Live**

**Charisma PGDL 1, 1983 (UK No. 8)**

The Rhythm Of The Heat / I Have The Touch / Not One Of Us / Family Snapshot / D.I.Y. / The Family And The Fishing Net / Intruder / I Go Swimming / San Jacinto / Solsbury Hill / No Self-Control / I Don't Remember / Shock The Monkey / Humdrum / On The Air / Biko

**Peter Gabriel Plays Live Highlights**
**Charisma PGDLCD 1, June 1985**
I Have The Touch / Family Snapshot / D.I.Y. / The Family And The Fishing Net / I Go Swimming / San Jacinto / Solsbury Hill / No Self-Control / I Don't Remember / Shock The Monkey / Humdrum / Biko

**Secret World Live**
**Real World/Virgin PGDCD 8, September 1994 (UK No. 10)**
Come Talk To Me / Steam / Across The River / Slow Marimbas / Shaking The Tree / Red Rain / Blood Of Eden / Kiss That Frog / Washing Of The Water / Solsbury Hill / Digging In The Dirt / Sledgehammer / Secret World / Don' Give Up / In Your Eyes

**Encore Series 8/03**
**Real World / Themusic.com, Summer 2003**
Typical tracklist: Red Rain / More Than This / Secret World / Games Without Frontiers / Mercy Street / Darkness / Digging In The Dirt / Don't Give Up / The Tower That Ate People / Growing Up / Animal Nation / Solsbury Hill / Sledgehammer / Signal To Noise / In Your Eyes / Shock The Monkey / Father, Son

**Encore Series The Warm Up Tour Summer 07**
**Real World, 2007**
Typical tracklist: The Rhythm Of The Heat / On the Air / Intruder / DIY / I Have The Touch / Washing Of the Water / Blood Of Eden / We Do What We're Told (Milgram's 37) / I Don't Remember / No Self Control / Moribund, the Burgermeister / Family Snapshot / Not One Of Us/ Mother Of Violence /I Grieve / Big Time / Steam / Lay Your Hands On Me / Solsbury Hill / Sledgehammer / In Your Eyes

**Live Blood**
**Real World/Virgin PGCD 14, April 2012**
Intruder / Wallflower / The Boy In The Bubble / Apres Moi / The Drop / Washing Of The Water / The Book Of Love / Darkness / The Power Of The Heart / Biko / San Jacinto / Digging In The Dirt / Signal To Noise / Downside Up / Mercy Street / The Rhythm Of The Heat / Blood Of Eden / Red Rain / Solsbury Hill / In Your Eyes (featuring Sevara Nazarkhan) / Don't Give Up (featuring Ane Brun) / The Nest That Sailed The Sky

## SOUNDTRACKS

**Music From The Film *Birdy***
**Charisma CAS 1167, March 1985 (UK No. 51)**
At Night / Floating Dogs / Quiet And Alone / Close Up (from Family

Snapshot) / Slow Water / Dressing The Wound / Birdy's Flight (from Not One Of Us) / Slow Marimbas / This Heat (from Rhythm Of The Heat) / Sketch Pad With Trumpet And Voice / Under Lock And Key (from Wallflower) / Powerhouse At The Foot Of The Mountain (from San Jacinto)

**Passion – Music For *The Last Temptation Of Christ***
**Real World/Virgin RWCD 1, June 1989 (UK No. 29)**
The Feeling Begins / Gethsemane / Of These, Hope / Lazarus Raised / Of These, Hope (reprise) / In Doubt / A Different Drum / Zaar / Troubled / Open / Before Night Falls / With This Love / Sandstorm / Stigmata / Passion / With This Love (choir) / Wall Of Breath / The Promise Of Shadows / Disturbed / It Is Accomplished / Bread And Wine

**Long Walk Home – Music From *Rabbit Proof Fence***
**Real World/Virgin PGCD 10, 2002**
Jigalong / Stealing The Children / Unlocking The Door / The Tracker / Running To The Rain / On The Map / A Sense Of Home / Go Away Mr Evans / Moodoo's Secret / Gracie's Recapture / Crossing The Salt Pam / The Return – Parts 1, 2 and 3 / Ngankarrparni (Sky Blue – Reprise) / The Rabbit-Proof Fence / Cloudless

## COMPILATIONS

**Shaking The Tree – Sixteen Golden Greats**
**Real World/Virgin PGTVD6, 1990 (UK No. 11)**
Solsbury Hill / I Don't Remember / Sledgehammer / Family Snapshot / Mercy Street / Shaking The Tree / Don't Give Up / San Jacinto / Here Coems The Flood / Re Rain / Games Without Frontiers / Shock the Monkey / I Have The Touch / Big Time / Zaar / Biko

**Hit – The Definitive Two CD Collection**
**Real World / EMI 595237 2 9, 2003 (UK No. 29)**
Solsbury Hill / Shock The Monkey / Sledgehammer / Don't Give Up / Games Without Frontiers / Big Time / Burn You Up, Burn You Down / Growing Up / Digging In the Dirt / Blood Of Eden / More Than This / Biko

Steam/ Red Rain / Here Comes The Flood / San Jacinto / No Self-Control / Cloudless / The Rhythm Of The Heat / I Have The Touch / I Grieve / D.I.Y./A different Drum / The Drop / The Tower That Ate People / Lovetown / Father, Son / Signal To Noise / Downside Up (Live) / Washing Of The Water

**So – 25th Anniversary Edition**
**Real World PG BOX 2, October 2012**
Red Rain / Sledgehammer/ Don't Give Up / That Voice Again / Mercy

Street / Big Time / We Do What We're Told (Milgram's 37) / This Is The Picture (Excellent Birds) / In Your Eyes

**So DNA**

**Live In Athens 1987**: This Is The Picture (Excellent Birds)/ San Jacinto / Shock The Monkey / Family Snapshot / Intruder / Games Without Frontiers / No Self Control / Mercy Street / The Family And The Fishing Net

Don't Give Up / Solsbury Hill / Lay Your Hands On me / Sledgehammer / Here Comes The Flood / In Your Eyes / Biko

**DVD: *SO* Classic Albums**

DVD: **Live In Athens 1987**: This Is The Picture (Excellent Birds)/ San Jacinto / Shock The Monkey / Family Snapshot / Intruder / Games Without Frontiers / No Self Control / Mercy Street / The Family And The Fishing Net / Don't Give Up / Solsbury Hill / Lay Your Hands On me / Sledgehammer / Here Comes The Flood / In Your Eyes / Biko

**VINYL**: Red Rain / Sledgehammer/ Don't Give Up / That Voice Again / Mercy Street

Big Time / We Do What We're Told (Milgram's 37) / This Is The Picture (Excellent Birds) / In Your Eyes

**12 :** Courage / Sagrada/ In Your Eyes (Alternative Version Piano and Bvox mix)

## SIGNIFICANT IMPORTS

**Ein Deutsches Album**

**Charisma, July 1980**

Eindringling / Keine Selbstkontrolle / Frag Mich Night Immer / Schnappschuß (ein Familienfoto) / Und Durch Den Draht / Spiel Ohne Grenzen / Du Bist Nicht Wie Wir / Ein normales Leben / Biko

**Deutsches Album**

**Charisma, September 1982**

Der Rhythmus Der Hitze / Das Fischernetz / Kon Takt! / San Jacinto / Schock Den Affen / Handauflegen / Nicht Die Erde Hat Dich Verschluckt / Mundzumundbeatmung

## COLLABORATIONS

### OVO

**Real World/Virgin PGCD 9, August 2000 (UK No. 24)**
The Story Of OVO/ Low Light / the Time Of The Turning / The Man Who Loved The Earth – The Hand That Sold Shadows / The Time Of The Turning (Reprise) – The Weaver's Reel / Father, Son / The Tower That Ate People / Revenge / White Ashes / Downside-Up / The Nest That Sailed The Sky / Make Tomorrow

**Big Blue Ball**
**Real World CDRW150, June 2008**
Whole Thing / Habibe / Shadow / altus silva / Exit Through You / Everything Comes From You / Burn You Up, Burn You Down / Forest / Rivers / Jijy / Big Blue Ball

## SINGLES

**March 1977**
Solsbury Hill / Moribund, The Burgermeister
(Charisma CB 301) (UK No.13)
**June 1977**
Modern Love / Slowburn
(Charisma CB 302)
**May 1978**
DIY / Perspective
(Charisma CB 311)
**September 1978**
DIY / Mother Of Violence / Me And My Teddy Bear
(Charisma CB 319)
**March 1980**
Games Without Frontiers / Start / I Don't Remember
(Charisma CB 354) (UK No. 4)
**May 1980**
No Self Control / Lead A Normal Life
(Charisma CB 360) (UK No. 33)
**August 1980**
Biko / Shosholoza / Jetzt Kommt Die Flut
(Charisma CB 370) (UK No. 38)
**September 1982**
Shock The Monkey / Soft Dog
(Charisma SHOCK 1) (UK No. 58)
**December 1982**
I Have The Touch / Across The River
(Charisma CB 405)

**July 1983**
I Don't Remember / Solsbury Hill (Live)
(Charisma GAB 1) (UK No. 62)
**May 1984**
Walk Through The Fire / The Race
(Virgin VS 689) (UK No. 69)
**April 1986**
Sledgehammer / Don't Break The Rhythm
(Virgin PGS 1) (UK No. 4)
**September 1986**
Don't Give Up / In Your Eyes (African Mix)
(Virgin PGS 2) (UK No. 9)
**February 1987**
Big Time / Curtains
(Virgin PGS 3) (UK No. 13)
**June 1987**
Red Rain/ Ga Ga (I Go Swimming)
(Virgin PGS 4) (UK No. 46)
**November 1987**
Biko / No More Apartheid
(Virgin PGS 6) (UK No. 49)
**June 1989**
Shaking The Tree / Old Tuscon
(Real World / Virgin VS 1167) (UK No. 69)
**December 1990**
Solsbury Hill / Shaking The Tree
(Real World / Virgin VS 1322) (UK No. 57)
**September 1992**
Digging In The Dirt / Digging In The Dirt (Instrumental) / Quiet Steam / Bashi-Bazouk
(Real World / Virgin PGSDX 7) (UK No. 24)
**February 1993**
Steam / Games Without Frontiers (Massive/DB mix) / Steam (Oh Oh Let Off Steam Mix 12") / Games Without Frontiers (Live)
(Real World / Virgin PGSDX 8) (UK No. 10)
**March 1993**
Blood Of Eden / Mercy Street (remix) / Blood Of Eden (Special Mix)
(Real World / Virgin PGS 9) (UK No. 43)
**September 1993**
Kiss That Frog / Kiss That Frog (Mindblender mix) / Across The River / Shaking The Tree (Remix)
(Real World / Virgin PGSDX 10) (UK No. 46)

**June 1994**
Lovetown / Love To Be Loved
(Sony 660480-7) (UK No. 49)
**August 1994**
SW Live EP: Red Rain / San Jacinto / Mercy Street
(Real World / Virgin PGSCD 11)(UK No. 39)
**September 2002**
The Barry Williams Show (Unadulterated Radio Edit) / The Barry Williams Show (Album Version) / My Head Sounds Like That (Remix by Royksopp) / Cloudless (Radio Edit)
(Real World / Virgin PGSCD 13)
**January 2003**
More Than This (Radio Edit) / More Than This (Polyphonic Spree Mix) / More Than This (Elbow Mix)
(Real World / Virgin PGSCD 14) (UK No. 47)
**June 2003**
Growing Up (Tom Lord Alge Radio Edit) / Growing Up (Album Version) / Growing Up (Trent Reznor Mix)
(Real World / Virgin PGSCD 15)
**December 2003**
Burn You Up, Burn You Down (Radio Edit) / Darkness (Engelspost Mix)
(Real World / Virgin GABRIEL003)
**April 2010**
The Book Of Love / Not One Of Us (Stephen Merritt)
(Real World / Virgin PGSV 15)
**May 2010**
Mirrorball / Mercy Street (Elbow)
(Real World / Virgin, download)
**June 2010**
The Boy In The Bubble / Biko (Paul Simon)
(Real World / Virgin, download)
**July 2010**
Flume / Come Talk To Me (Bon Iver)
(Real World / Virgin, download)
**August 2010**
The Power Of The Heart / Solsbury Hill (Lou Reed)
(Real World / Virgin, download)
**September 2010**
Listening Wind / I Don't Remember (David Byrne)
(Real World / Virgin, download)

## VHS

**CV**
**Virgin Music Video, 1987**
Big Time / Don't Give Up (version 2) / Shock The Monkey / Mercy Street / Sledgehammer / I Don't Remember / Red Rain / Don't Give Up (Version 1)

**PoV**
**Virgin Music Video, 1991**
This Is The Picture / San Jacinto / Shock the Monkey / Games Without Frontiers / No Self Control / Mercy Street / Sledgehammer / Lay Your Hands On Me /Don't Give Up / In Your Eyes / Biko

**All About *Us***
**Virgin Music Video, 1993**
Introduction / The Making Of Digging In the Dirt / Digging In the Dirt / The Making Of Steam / Steam / Steam: Live At The BRIT Awards / The Making Of The Blood Of Eden / Break the Barriers / Solsbury Hill / Zaar / Stusio Recording: Come Talk To Me / Come Talk To Me / The Making Of Kiss That Frog / Kiss That Frog / Digging In the Dirt / Steam / Blood Of Eden / Solsbury Hill / Kiss That Frog / Blood Of Eden

**Secret World Live**
**Real World / Picture Music International, 1994**
Come Talk To Me / Steam / Across The River/ Slow Marimbas / Shaking The Tree / Blood Of Eden / San Jacinto / Kiss That Frog / Washing Of The Water / Solsbury Hill / Digging In the Dirt / Sledgehammer / Secret World / Don't Give Up / In Your Eyes

## DVD

**Growing Up Live**
**Real World / Warner Vision, 2003**
Here Comes the Flood / Darkness / Red Rain / Secret World / Sky Blue / Downside-Up / The Barry Williams Show / More Than This / Mercy Street / Digging In the Dirt / Growing Up / Animal Nation / Solsbury Hill / Sledgehammer / Signal To Noise / In Your Eyes / Father, Son

**SPECIAL FEATURES:** The Story of Growing Up / Tony Levin's View

**Play: The Videos**
**Real World, 2004**
Father, Son / Sledgehammer/ Blood Of Eden / Games Without Frontiers / I Don't Remember / Big Time / Lovetown / Red Rain / In Your Eyes / Don't Give Up / The Barry Williams Show / Washing Of The Water / Biko / Kiss That Frog / Mercy Street / Growing Up / Shaking The Tree /

Shock The Monkey / Steam / the Drop / Zaar / Solsbury Hill / Digging In The Dirt

**SPECIAL FEATURES**: Programmable 16-Track Jukebox / Games Without Frontiers Live 2004 / Video Introductions / Trailer For *Growing Up On Tour – A Family Portrait* / The Nest That Sailed The Sky / Modern Love / Trailer For *Growing Up Live* / Trailer For *Secret World Live.*

**Still Growing Up – Live & Unwrapped**
**Real World, 2005**
The Feeling Begins / Red Rain / Secret World /White Ashes / Games Without Frontiers / Burn You Up, Burn You Down / The Tower That Ate People / San Jacinto / Digging In the Dirt / Solsbury Hill / Sledgehammer / Come Talk To Me / Biko

**Growing Up On Tour: A Family Portrait – A Film By Anna Gabriel**
Real World, 2004

**SPECIAL FEATURES:** My Head Sounds Like That / The Barry Williams Show / The Making Of . . . The Barry Williams Show / Shooting The Programme / Peter Gabriel Solo Performance at Newport International Film Festival Fundraiser

**Classic Albums: So**
**Real World/Eagle Vision, 2011**

**Peter Gabriel Secret World Live**
**Real World/Eagle Vision, 2011**
Come Talk To Me / Steam / Across The River/ Slow Marimbas / Shaking The Tree / Blood Of Eden / San Jacinto / Kiss That Frog / Washing Of The Water / Solsbury Hill / Digging In the Dirt / Sledgehammer / Secret World / Don't Give Up / In Your Eyes / Bonus Track: Red Rain

**BONUS FEATURES:** Making of Secret World / Timelapse film of stage set up / Quiet Steam (photo montage) / Rhythm Of The Heat (Hammersmith London 2011)

**New Blood – Live In London**
**Real World/Eagle Vision, 2011**
Intruder / Wallflower / The Boy In The Bubble / Apres Moi / The Drop / Washing Of The Water / The Book Of Love / Darkness / The Power Of The Heart / Biko / San Jacinto / Digging In The Dirt / Signal To Noise / Downside Up / Mercy Street / The Rhythm Of the Heat / Blood Of Eden / Red Rain / Solsbury Hill / In Your Eyes / Don't Give Up / The Nest That Sailed The Sky

**BONUS FEATURES:** Blood Donors

## MISCELLEANOUS RELEASES

### As Producer:

**Charlie Drake**
**You Never Know / I'm Big Enough For Me**
(Charisma CB 270, November 1975)
(Credited to 'Gabriel Ear Wax')

**Jimmy Pursey**
Animals Have More Fun / SUS
(Epic EPC A 1336, May 1981)

### Selected appearances as guest artist:

**Cat Stevens**
Mona Bone Jakon (Island, 1970)
Katmandu – flute

**Colin Scot**
Colin Scot (United Artists, 1971)
Confusion – backing vocals

**Robert Fripp**
Exposure (EG, 1979)
Preface – spoken word
Here Comes The Flood – vocals and piano

**Johnny Warman**
Walking Into Mirrors (Rocket, 1981)
Screaming Jets – backing vocals, screams

**Laurie Anderson**
Mister Heartbreak (Geffen, 1984)
Excellent Birds – co-write, vocals, synclavier
Langue D'Amour – backing vocals
Gravity's Angel – backing vocals

**Phil Collins**
No Jacket Required (Virgin, 1985)
Take Me Home – backing vocals

**The Call**
Reconciled (Geffen, 1986)
Everywhere I Go – backing vocals

**Nona Hendryx**
Female Trouble (EMI America, 1987)
Winds Of Change (Mandela to Mandela) – backing vocals, keyboards

**Robbie Robertson**
Robbie Roberston (Geffen, 1987)
Fallen Angel – backing vocals, keyboards
Broken Arrow – drum programming, keyboards

**Joni Mitchell**
Chalk Mark In A Rain Storm (Geffen, 1988)
My Secret Place – backing vocals

**Youssou N'Dour**
The Lion (Virgin, 1989)
Shakin' The Tree – co-write, vocals

**Manu Katché**
It's About Time (BMG France, 1991)
Warm Doorway – vocals
Silence – vocals

**Toni Childs**
The Woman's Boat (Geffen, 1994)
I Met A Man – Vocals

**Milton Nascimento**
Angelus (Warner Music, 1994)
Qualquer Coisa a Haver Com o Parais – vocals

**Paula Cole**
This Fire (Imago1996)
Hush, Hush, Hush – Vocals

**Afro-Celt Sound System**
Volume 3: Further In Time (Real World, 2001)
When You're Falling – vocals

**Jools Holland**
Friends 3 (Warners, 2004)
Washing Of The Water – vocals

**Anjelique Kidjo**
Djin Djin (Razor & Tie, 2007)
Salala – vocals

## SOUNDTRACK CONTRIBUTIONS

**All This And World War Two**
Riva Records, June 1976
Strawberry Fields Forever

**Hard To Hold**
BMG, April 1984
I Go Swimming

**Against All Odds**
Virgin Records, April 1984
Walk Through The Fire

**Gremlins**
Geffen Records, October 1984
Out Out

**Philadelphia**
Sony Music, June 1994
Lovetown

**Natural Born Killers**
Nothing, August 1994
Taboo (with Nusrat Ali Fateh Khan)

**Virtuosity**
Radioactive, September 1994
Party Man (with George Acogny)

**Strange Days**
Columbia, 1995
While The Earth Sleeps (with Deep Forest)

**City Of Angels**
Warner Bros, March 1998
I Greive

**Babe 2: Pig In The City**
Geffen, November 1998
That'll Do

**Red Planet**
Pangea, 2000
The Tower That Ate People

**The Wild Thornberrys**
Jive, November 2002
Animal Nation

**Gangs Of New York**
Polydor, December 2002
Signal To Noise (New Version)

**Shall We Dance**
Universal, 2005
The Book Of Love

**Barnyard**
Bulletproof, August 2006
Father, Son

**Sea Monsters**
National Geographic, 2007
Different Stories, Different Lives

**Wall–E**
Walt Disney, June 2008
Down To Earth

## OTHER APPEARANCES

**The Bristol Recorder 2**
Bristol Recorder, January 1981
Humdrum / Not One Of Us / Ain't That Peculiar

**Music And Rhythm**
WEA, July 1982
Across The River

**Raindrops Pattering On Banana Leaves**
WOMAD, June 1984
Lead A Normal Life (Live)

**Sun City**
EMI Manhattan, November 1985
No More Apartheid

**The Secret Policeman's Third Ball**
Virgin, September 1987
Biko

**The Glory Of Gershwin**
Mercury, February 1994
Summertime

**Woodstock 94**
A&M, October 1994
Biko

**Tower Of Song: The Songs Of Leonard Cohen**
A&M, October 1995
Suzanne

**Diana, Princess Of Wales: Tribute**
Sony, December 1997
In The Sun

## GABRIEL / GENESIS ALBUMS

**From Genesis . . . To Revelation**
**Decca SKL 4990, March 1969**
Where The Sour Turns To Sweet / In The Beginning / Fireside Song / The Serpent / Am I Very Wrong? / In The Wilderness / The Conqueror / In Hiding / One Day / Window / In Limbo / Silent Sun / A Place To Call My Own

**Trespass**
**Charisma CAS 1020, October 1970 (UK No. 98 1984)**
Looking For Someone / Visions Of Angels / White Mountain / Stagnation / Dusk / The Knife

**Nursery Cryme**
**Charisma CAS 1052, November 1971 (UK No. 12 1974)**
The Musical Box / For Absent Friends / The Return Of The Giant Hogweed / Seven Stones / Harold The Barrel / Harlequin / The Fountain Of Salmacis

**Foxtrot**
**Charisma CAS 1058, October 1972 (UK No. 12)**
Watcher Of The Skies / Time Table / Get 'Em Out By Friday / Can-Utility And The Coastliners / Horizons / Supper's Ready – i: Lover's Leap ii: The Guaranteed Eternal Sanctuary Man iii: Ikhnaton and Itsacon And Their Band Of Merry Men iv: How Dare I Be So Beautiful? v: Willow Farm vi: Apocalypse in 9/8 (Co-starring The Delicious Talents Of Gabble Ratchet) vii: As Sure As Eggs Is Eggs (Aching Men's Feet)

**Genesis Live**
**Charisma CLASS 1, July 1973 (UK No. 9)**
Watcher Of The Skies / Get 'Em Out By Friday / The Return Of The Giant Hogweed / The Musical Box / The Knife

**Selling England By The Pound**
**Charisma CAS 1074, October 1973 (UK No. 3)**
Dancing With The Moonlit Knight / I Know What I Like (In Your Wardrobe)/ Firth Of Fifth / More Fool Me / The Battle Of Epping Forest / After The Ordeal / The Cinema Show / Aisle Of Plenty

**The Lamb Lies Down On Broadway**
**Charisma CGS 101, November 1974 (UK No. 10)**
The Lamb Lies Down On Broadway / Fly On A Windshield / Broadway Melody of 1974 / Cuckoo Cocoon / In The Cage / The Grand Parade Of Lifeless Packaging / Back in N.Y.C. / Hairless Heart / Counting Out Time / The Carpet Crawlers / The Chamber Of 32 Doors / Lilywhite Lilith / The Waiting Room / Anyway / Here Comes The Supernatural Anesthetist / The Lamia / Silent Sorrow In Empty Boats / The Colony Of Slippermen – a: The Arrival b: A Visit To The Doktor c: Raven / Ravine / The Light Dies Down On Broadway / Riding The Scree / In the Rapids/ *it*

## GABRIEL / GENESIS COMPILATIONS

**Genesis Archive 1967– 1975**
**Virgin CD BOX 6, June 1998 (UK No. 35)**
**The Lamb Lies Down On Broadway: Recorded At The Shrine Auditorium, Los Angeles 24/1/75** – The Lamb Lies Down On Broadway / Fly On A Windshield / Broadway Melody of 1974 / Cuckoo Cocoon / In The Cage / The Grand Parade Of Lifeless Packaging / Back in N.Y.C. / Hairless Heart / Counting Out Time / The Carpet Crawlers / The Chamber Of 32 Doors / Lilywhite Lilith / The Waiting Room / Anyway / Here Comes The Supernatural Anesthetist / The Lamia / Silent Sorrow In Empty Boats / The Colony Of Slippermen – a: The Arrival b: A Visit To The Doktor c: Raven / Ravine / The Light Dies Down On Broadway / Riding The Scree / In the Rapids/ *it* / Dancing With The Moonlit Knight (Live at The Rainbow 1973) / Firth Of Fifth (Live at The Rainbow 1973) / More Fool Me (Live at The Rainbow 1973) / Supper's Ready (Live at The Rainbow 1973) / I Know What I Like (In Your Wardrobe) (Live at The Rainbow 1973) / Stagnation (BBC Session) / Twilight Alehouse / Happy The Man / Watcher Of The Skies (Single version) / In The Wilderness (Rough mix) / Shepherd (BBC Session) / Pacidy (BBC Session) / Let Us Now Make Love (BBC Session) / Going Out To Get You (demo) / Dusk (demo) / Build Me A Mountain (rough mix) / Image Blown Out (rough mix) / One Day (rough mix) / Where The

Sour Turns To Sweet (demo) / In The Beginning (demo) / The Magic Of Time (demo) / Hey! (demo) / Hidden In the World Of Dawn (demo) / Sea Bee (demo) / The Mystery Of The Flannan Isle Lighthouse (demo) / Hair On The Arms And Legs (demo) / She Is Beautiful (demo) / Try A Little Sadness (demo) / Patricia (demo)

**Genesis 1970–1975**

**Virgin CD BOX 14, November 2008**

**Trespass CD:** Looking For Someone / Visions Of Angels / White Mountain / Stagnation / Dusk/ The Knife. **Trespass DVD-A:** Looking For Someone / Visions Of Angels / White Mountain / Stagnation / Dusk/ The Knife / Reissues Interview 2007

**Nursery Cryme CD:** The Musical Box / For Absent Friends / The Return Of The Giant Hogweed / Seven Stones / Harold The Barrel / Harlequin / The Fountain Of Salmacis. **Nursery Cryme DVD-A:** The Musical Box / For Absent Friends / The Return Of The Giant Hogweed / Seven Stones / Harold The Barrel / Harlequin / The Fountain Of Salmacis / Reissues Interview 2007

**Foxtrot CD:** Watcher Of The Skies / Time Table / Get 'Em Out By Friday / Can-Utility And The Coastliners / Horizons / Supper's Ready – i: Lover's Leap ii: The Guaranteed Eternal Sanctuary Man iii: Ikhnaton and Itsacon And Their Band Of Merry Men iv: How Dare I Be So Beautiful? v: Willow Farm vi: Apocalypse in 9/8 (Co-starring The Delicious Talents Of Gabble Ratchet) vii: As Sure As Eggs Is Eggs (Aching Men's Feet). **Foxtrot DVD-A:** Watcher Of The Skies / Time Table / Get 'Em Out By Friday / Can-Utility And The Coastliners / Horizons / Supper's Ready – i: Lover's Leap ii: The Guaranteed Eternal Sanctuary Man iii: Ikhnaton and Itsacon And Their Band Of Merry Men iv: How Dare I Be So Beautiful v: Willow Farm vi: Apocalypse in 9/8 vii: As Sure As Eggs Is Eggs (Aching Men's Feet) / Reissues Interview 2007 / **Brussels, Belgium Rock Of The 70s:** The Fountain Of Salmacis / Twilight Alehouse / The Musical Box / The Return Of the Giant Hogweed / **Rome, Italy Piper Club 1972**: Stagnation / Interview

**Selling England By The Pound CD:** Dancing With The Moonlit Knight / I Know What I Like (In Your Wardrobe)/ Firth Of Fifth / More Fool me / The Battle Of Epping Forest / After The Ordeal / The Cinema Show / Aisle Of Plenty. **Selling England By The Pound DVD-A :** Dancing With The Moonlit Knight / I Know What I Like (In Your Wardrobe)/ Firth Of Fifth / More Fool Me / The Battle Of Epping Forest / After The Ordeal / The Cinema Show / Aisle Of Plenty / Reissues Interview 2007 / **Shepperton Studios, Italian TV:** Watcher Of The Skies / Dancing With The Moonlit Knight / I Know What I Like (In Your Wardrobe) / The Musical Box / Supper's Ready **Bataclan, France:** The Musical Box / Supper's Ready / The Return Of The Giant Hogweed / The Knife / Interview

**The Lamb Lies Down On Broadway CD:** The Lamb Lies Down On Broadway / Fly On A Windshield / Broadway Melody of 1974 / Cuckoo Cocoon / In The Cage / The Grand Parade Of Lifeless Packaging / Back in N.Y.C. / Hairless Heart / Counting Out Time / The Carpet Crawlers / The Chamber Of 32 Doors / Lilywhite Lilith / The Waiting Room / Anyway / Here Comes The Supernatural Anesthetist / The Lamia / Silent Sorrow In Empty Boats / The Colony Of Slippermen – a: The Arrival b: A Visit To The Doktor c: Raven / Ravine / The Light Dies Down On Broadway / Riding The Scree / In the Rapids/ *it.* **The Lamb Lies Down On Broadway DVD-A:** The Lamb Lies Down On Broadway / Fly On A Windshield / Broadway Melody of 1974 / Cuckoo Cocoon / In The Cage / The Grand Parade Of Lifeless Packaging / Back in N.Y.C. / Hairless Heart / Counting Out Time / The Carpet Crawlers / The Chamber Of 32 Doors / Lilywhite Lilith / The Waiting Room / Anyway / Here Comes The Supernatural Anesthetist / The Lamia / Silent Sorrow In Empty Boats / The Colony Of Slippermen – a: The Arrival b: A Visit To The Doktor c: Raven / Ravine / The Light Dies Down On Broadway / Riding The Scree / In the Rapids/ *it* / Reissues Interview 2007 / **Melody French TV 1974**: I Know What I Like (In Your Wardrobe) / Supper's Ready

**Extras CD:** Happy The Man / Twilight Alehouse / Shepherd (BBC Nightride 1970) / Pacidy (BBC Nightride 1970) / Let Us Now Make Love (BBC Nightride 1970) / Going Out To Get You (demo) **Genesis Plays Jackson:** Provocation / Frustration / Manipulation / Resignation

**Extras DVD-A:** Happy The Man / Twilight Alehouse / Shepherd (BBC Nightride 1970) / Pacidy (BBC Nightride 1970) / Let Us Now Make Love (BBC Nightride 1970) / Going Out To Get You (demo) **Genesis Plays Jackson:** Provocation / Frustration / Manipulation / Resignation / Reissues Interview 2007 / Box Set 1967–1975 (VH1 Special) **Midnight Special – American TV 1973**: Watcher Of The Skies / The Musical Box

**Genesis 1973–2007**

**Virgin CD BOX 17, September 2009. Box set including two Peter Gabriel-era discs:**

**Genesis Live CD**: Watcher Of The Skies / Get 'Em Out By Friday / The Return Of The Giant Hogweed / The Musical Box / The Knife / Back In New York City / Fly On A Windshield / Broadway Melody of 1974 / Anyway / Chamber of 32 Doors **Genesis Live DVD-A**: Watcher Of The Skies / Get 'Em Out By Friday / The Return Of The Giant Hogweed / The Musical Box / The Knife / Back In New York City / Fly On A Windshield / Broadway Melody of 1974 / Anyway / Chamber of 32 Doors

**Live At The Rainbow 1973 CD:** Dancing With The Moonlit Knight / the Cinema Show / I Know What I Like (In Your Wardrobe) / Firth Of Fifth / More Fool Me / The Battle Of Epping Forest / Supper's Ready. **Live At The Rainbow 1973 DVD-A:** Watcher Of The Skies / Dancing

With The Moonlit Knight / the Cinema Show / I Know What I Like (In Your Wardrobe) / Firth Of Fifth / More Fool Me / The Battle Of Epping Forest / Supper's Ready.

## GENESIS SINGLES

**February 1968**
The Silent Sun / That's Me
(Decca F 12735)
**May 1968**
A Winter's Tale / One-Eyed Hound
(Decca F 12775)
**June 1969**
Where The Sour Turns To Sweet / In The Beginning
(Decca F 12949)
**May 1971**
The Knife (Part One) / The Knife (Part Two)
(Charisma CB 152)
**October 1972**
Happy The Man / Seven Stones
(Charisma CB 181)
**February 1974**
I Know What I Like (In Your Wardrobe) / Twilight Alehouse
(Charisma CB 224) (UK No. 21)
**November 1974**
Counting Out Time / Riding The Scree
(Charisma CB 238)
**April 1975**
The Carpet Crawlers / The Waiting Room (Evil Jam)
(Charisma CB 251)

# Acknowledgements

To Jules and Flora Easlea. Shedding ever-changing colours in the darkness of the fading light.

To John Chadwick for being such a lovely fellow and the loan of his *Six Of The Best* programme.

To Graham Brown (and the family Brown – Wendy, Nathan and Katy, plus dear Phyl Brown, Bernard and Judy Brown, Eileen and Ken) for those many trips to the cinema to see *White Rock/ Genesis In Concert* (out of era, I know, but it was the only way to see them then).

To Johnny Jazz and Julie Grigg: the other 50 per cent of Tarmey and forever united because of side two of *The Lamb Lies Down On Broadway* that June evening at the pink. And the products of their later non-doomed relationships, Amelia and Isaac, Ellie and Amy. And to Nicky and Steve.

To David Barraclough for allowing me to write about my first love; Chris Charlesworth, Jacqui Black, Charlie Harris, Helen Donlon.

Mr Simon Benham

Sincere thanks to all those who agreed to be interviewed: Tony Banks, David Buckley, John Chadwick, Chris Charlesworth, Gail Colson, Paul Conroy, Bob Ezrin, Larry Fast, Dave Gregory, Steve Hackett, Peter Hammill, Nona Hendryx, Julian Huntly, David Lord, Richard Macphail, John Metcalfe, Kris Needs, Richard Norris, Anthony Phillips, Nile Rodgers, Mike Rutherford, David Stopps, Jon Webster, Julian Woollatt

Thanks to all of those who so politely declined

Thanks to Mark and Vicki Powell; Paul Conroy for his help and guidance; Penny Morgan; Tim Fraser-Harding; Sylvie Simmons; Sooze Plunkett-Greene; Chris O'Donnell; Guy Hayden; Chris Hewlett; Henry Scott-Irvine; Steve Hammonds; Andie Daw; Jo Greenwood; Todd Christensen, Vicki Wickham; Mike Large; Jim Chancellor, Peter Loraine, Kim Markovchick, Teddy Cummings, Elaine Gwyther, Sue Brearley, Declan Colgan, Jerry Marotta, Geoff Jukes, Clare Moon, Chris Carr, Tony Smith.

**To Middle Age Spread**

Adam Hasan, Alastair Johnson and Dan Newman. We rock. Sue, Ella and Dylan; Tania, Tallulah and Eloise; Rachel, David and Daniel

www.shipfullofbombs.co.uk

**The Wolstanton Cultural Quarter**:

Fiona Dutton, Nick Maslen, Audrey and Rob Ebrey, Barry Pitts, Lisa Walmsley Pitts and all the extended family

**To UMC/UMGI**:

Andie Daw, Karen Simmonds, Lutz Stoever, Johnny Chandler, Richard Hinkley, Captain Colin Smith, Adam Barker, Hannah Chadwick, Simon Li, Caroline Allen-Coyle, Suzie-Soo Armstrong, Belle Crocker, Katie Alley, Clive Cawley, Martina Pemac, Joe Howard, Julian Fernandez, Paul Fernandes, Ward Allen Ward, Greg Snowdon, Charlotte Wilson, Kathryn Gilfeather, Simon Li, Jack Thomson, Giancarlo Sciama, GK Skinner, David Manning, Kevin Phelan, Chris Dwyer, Jessie Duffy, Kate Hudspeth, Joe Black, Andy Street, Liam Lydon, Emma Shalless, Christine Atkins thank you for your support and patience.

**Previously unmentioned Brothers in Nan**:

Jason Day (and Helen), Nigel Reeve (and Debs), Hugh Gilmour (and Gail).

To all at *Mojo* and *Record Collector.* To Barney Hoskyns and all at www.rocksbackpages.com

**To the couples of the autumn**:

Bernice Owen and Kevin Simpson; Mark Wood and John Geddes.

**Sundries and unforgettables**:

Mish1 & 2, Steve, Joy, Lily and Maia Robins, Colette Bailey, Simon Fowler, Steven Hastings, Box, Chox and Lox, BMS, Lugubrious George, Pat, The legend that is Grant Philpott, Syd Moore, Sean and Riley, Zoë and Dylan Howe, Social hub Steph Stevenson, Robbie, Jack and Finn, Sean McLaughlin, Jo Hartle, Granddad Jonny Parsons, Sophie, Louis and bump, Andy, Ronnie and Harland, Nancy Wallace, Trevor Kiernander, Hannah Marsh, Paul Cotgrove, Matt and Emma Read – that was fun, Phil Alexander, Mike Diver, Alan Hodgson, Mark Paytress, Lois Wilson, Jon Harrington and forthcoming, Selvy and Esther Emmanuel, Pete, Debs and Emily Cunnane, Larry Mann, Richard Stanley, Sion, Agata, Jonasz and Konrad, Ben, Caroline, Alex and Lucy, Dave, Clare and Miracle Jack Clarke, Phillip DH Short, Phil Pavling, Simon, Saskia, Lillie and Maisie Dornan, Lester Mills, Stuart DeVoil, Kirtsy MacHattie, Simon Feather, Tricia North, Jessie Diss, Natalia Farran, Dave and Jo Collins, Jim Fry – Brutus love goes on forever and the memory of Nick Sanderson, who told superb Gabriel tales, John Birdy Bloomfield, Val Jennings, Chris Jones, Tom Doyle, Will Birch, Sue Zekai, Penny and Steve, Simon and Fi, Polly and Matilda, the Williams massive, Matt and Justine and co, Sue Cooper, Tom and Jo Seabrook and Nathan, Paddy Fraser, Sarah Rabia, Laura and Amelie Dutton.

Special thanks to the writers/editors of key Gabriel and Genesis texts – Spencer Bright's candid *Authorised Biography*; Philip Dodd's editorial skill with *Genesis Chapter and Verse*; Hugh Fielder and Phil Sutcliffe – remarkable Genesis scholars – with *The Book Of Genesis,* Chris Welch's writing for championing Genesis right from the off; Alan Hewitt's meticulous *Genesis Revisited* and finally to Armando Gallo, who was the first to chronicle and catalogue Gabriel firstly in *Evolution Of A Rock Band* and then the solo *Peter Gabriel* book.

Hair by Pam Weaver at Nicola's

Drink at the Ship, Leigh-On-Sea and at the Railway Hotel, Southend-On-Sea.

Go Jane!

Patricia Byford, Alan Byford, Chrissie Absalom, Sylvie Easlea, Win Batcock, Liz Rabeotti. All the Bushs and Easleas; and Katie, Thom, Beth, Ellie, Stephen and Sharon.

**To the dead**: Love your work: Hazel and Edgar Easlea, Rod Easlea, Deane Easlea, Eryl Batcock, Tom Clarke, Gwyneth Clarke, George Cook, who passed away in the final days of this book, Lorcan Devine and Jack Kane. Miss you much, but frankly it only feels like you all live in Madrid or somewhere.

Thanks to all, and for those I haven't mentioned but gave support and love in even the most passing of manners, what a pleasure.

A flower?

# Bibliography

Banks, Tony, Phil Collins, Peter Gabriel, Steve Hackett, Mike Rutherford. *Genesis, Chapter And Verse.* (Ed: Philip Dodd). Weidenfeld & Nicolson, London, 2007.

Boyer, Paul S., Clifford E. Clark Jr., Joseph F. Kett, Neal Salisbury, Harvard Sitkoff and Nancy Woloch (Eds.). *The Enduring Vision: A History Of The American People.* DC Heath, Lexington, Toronto, 1996.

Bono, The Edge, Adam Clayton and Larry Mullen, Jr, with Neil McCormick. *U2 By U2.* Haper Collins, London, 2006.

Bronson, Fred. *The Billboard Book Of Number 1 Hits, Updatde and Expanded 5th Edition.* Billboard Books, 2003

Brown, Allan. *Nileism. The Strange Course Of The Blue Nile.* Polygon, Edinburgh, 2010.

Bright, Spencer. *Peter Gabriel – An Authorized Biography.* Sidgwick & Jackson, 1988

Bruford, Bill. *The Autobiography.* Jawbone Press, London, 2009.

Buckley, David. *Strange Fascination – David Bowie The Definitive Story* (revised and updated edition). Virgin Books, London, 2005

Deneslow, Robin. *When The Music's Over: The Story of Political Pop.* Faber & Faber, London, 1990.

Dickson, Paul. *From Elvis To E-Mail: Trends Events And Trivia From The Postwar Era To The End Of The Century.* Federal Street Press, Springfield, MA, 1999.

Drewett, Michael, Sarah Hill and Kimi Kärki. *Peter Gabriel, From Genesis To Growing Up.* Ashgate Publishing, Farnham, Surrey, 2010.

Ertegun, Ahmet. *"What'd I Say" The Atlantic Story: 50 Years Of Music.* Orion, London, 2001.

Fielder, Hugh and Phil Sutcliffe. *Book Of Genesis.* Omnibus Press, London, 1984

Gallo, Armando. *Genesis – I Know What I Like.* Sidgwick & Jackson, London, 1980

Gallo, Armando. *Peter Gabriel.* Omnibus Press, London, 1986

Hewitt, Alan. *Genesis Revisited: The Genesis Story.* Willow Farm, Godalming, 2006.

Hewitt, Alan. *Sketches Of Hackett – The Authorised Steve Hackett Biography.* Wymer Publishing, Bedford, England, 2009.

Hipgnosis, George Hardie. *The Work of Hipgnosis: Walk Away René.* Paper Tiger, London, 1978.

Holm-Hudson, Kevin. *Genesis And The Lamb Lies Down On Broadway.* Ashgate, Farnham, 2008

King, Tom. *David Geffen – A Biography Of New Hollywood.* Hutchinson, London, 2000

Larkin, Colin. *The Virgin Encyclopedia Of Popular Music, Concise Fourth Edition*. Virgin, London, 2002.

Lanois, Daniel. *Soul Mining: A Musical Life*. Faber and Faber, New York, 2010.

Lynskey, Dorian. *33 Revolutions Per Minute – A History of Protest Songs*. Faber and Faber, London, 2010.

Milner, Greg. *Perfecting Sound Forever: The Story Of Recorded Music*. Granta, London 2009.

Morley, Paul. *Ask: The Chatter Of Pop*. Faber and Faber, London, 1986.

Myers, Paul. *A Wizard, A True Star: Todd Rundgren In The Studio*. Jawbone Press, London, 2010

Peel, John. *The Olivetti Chronicles – Three Decades Of Life and Music*. Bantam Press, London, 2008.

Palin, Michael. *Diaries 1969 – 1979: The Python Years*. Wiedenfield & Nicolson, London, 2006.

Palin, Michael. *Halfway To Hollywood: Diaries 1980 – 1988*.Wiedenfield & Nicolson, London, 2009.

Palmer, Tony. *All You Need Is Love: The Story Of Popular Music*. Wiedenfield & Nicolson and Chapell, London, 1976.

Radcliffe, Mark. *Reelin' In the Years: The Soundtrack Of A Northern Life*. Simon and Schuster, London, 2011

Rees, Dafydd and Luke Crampton. *Q Encyclopaedia Of Rock Stars*. Dorling Kindersley, Barnstaple, Mass., 1996

Roach, Martin (Ed.). *The Virgin Book Of British Hit Singles*. Virgin Books, London, 2008.

Roach, Martin (Ed.). *The Virgin Book Of British Hit Albums*. Virgin Books, London, 2009.

Robbins, Ira A (Ed.). *The All-New Trouser Press Record Guide*. Third Edition. Collier Books, New York, 1989.

Russell, Paul. *Play Me My Song: A Genesis Live Guide 1970–1975*. SAF Publishing, London, 2004.

Sandbrook, Dominic. *State Of Emergency, The Way We Were: Britain 1970–1974*. Allen Lane, London, 2010

Sandbrook, Dominic. *Seasons In The Sun: The Battle For Britain 1974–1979*. Allen Lane, London, 2012

Sheppard, David. *On Some Faraway Beach: The Life And Times Of Brian Eno*. Orion, London, 2008.

Southall, Brian. *The A–Z Of Record Labels. Second Edition*.
Sanctuary Publishing, London, 2003.

Strong, Martin C. *The Great Rock Discography Sixth Edition*. Canongate, Edinburgh, 2002

Stump, Paul. *The Music's All That Matters: A History Of Progressive Rock*. Quartet Books, London, 1997.

Tamm, Eric. *Robert Fripp – From King Crimson To Guitar Craft*. Faber & Faber, London, 1990.

Thomson, Graeme. *Under The Ivy: The Life And Music Of Kate Bush*. Omnibus, London, 2010

Thompson, Dave. *Turn It On Again: Peter Gabriel, Phil Collins & Genesis*. Backbeat Books, San Francisco, 2005.

Walker, John. *Halliwell's Film Video & DVD Guide* 2006.

Harper Collins, London, 2006.

Welch, Chris. *The Secret Life Of Peter Gabriel*. Omnibus Press, London, 1998.

Welch, Chris. *Genesis: The Complete Guide To Their Music*. Omnibus Press, London, 2005.

Wilkerson, Mark. *Who Are You: The Life Of Pete Townshend*. Omnibus Press, London, 2009

## Primary Newspapers and Magazines Articles:

Many publications including *The Metro; The Times; The Sunday Express; The Independent; Billboard; The Mirror; Q; Mojo; New Musical Express; Clash Magazine; The Guardian; The LA Times; Uncut; Newsweek; People Magazine; Classic Rock Presents Prog; USA Today; Entertainment Weekly; News Of the World, Record Collector*

### ***All other publications referenced in text***

## Websites

Many sites, including allmusic, discogs, imdb, metacritic, Wikipedia

www.petergabriel.com

www.facebook.com/PeterGabriel?fref=ts

www.realworld.co.uk

## Albums:

### Car:

www.allmusic.com/album/peter-gabriel-1-mw0000197419

www.rollingstone.com/music/albumreviews/peter-gabriel-20010726#ixzz2FJ6j0YIG

### Scratch:

All Music: www.allmusic.com/album/peter-gabriel-2-mw0000650173

### Melt:

www.allmusic.com/album/peter-gabriel-3-mw0000190091

Popmatters: www.popmatters.com/pm/review/gabrielpeter-st-3

**Security:**

www.allmusic.com/album/security-mw0000540147

**Plays Live:**

www.allmusic.com/album/plays-live-mw0000218484

www.rollingstone.com/music/albumreviews/plays-live-19830901#ixzz2AtqdKDG6

**Birdy:**

www.allmusic.com/album/birdy-mw0000189972

**So:**

www.allmusic.com/album/so-mw0000650174
consequenceofsound.net/2012/10/album-review-peter-gabriel-so-reissue

**So 2012**:

www.bbc.co.uk/music/reviews/2bhf

www.rollingstone.com/music/news/q-a-peter-gabriel-reflects-on-his-1986-landmark-album-so-20120904

**Passion:**

www.allmusic.com/album/passion-mw0000204174

**Shaking The Tree: Sixteen Golden Greats:**

www.bbc.co.uk/music/reviews/bdp2

**Us:**

www.allmusic.com/album/us-mw0000218150

**Secret World Live:**

www.allmusic.com/album/secret-world-live-mw0000118526

www.ew.com/ew/article/0,,303731,00.html

www.rollingstone.com/music/albumreviews/secret-world-live-19941020

**OVO:**

www.allmusic.com/album/ovo-mw0000461812

pitchfork.com/reviews/albums/3373-ovo-the-millennium-show

**Up:**

www.bbc.co.uk/music/reviews/v4gb

www.guardian.co.uk/music/2002/sep/19/artsfeatures.popandrock1

www.metacritic.com/music/up/peter-gabriel

www.popmatters.com/pm/review/gabrielpeter-up

www.rollingstone.com/music/news/peter-gabriel-gets-back-up-20020806#ixzz2FJ8IgwqF

**Long Walk Home**:

www.allmusic.com/album/long-walk-home-music-from-the-rabbit-proof-fence-mw0000220848

www.bbc.co.uk/music/reviews/c6mq

www.metacritic.com/music/long-walk-home-music-from-the-rabbit-proof-fence/peter-gabriel

**Big Blue Ball**:

bigblueball.realworldrecords.com

realworld.co.uk/podcasts/realworld_bigblueball.mp3

www.time.com/time/specials/2007/article/0,28804,1733748_1733756_1735249,00.html #ixzz2RNP3VsTp

**Scratch My Back:**

www.bbc.co.uk/music/reviews/fpnv

latimesblogs.latimes.com/music_blog/2010/03/album-review-peter-gabriels-scratch-my-back.html

www.metacritic.com/music/scratch-my-back/peter-gabriel/critic-reviews

www.prefixmag.com/reviews/peter-gabriel/scratch-my-back/35164

lifeasahuman.com/2010/arts-culture/music/peter-gabriels-secret-world/

**New Blood:**

www.bbc.co.uk/music/reviews/jpj9

www.bowers-wilkins.co.uk/Society_of_Sound/Society_of_Sound/Music/Peter-Gabriel_Half-Blood.html

**Live Blood:**

www.allmusic.com/album/live-blood-mw0002334859

**Chris Adams on Strat:** www.charismalabel.com/chrisadams.htm

**Amnesty:** www.amnesty.org/en/news-and-updates/news/peter-gabriel-ambassador-of-conscience-global-music-human-rights-tour-20080910

**Christmas Cottage:**
www.genesis-news.com/c-Take-A-Little-Trip-Back-To-The-Cottage-s293.html

**Back To Front**: www.superdeluxeedition.com/video/peter-gabriel-talks-at-google

**Bayete**: neverenoughrhodes.blogspot.co.uk/2008/08/lives-of-todd-cochran.html

**Bowers And Wilkins:**

www.bowers-wilkins.co.uk/Society_of_Sound/Society_of_Sound/Music/Peter-Gabriel_Half-Blood.html

**Box Mill**: www.pereds.com/cms/uploads/brochures/Box-Mill-Bath.pdf

**Thomas Brooman:**
www.tpimagazine.com/interviews/9606/thomas_brooman.html
www.swms.org.uk/about-us/mentorstutors/thomas-brooman

**John Burns**: www.worldofgenesis.com/JohnBurns-interview2006.htm

**David Byrne**:
www.realworldmusic.com/news/listening-wind-and-i-dont-remember

**Richard Chappell:**
www.soundonsound.com/sos/May03/articles/gabrielchappell.asp

**Charterhouse**: www.charterhouse.org.uk

**Charterhouse terms glossary:**
www.charterhouse.org.uk/Mainfolder/Glossary-of-Terms.pdf

**Gail Colson**: sofasound.wordpress.com/2011/12/31/gail-leaves-the-building

**Davies Laing and Dick**:
www.dldcollege.co.uk/the-college/the-history-of-dld.aspx

**Charlie Drake:** www.charismalabel.com/artists/drake.htm

**The Elders**: www.theelders.org

**EST training**: www.wernererhard.com/est.html

**Bob Ezrin**: http://performingsongwriter.com/bob-ezrin/

**Fairlight**:
petervogelinstruments.com.au/history/
www.hollowsun.com/vintage/fairlight

**Family background:** www.telegraph.co.uk/women/mother-tongue/familyhistory/3355127/Family-detective-Peter-Gabriel.html

**Larry Fast**: www.innerviews.org/inner/fast.html

**The Filter**: www.thefilter.com

**Friars, Aylesbury**: www.aylesburyfriars.co.uk

**The Filter:**
www.businessweek.com/magazine/content/10_16/b4174046688330.htm#p3

**Robert Fripp:**
www.elephant talk.com/wiki/Interview_with_Robert_Fripp_in_Melody_Maker_%281979%29

**Luc Gabriel**:
www.dailymail.co.uk/tvshowbiz/article-1034232/Former-Genesis-frontman-Peter-Gabriel-dad-fourth-time-aged-58.html#ixzz2CffgSyY7
www.celebritybabies.people.com/2008/07/11/peter-gabriel-l/

**Lady Gaga**:

www.spinner.com/2009/06/23/lady-gaga-covers-kate-bush-peter-gabriel-with-canadian-rockers/

**Genesis:**

www.genesis-music.com

www.genesis-discography.org

www.genesisfan.net

www.genesis-fanclub.de

www.genesis-movement.org

www.genesismuseum.com

www.genesis-news.com

www.twronline.net

www.worldofgenesis.com

**Genesis Live:** www.progarchives.com/forum/forum_posts.asp?TID=17117

**Genesis reunion 2010:**

www.rollingstone.com/music/news/peter-gabriel-possibility-of-a-genesis-reunion-is-slim-20110927#ixzz20cNtTSGs

**Genesis 1972 tour programme:**

www.genesismuseum.com/features/UKSouvenir.htm

**Glaspant Farm**: www.companiesintheuk.co.uk/ltd/glaspant-farm

**Gremlins**: popdose.com/lost-in-the-80s-peter-gabriel-out-out

**Hats**: www.contactmusic.com/news/peter-gabriels-hats-were-a-hit-with-the-stones-set_1247785

**Headley Grange**:

www.johnowensmith.co.uk/headley/grange.htm

**Hop Farm Reviews**:

www.independent.co.uk/arts-entertainment/music/reviews/hop-farm-festival-paddock-wood-kent-7903541.html

www.kentnews.co.uk/home/review_hop_farm_festival_2012_1_1428332

**Hurricane Irene:** books.google.co.uk/books?id=ozV_Wa_c470C&pg=PA27&lpg=PA27&dq=hurricane+irene+peter+gabriel&source=bl&ots=nFz2EhmGSS&sig=twLi_UOG4CxTV_voSO6l245WEl4&hl=en&sa=X&ei=55lJUY35NIaZ0AWW_oBw&ved=0CEAQ6AEwBA#v=onepage&q=hurricane%20irene%20peter%20gabriel&f=false

**Knebworth 1978**:

www.ukrockfestivals.com/Kneb-fest-recording-9-9-78.html

**Daniel Lanois**:

blog.discmakers.com/2009/10/nothing-is-sacred

www.freethescene.com/2006/11/15/daniel-lanois-interview/

**Mike Large:**

investing.businessweek.com/research/stocks/private/person.asp?personId=35269349&privcapId=34121601&previousCapId=34121601&previousTitle=We7%20Ltd.

**Li Capanni**: www.licapanni.com

**Live8:**

www.redorbit.com/news/entertainment/162131/peter_gabriel_has_mixed_feelings_over_live_8

www.billboard.com/articles/news/62576/live-8-expands-with-africa-calling

**Lunapendium:** www.lunapendium.com

**Hats**:

www.contactmusic.com/news/peter-gabriels-hats-were-a-hit-with-the-stones-set_1247785

http://www.dailymail.co.uk/travel/holidaytypeshub/article-592416/Peace-quiet-rock-hotel.html#ixzz2DtOOy0ru

**The Lamb Lies Down On Broadway**: www.bloovis.com/music/lamb.html

**The Lamb Lies Down On Broadway reunion:**

www.classicrockmagazine.com/news/competitive-genesis-reunion-unlikely-steve-hackett/

**Tony Levin**: www.papabear.com

**Madness**: www.robomod.net/pipermail/madness/2008-February/000439.html

**Man Of Peace**: www.nobelforpeace-summits.org/peace-summit-award

**Massey Hall**: www.guardian.co.uk/music/2011/aug/04/musicians-worst-gigs

**Miami Vice**: miamivice.wikia.com/wiki/Peter_Gabriel

***The Mirror:***

www.mirror.co.uk/news/allnews/page.cfm?objectid=12690202&method=full&siteid=50143

**Mozo**:

davewainscott.blogspot.co.uk/2011/01/peter-gabriels-mercurial-disruptive.html

www.genericsubject.com/MBW/blog-2012/peter-gabriels-mozo-song.html

**MUDDA**:

www.synthtopia.com/content/2004/02/04/mudda-eno-and-gabriel-behind-music-manifesto/

news.bbc.co.uk/1/hi/business/3424483.stm

**NPR**:

www.npr.org/2012/10/16/162937338/guest-dj-peter-gabriel

**Notting Hill**:

www.dailymail.co.uk/tvshowbiz/article-203657/Singer-battles-home.html

**Nursery Cryme:** www.robertchristgau.com/get_artist.php?name=genesis

thequietus.com/articles/09210-rush-geddy-lee-interview-favourite-albums?page=

**The Peter Gabriel Trust**: opencharities.org/charities/1094058

www.charitycommission.gov.uk/Showcharity/RegisterOfCharities/CharityWithoutPartB.aspx?RegisteredCharityNumber=1094058&SubsidiaryNumber=0

**Plus From Us**: realworldrecords.com/release/67/plus-from-us

**Punk Gabriel:** www.heartofapunksoulofarasta.com/when_peter_was_a_punk.html

**David Rhodes**: www.davidrhodes.org

www.davidrhodes.org/GP1987.html

**Allan Schwartzberg**: www.stereosociety.com/schpayne.shtml

**Secret World:** www.songfacts.com/detail.php?id=776

**Selling England By The Pound**: www.bbc.co.uk/music/reviews/vxhj

**The Silent Sun**: news.bbc.co.uk/dna/place-lancashire/plain/A18463827

**Solid State Logic**:

www.solid-state-logic.com

http://broadcastengineering.com/audio/peter-gabriel-and-david-engelke-purchase-solid-state-logic

**South Bank Show**: epguides.com/SouthBankShow/

**Surname**: www.surnamedb.com/Surname/gabriel

**Swingos Hotel**: www.cleveland.com/visit/plaindealer/index.ssf?/visit/more/pd/touringcleveland.html

**Time:** www.time.com/time/specials/2007/article/0,28804,1733748_1733756_1735249,00.html

**Tony Stratton-Smith:**

www.themarqueeclub.ne

www.vandergraafgenerator.co.uk/tony.htm

**Trespass:** web.archive.org/web/20080502020946/http://www.rollingstone.com/artists/genesis/albums/album/127085/review/5946324/trespass

**TV TROPES**: tvtropes.org/pmwiki/pmwiki.php/Music/Genesis

**Uncut**:

http://www.uncut.co.uk/peter-gabriel/peter-gabriel-blooming-marvelous-feature#dbGWJ57RKqZf4946.99

**University Of Peace**: www.upeace.org/about

***Us* paintings**:

www.independent.co.uk/arts-entertainment/art—breaking-out-of-the-box-peter-gabriel-asked-11-artists-to-respond-to-tracks-on-us-an-album-he-wrote-to-deal-with-his-failed-relationships-he-tells-dalya-alberge-of-plans-to-improve-relations-between-music-and-visual-art-1479459.html

**Vampire Weekend**:

www.gigwise.com/news/43639/peter-gabriel-unveils-plans-to-cover-vampire-weekend

**Wall_E**:

www.rollingstone.com/music/news/peter-gabriel-not-performing-at-oscars-out-of-protest-20090213

**We7**:

www.we7.com

www.theregister.co.uk/2007/04/30/we7_music_downloads

www.guardian.co.uk/media/2012/jun/14/tesco-buys-we7

**Wedding**:

www.inthemix.com/news/41300/Gilles_Peterson_a_terrible_wedding_DJ

**Paul Whitehead**:

www.vandergraafgenerator.co.uk/paulw.htm

www.worldofgenesis.com/PaulWhitehead-interview.htm

**WITNESS**: www.witness.org

**WOMAD**:

womad.org

www.genesismuseum.com/pgsfxmagsummer82.mp3

www.chicagoreader.com/chicago/womad/Content?oid=882757

**WOMAD 30 Years**:

www.guardian.co.uk/music/2012/jul/26/peter-gabriel-30-years-womad

**Woolley Valley**:

www.telegraph.co.uk/earth/earthnews/7741147/Peter-Gabriel-joins-campaign-to-save-valley-he-sang-about.html

**Xplora1:** www.adventureclassicgaming.com/index.php/site/reviews/483

## Selected You Tube:

**Al Jazeera One On One**:
www.youtube.com/watch?v=dPqsUJF2Iqo&feature=endscreen

**Andrew Marr Show:** www.youtube.com/watch?v=yR2DIyop-K0

**Back To Front Google Interview:** www.youtube.com/watch?v=xPL7cebKI5o

**Biko:** www.youtube.com/watch?v=L0nMCwVt6GY

***Car*:**
www.youtube.com/watch?v=PUD3S07cQDI&list=PL3DAFD1144095EC37&index=5

**Five Bob Tour**: www.youtube.com/watch?v=f4XvdoSwrt4

**Daniel Lanois**: www.youtube.com/watch?v=5uAcgxXJgXc

**Conspiracy Of Hope**: www.youtube.com/watch?v=Xcj9CRdSYEI

**Entertainment UK**: www.youtube.com/watch?v=MK1rR478AoQ

**Father, Son**: www.youtube.com/watch?v=0PMEuJmz3CU

**Genesis:** www.youtube.com/artist/genesis

**Growing Up On Tour**: www.youtube.com/watch?v=j4bItaDML0M

**Here Comes The Flood on Kate Bush Christmas Special**:
www.youtube.com/watch?v=G0GcqYGv1AA

**Intruder Live on Letterman:**
www.youtube.com/watch?v=1OCGJRAtpfA&list=ALNb4maWNoT6RWzzwmM7O3IKQ054h95Ksn

**Later With Jools Holland**: www.youtube.com/watch?v=-ds4M59-79A

**Old Grey Whistle Test 1982**: www.youtube.com/watch?v=bFha7IVlRac

**Peter Gabriel**: www.youtube.com/artist/peter-gabriel

**Rock and Roll Hall Of Fame**:
www.youtube.com/watch?v=Sxitq0VmZmE&feature=related

***Security***: www.youtube.com/watch?v=DaT_V2kL9YY

**Six Of The Best**: www.youtube.com/watch?v=KPdEPC2AsB8

**South Bank Show**: www.youtube.com/watch?v=jayZFCo-mvw&feature=relmfu

**Star Test**: /www.youtube.com/watch?v=0_hn2s0jBt8

**Wogan**: www.youtube.com/watch?v=Jl9At0qADuY

★ ★ ★

## Rocks Back Pages:

**1971**: Genesis/1971/Chris Welch/Melody Maker/In The Beginning There Was... Genesis/07/10/2012 13:36:01/http://www.rocksbackpages.com/article.html?ArticleID=8320

**Dublin**: Genesis, Lindisfarne/1972/Chris Charlesworth/Melody Maker/Lindisfarne, Genesis: Dublin Stadium, Dublin/21/01/2013 10:07:11/http://www.rocksbackpages.com/Library/Article/lindisfarne-genesis-dublin-stadium-dublin

**Foxtrot**: Genesis/1972/Jerry Gilbert/Sounds/Genesis: *Foxtrot* (Charisma)/11/10/2012 17:18:11/http://www.rocksbackpages.com/article.html?ArticleID=8562

**1972**: Genesis/1972/Jerry Gilbert/Sounds/Peter Gabriel/30/10/2012 14:33:23/http://www.rocksbackpages.com/article.html?ArticleID=8349

Genesis/1971/uncredited writer/ZigZag/Genesis/07/10/2012 14:22:28/http://www.rocksbackpages.com/article.html?ArticleID=226

**1973**: Genesis/1973/Chris Welch/Melody Maker/Genesis: What Genesis Did On Their 'Holidays'/30/10/2012 14:00:26/http://www.rocksbackpages.com/article.html?ArticleID=17462

**1973**: Genesis/1973/Barbara Charone/NME/Genesis: Peter Gabriel Talks/30/10/2012 17:04:41/http://www.rocksbackpages.com/article.html?ArticleID=6740

**1974**: Drury Lane: Genesis/1974/Chris Welch/Melody Maker/Genesis: Drury Lane Theatre, London/02/02/2013 17:07:21/http://www.rocksbackpages.com/Library/Article/genesis-drury-lane-theatre-london

**1975**: Genesis, Peter Gabriel/1975/Chris Welch/Melody Maker/Peter Gabriel: Behind Peter Gabriel's Mask/06/07/2012 09:04:56/http://www.rocksbackpages.com/article.html?ArticleID=15665

**1981**: Mick Gold audio interview. www.rocksbackpages.com/audio/gabriel_gold.mp3

**1986:** Peter Gabriel/1986/John Hutchinson/Musician/Peter Gabriel: From Brideshead to Sunken Heads/18/11/2012 13:30:27/http://www.rocksbackpages.com/article.html?ArticleID=21043

**1989**: Peter Gabriel, Youssou N'Dour/1989/Len Brown/NME/Black Steel In The Hour Of Chaos/03/12/2012 13:17:53/http://www.rocksbackpages.com/article.html?ArticleID=5363

**1993**: Peter Gabriel/1993/Robert Sandall/Q/Peter Gabriel: Gawp Factor Ten/29/01/2013 16:17:06/http://www.rocksbackpages.com/Library/Article/peter-gabriel-gawp-factor-ten

**The Lamb Lies Down On Broadway**: Genesis/1974/Chris Welch/Melody Maker/Genesis: *The Lamb Lies Down On Broadway* (Charisma) /11/10/2012 17:21:16/http://www.rocksbackpages.com/article.html?ArticleID=884

**The Lamb Lies Down On Broadway**: Genesis/1975/Ron Ross/Circus/Will America Swallow The Lamb? Why Genesis wouldn't chop up *The Lamb Lies Down on Broadway*/31/10/2012 14:45:15/http://www.rocksbackpages.com/article.html?ArticleID=3583

**New Blood**: Peter Gabriel/2011/John Doran/Quietus, The/Peter Gabriel: An Invasion Of Privacy/03/12/2012 17:24:50/http://www.rocksbackpages.com/article.html?ArticleID=20185

**New York Philharmonic Hall**: Genesis/1973/Ron Ross/Phonograph Record/Genesis at Philharmonic Hall, New York/18/05/2013 15:37:26/http://www.rocksbackpages.com/Library/Article/genesis-at-philharmonic-hall-new-york

**Nursery Cryme**: Genesis/1972/Richard Cromelin/Rolling Stone/Genesis: *Nursery Cryme*/11/10/2012 17:14:38/http://www.rocksbackpages.com/article.html?ArticleID=6418

**Peter Gabriel departure**: Genesis, Peter Gabriel/1975/Chris Welch/Melody Maker/Peter Gabriel Quits Genesis/09/07/2012 09:39:51/http://www.rocksbackpages.com/article.html?ArticleID=4744

**Peter Gabriel departure**: Genesis/1975/Barbara Charone/Sounds/Genesis: The Lamb Lies Down But Genesis Carries On/30/10/2012 10:40:11/http://www.rocksbackpages.com/article.html?ArticleID=19845

**Peter Gabriel 1**: Peter Gabriel/1977/Barbara Charone/Circus/Peter Gabriel: Say Goodbye to the Bubble Creature/09/10/2012 09:23:01/http://www.rocksbackpages.com/article.html?ArticleID=10332

**Peter Gabriel 1**: Genesis, Peter Gabriel/1977/Tony Stewart/NME/The Re-Genesis Of Peter Gabriel/29/10/2012 18:13:16/http://www.rocksbackpages.com/article.html?ArticleID=13709

**Peter Gabriel II**: Peter Gabriel/1978/Barbara Charone/Sounds/Peter Gabriel: *Peter Gabriel (2)*/08/10/2012 21:03:06/http://www.rocksbackpages.com/article.html?ArticleID=18307

**Peter Gabriel III**: Peter Gabriel/1980/Phil Sutcliffe/Sounds/Mr. Clean: Peter Gabriel/08/10/2012 20:40:27/http://www.rocksbackpages.com/article.html?ArticleID=5306

**Peter Gabriel III**: Peter Gabriel/1980/Dave Marsh/Rolling Stone/Peter Gabriel: *Peter Gabriel*/07/10/2012 16:28:35/http://www.rocksbackpages.com/article.html?ArticleID=8791

**Peter Gabriel IV**: Peter Gabriel/1982/Gavin Martin/NME/Peter Gabriel: *Four* (Charisma)/29/10/2012 11:20:13/http://www.rocksbackpages.com/article.html?ArticleID=8591

**Peter Gabriel IV**: Peter Gabriel/1982/Sandy Robertson/Sounds/Peter Gabriel :*Peter Gabriel* (Charisma)/29/10/2012 13:08:42/http://www.rocksbackpages.com/article.html?ArticleID=8961

***Peter Gabriel IV***: Genesis, Peter Gabriel/1982/Richard Cook/NME/Rhythm Of The Pete/29/10/2012 15:07:09/http://www.rocksbackpages.com/article.html?ArticleID=133

***Rolling Stone***:
www.rollingstone.com/music/news/peter-gabriel-story-that-bruce-springsteen-was-inspiration-for-solsbury-hill-is-hogwash-20111010#ixzz1zrrM4kZ6

**Selling England**: Genesis/1973/Barbara Charone/NME/Genesis: *Selling England By the Pound* (Charisma)/03/07/2012 15:03:17/http://www.rocksbackpages.com/article.html?ArticleID=623

**UP**: Peter Gabriel/2002/Sylvie Simmons/MOJO/Peter Gabriel: Gods And Monkeys/08/04/2013 14:28:08/http://www.rocksbackpages.com/Library/Article/peter-gabriel-gods-and-monkeys

## Sleevenotes:

***The Famous Charisma Box.*** Charlesworth, Chris (Ed.), Colson, Glen, Roy Hollingsworth, et al, 1993

***Genesis Archive 1967–1975***. King, Jonathan, Richard Macphail et al, 1998

***Big Blue Ball***. Gabriel, Peter, 2008

***Birdy***. Gabriel, Peter, 2002 reissue

***Passion***. Gabriel, Peter, 1989.

***Scratch My Back***. Gabriel, Peter, 2010

## DVD:

***Genesis 1970–1975*** set. Virgin, 2007

***The Genesis Songbook***. Eagle-Rock, 2000

## Interviews

All interviews conducted between October 2012 – May 2013:

Tony Banks, David Buckley, John Chadwick, Chris Charlesworth, Gail Colson, Paul Conroy, Bob Ezrin, Larry Fast, Dave Gregory, Steve Hackett, Peter Hammill, Nona Hendryx, Julian Huntly, David Lord, Richard Macphail, John Metcalfe, Kris Needs, Richard Norris, Anthony Phillips, Nile Rodgers, Mike Rutherford, David Stopps, Jon Webster, Julian Woollatt.

# Index

*Singles releases are in roman type and albums are in italics.*

10/13(188426)